Developmentally Appropriate Practice

Curriculum and Development in Early Education

Carol Gestwicki

*Central Piedmont
Community College*

Delmar Publishers Inc.™

I(T)P™ An International Thomson Publishing Company

Albany • Bonn • Boston • Cincinnati • Detroit • London • Madrid • Melbourne
Mexico City • New York • Pacific Grove • Paris • San Francisco • Singapore • Tokyo
Toronto • Washington

NOTICE TO THE READER

Cover design by: Doug Hyldelund   Cover background by: Jennifer McGlaughlin

Delmar Staff
Acquisitions Editor: Jay Whitney
Developmental Editor: Christopher Anzalone
Project Editor: Theresa M. Bobear

Production Coordinator: Jennifer L. Gaines
Art and Design Coordinator: Doug Hyldelund

Delmar Publishers' Online Services
To access Delmar on the World Wide Web, point your browser to:
http://www.delmar.com/delmar.html
To access through Gopher: gopher://gopher.delmar.com
(Delmar Online is part of "thomson.com", an Internet site with information on more than 30 publishers of the International Thomson Publishing organization.)
For information on our products and services:
email: info@delmar.com
or call 800-347-7707

Copyright © 1995
BY DELMAR PUBLISHERS
a division of International Thomson Publishing Inc.
The ITP logo is a trademark under license.

Printed in the United States of America

For information, contact:

Delmar Publishers Inc.
3 Columbia Circle, Box 15-015
Albany, New York 12212-5015

International Thomson Publishing Europe
Berkshire House 168-173
High Holborn
London, WC1V7AA
England

Thomas Nelson Australia
102 Dodds Street
South Melbourne, 3205
Victoria, Australia

Nelson Canada
1120 Birchmont Road
Scarborough, Ontario
Canada, M1K 5G4

International Tomson Editores
Campos Eliseos 385, Piso 7
Col Polanco
11560 Mexico D F Mexico

International Thomson Publishing GmbH
Königswinterer Str. 418
53227 Bonn
Germany

International Thomson Publishing Asia
221 Henderson Road
#05-10 Henderson Bldg.
Singapore 0315

International Thomson Publishing - Japan
Hirakawacho Kyowa Building, 3F
2-2-1 Hirakawacho
Chiyoda-ku, Tokyo 102
Japan

5   6   7   8   9   XXX   01   00   99   98

Library of Congress Cataloging-in-Publication Data

Gestwicki, Carol, 1940-
    Developmentally appropriate practice: curriculum and development in early education / Carol Gestwicki.
        p.   cm.
    includes index.
    ISBN 0-8273-6240-4
    1. Early childhood education—United States.   2. Child development—United States.   I. Title.
LB1139.25.G47   1995
372.21—dc20
                                                                    94-8229
                                                                    CIP

Contents

CHAPTER **12**

For Toddlers **231**

CHAPTER **13**

For Preschoolers **253**

CHAPTER **14**

For Primary-Aged **281**

SECTION FIVE

Steps Toward More Developmentally Appropriate Practice

CHAPTER **15**

Helping Teachers Change to More Appropriate Practice **311**

CHAPTER **16**

Helping Parents and Communities Understand Developmentally Appropriate Practice **323**

CHAPTER **17**

A Look at Developmentally Appropriate Programs **339**

Index **357**

Preface

*I*n our world today, increasing numbers of young children are cared for by others beyond family in their earliest years. This has naturally led to questions about the most helpful practices to nurture their development. In addition, the educational systems have been increasingly under scrutiny, with report after report revealing declining scores in every area. Concern on both fronts has led many teachers, parents, and communities to devise their own best solutions. Unfortunately in many cases, the solution has become part of the problem. A recent response to this complex issue of what is the most appropriate learning for children from birth through the early primary years has been the publication of a number of position statements defining what should and should not be happening to young children.

The early childhood profession has been enriched and stimulated by the series of position statements on developmentally appropriate practice issued by a variety of professional organizations in the past several years. While these statements have formed the basis for continuing discussion among academics and professionals, classroom teachers are struggling to discover how the philosophy translates into everyday decisions and actions in their particular situations. This book is designed to help teachers who work with children through the early childhood years as they try to implement the philosophy daily. The ideas found in the book are practical and comprehensive, applicable in the wide variety of private and public settings with the various client populations that early childhood teachers encounter today.

In addition, others are involved in the wider conversations about helpful practices in the early years. Administrators and decision-makers in the community also gain clear understandings of positive learning environments for young children. Parents who are making choices for the care and education of their young children can learn what good practice looks like.

In the first two chapters, the concepts of developmentally appropriate practice are explored by the introduction of general principles that are made specific and concrete in subsequent chapters. After the general introduction, students examine developmentally appropriate physical environments, social/emotional environments, and cognitive/language environments. "Environment" is used here to include comprehensively the materials, activities, arrangements, relationships, and interaction that adults provide in the classroom. In each of these sections, there are separate chapters describing appropriate practice for infants, for toddlers, for preschoolers, and for primary-aged children. The last section includes chapters that explore the process of making changes for teachers, and for gaining support for those changes. Examples of programs implementing developmentally appropriate practice are included in the final chapter.

For those instructors or students who prefer to use an age/stage rather than topic approach, it will be easily seen how the chapters on infancy may be designated for consecutive reading and discussion (e.g., Chapters 3, 7, and 11), then those on toddlers (Chapters 4, 8, and 12). The author assumes that students who use this text have already been exposed to a child development course, since the body of current child development knowledge is beyond the scope of this book. However, both in the introductory chapters and where appropriate throughout, reference and/or summary of the necessary theoretical base is included. Whether students are at beginning levels or more advanced ones, the references and ideas for further study meet individual needs. Instructors will find suggestions for classroom activities at chapter end and additional resources in the Instructors' Guide.

A critical component of the philosophy of developmentally appropriate practice is the idea of individual appropriateness; that is, that no absolute standard can be set that precisely meets the needs of every individual. This principle also holds true for the particular teachers and programs that work to find their optimum functioning. So this book is intended as a guide for thoughtful consideration of classroom practices, not as an absolute prescription that would push every classroom mindlessly into the same mold. It is assumed and planned that the dialogue in the profession will continue, expanding our thought and our horizons. This book is offered in the hope that young children will be offered the best experiences that caring and knowledgeable adults can provide.

Acknowledgments

There are many conversations and experiences that contribute to a work such as this. Over twenty years of college classroom discussions with new and experienced teachers have shaped my questions and assumptions, and I am grateful to students who have pushed me to find better ways to explain. I have been fortunate to have had colleagues all along the way to support and stimulate my growth as an educator. In particular, I want to thank Saunie Wood and Cliff Hammond, two good friends who have provided strong leadership in the early childhood program at Central Piedmont Community College; Vaughn Luckadoo and the rest of the Human Services Department, who help make teaching a pleasure; Betty High Rounds, a valued friend and colleague who first gave me the idea, then gave helpful feedback on chapters in an early draft, and who provided both the excitement and many materials on Reggio Emilia; Jean McDuffie of the library at CPCC; and Anne Siekman, of the Norway Memorial Library in Norway, Maine, who provided exceptional library resource assistance to a "summer resident." Thanks also to Jay and Kylie who made a trip to get the photos at Scarborough. I am grateful in acknowledging the importance of the comments of Lella Gandini in shaping the final section on Reggio Emilia, and her time in reading the original draft. I am also grateful to Beth Bellemere for her time in explaining the GOLD program to me. All of the materials acknowledged to the Scarborough School Department in this book may be used only with Ms. Bellemere's written permission. All photos from the Scarborough School Department are also courtesy of Jay Gestwicki. I appreciate the willingness of the centers that permitted me to photograph their children and classrooms: Avondale Children's Center; CPCC Child Care Training Center; the Methodist Home Child Development Center; and Nations Bank Child Care Center, all in Charlotte N.C., as well as the children in the multi-aged program in Scarborough, Maine. I appreciate the thoughtful comments of reviewers: Kathleen Glascott, Middle Tennesee State University, Tennessee; Mary Jennings, Northland College, Wisconsin; Penny Luken, Broward Community College, Florida; and Tamra Bottomlee, Purdue University, Calumet, Indiana. And of course, much love and gratitude to my family—Ron, Tim, and Jay—who are always developmentally appropriate, and willing to ignore the many shortcomings a work such as this produces.

Note to the Reader. I am well aware that a work of this kind could always be larger and more comprehensive; it is my assumption that a text such as this might be used in several courses, covering the age spans. It may well supplement development texts and courses. I have endeavored to convey the ongoingness of the discussion on developmental appropriateness.

SECTION ONE

Guest Editorial by David Elkind

What is happening in the United States today is truly astonishing. In a society that prides itself on its preference for facts over hearsay, on its openness to research, and on its respect for "expert" opinion, parents, educators, administrators, and legislators are ignoring the facts, the research, and the expert opinion about how young children learn and how best to teach them.

All across the country, educational programs intended for school-aged children are being appropriated for the education of young children.... Many... kindergartens have introduced curricula, including work papers, once reserved for first-grade children. And in books addressed to parents a number of writers are encouraging parents to teach infants and young children reading, math, and science.

When we instruct children in academic subjects, or in swimming, gymnastics, or ballet, at too early an age, we miseducate them; we put them at risk for short-term stress and long-term personality damage for no useful purpose. There is no evidence that such early instruction has lasting benefits, and considerable evidence that it can do lasting harm.

Why, then, are we engaging in such unhealthy practices on so vast a scale? Like all social phenomena, the contemporary miseducation of large numbers of infants and young children derives from the coming together of multiple and complex social forces that both generate and justify these practices. One thing is sure: miseducation does not grow out of established knowledge about what is good pedagogy for infants and young children. Rather, the reason must be sought in the changing values, size, structure, and style of American families, in the residue of the 1960s effort to ensure equality of education for all groups, and in the new status, competitive, and computer pressures experienced by parents and educators in the eighties.

While miseducation has always been with us— we have always had pushy parents—today it has become a social norm. If we do not wake up to the potential danger of these harmful practices, we may do serious damage to a large segment of the next generation (Elkind, 1988, pp. 3–4).

Defining Developmentally Appropriate Practice

INTRODUCTION

In Chapters 1 and 2, we will explore what is meant by the term *developmentally appropriate practice*, or DAP. The chapters examine the general definitions, understandings, and implications of DAP, and will also delineate an understanding of practices that are not developmentally appropriate for children under the age of eight.

Defining Developmentally Appropriate Practice:
What It Is

*S*eth Adams and Maria Jimenez are two of the nation's millions of pre-schoolers who will begin attending early childhood programs this year. Seth is entering the two-year-old class at Busy Learners Day Care Center and Maria is enrolled in the half-day program at Happy Days Nursery School. Their parents have looked at several programs in their communities before making their choice.

Seth's parents chose his center because of its philosophy and the activities they saw during a visit. The center handbook states:

> We believe young children are capable of serious learning, so our day is arranged to provide opportunities for your child to gain the important academic skills that will gain him/her entrance to the school of your choice. Our curriculum includes beginning reading skills, with emphasis on phonics, and introductory math activities. Before your child leaves our two-year-old class, he/she will be able to recite the alphabet and recognize many letter sounds, name the shapes and colors, and count to twenty. Our Spanish teacher spends an hour a week with the two-year-old class.

Their visit to the classroom found children quietly sitting at tables coloring a sheet that had a big D and a picture of a dog. The work from the day before was hanging on the walls; the children had pasted the precut outline of a dog. The teachers seemed competent and completely in control as they gave instructions to the toddlers. This school matched their concept of what a school should be.

Maria's parents also chose their school based on its philosophy and their visit. The handbook states:

> We believe that children should be actively involved in play to develop the whole child. Teachers prepare a variety of interesting choices for children each day. Children make their own discoveries about the world as they are able to explore materials and learn to play with other children.

A visit to this classroom showed groups of children busy all around the room. One child painted at an easel. Three were building with blocks in an area where another was pushing a truck. Three children were talking as they dressed in grown-up finery. Another group was helping the teacher mix up some play dough at a table. There was a lot of conversation.

Both of these sets of parents were confident that they had made the best decision for their child's entry into the world of school. Yet it seems obvious to any observer that the children in these programs will encounter very different experiences. The philosophies as stated by the two programs seem to claim very different methods of educating young children. How do we reconcile such differing views on what is the appropriate education and nurturing of development for young children?

The debate is not new; nor is it finished. But it has entered a new stage since the publication in the 1980s and early 1990s of several position statements about developmentally appropriate practice by several major educational organizations in this country.

The first definitive position on developmentally appropriate practice was published by the National Association for the Education of Young Children (NAEYC) in 1986. With the development of NAEYC's accreditation system (the National Academy of Early Childhood Programs), it had become obvious that there was a need for a more specific definition of developmentally appropriate practice. Otherwise, statements like "using developmentally appropriate activities or materials" were too open to varieties of interpretation. That first publication was soon followed by a statement expanded to include specifics for programs serving children from birth through age eight, and outlines of both appropriate and inappropriate practices (Bredekamp, 1987). The Association for Childhood Education International (ACEI) published an article corroborating the importance of play in 1988 (Isenberg and Quisenberry, 1988), and the National Association of Elementary School Principals (NAESP) elaborated its own standards for quality programs for young children in 1990 (NAESP, 1990). The National Association of State Boards of Education (NASBE) followed with statements as part of the report of the National Task Force on School Readiness (NASBE, 1991). NAEYC has since published jointly with the National Association of Early Childhood Specialists in State Departments of Education (NAECS/SDE) a position statement, *Guidelines for Appropriate Curriculum Content and Assessment in Programs Serving Children Ages 3 Through 8* (Bredekamp and Rosegrant, 1992). The endorsers of this statement include the Association for Childhood Education International, the Association for Supervision and Curriculum Development, the National Association of State Boards of Education, the National Council for the Social Studies, the National Council of Teachers of Mathematics, and the Southern Early Childhood Association. A joint statement of concerns about present practices in reading instruction and recommendations for improvement was made by the Association for Childhood Education International, the Association for Supervision and Curriculum Development, the International Reading Association (IRA), the National Association for the Education of Young Children, the National Association of Elementary School Principals and the National Council of Teachers of English (IRA, 1989).

The conversations continue. Many early childhood professionals, parents, and communities have been grateful for the guidelines as they endeavor to chart the path in ever-changing territory. New trends and concerns encountered in the early childhood field include the ever-increasing numbers of infants and toddlers being cared for in groups and the increasing emphasis on academic assessment and readiness requirements for kindergartens and even prekindergartens. Pressure to achieve in standardized tests haunts teaching and learning in the early elementary years. The position statements help us make judgments and inform our decision making. If you have not already seen these position statements, especially the NAEYC "green book" (Bredekamp, 1987), obtain a copy for your reading and professional library. It will give a useful summary of the principles that lie behind this book.

The NAEYC statement contains an introductory position statement with guidelines on curriculum, adult-child interaction, relations between the home and the program, and developmental evaluation of children. There are separate sections on developmentally appropriate practice for infants and toddlers, for three-year-olds, for four- and five-year-olds, and for the primary grades, serving five- through eight-year-olds. Practitioners can use the guidelines for initial assessment of programs for developmentally appropriate practices.

Nevertheless, programs as different as those for Seth and Maria exist everywhere. And the differences extend downward into the nursery and upward into the elementary school classroom. In many centers and schools, the statements on developmentally appropriate practice appear to have had no impact or recognition at all. This may be due, in part, to the human tendency to avoid recognizing ideas or information that conflict with past experience or present comfort levels. This book is intended to help students, professionals, parents, and concerned communities to consider the definitions and implications of the developmental appropriateness of programs for children from birth through age eight. Together we will consider ideas that can help translate theoretical statements into actions applicable in particular situations.

OBJECTIVES

After completing this chapter, students should be able to:

- define developmentally appropriate practice (DAP).
- describe the essential components of DAP.
- identify seven developmental principles relevant to understanding DAP.
- discuss ten positive interpretations of misunderstandings related to DAP.

Developmentally Appropriate Practice—What Is It?

Developmentally appropriate practice refers to applying child development knowledge in making thoughtful and appropriate decisions about early childhood program practices. Everything that has been learned through research and formulated into theory about how children develop and learn at various ages and stages is used to create learning environments that match their abilities and needs. This means that developmentally appropriate practice is based only on what is presently known and understood about children. It is not based on what adults wish children were like, or hope they will be like, or even surmise they might be like.

Developmentally appropriate practice is based on the accumulation of data and facts of what children are like. Developmentally appropriate practice "is not a curriculum; it is not a rigid set of standards that dictate practice. Rather, it is a framework, a philosophy, or an approach to working with young children" (Bredekamp and Rosegrant, 1992, p. 4). This is important to understand at the outset. Those concerned about narrowing the standards of good practice until all programs look the same and do the same things need to realize that there is no such intention. Rather, the intention is to focus philosophically on what we know about children and what we can learn about individual children as a basis for decision making.

In order to translate knowledge of child development into the practical implications for nurturing and educating children, adults have to make many decisions. The deciding question when designing program curricula and formulating plans is, How does this fit with what we know about children? If our practice complements and accommodates our knowledge of children, then the decision can be said to be based on developmentally appropriate practice. If it is not compatible, then the practice should be questioned and changed.

The clear implication is for early childhood practitioners to be steeped in child development knowledge. Without that background, it is too easy for teachers and caregivers to fall back on making decisions based only on vague notions that are part personal values, part memories, part expediency, and part images of desirable future behavior. If you have not completed basic child development courses and/or reading, that is an important place to start before attempting to plan and evaluate quality programs for young children. This book briefly reviews pertinent developmental knowledge to remind readers of the theoretical basis for the suggested actions in the classroom.

Obviously child development knowledge alone will not give practitioners all the answers they need in planning programs and curricula for young children (Spodek and Brown, 1993). Educational programs are products of decisions about curriculum content (what children will learn), learning processes (how children will learn), instructional strategies (how teachers will teach), and assessment methods (how to know what children have learned and how to plan for the future) (Bredekamp and Rosegrant, 1992). Decisions are made on the basis of child development knowledge, and also on the basis of family, community, and cultural values and priorities. Finding the correct balance between professionals' knowledge and parent and community expectations is an important component of the philosophy of developmental appropriateness.

As Bredekamp reminds us in the opening of the NAEYC position statement, there are two dimensions of developmental appropriateness: age appropriateness and individual appropriateness.

❝ Human development research indicates that there are universal, predictable sequences of growth and change that occur in children during the first nine years of life. These predictable changes occur in all domains of development—physical, emotional, social, and cognitive. Knowledge of typical development of children within the age span served by the program provides a framework from which teachers prepare the learning environment and plan appropriate experiences (Bredekamp, 1987, p. 2). ❞

Most teachers of twos would refer to their increasing abilities with language, their beginning interest in toilet control, their short episodes of parallel play, and their limits on emotional control. Teachers of fours are likely to refer to exuberant, active, out-of-bounds behaviors, representational art and imaginative fantasy play, fascination with friends and talk, and abilities to button, snap, and zip. Teachers of sixes would talk about the increasing dependence on peer approval, interest in games and developing physical skills, interest in collections, and desire for competence. Such typical characteristics help teachers plan appropriately for particular age groups, and also to note when children's behavior seems far from developmentally typical.

But age/stage norms do not explain the infinite variations in behavior and skills that teachers see in any classroom. Individual children have followed their own patterns of development.

> *Each child is a unique person with an individual pattern and timing of growth, as well as individual personality, learning style and family background. Both the curriculum and adults' interactions with children should be responsive to individual differences. Learning in young children is the result of interaction between the child's thoughts and experiences with materials, ideas, and people. These experiences should match the child's developing abilities, while also challenging the child's interest and understanding (Bredekamp, 1987, p. 2).*

Children must be considered within the context of their family, culture and community, past history, and present circumstances. Developmentally appropriate practice does not approach children as if they were equal members of an age grouping, but as unique individuals. The knowledge of specifics of uniqueness does not come through courses or books, although awareness and sensitivities to diversity may start by using these methods. This knowledge primarily comes through relationship and interaction with children, and also with their parents, who are important resources of knowledge of their children. Developmentally appropriate practice is based on parents' active involvement, both as resources of knowledge and as decision makers about what is individually appropriate for their children.

Both of these dimensions, age and individual appropriateness, must be given attention in planning developmentally appropriate programs. Attention only to age appropriateness would lead to too much uniformity in classroom practice, which is something that advocates of the standards want to move away from.

Bredekamp (1987) points out that the actual content of the curriculum in developmentally appropriate programs may differ according to community tradition, social and cultural values, and parental desires. But for content and teaching strategies to be developmentally appropriate, they must be both age and individually appropriate.

In the position on developmentally appropriate practice, play is stated to be the primary vehicle by which young children learn and show the progress in their learning in all domains. Piaget's ideas about play (see Chapters 11, 12, 13, and 14) are referred to as the standard for developmentally appropriate practice. "Child-initiated, child-directed, teacher-supported play is an essential component of developmentally appropriate practice" (Bredekamp, 1987, p. 3).

Thus far, these definitions make it sound fairly straightforward: get as much developmental knowledge as possible about both the age group taught and individuals within that group, and then plan play environments and experiences that will nurture and enhance development.

But before appropriate decisions can be made for the care and nurturing of young children, one more component of developmentally appropriate practice needs to be identified. This is an attitude: an attitude of respect (Kostelnik, 1993). It is this attitude that allows adults to accept children's developmental behaviors and differences without wanting to change them or hurry them on to a subsequent stage. Respect demands that teachers recognize and accept the diverse backgrounds from which children come and the contributions of their families. (Diversity may mean differences in family structure and experiences, racial or ethnic heritage, community lifestyles and traditions, special needs related to physical or mental conditions, etc.) Respect demands that teachers and families continue a dialogue of negotiation in making decisions for the benefit of the children. Respect for the developmental process allows adults to have faith in children's capacity to develop and change in their own ways, in their own time. Respect demands that adults search for developmentally compatible answers in each particular situation, not just move around solutions that have seemed to "work" with other groups. Just because group time seemed like an appropriate learning experience for four-year-olds, doesn't mean the director decides to institute it for toddlers as well. Respect for toddlers' current learning styles will prevent the director from imposing the practice. The attitude of respect for development allows early childhood professionals to feel unpressured in the face of questions about proving accountability. They know that development ultimately moves children on to increased knowledge and skills, given an environment that supports appropriately and does not thwart.

To summarize our discussion to this point, developmentally appropriate practice is a philosophy of making decisions related to children's programs based on child development knowledge. Professionals base their knowledge of age appropriateness on research and recognized theory, and do their own research to learn what is also individually appropriate for each child in their care. The standards recognize that active play is the primary curriculum method in early childhood, and that child-initiated and teacher-supported activity is developmentally appropriate. The component of respect in the philosophy governs teachers' interactions with children and their families in searching for the best responses. An understanding of development is critical to making developmentally appropriate decisions.

Basic Principles of Development

There are certain basic principles of child development that begin every text or course in development. These principles represent the distillation of decades of research, study, theory, and practice. They merit brief restating here, as we consider practices based on developmental knowledge. (A reminder for students who have not completed child development courses: these principles would be considered in depth in most child development texts.)

1. *There is a predictable sequence in development.* Understanding the behaviors necessary at a particular stage, and those that are likely to emerge next, helps practitioners to recognize typical development and to challenge appropriately for the next phase.

2. *Development at one stage lays the base for later development.* It is impossible for development to continue well when attempts are made to push children to skip or hurry through earlier stages. Children must be allowed to take the time needed for learning before they are encouraged to proceed on.

3. *There are optimal periods in development.* Times of readiness need to be recognized through careful observation and taken advantage of. Learning occurs most easily at the optimal period. Conversely, all the teaching in the world won't make learning happen easily before a time of readiness.

4. *Development results from the interaction of biological factors (maturation) and environmental factors (learning).* It is in fact maturation that is a prerequisite to readiness for learning. The environment determines just what direction development will take.

5. *Development proceeds as an interrelated whole, with all aspects (physical, cognitive, emotional, social) influencing the others.* A program that strives to nurture development supports all domains as having equal importance. All learning experiences are recognized as integrated opportunities for growth, instead of separate skill or content entities.

6. *Each individual develops according to a particular timetable and pace.* It is impossible and dangerous to compare individuals of similar chronological ages. Each child has unique needs and characteristics at any particular stage. When activities provide for differences and choice, this principle is supported.

7. *Development proceeds from simple to complex, and from general to specific.* Recognition of this principle again cautions against skipping or rushing children on to behaviors they are not yet ready for.

Having defined the essential components of developmentally appropriate practice, and considered developmental principles, it is important to state that nothing is so clear-cut as to be either/or: either child-initiated or adult-directed; either process-oriented or product-oriented. The variables are not meant to be absolutes—the good versus the bad. Developmentally appropriate practice demands finding a balance, including a balance that each teacher finds compatible with personal experience and values. Many programs include practices that are somewhere along a continuum between the two poles (Kostelnik, 1992). Some include practices that are developmentally appropriate along with others that are less appropriate. The goal of developmentally appropriate practice is to examine all aspects of programs for young children to determine whether actions "enhance or detract from the quality of children's lives" (Kostelnik, 1993, p. 74).

Many of the developmentally inappropriate practices noted by the position statements relate to the early teaching of academic skills that focus purely on cognitive development, particularly in the preschool years. Bredekamp and Rosegrant note that the "goal [of the position statement] was to 'open up' the curriculum and teaching practices and move away from the narrow emphasis on isolated academic skills and the drill-and-practice approach to instruction"

(Bredekamp and Rosegrant, 1992, p. 4). The crux of the "appropriate/inappropriate" discussions is probably in the differing answers to these three questions:

 How do children most effectively learn at this age?

What is most important for children to learn at this age, whether they are in a program of one sort or another or at home?

What are the repercussions later in the child's school years, adolescence, and adult life of the academic preschool experience versus experience in a developmentally appropriate program? (Greenberg, 1990, p. 75). "

Greenberg also notes that another question of interest is, Why do so many teachers, parents, and others prefer the academic-style preschool? This question, along with the issue of later repercussions, will be addressed in Chapter 2. The answers to the first two questions, what and how children of various ages should be learning, form the content of Sections Two, Three, and Four of this book.

Positive Interpretations of Misunderstandings Regarding DAP

We should realize that some of the resistance to instituting developmentally appropriate practice comes because certain misunderstandings about what it means have arisen (Kostelnik, 1992). Some of the misunderstandings result from a less than thorough grounding in child development knowledge; others come from trying to simplify and close a complex discussion that should remain open-ended as early childhood professionals continue to puzzle through its implications. There is certainly a danger that standards of practice be interpreted as crystallized and fixed.

Ten Misunderstandings About DAP

Whatever their source, the misunderstandings cloud the issue of acceptance of developmentally appropriate practice. It is advantageous to consider these misunderstandings here as we try to understand the nature of developmental appropriateness.

Misunderstanding 1—There is only one right way to do developmentally appropriate practice. Bredekamp and Rosegrant suggest that this misinterpretation resulted from the format of the 1987 position statement, contrasting appropriate and inappropriate practice as if they were two opposite poles and not differences on a continuum with differing gradations in between. Obviously the misinterpretation of only one right way contradicts precisely what is intended in terms of uniqueness. Some children will need more adult guidance and classroom structure than others. Children whose experiences are limited, who bring less knowledge and skills to the classroom than others, need teachers who can continually modify their teaching strategies, learning what works best at any particular time. If a program needs to match its practices to the unique population served, there will be a multitude of appearances to developmentally appropriate practice. A program that serves mostly white upper middle-class children who live in a big city will likely offer different curriculum experiences from one found in a rural desert community, serving Hispanic children whose families are involved in farming. What any program looked like and did last year may be quite different as it tries to work with this year's children. Developmentally appropriate teachers aren't looking only for the right answers, but for the best answers for these particular children at this particular time.

Misunderstanding 2—Developmentally appropriate classrooms are unstructured. Understandably, to some this sounds like an environment of chaos they'd prefer to avoid; to others, structure sounds so rigid and teacher-driven they want to avoid it. Structure refers to the teachers' formulations of instructional plans, and their careful organization of materials and interaction in the physical, social/emotional, and cognitive/language environments to achieve their instructional goals. As we will see in our discussion of these environments later in the book, developmentally appropriate classrooms are highly structured. There is purposeful planning and interaction to support children's growth in all of these areas. Children actively participate in and influence planning, but teachers are in control. Casual visitors may not perceive the organization, the planning, and the evaluation that go on behind the scenes in classrooms where children learn through play. While developmentally appropriate classrooms contain movement, diverse activity, conversation, and play, they do not contain chaos or aimlessness.

Misunderstanding 3—Teachers teach minimally or not at all in developmentally appropriate classrooms. Once again, the misunderstanding relies on a limited view: that teachers teach only by directing and controlling all learning in a classroom—instructing, assigning tasks, correcting errors. The implication in this misinterpretation is that teachers are merely passive observers in developmentally appropriate classrooms—again, these environments are seen as chaotic. Teachers in developmentally appropriate classrooms use a variety of teaching strategies. Some of the strategies—the observing, planning, scheduling, arranging, and organizing—create the invisible structure that supports learning activity. Some of the strategies are embedded in the personal interaction with children busy at play; teachers comment, ask, suggest, and provide information and additional materials. They model, challenge, and help children change direction. They also teach with large group activities, although these play a lesser role in developmentally appropriate classrooms, where matching individual needs is a priority. They recognize that learning doesn't happen only when their mouths are open. When they intervene in learning situations, it is because their observation and judgment have led them to conclude that learning will be enhanced by their teaching. Teachers in developmentally appropriate classrooms teach by supporting children's active learning with a multitude of direct and indirect strategies.

Misunderstanding 4—Developmentally appropriate programs don't include academics, generally interpreted to be the formal skills of learning reading, writing, and arithmetic. This misunderstanding stems from a passionate disagreement between those who feel that children not exposed to academics will be unable to achieve at expected levels in later education and those who feel young children are not yet ready for this style of learning. Each side ignores the real nature of how children's learning and interest in materials naturally brings them to literacy- and mathematical-related activity and exploration: "Read it again!"; "What does that say?"; "I need two more plates for the table!"; "Timmy's got too many—I've only got one!" Children's interest brings opportunities for academic content into the teaching day of any preschool and drives them to continue learning the skills they need in the primary years; thus, it is a simplification to say that academics are not developmentally appropriate. What is really meant is that curriculum activities that focus on aspects of isolated skill development, and teaching strategies of whole-group teacher instruction and teacher-directed abstract worksheet drills are not appropriate methods of teaching young children. Academic content of literacy- and mathematical-related content is presented by integration with all other classroom experiences in a developmentally appropriate classroom; most formal methods of traditional teacher-directed instruction are not included.

A comment from David Elkind is pertinent here:

 A developmental approach to education does not deny the importance of such knowledge. The difference between the two approaches is a matter of which acquisition comes first.... From a developmental perspective, the creation of curious, active learners must *precede* the acquisition of particular information.... To put the difference more succinctly, the developmental approach seeks to create students who *want to know*, whereas the psychometric approach seeks to produce students who *know what we want* (Elkind, 1989, p. 115).

One of the voices in the debate on developmentally appropriate practice (Walsh, 1989) suggests that the issue is not that

 ...such-and-such is bad because it is happening in preschool or kindergarten... but the reality that many of these practices are inappropriate for any child....The problem is not that kindergarten looks like first grade; the problem is what kindergarten and first grade (and second and third), that is, what the elementary school is beginning to look like (Walsh, 1989, p. 389).

The real irony is that, when children are judged "unready" for the rigors of academic kindergartens or first grades, they are often tracked into "developmental" kindergartens or "transitional classes" that emphasize active, hands-on learning experiences for young children. Developmentally appropriate practices are offered to these children who are "failing" in the less appropriate, traditional settings.

Misunderstanding 5—Developmentally appropriate programs are only effective for particular populations, "usually assumed to be typically developing, White, middle-class children" (Bredekamp and Rosegrant, 1992, p. 5). This implies that children of diverse racial, cultural, or socioeconomic backgrounds, or children with special needs, will not be well-served in such programs (Jipson, 1991). A number of experts planning intervention programs for children from lower socioeconomic backgrounds feel that a directly academic approach is essential to counteract the early lack of experiences and stimulation in the preschool years. The DISTAR method of working with preschoolers and kindergartners, developed by Bereiter and Englemann, relies heavily on drill and rote-learning style of letter sounds and number skills in preplanned curriculum packages (Bereiter and Engelmann, 1966).

Others disagree, notably David Elkind, contending that the DISTAR approach is inappropriate for most young children of all socioeconomic backgrounds.

❝ DISTAR is even worse for young disadvantaged children, because it imprints them with a rote-learning style that could be damaging later on. As Piaget pointed out, children learn by manipulating their environment, and a healthy early education program structures the child's environment to make the most of that fact. DISTAR, on the other hand, structures the child and constrains his learning style (Elkind, in Shell, 1989, p. 53). *❞*

It is not only early childhood professionals who are unsure about the benefits of direct instruction vs. developmentally appropriate.

❝ Many parents (of minority children) view the non-didactic and child-initiated activity characteristic of a developmentally appropriate classroom as inimical to their children's success; these parents believe that worksheets and other evidence of information and skills are more appropriate than the "messing around" characteristic of informal classrooms (Bowman, in Bredekamp and Rosegrant, 1992, p. 132). *❞*

Parents of children with special needs voice similar concerns, that their children need all the direct instruction they can get.

According to the basic principles of developmentally appropriate practice, modification to curriculum experiences, environments, and strategies are made to respond to individual needs and abilities. This makes the developmentally appropriate classroom suited for every child, no matter what the experience or ability; and because there are no uniform standards of achievement for all children in the class, it is more likely that children with special needs will grow comfortably and successfully without fear of failure. Everyone learns at their own rate, in their own way in a developmentally appropriate classroom.

In addition, to be individually appropriate, programs must attend to cultural variations in the children they serve. Programs must adapt themselves to all individual needs, interests, and heritages. Those who criticize developmentally appropriate practice on the basis of "failing to fully acknowledge the role of personal voices, cultures, caring and care-taking, interconnectedness, and shared responsibility" (Jipson, 1991, p. 133) seem not to understand that the standards make an essential part of the curriculum to be a relationship between children's personal and cultural histories and the classroom environments. And as Elizabeth Jones points out, teachers who want to work in developmentally appropriate ways have

❝ ...both a political and a moral obligation to be accountable to those unfamiliar with the rationale for this view of learning. While skepticism about the value of play is widespread, it is no accident that parents in those groups that have traditionally lacked power in our economic system are particularly concerned when teachers let children play. Their children have been ill-served in our schools,

often by teachers who lacked belief in their ability to learn. "You teach my kid" is an understandable and justifiable demand by any parent, and especially by those whose suspicion is well founded (Jones and Reynolds, 1992, pp. 86–87).

Teachers using developmentally appropriate practice must work to make their classrooms individually appropriate for every child and supported by every parent.

Misunderstanding 6—In developmentally appropriate classrooms, there is no way to tell if children are learning. The misunderstanding here is that methods other than the traditional, easily applied techniques of testing children's retention of material are used. The pressure for accountability has brought standardized testing into classrooms for young children. Even the youngest children are frequently subjected to pop quizzes (What color is this? How many balls do I have?). Children's learning in all domains cannot be so easily quantified and measured as these tests for achievement of cognitive concepts suggest. Children's constructed understanding of the world, its objects, and people is indicated in their increasingly complex use of materials and style of interaction. Their language, questions, and concentration indicate development. The essence of teaching in a developmentally appropriate classroom lies in continual observation of children's play, language, and interaction, and increasing abilities to use literacy skills to communicate their learning. As teachers record specific observations, they identify patterns of growth and change in each child. These observations lead to creating the next challenges for children. The observations also answer adult questions about learning. Teachers who have respect for children's innate ability and desire to teach themselves have faith that children will develop and learn in a responsive environment, and their observations are a concrete way of justifying that faith.

Misunderstanding 7—Developmentally appropriate practice can be achieved simply by acquiring certain kinds of toys and materials (Kostelnik, 1993). This is just nonsense, and a gross simplification of important ideas. It is the same kind of gross misunderstanding evidenced when centers purchase selections of toys designed by Montessori and then call themselves a Montessori program. Without a thorough understanding and grounding in the educational philosophy, the toys are just additional materials in the classroom. The misunderstood truth here is that materials are indeed important components in the active learning environment. The standards for developmentally appropriate practice state the concern with too much emphasis on pencil-and-paper kinds of learning activities. Teachers in developmentally appropriate classrooms understand that children's actions and interactions with materials help them create their own sensorimotor understandings and preoperational and concrete concepts. Thus, much time and effort goes into making thoughtful choices of the toys and materials made available for children's play. Because children need materials they can act upon with success regardless of their ability and skill, many of the toys in the developmentally appropriate classroom are open-ended; that is, open for use in a multitude of ways. But beyond this, materials include both traditional toys of early childhood, such as blocks, books, and small items to manipulate, and materials from the real world, such as water, sand, grown-up clothes, kitchen utensils, and old clocks. The one criterion for inclusion of materials in a developmentally appropriate classroom is that they support a specific learning interest or goal. (See Figure 1-1.)

Misunderstanding 8—Developmentally appropriate practice uses no goals or objectives (Bredekamp and Rosegrant, 1992). Children alone decide on what they will learn and how they will learn it. This results from the misunderstanding of the phrase "child-centered," often interpreted to mean child-determined, child-dictated, or child-indulgent, when a more accurate understanding would be "child-sensitive" (Bredekamp and Rosegrant, 1992). While emphases on narrowly academic skills have been rejected by NAEYC as inappropriate practice for young children, developmentally appropriate practice does use goals and objectives. "All effective educational programs have clearly stated objectives (or outcomes) toward which the teacher plans and works with children to achieve" (Bredekamp and Rosegrant, 1992, p. 5). The difference in developmentally appropriate classrooms is that those goals are for all areas of development, based on knowledge of the children's age-level development and on individual needs in learning and development. Children's needs, questions, and interests play a major role in influencing teacher planning in a child-centered curriculum. But teachers also know how, why, and when to extend learning possibilities in play and projects. They monitor children's progression through specific lessons they need to acquire as they move toward acquiring literacy and numerical abilities, as well as in social skills, emotional control, and physical competency.

Misunderstanding 9—In developmentally appropriate practice, the curriculum is child development (Bredekamp and Rosegrant, 1992). This misinterpretation loses sight of the fact that other knowledge must work together with child development to ensure that all children reach their individual potentials. While child development knowledge is crucial to determine appropriate teaching practice, there are other considerations that influence decisions about curriculum. Spodek and Brown suggest that development is only one of three dimensions that influence classroom practices. The other dimensions include the cultural dimension, considering a society's values of what its members want their children to be like; and the knowledge dimension, what children need to know (Spodek and Brown, 1993). This implies a continuing need for conversations between educators and communities to make decisions about skills and dispositions children will need as citizens of the twenty-first century; values of the family and community; identification of necessary knowledge and subject areas; and areas of interest to the child/children. Consideration of these dimensions does not conflict with concepts of developmental appropriateness. Rather, it is this process of dialogue that results in making decisions that are truly individually appropriate.

Misunderstanding 10—Developmental appropriateness is just one in a sequence of changing trends in education (Kostelnik, 1992). Obviously there have been changes in what educators have been asked to do in the past, and teachers tend not to take too seriously that which they think may not last too long. However, if developmental appropriateness is conceived of as "an evolution in professional thinking that will continue to emerge over the coming decades" (Kostelnik, 1992, p. 23), the philosophy is likely to be integrated into professional thinking and practice. Teachers are not being asked to change everything they do; they are instead being asked to con-

EDUCATIONAL TOYS

"If we buy it, what are his chances of getting into Harvard?"

Figure 1-1 The "right" materials alone do not guarantee developmentally appropriate activities, or the kind of success parents or teachers may be looking for. *Used by permission of Phi Delta Kappan and Bo Brown.*

sider their actions in the light of integrating their developmental knowledge of children. The abiding question will be, Is what I do supported by what I know to be true about this child/children? The strategies may change, but the knowledge and attitude will remain constant. Developmentally appropriate practice should remain as the unifying value that draws early childhood professionals together. There is recognition that the subject is an ongoing conversation. NAEYC has called for comments and suggestions to be sent to them for a forthcoming revision of the position statement.

It would be misleading to suggest that there is complete consensus within the early childhood professional community about the statements of developmentally appropriate practice. Jipson suggests that DAP ignores issues of cultural variation in what constitutes "appropriate" (Jipson, 1991). Spodek points out that questions of the "what" of curriculum are not addressed by a focus on development (Spodek and Brown, 1993). Kessler warns that professionals should be wary of prescriptions for practice based on the perspectives of a particular group of individuals, and suggests the multiplicity of views of purposes of education (Kessler, 1991). Walsh suggests that the consensus about child development is more apparent than real and ignores important alternative perspectives on learning and development (Walsh, 1991). It is important that the conversations about the position statements continue, in order to ensure the inclusion of all arguments and perspectives.

This book is intended to help practitioners and others interested in developmentally appropriate practice consider specific implications for action in their particular environments. While it is not presented as a definitive statement or an absolute plan of action—the assumption is that no such statement would be developmentally appropriate for adults—rather, it is intended to stimulate questions and examinations of current practice.

SUMMARY

Within recent years NAEYC and other professional educational organizations have published statements defining developmentally appropriate practice as actions based on developmental knowledge of both age-level ability and individual interest and need. Developmentally appropriate practice specifies the provision of child-centered, child-initiated, teacher-supported play learning environments. In NAEYC's publications specifics are defined as appropriate and inappropriate for each age group from birth through age eight, and guidelines given for curriculum and assessment. A number of misunderstandings have arisen among practitioners about the implications of DAP. The most important component may be the respect of children and their characteristics. This respect leads adults to continually question whether their practices match what they know about child development. A thorough grounding in developmental knowledge is essential.

THINK ABOUT IT

1. Talk with several early childhood teachers. Ask them what the term "developmentally appropriate practice" means to them. Ask them to give examples of ways they feel their classroom practices are developmentally appropriate. Ask them to describe ways they meet individual needs in their classrooms. Discuss your thoughts about their responses later with your classmates.

2. Talk with parents of young children about their feelings and concerns about a play curriculum. Discuss with your classmates the implications of their responses as if you were teachers who were implementing DAP.

3. Obtain and read through NAEYC's Developmentally Appropriate Practice book (Bredekamp, 1987) to note the major areas discussed.

QUESTIONS TO REVIEW OBJECTIVES

1. Describe, as fully as you can, what is meant by developmentally appropriate practice. Identify the professional organization that first published a position statement on DAP.

2. Identify and describe the various essential components of DAP.

3. List and discuss implications of several principles of development.

4. Discuss several concepts related to DAP that have been misunderstood. Discuss a more accurate interpretation for each.

REFERENCES AND SUGGESTIONS FOR READING

Bereiter, C., & Engelmann, S. (1966). *Teaching disadvantaged children in the preschool.* Englewood Cliffs, NJ: Prentice-Hall.

Bredekamp, S. (ed.). (1987). *Developmentally appropriate practice in early childhood programs serving children from birth through age 8.* Washington, DC: NAEYC.

Bredekamp, S., & Rosegrant, T. (eds.). (1992). *Reaching potentials: Appropriate curriculum and assessment for young children, Vol. 1.* Washington, DC: NAEYC.

Elkind, D. (1988). *Miseducation: Preschoolers at risk.* New York: Alfred A. Knopf, 3–4.

Elkind, D. (1989, October). Developmentally appropriate practice: Philosophical and practical implications. *Phi Delta Kappan*, 113–117.

Greenberg, P. (1990, January). Why not academic preschool? (Part I). *Young Children.* 46(2), 70–79.

Isenberg, J., & Quisenberry, N. (1988). Play: A necessity for all children. *Childhood Education,* 64(3), 138–145.

Jipson, J. (1991, April). Developmentally appropriate practice: Culture, curriculum, connections. *Early Education and Development, 2(2),* 120–136.

Jones, E., & Reynolds, G. (1992). *The play's the thing: Teacher's roles in children's play.* New York: Teachers College.

Kessler, S. (1991, April). Early childhood education as development: Critique of the metaphor. *Early Education and Development, 2(2),* 137–152.

Kostelnik, M. J. (1992, May). Myths associated with developmentally appropriate programs. *Young Children,* 45(4), 17–23.

Kostelnik, M. J. (1993, March). Recognizing the essentials of developmentally appropriate practice. *Child Care Information Exchange,* 73–77.

NAESP. (1990). *Early childhood education and the elementary school principal: Standards for quality programs for young children.* Alexandria, VA: Author.

NASBE. (1988). *Right from the start.* Alexandria, VA: Author.

NASBE. (1991). Caring communities: Supporting young children and families. *The Report of the National Task Force on School Readiness.* Alexandria, VA: Author.

Shell, E. R. (1989, December). Now, which kind of preschool? *Psychology Today,* 52–53, 56–57.

Spodek, B., & Brown, P. (1993). Alternatives in early childhood education: A historical perspective. In Spodek, B. (ed.), *Handbook of Research on the Education of the Young Children.* New York: Macmillan Publishing Co.

Strickland, D.S. & Morrow, L.M. (eds.). (1989). *Emerging literacy: young children learn to read and write.* Newark, Delaware: International Reading Association.

Walsh, D. J. (1989). Changes in kindergarten: Why here? Why now? *Early Childhood Research Quarterly, 4,* 377–391.

Walsh, D. J. (1991, April). Extending the discourse on developmental appropriateness: A developmental perspective. *Early Education and Development, 2(2),* 109–119.

CHAPTER 2

Defining Developmentally Appropriate Practice:
What It Is Not

*I*n understanding and describing a developmentally appropriate program for young children, it is also helpful to state what practices are not part of developmental appropriateness. This chapter explores these practices, contrasting them with those defined by position statements on developmentally appropriate practice, and examines some results of children who have been exposed to developmentally inappropriate curriculum and teaching methods. Sadly, many of these are a part of too many classrooms in every community.

OBJECTIVES

After completing this chapter, students should be able to:

- discuss reasons why adults choose less appropriate practices.
- identify practices that are not developmentally appropriate.
- discuss why these practices are not appropriate.
- identify results when young children are exposed to curricula that emphasize formal academics.

Reasons for Developmentally Inappropriate Practice

If developmentally appropriate practice is based on child development knowledge, it follows that developmentally inappropriate practice (or DIP) is *not* based on that knowledge. What, then, are the motivations for the frequently seen emphases on more rigidly academic and adult-controlled learning experiences that are offered to young children? Most of the reasons are related to changes in the social milieu in which we live.

Since the early 1960s, attempts to accelerate children's acquisition of academic skills have preoccupied parents and institutions. The panic precipitated by the launching of the Russian satellite Sputnik brought our education system and curriculum under scrutiny. It is interesting to note that at each period of societal change (the Industrial Revolution, the influx of immigrants to the United States in the early 1900s, the Great Depression, World War II, the Great Society reforms of the 1960s), educational reformers have turned to proposing programs for young children (Curry, 1990). In the most recent cycle of this pattern, as experts were consulted to quickly improve the situation, attention focused on getting the academic learning process started as early as possible. In a frequently quoted statement, Jerome Bruner of Harvard theorized that "any subject can be taught effectively in some intellectually honest form to any child at any stage of development" (Bruner, 1962, p. 33). Unfortunately his idea was not based on knowledge of what real children could do, rather, it was merely a hypothesis preceding curriculum recommendations; it was, nonetheless, generally adopted. This was followed by the statement from Benjamin Bloom, interpreting his statistical summaries of IQ data, that four-year-olds had attained half of their intellectual development. The implication was that we must "impose formal learning on young children because otherwise we might lose out on this period of phenomenal mental growth" (Elkind, 1987, p. 9). A number of commercial attempts to capitalize on this idea of early teaching have proliferated into flashcards and methodologies to teach reading, math, foreign language, and esoteric knowledge such as fine art to babies.

Continuing failure in school systems has heightened social concern. The publication of *A Nation at Risk* in 1983 created serious concern about the poor performance of American students on achievement tests, especially when compared with students of other countries. This was followed by other books about failures in learning, which hit the best-sellers lists (Bloom, 1987; Hirsch, 1987). Parents and communities were truly panicked by the studies and predictions.

As the schools came under increasing pressure, educators defended themselves by pointing out that many children from low-income families came to school unprepared for rigorous academics. Among the many programs that were developed to allow disadvantaged children to receive early learning foundations were some that stressed early academics in a highly structured, teacher-controlled system. The debate among early childhood professionals continues regarding the merits of early academic instruction for children who particularly need early intervention to succeed in later education.

❝ Whether or not academic preschools are best for this group of children has been extensively investigated; see, for example, the work of David Weikart. [Author's note: references to Weikart at end of chapter.] It seems paradoxical, but academic preschools are not the most helpful way for low-income children to achieve later academic success. The explanation lies, of course, in the maturation theories of Gesell (physical) and Piaget (mental). (Greenberg, 1990, p. 74) ❞

In fact, the emphasis on early intellectual stimulation has caused the concept of readiness for learning—or developmental appropriateness—to be ignored. Early intervention planning continues to the present, as more and more states move to include public prekindergarten programs into their school systems. Public prekindergarten programs usually serve children from less advantaged socioeconomic backgrounds, and today the same questions about "too much, too soon" in these programs are being raised by child development professionals (Kagan, 1988; Mitchell, 1989). It is not the programs themselves that are brought to question, but the inclusion of practices that many are calling developmentally inappropriate.

Another social factor that has contributed to inappropriate practice is the phenomenon of working mothers and the care of very young children in groups.

Increasingly since the 1960s, women have joined the work force, necessitating finding substitute care for their children, often shortly after birth. Unfortunately in many cases, this has not led to programs that "are more of an outward extension of the home, but instead more a downward extension of the school." (Elkind, March, 1987, p. 14). Directors, teachers, and parents, unless trained in child development, are all more familiar with the kind of education that begins later and is associated with teacher-directed lessons. It has been too easy to "dribble down," to use James Hymes's well known phrase, or to begin earlier and earlier to teach the skills and subskills of academics. Teachers are eager to justify themselves as not merely "babysitters" and parents want to feel they are getting something measurable for their money.

Modern families have been under stress, and we have the statistics on divorce, single parent families, and stepfamilies to prove this. As parents have to contend with their own concerns, it has often been easier or necessary for parents to believe their children are more mature and capable than they really are. This assumption has enabled parents to accept the commonly held view that today's children are ready for learning earlier than in past generations.

Societal pressures to compete, achieve, and succeed push parents to be competitive about their children also. Parents who are trying to have it all may need to give their children as much as they can, including a competitive edge, or head start. It is felt that the sooner children can get started on the "right track," the better chance they will have against the competition. Parents seem driven to make sure their child will have learned the necessary skills to be accepted into the right school or talent program.

To summarize, the educational systems have moved to earlier academics to attempt to try to answer some of their own questions on how to best achieve learning results and how to define their role in serving very young children. Parents are playing new roles as working or single parents, and are therefore needing child care for very young children. Unfamiliar with forms other than traditional school systems and learning, and driven by the pressure to compete and succeed, parents have accepted the guidance of both professionals and entrepreneurs who are promoting ideas for early teaching.

The problem is that the real learning that goes on in a developmentally appropriate classroom goes unrecognized by those who define learning in a narrow hierarchy of cognitive skills. As David Elkind says in *Miseducation: Preschoolers At Risk*:

> Infants and young children are not just sitting twiddling their thumbs, waiting for their parents to teach them to read and do math. They are expending a vast amount of time and effort in exploring and understanding their immediate world. Healthy education supports and encourages this spontaneous learning. Early instruction miseducates, not because it attempts to teach, but because it attempts to teach the wrong things at the wrong time. When we ignore what the child has to learn and instead impose what we want to teach, we put infants and young children at risk for no purpose. (Elkind, 1988, p. 25)

Young children have important things to learn and important skills to develop, and these are nothing like the education most adults understand or remember.

It is important that we examine practices that do not belong in any developmentally appropriate classroom before moving to the specifics of how to implement developmentally appropriate practice for children from birth through age eight. As pointed out by Bredekamp and Rosegrant (1992) in the NAEYC's most recent position statement, it is misleading to suggest that developmentally appropriate practice is at one side (the good side) of a chasm and developmentally inappropriate practice is at the completely opposite extreme. It is not a matter of either/or, rather than positions on a continuum. The intention is to encourage practitioners to examine practices with a view to what is best for children's development. So too, as these contrasts are presented here, the intention is to help see the contrast broadly. With almost every statement, it is possible to add, "at least most of the time," or "unless there are particular occasional circumstances." This is not intended to be a hedging of statements, but to be a real recognition that responding genuinely to individual circumstances might cause teachers to change strategies or practice. However, the contrasts may help readers recognize the areas of concern about standards of good practice.

Contrasting Developmentally Inappropriate and Appropriate Practice

In the following pages, sixteen contrasts between developmentally appropriate and inappropriate practices are made.

Sixteen Points of Contrast Between Developmentally Appropriate and Inappropriate Practice

Contrast 1. It is developmentally inappropriate to direct children to all do the same activity at the same time. Examples might include: asking all the kindergartners to turn to work on page 26 in their language workbooks; directing all the three-year-olds to work on cutting out and coloring an outlined shape of a house; or placing all infants on the same feeding and napping schedule. For one thing, these practices incorrectly assume that young children of like chronological ages are developmentally similar, rather than recognizing unique learning styles and paces, abilities and interests, needs and experiences. Children who are not permitted choices that allow them to find their own developmental opportunity for success will not develop self-confidence in their ability as learners. Very young children who do not have their personal needs met predictably do not have the opportunity to develop confidence in other people.

In developmentally appropriate classrooms, teachers recognize that children develop uniquely, on their own timetable, and have individual needs and differing abilities at any given point in time. Their classrooms are planned to respond to individuality.

Contrast 2. In addition, requiring children to do the same thing at the same time requires teachers to be entirely in charge, directing, telling, instructing—in short, they become the focus of attention. It makes the teacher the most active participant, with the children becoming quite passive recipients of whatever the teacher has decided they will learn on a given day.

In developmentally appropriate classrooms, teachers function as facilitators first and instructors second, stimulating and expanding on learning possibilities in activities, and responding to children's indications of interest and ability.

Contrast 3. Developmentally inappropriate programs ask young children to sit and listen or work on assigned tasks much of the time. This ignores their need to be physically active and interactive with materials and people, as their major form of learning. The physical set-up of a classroom quickly indicates whether it is a sit-at-the-table-or-desk-and-work kind of place, or one where children learn by action and interaction. Developmentally appropriate classrooms for young children have little room for worksheets, coloring books, workbooks, flash cards, or drill sessions for rote learning.

Developmentally appropriate practice allows for most of the learning to take place in a variety of interest centers or choice of work areas, with individuals or small groups of children using a wide variety of open-ended materials. Children may move freely, much of the time, to many areas in the classroom, choosing places to play that are most comfortable for them. Some children will stand to work, some will sit at tables, and others will sit on the floor.

Contrast 4. In developmentally inappropriate practice, little emphasis is put on the kinds of materials offered to children. Many materials are related to pencil and paper tasks, or other items used with direct teacher instruction. Materials are usually used in conjunction with instruction sessions according to specific regulation of how to use the material correctly.

Materials for children's direct, hands-on learning are a vital part of any developmentally appropriate classroom. Teachers carefully select and present to children materials that allow them to construct their own understandings of the world.

Contrast 5. Developmentally inappropriate practice for children emphasizes the product of specific learning—in other words, narrow definitions of subject and content to be learned in a given period, with adult-established concepts of correctness, completion, achievement, and failure. Teachers set very specific learning objectives and interpret their function to make sure that all children accomplish these objectives by following the teacher's plans. An example of this would be expecting all two-year-olds to correctly identify five color flash cards in a given morning; all four-year-olds to correctly print their first names at the top of their worksheets; and every six-year-old to complete the basal reader by November.

Developmentally appropriate classrooms recognize that early childhood learning is an ongoing process that is less easily measured and quantified. Teachers do not plan for specific behavioral objectives (e.g., The children will demonstrate learning of _____ by _____), recognizing that such preplanning is typically linear, with only one way to go (Jones, 1992). Instead, the planning is for children to "have opportunities to do_____" (Jones, 1992, p. 91) many different things. There will be different learning in the same activity for different children. In the block corner, Allison is discovering how to get a stack of blocks to balance, while LaKeisha is learning that talking with a peer may accomplish the same thing as grabbing. And Sam has just noticed that two half-units will make the same size side as the long unit block.

Contrast 6. Inappropriate practice focuses narrowly on cognitive learning and on specific fragmented content areas, such as science, math, language, and physical education, with separate times and methods of studying each. For preschool and elementary-aged children, this results in days being broken up into small, teacher-controlled compartments of times.

Instead, in a developmentally appropriate classroom there is recognition that each aspect of development—physical, social, emotional, cognitive, and language—is interrelated with the others, and all early childhood learning connects all aspects. Even in elementary classrooms, and most especially in preschool classrooms, "the curriculum is integrated so that learning occurs primarily through projects, learning centers, and playful activities that reflect current interests of children" (Bredekamp, 1987, p. 68). In the infant room, learning is inseparably intertwined with caregiving encounters that nurture social/emotional, cognitive/language and physical sensory learning all at the same time.

When the children work with unit blocks, for example, they absorb concepts of size, shape, quantity, density, and balance. Beyond the concepts they are also physically manipulating and gaining a sense of physical space, labeling and verbally communicating with peers, conceptualizing their knowledge of their world, and planning and following a project through to completion. There is too much real learning going on to fit into neat little subject compartments.

Contrast 7. Less developmentally appropriate learning focuses on abstract structured materials that emphasize symbols such as letters and numbers, isolated skill development, and memorizing of these. Singing the alphabet song and printing a page of M's are examples of this. Tasks are selected arbitrarily by the teacher, and while they may make some sense of connectedness to the adult, children often see no connection between the assigned learning tasks and their real experiences.

A developmentally appropriate curriculum offers children concrete learning activities with familiar materials and people, easily recognized and selected as relevant to their life experiences. Examples might be children working with a variety of art media to represent a recent trip to the post office and dictating a story to the teacher to describe the trip, or following simple pictures giving instructions to prepare, measure, and mix ingredients for a fruit salad that they will eat for lunch.

Contrast 8. Developmentally inappropriate curriculum and lesson plans are designed by teachers who make decisions arbitrarily on the basis of what they feel should be learned by the group on any given day or by following the school system curriculum guide. The amount of time spent on any activity or topic is decided by teachers and determined in advance. Teachers have a fairly rigid schedule to follow, and change activities according to the clock and the calendar, rather than children's interest and involvement. Often prepackaged curricula are purchased and implemented, and in primary classrooms, teachers follow texts and teacher guides quite exclusively.

Instead, in developmentally appropriate classrooms, teachers' plans are based on regular observation and assessment of children's activities, interests, needs, and involvement. Materials are selected that seem to match children's current levels of interest. Teachers decide when to supplement or change materials based on the children's use of the materials. When interest declines it is time for change. Teachers plan, but know when to depart from the plan for spur-of-the-moment teaching to respond to the direction of the children's activities. While children continue using materials constructively and enthusiastically, teachers allow them to have as much time as can be productively used.

Contrast 9. Teachers make all the decisions in developmentally inappropriate classrooms. Such decisions may include assigning children to activities, insisting that all children participate in an activity, or assigning them to work or play with a particular child or group, arbitrarily moving them on to another activity with the signal of a bell.

Developmentally appropriate classrooms recognize that children learn when they are truly involved with an experience, and such involvement comes when children are able to freely choose with what and whom they interact, and are given enough time for deep involvement. Teachers may support and encourage children to reach out to new challenges, but will not force activities or friends. Many choices are offered to children, recognizing that the opportunity to make choices is related to both a sense of competence and self-control.

Contrast 10. In developmentally inappropriate classrooms, teachers do most of the routines, cleanup, and tasks themselves, because it seems more efficient to do so, and they do not see the value of children's participation in these activities. Routines are usually rushed and chaotic, as teachers hurry to get the entire group through them and on to the "real" learning. Children get neither the opportunity to practice self-help skills nor to sense themselves becoming independent and responsible.

Developmentally appropriate management of routines is based on a recognition that every experience is a real learning opportunity for children. Teachers involve children, taking time to help them learn and practice skills and get a sense of completion. Equipment and utensils designed for children to manage are provided to help them feel competent. Children's abilities are reinforced with recognition. Children are encouraged to feel that their responsible participation offers a necessary contribution to the group.

Contrast 11. In less appropriate classrooms, teachers occupy the dominant position, a place of power, which they exert to reward acceptable behavior and punish unacceptable behavior. Their primary goal is maintaining control in the classroom so they can accomplish their teaching goals, and they spend much time enforcing rules and carrying out management systems (e.g., "The first time, your name goes on the board"). Teachers intervene to solve problems for children. Their actions are often cold and arbitrary. Social development and the gradual acquisition of self-control and interpersonal skills are not seen as a valuable part of the curriculum for young children.

In developmentally appropriate classrooms, teachers recognize that facilitating the development of self-control and social communication is both an important role and a slow, gradual process, which is developmentally related to language ability and cognitive understanding. They are friendly grown-ups who recognize and accept feelings, and who teach appropriate behavior by example and by treating children with respect, not demeaning their attempts at social interaction. They maintain limits and help children understand the reasons behind the limits. They interpret conflict not as an annoying interruption to their teaching, but as opportunities to help children learn more about problem-solving communication with others and developing self-control.

Contrast 12. It is developmentally inappropriate for children to be mostly silent in their classrooms. Verbal interaction with both adults and other children is necessary to develop the language base that is the foundation for later academic skills, and to move gradually to a less egocentric view of the world. When the environment and learning activities do not encourage language, when speech is in fact actively discouraged, and when adults do not respond positively and attentively to children's speech, learning is impeded.

In developmentally appropriate practice, teachers clearly value children's use of language by responding, making time for one-on-one conversations with children, and facilitating verbal interaction from child to child by the way space is arranged, the structuring of activities, and with deliberately planned language experiences. Speaking and listening experience is seen as important to the simultaneous development of literacy skills, with reading and writing opportunities offered in an integrated language program.

Contrast 13. In developmentally inappropriate settings, outdoor play is viewed as a brief period when children can blow off steam before getting back to the important learning inside the classroom. Teachers view their role outdoors as purely supervisory, and often use this time to relax and socialize with other adults.

In a developmentally appropriate program, integrated learning is believed to take place both indoors and outdoors, and teachers interact, observe, and facilitate in both places. Varieties of interesting materials and experiences are planned for outdoor learning opportunities.

Contrast 14. In a program that does not rely on developmentally appropriate practice, communication with parents is minimal and perfunctory. Staff believe that they are the professional experts on children, and neither solicit nor value parents' contributions in the form of information, suggestions, questions, or assistance. Frequently, parents are subtly and not-so-subtly excluded.

In a developmentally appropriate program, teachers value the information and ideas gained from parents to help with their knowledge of individual children. Communication is regular and builds mutual understanding, as well as appropriate plans and consistent responses for children. Children feel comfortable moving back and forth between home and school where there is obvious respect for their parents. The primary role of parents in children's development is recognized and supported.

Contrast 15. It is developmentally inappropriate practice to use chronological age and/or specific tests and assessments to determine when children are eligible to enter a program or be moved on to the next level within a program. Observation quickly shows marked differences in ability within children of exactly the same age. Young children are not good test takers, and tests narrow the focus to assessing purely cognitive learning. In addition, children often exhibit wide variation in their own levels of developmental abilities. A three-year-old may have language ability that is closer to the four-year-old norm, while having the gross motor skills shown on the developmental scale for a child of thirty months. Another three-year-old may be able to sustain periods of cooperative play, yet still not have achieved toilet control.

Developmentally appropriate programs recognize these variations and do not exclude children on the basis of readiness tests or arbitrary standards. The program recognizes it must adjust to the developmental needs and levels of the children served, not demand that children come ready to fit the system. Equipment and activities in any classroom are chosen to match a developmental span of several years. Groupings may be multi-aged, to allow children to function comfortably, without loss of self-esteem, at their developmental rather than chronological level. Decisions about moving on are made jointly by teachers and parents, as they consider direct observations and assessment of the individual child.

Contrast 16. Inappropriate practice is often the result of teachers who are not trained in child development theory and who have not had opportunities to practice in developmental programs. When teachers are arbitrarily moved around in school systems, teachers who are not trained specifically in early childhood developmentally appropriate practice may end up in classrooms with the youngest elementary grades, without a full understanding of the special learning style and needs of five through eight-year-olds. In infant/toddler or preschool classrooms where the adult-child ratios are so high that time for individual observation and interaction does not exist, it is extremely difficult, even for trained teachers, to provide appropriate experiences for children.

Developmentally appropriate programs offer opportunities, training, and support for staff to acquire the child development knowledge base necessary to nurture optimum development.

Results of Developmentally Appropriate vs. Inappropriate Practice

Why do many early childhood educators believe it is crucial to delineate and discard the kinds of developmentally inappropriate practice just described? The answer lies primarily in four directions: the development of self-esteem, self-control, stress, and later academic patterns.

Self-Esteem   "Self-esteem is generated in children in large part through the process of frequently meeting and mastering meaningful new challenges" (Greenberg, 1990,

"Don't bother calling my parents—I'm sure it's genetic."

Figure 2–1 Premature academic expectations for young children may damage self-esteem.

p. 76). Children come to regard themselves as capable when they are able to succeed at things that are important to them, not to someone else.

A key concept here is *mastering*. As adults expect children to engage in learning activities that are beyond their developmental level, an unnecessary sense of failure is created. When children do not succeed in mastering a task, they have no way of judging whether or not adults have in fact been mistaken in their selection of the style or tasks of learning they expect of children. Children simply know that the learning style is alien and difficult for them and that they have not measured up to the adult standards. Continually getting disapproval because he can't sit still during teacher instruction hurts a child's self-esteem. Being directed over and over again to cut on the lines when she just can't do it, hurts her self-esteem. Programs centered around academic learning stress mastery of narrowly defined cognitive skills and imply to children that mastery in other areas is of little value. "Another risk that may attend introducing young children to academic work prematurely is that those children who cannot relate to the content or tasks required are likely to feel incompetent" (Katz, 1988, p. 30). Such negative experiences impact on the development of self-esteem (Figure 2-1).

Another key word is *meaningful*. "If we expect a young child to master tasks that are meaningless to her as an individual, she has little satisfaction or feeling of self-worth in doing the chore, even if she succeeds." (Greenberg, 1990, p. 76). The rote learning of abstract skills and sub-skills is far from the natural interest and active curiosity of young children. Self-esteem suffers when the child has not chosen the learning as important to him. Detailed discussions in later chapters will help students see the contrasting kinds of experiences and practices that help generate self-esteem.

Self-Control

As children mature cognitively, they are increasingly able to govern their behavior according to their understanding of the guidance they have received from adults. If children have been disciplined by adults who primarily use arbitrary, power-driven techniques, there is little opportunity to learn and slowly internalize the information needed to gradually be able to take over more control in their lives. These children are so controlled by external power that they not only suffer in self-esteem ("Nothing I do seems to please my teacher or parents"), but suffer also in self-control ("I'll go as far as I can because I know sooner or later they'll stop me, and then I'll pay for it").

All early childhood teachers believe that children need discipline in the form of limits on behavior and impulses. The difference between developmentally appropriate and inappropriate guidance techniques, or those likely to lead toward eventual self-control (as opposed to others that only temporarily stop misbehavior), is how well adults select teaching techniques that match what is known of the young child's learning ability. Adults are more likely to use power disciplinary techniques when they do not understand the developmental capabilities and limitations of children in verbal expression, cognitive reasoning and judgement skills, or abilities to empathize or de-center mentally. For example, when adults become annoyed with toddlers who cannot share no matter how many times they are asked to, then ask them to sit in "time-out" to emphasize this point, they are paying no attention to the real nature of the toddler, who is truly unable to comprehend or internalize the notion of others' rights or control of his own impulses. More developmentally appropriate discipline would recognize the developmental limitations, and redirect the child toward a positive substitution or alternative. Later, when the preschooler is able to be helped to recognize others' wishes as well as her own, she will be encouraged to help find a solution for taking turns or cooperating on the use of the sought-after toy. Such disciplinary techniques put the adult in the position of facilitator and guide, rather than the adult who manages all behavior for the child. Self-control cannot grow when children are not helped to understand and experience the sense in behaving in desirable ways, but are simply stopped when the adult decides to stop them.

The impact on future behavior of developmentally inappropriate discipline practices may be suggested by findings in a study that indicated that first-grade students who had been in developmentally inappropriate kindergarten classrooms were perceived by first-grade teachers as being more hostile and aggressive, anxious and fearful, and hyperactive and distractible than children who had attended kindergartens using developmentally appropriate practices (Hart, 1991).

Learning to make good choices is an important component of self-discipline. An environment and interaction that informs and supports choices is crucial to healthy self-control.

The impact of developmentally appropriate programs on both self-esteem and self-control has been highlighted by the longitudinal studies reported by David Weikart and his colleagues (Berreuta-Clement et al., 1984; Schweinhart et al., 1986; Schweinhart and Weikart, 1993). The purpose of the study was to assess whether high-quality preschool programs could provide both short- and long-term benefits to children living in poverty and at high risk of school failure.

Children who had participated in three different models of preschool programs in Ypsilanti, Michigan, were followed from after they left the preschool programs until they reached age twenty-seven. The three approaches used with the group of disadvantaged preschoolers were: a direct-instruction program, emphasizing academic objectives and teacher-directed instruction, now called DISTAR; a traditional nursery school program that encouraged children's active involvement in free play organized around themes, such as community helpers, seasons of the year, holidays, etc., with teachers supervising for safety and responding to children's expressed needs and interests; and an "open-framework" approach, now called the High/Scope curriculum. In this approach both teacher and child plan learning activities jointly with a variety of interest centers, the teachers interacting with an open-ended questioning style to facilitate active learning. Both of these latter two programs included social and academic objectives, and called for child-initiated activity (Schweinhart, 1988). Although the study involved relatively small numbers of children, the results are thought-provoking.

When the study initially found that all children who had participated in any of the preschool programs showed dramatic gains in IQ over children without preschool experience, and that these gains in achievement remained over time at a higher level through their tenth year, it was concluded that any preschool program of high quality could make a significant difference in a disadvantaged child's educational life. (As the participants were contrasted with the control group at age nineteen and most recently at age twenty-seven (Schweinhart and Weikart, 1993), it was discovered that those who had participated in any preschool program were significantly more likely to graduate from high school, enroll in postsecondary education, and be employed. They were significantly less likely to be assigned to special education classes, commit crimes, have children themselves during their teen-age years, or receive welfare assistance (Berrueta-Clement et al., 1984). At age twenty-seven the adults who had participated in the preschool programs completed higher levels of schooling, earned significantly higher salaries; were more likely to own their own homes, second cars, and be married; received significantly fewer social services; and had fewer arrests.

When the study looked at the participants of the three different programs at their fifteenth year, a differentiation was shown in various socioeconomic factors between the participants of the direct-instruction program and the two programs in which children initiated their own activities. In the structured academic program, much larger percentages of teenagers had been involved in a variety of delinquent and antisocial activities, were much less involved socially in their schools with peers, and were having much more difficulty with their families. Of the other two groups, about half as many delinquent acts were reported, and more were reported to have made positive social adjustments at school and with their families. Such marked differences suggest the gains by the young children in the programs who had opportunities to make choices, build up their self-confidence as learners, and gradually develop self-control (Schweinhart et al., 1986).

> The essential process connecting early childhood experience to patterns of improved success in school and the community seemed to be the development of dispositions that allowed the child to interact positively with other people and with tasks. This process was based neither on permanently improved intellectual performance nor on academic knowledge.... *It was the development of specific personal and social dispositions that enabled a high-quality early childhood program to significantly influence participants' adult performance* (Schweinhart and Weikart, 1993, p. 11, 12).

In light of this finding, the researchers concluded that a high-quality preschool curriculum must have an abundance of child-initiated learning activities, as described in recommendations for developmentally appropriate practice.

> These results call into question the advisability of pushing formal academics on four-year-olds. In particular, such programs, focusing on teacher-directed activities, may not be the best way to improve a disadvantaged child's chance for a successful life. To overcome obstacles to success, disadvantaged children must have opportunities to chart their own course. To be self-directed, they must initiate their own learning, follow through with their plans, and evaluate the outcomes (Schweinhart et al., 1986, p. 43).

The results of the study suggest that children in developmentally appropriate programs—who plan and have responsibility for their own activity, and who initiate their own work—develop dispositions toward lifelong learning, with "initiative, curiosity, trust, confidence, independence, responsibility, and divergent thinking" (Schweinhart and Weikart, p. 12). The suggestion is also that children who are taught directly what to do, working within limits and on objectives determined by adults, have no sense of investment in either themselves or in the educational systems (Weikart, 1989).

Stress

There are child psychologists today who claim that our children are at risk, because of the stresses involved in being hurried through childhood (Elkind, 1981, 1988). Hurrying can take many forms, including early entry into competitive sports and specialized lessons, early exposure to the problems and rapid changes in the adult world, or bearing increased emotional and physical responsibility in families that are themselves under stress, for example, with divorce and single parents. The earlier introduction of academics to educational programs for young children is the kind of hurrying this book is most concerned with.

Stress is a common "risk seen in children when excessive and inappropriate demands are made on them through formal instruction" (Bullock, 1990, p. 15). When young children are asked to learn subject matter and methods that are contrary to their natural learning style, they experience a natural conflict between their desires and the systems imposed and expected by the adults. In having to deny their natural instincts in order to win adult approval, children must make enormous efforts to suppress and control their behavior. An example of this is the five-year-old boy who seems to be physically unable to sit and listen as the teacher has asked him to, or the eighteen-month-old who is driven to climb and is removed every time she does so. This is true stress.

A number of studies corroborate the increased stress on children in developmentally inappropriate settings. Children in DIP kindergarten classrooms were found to exhibit significantly more stress behaviors than children in DAP classrooms. Stress was particularly evident in boys, with more stress behaviors found in boys in DIP classrooms than in DAP ones. The activities found to be most stressful for kindergarten children were workbook and worksheet assignments, waiting, and transition activities (Burts, et al., 1992). Similar findings have been made about stress in developmentally inappropriate vs. appropriate preschool classrooms (Durland et al., 1992). Children from racial minority or lower socioeconomic backgrounds were found to exhibit more stress behaviors in either developmentally appropriate or inappropriate classrooms (Burts, et al. 1992). However, when low socioeconomic status African-American children were taught literacy using developmentally appropriate whole language methods, they progressed rapidly while, simultaneously, stress behaviors were observed to decrease in frequency (Weems-Moon, 1991).

To see how developmentally inappropriate expectations of uniform learning styles or timing put children under unnecessary stress, consider the following scenes that occur in too many early childhood settings. Watch the acute frustration of the toddler who can't sit still for the teacher's instruction period when asked. Imagine the anxiety of the four-year-old who wants to, but can't, form the letters to copy the teacher's perfect example. Picture the six-year-old who just can't seem to distinguish the letters and stumbles through the reading page, shame-faced and shaking each time the teacher corrects her. The fear of failure can become overwhelming, and is a hazard that is unnecessary when adults learn what is developmentally appropriate.

Later Academic Patterns

Do the benefits in later academic situations justify the stress when academic learning is pushed prematurely onto younger children? In fact, children who are asked to learn through methods unsuited to their stage of development may become turned off very early to education.

> Certainly young children can be successfully instructed in beginning reading skills; however the risk of such early achievement is that in the process of instruction, given the amount of drill and practice required for success at an early age, children's dispositions to be readers will be undermined.... What is sad to see in kindergartens is children so willing to do so many things that are so irrelevant to them at that age and so frivolous, and by second grade find many of them turned off. It isn't either-or. You don't acquire dispositions or skills. The challenge for educators—at every level—is to help the learner with *both* the acquisition of skills and the strengthening of desirable dispositions (Katz, 1988, p. 30).

There is a real risk that these children may learn helplessness; that is, they may become dependent on the kind of learning structured only by adults, rather than learning to take their own initiative, raise their own questions, and solve their own problems. Thus the child's natural motivation to learn may be seriously disrupted (Elkind, 1986).

In fact, there is some evidence that delaying rather than speeding up children's exposure to the learning of abstract academics has positive effects, and certainly appears to have no handicapping effects. First graders who attended developmentally inappropriate kindergarten classrooms received lower reading report-card grades when compared with children from developmentally appropriate classrooms (Burts, et al., 1992). Results on CAT test scores do not indicate the differences that justify the stress on young children of being exposed to developmentally inappropriate instruction methods. Children in kindergarten classrooms using developmentally appropriate practices scored no differently than children in kindergarten classrooms that used inappropriate practices (Burts et al., 1991). At the end of the first and second grades, children who had experienced developmentally appropriate practice in kindergarten scored no differently on the CAT average than children who had spent kindergarten in developmentally inappropriate classrooms (Verma, 1992).

An implication worth considering may be that early exposure to academics has in fact jeopardized later success, and delaying exposure has been beneficial. It may be worthwhile to heed the words of Lillian Katz: "While there is no compelling evidence to suggest that early introduction to academic work guarantees success in school in the long term, there are reasons to believe that it can be counterproductive" (Katz, 1988).

SUMMARY

Parents and teachers need to be aware of social pressures that produce developmentally inappropriate practices, and recognize these inappropriate practices that are prevalent in early childhood education today. These include the following.

1. asking all children to learn the same things at the same time

2. relying on direct teacher instruction

3. keeping children passive and immobile

4. using worksheets, flash cards, and drill sessions predominatcly

5. emphasizing product learning, using adult standards of completion and correctness

6. emphasizing cognitive learning and content fragmented into subject compartments

7. focusing on abstract symbolic concepts, such as letters, sounds, and numbers

8. lesson plans designed arbitrarily by teachers

9. teachers making all the decisions

10. teachers doing all routines themselves

11. teachers controlling behavior by rules, reward, and punishment

12. teachers keeping children quiet most of the time

13. viewing outdoor play only as an energy release

14. teachers excluding parents from partnership

15. using testing and chronological age to determine children's placement in programs

16. high adult-child ratios and inadequate staff training preventing optimum functioning

Results of developmentally inappropriate practices include putting children at risk for development of both self-esteem and self-discipline, and putting children under unnecessary stress, with no academic gains to justify these negatives.

Having examined general principles to help us understand developmentally appropriate practice, we will now move on to examine specific ideas for teachers trying to implement developmentally appropriate practices in learning environments for children from infancy through the early primary years. The reader should understand that the term *environment* is used broadly to suggest the materials and activities, physical arrangements, relationships with others, adult guidance, and interaction that are part of every classroom. For purposes of clarity in discussion, environments will be discussed as physical, social/emotional, and cognitive/language. Nevertheless, it will be obvious that these aspects are interrelated so completely that they cannot be completely separated.

THINK ABOUT IT

1. Interview two teachers and two parents of children under age eight. Ask them to describe what they think are the most important and appropriate learning activities for the children they are concerned with, and their reasons. How do their answers compare with: (a) the developmentally inappropriate practice discussed in this chapter; (b) the reasons behind their beliefs, compared with those discussed on pages 19–21. Discuss your findings with your classmates.

2. Visit a classroom for infants and toddlers, preschool children, and/or early elementary-aged children. (Instructors may wish to assign students to the various age levels. It may also be useful for students to visit in pairs, for comparison and discussion at a later time.) After observing the physical and social environments, and the schedules and lesson plans, read back through the sixteen comparisons in this chapter. Be prepared to discuss with your classmates specifics related to the ideas in this chapter.

3. As time permits, read some of David Elkind's comments in the books listed in the bibliography.

QUESTIONS TO REVIEW OBJECTIVES

1. Discuss some of the reasons why adults choose less developmentally appropriate practices.

2. Of the sixteen comparisons of developmentally inappropriate and appropriate practice, see how many you can recall.

3. For each of the practices identified above, discuss a reason why it is not developmentally appropriate.

4. Identify four possible results for children of early academics and other developmentally inappropriate practices.

REFERENCES AND SUGGESTIONS FOR READING

Berreuta-Clement, J., et al. (1984). *Changed lives: The effects of the Perry preschool program on youths through age 19.* Ypsilanti, MI: High/Scope Press.

Bloom, A. (1987). *The closing of the American mind.* NY: Simon & Schuster.

Bredekamp, S. (ed.). (1987). *Developmentally appropriate practice in early childhood programs serving children from birth through age 8.* Washington, DC: NAEYC.

Bredekamp, S. & Rosegrant, T. (eds.). (1992). *Reaching potentials: Appropriate curriculum and assessment for young children. 1.* Washington, DC: NAEYC.

Bruner, J. (1962). *The process of education.* Cambridge, MA: Harvard University Press.

Bullock, J. (1990, Winter). Child-initiated activity: Its importance in early childhood education. *Day Care and Early Education,* 14–16.

Burts, D. C., Charlesworth, R., & Fleege, P. O. (1991, April). *Achievement of kindergarten children in developmentally appropriate and developmentally inappropriate classrooms.* Paper presented at Society for Research in Child Development.

Burts, D. C., et al. (1992). Observed activities and stress behaviors in developmentally appropriate and inappropriate kindergarten classrooms. *Early Childhood Research Quarterly, 7,* 297–318.

Curry, N.E. (1990, March). Presentation to the Pennsylvania Board of Education. *Young Children, 45(3),* 17–23.

Durland, M., et al. (1992, November). *A comparison of the frequencies of observed stress behaviors in children in developmentally appropriate and inappropriate preschool classrooms.* Unpublished information included in paper at NAEYC.

Elkind, D. (1981). *The hurried child: Growing up too fast too soon.* Reading, MA: Addison-Wesley Publishing Co.

Elkind, D. (1987, March). Superbaby syndrome can lead to elementary school burnout. *Young Children, 42(3),* 14.

Elkind, D. (1987, May). The child yesterday, today, and tomorrow. *Young Children, 42(4),* 6–11.

Elkind, D. (1988). *Miseducation: Preschoolers at risk.* New York: Alfred A. Knopf.

Greenberg, P. (1990, January). Why not academic preschool? (part 1). *Young Children, 45(2),* 70–79.

Hart, C.H. (1991, November). Behavior of first and second grade children who attended developmentally appropriate and developmentally inappropriate classrooms. Paper presented at NAEYC. Denver, CO.

Hirsch, E.D. Jr. (1987). *Cultural literacy: What every American needs to know.* Boston: Houghton Mifflin Co.

Jones, E., & Reynolds, G. (1992). *The play's the thing: Teachers' roles in children's play.* New York: Teachers College Press.

Kagan, S. L. (1988, January). Current reforms in early childhood education: Are we addressing the issues? *Young Children, 2,* 27–32.

Katz, L. (1988, Summer). What should young children be doing? *American Educator,* 28–33 , 44–45.

Mitchell, A. (1989, May). Old baggage, new visions: Shaping policy for early childhood programs. *Phi Delta Kappan,* 665–672.

Schweinhart, L. J. (1988, May). How important is child-initiated activity? *Principal,* 6–10.

Schweinhart, L., & Weikart, D. P. (1993, Summer). Changed lives, significant benefits: The High/Scope Perry preschool project to date. *High/Scope Resource, 12(3),* 1, 10–14.

Schweinhart, L., Weikart, D., & Larner, M. (1986). Consequences of three preschool curriculum models through age 15. *Early Childhood Research Quarterly, 1,* 15–45.

Verma, A. K. (1992, November). *Achievement of kindergarten, first, and second grade children from developmentally appropriate and inappropriate kindergarten classrooms.* Unpublished master's thesis. Baton Rouge:

Louisiana State University. Included in paper at NAEYC, Nov. 1992.

Weems-Moon, N. (1991). *An ethnographic study of kindergarten students' literacy skills and stress-related behaviors before and after teacher demonstrations in bookreading strategies.* Unpublished doctoral dissertation. Baton Rouge: Louisiana State University. Included in paper at NAEYC, Nov. 1992.

Weikart, D. P. (1989, March). Hard choices in early childhood care and education: A view to the future. *Young Children, 44(3),* 25–30.

SECTION TWO

Guest Editorial by James Greenman

An environment is a living, changing system. More than the physical space, it includes the way time is structured and the roles we are expected to play. It conditions how we feel, think, and behave; and it dramatically affects the quality of our lives. The environment either works for us or against us as we conduct our lives... (p. 5).

Space speaks to each of us. Long corridors whisper "run" to a child; picket fences invite us to trail our hands along the slats. Physical objects have emotional messages of warmth, pleasure, solemnity, fear; action messages of come close, touch me, stay away; "I'm strong," "I'm fragile."... (p. 16)

Space speaks to our emotions. We build images of *places*, meaningful spaces, out of fragments of experiences, experiences significant to us for reasons of our own. Our memories, imaginings, hopes, and dreams transform places and things.... (pp. 16–17)

Children and adults inhabit different sensory worlds. Imagine a young infant's world of touch and taste—a world where you see and hear more than you look and listen—where you, in effect, think with your body and actions, and your whole body is your only means of reacting. Consider the way that young children run from place to place. Children respond to the sensory and motor mes-

sages of space, while adults are more utilitarian: "Adults notice whether an environment is clean or attractive to an adult eye" (Prescott in Greenman, 1988).

What we often don't notice are the elements that a child will zoom in on: the right place with the right shape, like a tight angular corner between the wall and a couch or the excitement of a perch; the right sight and sound, like a vantage point from which to watch and hear the torrential rain pouring out of the gutter and splashing to the ground below; or the right feel. We, who don't inhabit the floor, undervalue the hot, sunny spot on the floor that draws cats and babies. We are not drawn to the pile of dirt or the hole, to the puddle or dew, or to the rough spot where the plaster is chipping away that beckons small fingers. Our cold, utilitarian eyes assess for order and function, cleanliness and safety. We assess how the space will bend to our will.... (p. 21)

Good space for children (and adults) is the result of asking the right questions to establish goals and thinking through the important feelings and behaviors that are to be supported. Good space doesn't force behavior contrary to goals, such as dependency, or overemphasize unimportant goals, such as tolerance for waiting (Greenman, 1988, p. 23).

Developmentally Appropriate Physical Environments

INTRODUCTION

In this section we will examine the nature of the physical environments that set the stage for developmentally appropriate practice. The discussion of physical environments will include: the arrangement of space into areas created for learning; the kinds of materials and equipment available for children; and the structuring of time. Recognizing the particular developmental tasks of various stages, the section is divided into four chapters: infants, covering the first year of life; toddlers, including children from about one to three years; preschoolers, from age three to school entry; and primary-aged children, from kindergarten through age eight.

CHAPTER 3

Developmentally Appropriate Physical Environments:
For Infants

*I*n the past decade or so, the number of infants entering child care settings has grown faster than any other group. While many families try to replicate home care by finding substitute care in a family day care home, many have no choice but to look for care in a more traditional day care center. Nationwide, centers are faced with the dilemma of trying to adapt physical settings and schedules to the needs of ever growing numbers of babies. The care of babies in groups represents some unique questions and problems that require a thorough rethinking of long-held assumptions and practices of programs that are more accustomed to dealing with older children. (This may also lead us to discover more developmentally appropriate practice for those older children!) Infant programs have the choice of relying on what they know about settings for older children and preschoolers and moving those ideas down, with the addition of cribs, or creating environments that more closely resemble home-rearing practices. Decisions need to be based on knowledge about development during the first year.

OBJECTIVES

After completing this chapter, the student should be able to:
- identify several developmental needs of infants that must be considered when planning physical environments.
- identify several ways the environment can meet each of those developmental needs.
- discuss considerations in outdoor environments for infants.
- list several practices in providing for health and safety in infant rooms.
- identify several appropriate materials for infant rooms.
- discuss appropriate schedules for infant rooms.
- identify inappropriate components in infant rooms.

The Nature of Babies

Babies are very different from people at all later stages of development. In the first rapidly changing year of their lives, they move from helpless dependence to mobile independence; from communicating with cries and coos, to understanding quite a vocabulary and using some words of their own; from demands for physical needs being met quickly by anyone, to very particular demands for social responses from very specific people. As they progress through these changes, babies spend a good deal of time being cared for by adults.

In planning an environment for babies, the starting point is to ask what babies do, and what they need.

What Do Babies Do?

Babies sleep, eat, cry, are bathed and changed, quite a lot. They use all their five senses and their unfolding motor and manipulative abilities to explore their immediate world. They become attached to a few very special people in their worlds. Behind these objective statements lies a world of small and important steps and actions, which need to be recognized in planning environments for babies.

Among other things, young babies:

see	squeeze	sit up
watch	pinch	pull up
look	drop	crawl to, in, out, over
inspect	transfer hand to hand	
hear		creep around, in, and under
listen	shake	
smell	bang	swing
taste	tear	rock
feel	clap together	coo, babble
touch	put in	imitate sounds
mouth	take out	react to others
eat	find	accommodate to others
reach out	look for	
reach for	kick	solicit from others
knock away	turn	
grasp	roll	experiment endlessly
hold	lift their heads	

(Greenman, 1988, p. 49)

Add to this list later infancy accomplishments, which may include cruising, holding on, walking, holding a bottle, drinking with a cup, maneuvering a spoon, playing peek-a-boo, and making a loud raspberry sound. (There are a lot more left off this list—what else can you add?)

There is another point that needs to be stated here: Each baby is unique, with her own temperament, his own activity level, her own particular need for sleep. No two six-month-old infants will be ready for, or interested in, the same kind of exploring.

What Do Babies Need?

Now that we know what babies do, the next question is, What do they need to grow well? The previous list suggests some components. Babies need space and opportunity to move at their current capabilities. They need a place rich with objects to explore sensorily. They need key adults to respond to them promptly, consistently, and warmly, and to interact with them, giving them language, face to face, so they can begin to understand the process of human communication. They need a place that is safe for them to be in, but one that does not restrict free movement and active curiosity.

Look back at those statements again. In fact, they are applicable to children at any stage throughout the early years. Clues about how to make these general statements more specific in the design of an infant room come when we watch babies in action and consider: What do they like? How do they move? What attracts their attention? How far can they look? How far can they reach? What do they do when they encounter a new object? What disturbs or frustrates their activity and exploration? What comforts them? How do they seek attention? (Greenman, 1984).

A reconsideration of child development theory related to infancy is also necessary in this preliminary phase of considering what environments need to offer infants. Erikson describes the central task of infancy as the need to form a sense of trust against a negative component of mistrust. During the first year, as infants find that their needs are met consistently and warmly, they come to believe that the world and the people in it are good. This basic sense of trust forms a component of personality—an orientation toward positive outlooks and interactions (Erikson, 1963). Ainsworth refers to forming primary and secondary attachments during the first year, through patterns of repeated, mutually responsive behaviors between baby and adult (Ainsworth, 1982). Attachment refers to a deep, long-lasting emotional tie between people who prefer each other's company. Piaget described the first stage of cognitive development, during the first two years as the *sensorimotor stage*. During this period, the infant increasingly coordinates information from the senses and the movements and manipulation of the body to move toward a practical understanding of the surrounding world. The sensorimotor stage involves this practical, physical intelligence (Piaget, 1963).

In recalling what babies do, what they need, and these theories, we get our first clues about what needs to inform our environmental planning. Adults planning developmentally appropriate physical environments for infants need to consider environments that nurture these developmental tasks: formation of trust; development of attachment; mobility; sensory learning; and language.

Environment to Nurture Trust

An environment of trust for babies includes the capacity to provide a consistent responsiveness as infants express their needs. In physical environments this means an allowance for differences in babies' schedules for feeding, sleeping, and playing. Babies must not be required to fit into an arbitrarily drawn schedule; thus, in an infant room, some children will need to sleep, while others are being fed or exploring their bodies and surroundings. Separating crib areas from play areas as far as possible is helpful; a quiet, dark alcove adjoining the activity area

Figure 3-1 When play and caregiving areas are separated from sleeping areas, infants can be on their own individual schedules. *Courtesy NationsBank Child Care Center, Charlotte, NC.*

is preferable, since it allows caregivers to observe the crib while interacting with the other babies. (See Figure 3-1.)

An environment of trust includes consistent responsiveness by the same adults. This is provided when infant caregivers are trained about the crucial importance to later development of the relationships of the first year. The very best teachers need to be given the important responsibility of infant care, not the least trained, who will be most likely to leave the position, or unable to see the value in prompt attention to infant needs.

Centers that understand the need for consistent responsiveness are likely to institute primary caregiving patterns in the room; this means that each adult is primarily responsible for the care of her own small group of babies. For example, Mary is the primary caregiver for Seth, Sarah, and Kenyetta. LaTonya is the primary caregiver for Jon, Julio, and Anna-Li. As their babies need diaper changes, feeding, comfort, playtime, etc., the caregivers respond to them as they are able. Of course, if one of the caregivers is occupied with a baby already, her co-worker may step in to assist if one of the other babies needs something. Not only are there fewer babies for a caregiver to focus on interacting with and responding to, but also this system allows her to get to know the individual babies and their families intimately, and to individualize care accordingly. Parents feel more confident leaving their infants with someone who has become close to the family and reports to them at the end of the day the details they want to hear. Infants benefit by this consistent closeness with a particular person.

Staff continue to advocate the small adult-child ratios that allow for true responsiveness. The best standards recommend one adult caring for three, or at most four, infants. Check and see what the ratio is in your community.

Consistent responsiveness and meeting of individual needs are facilitated by regular communication between caregivers, including staff members and parents. Systems for ensuring regular exchange of information that will help plan appropriate responses are needed here. Notebooks in each baby's cubby for caregivers and parents to jot down items regarding daily routines and developmental changes are one example of such a system.

An environment of trust considers size and perspective from infants' points of view of comfort and security, recognizing that the smaller the baby, the smaller the group size and space around the infant should be. It is preferable to create small groups rather than doubling the size, even with double the adult caregivers; when groups are larger, there is more noise and sense of chaos. Newborns like confined space, such as a bassinet; older infants who are mobile are ready to move beyond furniture that restricts movement. Arranging the furniture and layout of an infant room to provide smaller nooks creates this sense of enclosure.

An environment of trust is a safe, familiar place. It is *predictable* in the patterns of things, people, and events. Caregivers provide this predictability by ensuring a place for everything, easily restorable from the clutter of infants' active exploration. Clearly marked storage bins, trays, baskets, and boxes help return things to the same places for babies to find again. Rituals of repeated experiences form the predictable sequence even babies can comprehend: always a song before being tucked in the crib for a nap; the few minutes to make funny noises and laugh that accompany a diaper change.

Emotional safety is also included in a physical environment where the prohibitions and restrictions are built in by thoughtful caregivers, instead of becoming verbal contests of will. When the fragile ornament is removed, or a gate added to prevent access to a forbidden area, infants are safe from having to contend with a barrage of "Nos." The environment is positive and trustworthy because of adults' recognition of babies' inability to limit themselves.

Make sure your trustworthy environment includes:

- separate sleeping, caregiving, and active play areas
- well-trained adults who are committed to nurturing infants' development
- primary caregiving systems
- small adult-child ratios, and small groups
- systems for oral and written communication
- space suited to the perspective of babies
- a familiar place, through environmental organization for easy restoration, and predictable patterns to accompany routines
- an environment where verbal prohibitions are avoided by a carefully prepared space for free exploration

Environment to Nurture Attachment

Figure 3-2 A couch makes a comfortable setting for adults to care for babies. *Courtesy NationsBank Child Care Center.*

Obviously the consistent responsiveness and stability of caregivers we've discussed are components of attachment. But there are other considerations as well.

" Assume that the most important times for the child are those one-to-one moments of real nurturing and communication, where the baby has the caregiver's full human presence. These are the times that need to be relaxed and even extended prime times (Greenman, 1988, p. 53). *"*

The environment needs to provide for adult comfort for such encounters; rocking chairs and couches allow adults to sit and hold a child while feeding or talking to her (See Figure 3-2), and soft, cushioned areas on the floor invite staff to interact with babies as they play. Staff also need to consider their role in nurturing parent-infant attachment. The environment needs to convey a clear sense of welcome for parents who have time to visit the center to nurse or play with their baby. Having a quiet corner chair labeled for parents who might like a private time with the baby encourages such interaction.

The arrangement of areas for routine care, such as diaper-changing or feeding areas, may help caregivers avoid the sense of having to rush through the routine without time for interaction. If the work areas are positioned so the adult can still see the rest of the room while providing care to one baby, the routine is less likely to be hurried. If all materials the adult may need are conveniently stored together, time for interaction is gained and attention can be given to the infant.

When adults are interacting with babies, they will want to screen out as many distractions as possible, so that the human interaction is the focus. This means removing the distracting toys or mobiles from over the changing table; the adult's face and words are the only stimulation necessary. This is quite the opposite of what many caregivers do when they hand the baby a toy to occupy him during the diaper changing routine. Toys are used then to distract the baby so the adult can efficiently complete the caregiving task. Such efficiency prevents the eye contact and sheer enjoyment of each other that are important compo-

BUT WHAT ABOUT?

But what about the grandmother who has terrified her daughter by saying that if she responds to the baby's every need he'll be spoiled?

How do the infant room staff respond to this family who wants them to follow the practice of not responding to the baby's cries unless it is to meet a physical need?

This is difficult, because people have such deeply felt opinions about how children ought to be raised, and mothers who have raised children may be quite closed in their opinion, in the face of research or theoretical beliefs. No one wants to be around children who have become nuisances because of their insistence on demanding their own way; we can certainly sympathize with that.

It may be useful to help those parents to state what their goals actually are for the infant; no doubt they really want him to care for others, to be a happy, learning child— perhaps even self-sufficient, though this may itself depend very much on their cultural orientation toward independence vs. interdependence. These are probably goals that caregiver, parent, and grandmother can agree upon. What may need to be discussed is the means by which developmentalists tell us these goals are reached.

The prompt responsiveness to young babies slowly, over repeated experiences, adds up to an impression that the world is a good place, that people in it care for him, and that he *will* be cared for. Because he simply doesn't have the mental capacity until he's nearly eight months or so to connect cause and effect, he simply can't do the devious plotting that grandmother fears might be going on in the baby's head. To lie in his crib and plan to cry to get someone to come to him because he recalls that the last time that's what happened is simply beyond the baby who hasn't yet achieved object permanence (see Chapter 12) and can thus call back an earlier mental image to make adults do what he wants the next time. Knowing something about the baby's abilities allows adults to respond more appropriately to him, instead of being afraid that he can learn to manipulate them in ways not yet possible.

As certainty builds, babies in fact cry less and less toward the end of their first year, confident that they will be cared for. They also come to feel so comfortable in the world that they are able to move away from adults and concentrate on learning. What a good first lesson about love and about respecting others' needs, which infants learn just by example! The responsiveness of the infant room staff can be seen as a very developmentally appropriate component of the physical environment.

nents for attachment. (Magda Gerber's philosophy describes using such caregiving times as opportunities for respectful interaction, and suggests that handing the baby toys to distract trivializes the baby's role in active participation. Read more about this in Gonzalez-Mena and Eyer, and Gerber; references on page 54.)

Be sure your environment for attachment contains:

- comfortable chairs and floor areas for adults to relax and enjoy one-to-one interaction with babies

- a designated parent space for private parent interaction

- work areas located to allow supervision of the room while caring for an individual baby, and access to all necessary materials

- no toys and other stimulation from the areas of caregiving, such as the feeding and diapering area, so babies can focus on the adult

Environment to Nurture Mobility

The unfolding physical abilities of the first year are inextricably tied to the development of sensorimotor intelligence. It therefore follows that babies need to have all the space and opportunity to use their bodies that they can safely use. There are several key implications here.

When babies are awake, they need to be removed from the confines of a crib and the soft mattress that gives entirely different support for muscles than does the firm floor. Next, methods need to be created to protect immobile babies from older mobile ones. Too often the little ones are left in the crib "for their own protection," or are confined out of reach of the older ones in devices such as infant seats, swings, walkers, or jumpers. The biggest problem with such items is that they hold young babies in positions the babies often cannot assume for themselves, which is certainly physically stressful, and they do not permit the freedom to practice whatever skill the baby is currently ready for. In addition, infants are at risk for injury from such devices. A better solution needs to be created for separating infants who are able to move about from those who are less mobile—a solution in which no one needs suffer. A pile of large boxes, a sturdy shelf arrangement, a gate, a pile of sofa cushions—all might serve as easily portable barriers at various stages. Allowing very little ones opportunities to lie in empty plastic swimming pools, foam circles, or in playpens gives them a protected play space, suitable until they begin to need the space to roll over. This may be the only age for whom a playpen is suitable, since the older babies who need to creep or walk around become justifiably frustrated by its limitation. It must be emphasized, though, that overuse of a playpen is not intended with this suggestion. Infants are at risk of retarding motor development, or possible injury, from playpens that are used too much. (See Figure 3-3.)

All the freedom a baby can *safely* use is a necessary part of the environment for mobility. This requires that adults lie on the floor regularly to see from the perspective of babies. Then any potential hazards are removed before they become tempting or there is a need for verbal restrictions. The environment is then an inviting place, not one where babies continually have to be removed or restricted. See more about safe environments later in this chapter.

Environmental planners need to remember that space is relative to size; quite a small space offers freedom to a small infant. Large room areas need to be broken up for a feeling of security for babies. It can be quite frightening to a new walker to see a huge space to traverse before getting to the comfort of the shelf he plans to grab on to.

Figure 3-3 Foam circles may be used to keep immobile babies protected from the more mobile, who need the scope of large space. *Courtesy Methodist Home Child Development Center, Charlotte, NC.*

Provide an environment for mobility by:

- allowing babies to play freely on the floor when awake and protecting less mobile babies by creating barriers
- removing devices that restrict the free movement of infants
- safety-proofing the environment completely and regularly
- creating smaller movement zones within the larger space available

Environment for the Senses

Figure 3-4 Since infant curriculum takes place below a height of 24 inches, interesting things should be provided to look at on the floor, or on the ends of cribs. *Courtesy Avondale Children's Center.*

Consider the sensory stimulation offered to infants by a typical home. An ever-changing variety of interesting things to look at is available close by: the interesting pattern of light and shadow as the sun comes through the curtains; the movement of the leaves on a plant near an open window; the colors of furnishings, kitchen dishes, clothing on people who move in and out of rooms. There are smells of flowers, coffee perking, clean, wet laundry, and onions frying. Babies can hear the thump of the clothes drier, the chiming of the clock, the soft hum of radio music, the rhythm of voices, or the birds in the yard. They feel the soft carpet, the cool kitchen linoleum, the prickly grass in the back yard, and the warm breeze. And they taste everything from the rubber of the pacifier to the sweetness of applesauce.

Babies in a child care center need to have an environment as rich in sensory stimulation and variety. Adults need to beware of providing so clinical a setting that there is no sense of this myriad of sensations.

It is probably useful to environment planners to realize that everything in the life of infants goes on below the height of twenty-four inches or so, and even less for babies who are rolling, sitting, or crawling. Certainly there are times when adults hold or carry babies to look at mobiles or out windows, but the majority of time babies should be able to make their own discoveries and explore freely without the adult having to stimulate them so directly.

The area under twenty-four inches, therefore, needs to offer babies a rich variety of materials to stimulate all of the senses. There should be interesting things to look at: unbreakable stainless steel mirrors attached along the baseboards; large, colorful photos firmly attached under clear Contac paper, to baseboards, linoleum, (See Figure 3-4) low on doors and cabinets, on the ends and undersides of cribs and chairs (be sure to use circles of Contac paper, rather than leaving tempting corners for exploring fingers to pick at); goldfish swimming in an aquarium; prisms hung at windows to reflect rainbow colors around the room; low windows or gates at the door that allow babies to look out at the passing world; streamers attached to catch the breeze.

And what will the babies touch? Squares of various kinds of carpet can be firmly attached at intervals on the floor, lower walls, and pieces of furniture—be sure to include the surprise of a rope mat or grass indoor-outdoor carpeting. Balls of yarn scraps, velvet and chore-girl can hang down from the ceiling within grasping reach. Different surfaces in the room—soft carpet, hard linoleum, cushioned pad—offer challenges in traction as well as variety in sensation. Imagine the surprise of a young crawler who discovers a square of clear Contac paper positioned sticky side up! (Goldhaber and Smith, 1993). (See Figure 3-5.)

Elizabeth Prescott defines the importance of softness in the environment, found in the "presence of objects which are responsive to one's touch—which provide a variety of tactile sensory stimuli" (Prescott, p. 1). Objects like couches, large pillows, rugs, swings, grass, sand, and water are included in her list, as well as laps to sit on.

Don't forget the smells. Leave the windows open when the grass is being cut, as well as the door when the cook is preparing lunch for the older children or the cleaning staff is working with wax and cleansers. Prepare snack foods for adults and older babies in the room, so the natural odors of hot chocolate and apple pieces linger in the air.

Particularly in the sense of sound, adults must be careful to be sensitive to the natural sounds in the environment—the murmurs of soft language and the louder sounds of adult conversations, the hum of the lawn-mower, and the roar of a plane passing by. It is too tempting to surround babies with more artificial sounds such as nursery rhyme songs on a cassette player, or the radio playing music for the adults to enjoy as they work. While some of this is certainly appropriate stimulation, too much of it provides a sort of sound overlay that masks the important sounds of human speech, or creates an unnecessarily chaotic atmosphere. Let the infants focus frequently on the real sounds in their environment, occasionally supplementing them with deliberate variety: the banging of a couple of aluminum pie plates hanging on yarn (also fun visually); an occasional wind chime, or the fun of an old-fashioned metronome set on the shelf.

Let's assume varieties of tastes are provided with additions of new foods at regular intervals.

The usual array of infant toys—rattles, chime balls, bells, soft blocks and animals, teethers, and mobiles—also provide sensory stimulation. Sturdy homemade toys can be replaced when babies get bored more easily than expensive commercial ones. Examples include dried beans or a mixture of colored water, oil, and glitter in a plastic soft drink container (be sure the cap is on tightly with a super glue); texture blocks; or a clear plastic mailing cylinder with an assortment of items inside that make sounds when rolled. Simple, open-ended materials, such as Mylar paper to crumple or a silk scarf for handling, offer varied sensory experiences. At all times, caregivers must recall that babies get most of their sensory information by mouthing objects, so realize that everything will go into babies' mouths—please don't try to stop them! Instead, simply ensure that *absolutely everything* is safe, in sizes too large for swallowing or choking, with no pieces that could come off, and decorated with no substances that would harm.

When planning the sensory environment, sensory overload must be considered. The walls and floor must not be filled or cluttered with so much that the infant becomes distracted and overstimulated. It is better to remove the things that babies just don't comprehend and are included only for adult amusement, such as a mural of Big Bird or Mickey Mouse, which are beyond meaning to infants. As materials seem to attract less and less of the babies' attention, replace them and find newer objects of interest.

The only place where sensory stimulation should *not* be provided is in the infant's crib. Despite the fact that many manufacturers deliberately market toys for cribs, and too many caregivers get tricked into thinking the baby's bed should be a mini-playground, the baby's bed should be kept for sleeping. When infants are awake, they need to be removed from their cribs to play elsewhere, so the bed

Figure 3-5 A collection of colorful feathers taped to the floor offers interesting opportunities for exploration. *Courtesy NationsBank Child Care Center.*

needs to be quietly and soothingly dull, to encourage only sleep when babies are tucked in.

Provide a sensory environment by:

- using the areas and furniture twenty-four inches above the floor to place materials that infants may explore independently
- considering all the senses when preparing the environment
- making homemade toys that have sensory appeal, as well as commercial ones, and continually checking all toys for safety
- avoiding sensory overload by removing things beyond direct understanding by infants
- removing sensory stimulation from cribs

Environment for Language

Much of what has already been said contributes to an environment that nurtures infant language development. Opportunities for one-to-one interaction during caregiving and playtimes and a room that is not too noisy from the sounds of too many babies and adults, or from constant artificial sound, are both important factors. In addition, a variety of interesting objects, views and experiences, and pictures encourage talk.

Caregivers sing and play rhyming and simple action games with infants. There are appropriate books, some of them homemade picture books, as well as books that adults can read to infants; reading is done regularly with infants. Read more about specifics in the language environment in Chapter 11.

Rethink the Traditional

Figure 3-6 Rethink the traditional! These photos on the wall under a table are just right for infant viewing. *Courtesy Avondale Children's Center.*

Babies are different in most respects from the older children in the child care center, so there is no reason to feel that their physical environment should not also look very different. Thus, it may be very useful to consider using items that might be seen in homes more frequently than in classrooms. An example of this is a couch. Besides the obvious comfort for adults, a couch offers versatility of use. A perfect spot for caregivers and parents to sit with babies—several at a time when necessary—the couch can be moved out from the wall to create a new pathway when babies have become crawlers. For those ready to pull up and cruise along holding on, the couch is a perfect height and casual support (Greenman, 1984). Also rethink the traditional when it comes to the decor of the classroom. See things from the perspective of infants—then you will discover that the bottoms of things like chairs and cribs need something interesting on them, or the ceiling for babies who are spending much time gazing upward. (See Figure 3-6.)

Babies play alone, and when they get crowded together, there is more likely to be unintentional hurting. The traditional classroom arrangement that has learning centers with space for several children is less appropriate for infants. More appropriate individual infant learning centers are created when caregivers observe what babies are ready for. For example, when an infant is ready to reach and grasp, a small area on the floor at one protected end of a couch, might be made into a reaching center, with a changing array of materials suspended from a dowel. The space under a table, or in the lowest cabinets (with the door

removed) might be the spot for a sitting baby to explore the box of different textured materials—a curly wig, a piece of sandpaper, a large end of packing Styrofoam. A baby ready to fingerpaint with flour or pudding can sit in his high chair. A small packing box with pillows makes a cozy spot for an infant who is looking at some cardboard-paged books. Individual playing spots are most appropriate for infants who will be at their own developmental level, for solitary play and for interaction with a caregiver.

Separate areas appropriate for an infant room might include: a rattle corner, a reaching center, a sensory corner, a manipulative area, an exercise mat, a cozy corner, and an area for interaction (Cataldo, 1983). (See Figures 3-7 and 3-8.)

Outdoors for Infants

Figure 3-7 and 3-8
Appropriate centers in an infant room may include a cozy corner and an exercise mat. *Courtesy Avondale Children's Center.*

Babies need to be taken outdoors regularly—how else can they experience the unique sensory and mobility environments of the larger world around? Many of the same principles apply to the infants' outdoor environment as apply indoors. The primary component of the environment is an alert, available adult, who enjoys being outdoors himself, and who doesn't feel babies have to be protected totally from the world around. To be sure, adults will have to be watchful for items dangerous to mouth: small rocks, acorns and berries, and discarded wrappers. The surface for babies needs to be both soft and level. It is best for babies to be separated from toddlers outdoors, however possible. It is assumed that much of the time outdoors for babies will be spent in gross motor play—"tummy time," crawling, cruising, perhaps climbing. Clean blankets will provide a safe surface for the youngest, who will also occasionally enjoy watching from the adult's lap. This may be the best time to use infant seats or walkers, to give less mobile babies a vantage point. Being close to a fence allows the young "cruisers" a natural support. (See Figure 3-9.) Tiny ramps and low steps may add variety for these children. (See more ideas about design in Greenman, 1991.) Partially filled inner tubes are useful for infants at several stages. Shade is important for tender skin, even if created from a canopy. Large strollers or "baby-buggies" will allow caregivers to transport the babies outdoors, as well as take walks into the neighborhood. (See Figure 3-10.) There will be lots of natural kinds of sensory stimulation outdoors. (For ideas for some additions, see Miller, 1989; Wortham and Wortham, 1992.)

Health and Safety

Surely an extremely important component of the physical environment for infants is the consideration of health and safety. Babies are totally dependent on alert adults to keep them safe at all times and to prevent the spread of infection. Statistics indicate that accidents are leading causes of death in infants, and that babies cared for in groups are at greater risk for many kinds of infections and diseases than babies cared for at home (Kendall and Moukaddem, 1992). This indicates the seriousness of the caregiver's responsibilities in this area.

Safe environments for infants include:

- shatterproof mirrors and protection from windows that could break, as well as from windows open at the bottom

Figure 3-9 Varying flat surfaces and a nearby fence will offer different experiences for infants. *Courtesy NationsBank Child Care Center.*

- covered electrical outlets, and removal of electrical cords that could trip or be chewed on
- protection from radiators, hot water taps, light bulbs, heaters, or other potential sources of burns and scalds
- nonpoisonous plants
- all medicines, cleaning substances, and other hazardous chemicals kept locked away from infants
- no broken or damaged toys, no toys with easily removable small parts, and no toys painted with lead or other toxic materials
- completely stable furniture that cannot be pulled over by or fall onto babies; be sure cribs and other furniture follow consumer protection standards, so babies cannot get their heads stuck
- staff knowledgeable regarding emergency procedures, including infant CPR and first aid, location of emergency equipment and emergency numbers, and firedrill procedures
- constant supervision of babies, who are not left unattended even for a moment; safety restraints are used in high-chairs, strollers, changing tables (See Figure 3-11.)
- supervision of babies as they eat and drink; no leaving them with bottles propped
- no overprotection of babies; staff work on finding ways of safely allowing babies to practice a challenging skill, such as putting pillows by the step the baby is drawn to climb on, rather than continually removing the baby

Healthy environments for infants include:

- scrupulous standards of adult hand-washing after coughing, sneezing, wiping an individual nose, changing diapers, and before handling food or bottles; adults use paper towels to touch faucets or waste containers after washing
- staff who follow licensing standards for cleanliness of the changing area, providing a cleansed and covered surface for each diaper change
- refrigeration of food and bottles until time of use
- staff that wash babies' hands frequently, with individual washcloths
- staff that wash toys and surfaces daily, even more often when they are aware that children are sharing and mouthing toys
- staff and parents that remove street shoes before walking on floors where babies lie
- cleanliness of individual cribs
- good record-keeping confirming up-to-date immunizations for all babies
- exclusion of babies with signs of illness, according to standards and symptoms defined by the program
- administration of medicine to babies only from prescribed medications with written permission and instructions from parents. (For more about healthy infant environments, see Kendall and Moukaddem, 1992.)

Care to health and safety is an important part of the physical environment.

Figure 3-10 Baby-buggies will help caregivers take infants outdoors regularly to enjoy walks in the neighborhood. *Courtesy NationsBank Child Care Center.*

Materials for Infant Rooms

Figure 3-11 Caregivers always use safety restraints in strollers. *Courtesy NationsBank Child Care Center.*

Figure 3-12 Reaching gyms and infant seats are appropriate equipment for infant rooms. *Courtesy NationsBank Child Care Center.*

Every infant room should contain the following:

mats or rugs to lie on

cribs to sleep in

infant seats, to be primarily used for feeding before the baby sits alone, or an occasional change of scene

high chairs, or some substitute that takes less room, such as seats that snap on low tables, for babies who sit

soft balls, animals, and blocks

rattles

plastic keys and beads

squeeze toys

cloth and cardboard books

nesting toys

simple busy boxes

kitchen utensils and safe discards

stacking cones

unbreakable mirrors

mobiles

reaching gyms

telephones

simple dolls

collections of objects with diameters from 2–5 in. to hold and explore (See Figure 3-12)

Most of these items are the toys traditionally seen in homes and centers. It should be recalled that caregivers will know which items babies are ready for as they watch their individual motor and cognitive development (more about this in Section Three). It should also be repeated that well-constructed toys made from ordinary discards allow caregivers to ensure novelty for babies.

Burton White's *The First Three Years of Life* has useful suggestions in each section for appropriate simple toys, including some brand name recommendations, as well as other toys not appropriate for the advertised age group (White, 1985).

Schedule Considerations

A schedule, if it is defined as an unchanging, predictable sequence of daily events for the children in a group, does not exist in an infant room, since each infant has individual daily patterns for rest, feeding, changes, and playtime that need to be responded to.

When five-month-old Andrea arrives one morning at eight o'clock, her mother tells the caregiver that the baby did not sleep well the previous night,

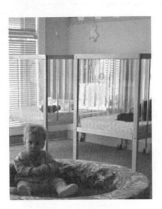

Figure 3-13 Babies on self-demand schedules may play while others sleep. *Courtesy Methodist Home Child Development Center, Charlotte, NC.*

and she is put directly into her crib to see if she needs more sleep. When she awakens, she is very hungry. After an immediate feeding, she is relaxed and ready to play with some rattles, lying on her back on the carpet, and rolling from side to side. The next day, she arrives rested, but ravenous, so the caregiver immediately prepares some cereal for her. After a bottle, she wants to lie drowsily on her caregiver's lap for a while before being placed on the carpet to play. It would be impossible to post a schedule that would meet her needs, as well as those of eleven-month-old Ben, who is trying to change his napping schedule to a short morning nap and a much longer afternoon one. (See Figure 3-13.)

Caregivers do not attempt to move babies to fit into a predetermined schedule. Instead, they communicate daily with parents to learn what current needs might be, and then watch the baby's reactions to determine what is needed next. This has been called a *self-demand schedule*; what this implies is that infants communicate their own needs, and adults respond appropriately. This rhythmic responsiveness is what slowly builds to a baby's inner sense of certainty that needs will be met by trustworthy people. A self-demand schedule builds healthy social/emotional development.

Much of the daily timeframe is spent on routine caregiving. Caregivers who regard these times as important for interaction and communication —in fact, the heart of the curriculum—do not rush through them, but allow for a relaxed and responsive pacing.

Things Not Seen in a Developmentally Appropriate Environment for Infants

Note that conspicuously missing from the list of materials for the infant room are the large pieces of equipment such as traditional playpens, swings, walkers, jumpers, etc. While there is some limited use for all of these items at various stages, they are too space-consuming and expensive to justify their value. Besides, when they are present, it is too tempting for caregivers to overuse them, to the detriment of optimum development. While it may be an exaggeration to say they are never present in a developmentally appropriate environment, they are certainly not a dominant feature, and may well be done without.

Another component not seen in a developmentally appropriate environment for infants is a by-the-clock sequence of scheduled events for all infants. Each infant needs to be responded to more individually than a set schedule permits.

The chaos of a large group of infants and several caregivers, perhaps with ratios as high as one adult caring for five to seven babies together in one room, simply does not allow for developmentally appropriate interaction, mobility, or individualization. Be sure to know what your state licensing requirements mandate for caregiving ratios, and work to change ratios too high for developmentally appropriate practice.

BUT WHAT ABOUT?

Mary Cassidy is a single mother of a five-month-old in your child care center. She asks you to keep Sam on a by-the-clock schedule so she can feed him his evening meal as soon as she gets home from work, and put him right to bed, leaving her free to do the household chores. You find it difficult to keep to the schedule, since it sometimes means waking him from a nap to feed him, and other times it means he's hungry before the prescribed hour. How do you respond?

When parental needs seem to interfere with the self-demand schedule that is considered developmentally appropriate by the caregiver, both caregiver and parent may be frustrated. A continuing dialogue focused on infant needs is necessary. The caregiver may help the parent to realize that infants become much more amenable to a more regulated schedule in the latter months of their first year, as they move more naturally to two long naps and a three-meal-a-day pattern. Perhaps mom will be able to defer her needs for a few more weeks. It is important to help parents of infants realize that developmental needs are specific and different at each age, and appropriate responses help infants build the developmental base for later stages.

SUMMARY

The physical environment for infants provides for meeting developmental needs of trust, attachment, mobility, sensory exploration, and language in a world that provides for safety and health considerations. Individual needs dictate daily schedules as well as the kind of materials that caregivers provide for babies at various stages. This environment serves as the framework for the interaction that will form the basis for the social/emotional environment and the cognitive/language environment, as we will discuss in Sections Three and Four.

THINK ABOUT IT

1. Visit a center that has an infant room. See if you can identify and note down:

   - health and safety practices

   - components to nurture trust and attachment; mobility; sensory exploration; language

   - communication methods between parents and staff

   - outdoor play area for infants

   - materials and arrangement of furniture in the room

   - Compare your findings with the ideas discussed in this chapter. Share your findings with those of classmates who visited other centers.

2. Write a brief report that could (but won't) be presented to the staff of the center of the infant room you visited, suggesting some changes you feel would improve the quality of the physical environment provided for infants. Be sure your writing includes the reasons why you recommend these changes. Share these ideas with other students.

QUESTIONS TO REVIEW OBJECTIVES

1. What are several of the developmental needs of infants that must be considered when planning the physical environment?

2. For each of the developmental needs listed above, describe several things that can be done in the environment to meet each need.

3. Discuss things to be considered when planning outdoor environments for babies.

4. List as many things as you can that provide safe and healthy environments for infants.

5. What are several appropriate materials for infant rooms?

6. What is an appropriate schedule for infants?

7. What is unlikely to be found in a developmentally appropriate environment for infants?

REFERENCES AND SUGGESTIONS FOR READING

Ainsworth, M.D.S. (1992). Attachment: Retrospect and prospect. In C.M. Parks & J. Stevenson Hinde (eds.). *The place of attachment in human behavior.* NY: Basic Books.

Cataldo, C. (1983). *Infant and toddler programs.* Reading, MA: Addison-Wesley.

Erikson, E. (1963). *Childhood and society.* New York: Norton.

Gerber, M. (ed.). (1991). *Resources for infant educarers.* Los Angeles, CA: RIE.

Goldhaber, J., & Smith, D. (1993, Spring). Infants and toddlers at play: Looking for meaning. *Day Care and Early Education,* 9–12.

Gonzalez-Mena Widmeyer Eyer, J., & Widmeyer Eyer, D. (1992). *Infants, toddlers, and caregivers.* Mountain View, CA: Mayfield Publishing Co.

Greenman, J. (1984, Summer). Worlds for infants and toddlers: New ideas. *Beginnings,* 21–25.

Greenman, J. (1988). *Caring spaces, learning places: Children's environments that work.* Redmond, WA: Exchange Press, Inc.

Greenman, J. (1991, May/June). Babies get out: Outdoor settings for infant toddler play. *Child Care Information Exchange,* 21–24.

Harms, T. et al. (1990). *Infant toddler environment rating scale.* New York: Teacher's College Press.

Kendall, E. D., & Moukaddem, V. (1992, July). Who's vulnerable in infant child care centers? *Young Children, 47(5),* 72–78.

Miller, K. (1989). *The outside play and learning book.* Mt. Rainier, MD: Gryphon House, Inc.

Piaget, J. (1963). *The origins of intelligence in children.* NY: Norton.

Prescott, E. The physical environment: A powerful regulator of experience. *Child Care Information Exchange, Reprint #4.*

White, B. (1985). *The first three years of life.* New York: Prentice Hall.

Wilson, L. V. C. (1995). *Infants and toddlers: Curriculum and teaching.* Albany, NY: Delmar Publishing Inc.

Wortham, S., & Wortham, M. R. (1992, Summer). Nurturing infant and toddler play outside. *Dimensions of Early Childhood,* 25–27.

CHAPTER 4

Developmentally Appropriate Physical Environments:
For Toddlers

N ear the end of their first year, when babies begin to move around freely, we begin to call them toddlers, and do so for the next one and a half to two years. In only about a year, toddlers make dramatic gains in physical mobility and dexterity, in language understanding and sound production, in their ability to explore actively the world around them. Their needs for sleep have decreased, and many hours each day are spent in physical activity.

They are definitely not "group" creatures, being centered on exploring their concept of self and everything which that means. It is fairly obvious to an impartial observer that they care little about rights or needs of other toddlers, though they are as intrigued by exploring other children in their environment as they are in exploring any other interesting object they come upon.

All of this has implications for planning appropriate physical environments that will match toddler development and nurture the tasks of toddlerhood.

OBJECTIVES

After completing this chapter, students should be able to:

- identify several developmental characteristics and needs of toddlers.
- identify several ways the environment can meet each of these developmental needs.
- identify several appropriate materials for toddler rooms.
- discuss schedule and transition considerations for toddlers.
- identify inappropriate components in physical environments for toddlers.

What Are Toddlers Like?

Imagine what the reaction would be of a bright young explorer from another planet who first stepped foot on planet Earth! Every waking moment would be spent in busily attempting to figure out this strange new place, its inhabitants, and everything else encountered. Not knowing any of the rules or customs of the place, the newcomer would undoubtedly make some errors along the way, breaking either physical objects or social norms. Not being very familiar with the language, attempts to teach or explain might be frustrating for both the visitor and those who tried to enlighten him.

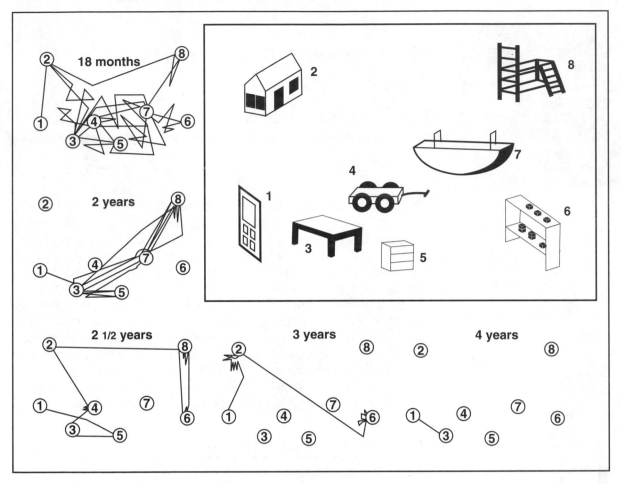

Figure 4-1 As the drawing shows, toddlers are almost constantly on the move. *Adapted from a drawing in the Sept. 1986 issue of Child Care Center.*

It is not very different for the toddler, suddenly able to move about the world and come to a firsthand understanding of it. Full of a sense of this new power, the toddler is at a peak of curiosity, and frustrated (but undaunted) by any sense of limitation. What the toddler has is a drive to use the body, to explore everything and everybody she comes in contact with, and the tireless energy to keep exploring even when others make it difficult. What the toddler does not yet have is much language for self-expression, much of the self-control that goes along with the understanding of concepts and language, or much concern about the needs, wishes, or rights of others in the world. It is precisely the contrast of what toddlers have and do not yet have that makes them such interesting and challenging individuals to care for in groups.

This may be one of the places where a picture is worth many thousands of descriptive words. Take a look at the diagram in Figure 4-1. In it you see the approximation of the movements of an eighteen-month-old around a typical preschool classroom, set up with a variety of interest centers and activities. The movements were recorded over a period of seven minutes. From the lines, you

Figure 4-2 Toddlers are so interested in exploring that they may leave a trail of disorder and things "undone." *Courtesy NationsBank Child Care Center, Charlotte, NC.*

can see the nearly ceaseless movement from one area to another, retracing pathways, obviously not staying with one thing for longer than seconds. The need for physical movement, the bottomless curiosity, the short attention span, the sense of autonomy and personal will—all of that can be seen as the lines on paper trace ceaseless toddler exploration. Incidentally, what is not seen in this drawing is what would happen if a group of equally busy toddlers were moving about the same space; undoubtedly there would be numerous physical clashes and conflicts of will as each independent explorer, intent on personal goals, encountered another. It might be comforting for caregivers to share this drawing with parents of toddlers, who despair of their frenetic children! Look at the much more controlled behaviors of the older twos, let alone the supremely confident four-year-olds who can focus on one interest, without change, for the full period. Maturation and development will soon change some things that no amount of teaching or scolding can!

This, then, is the nature of toddlers: exuberant physical energy, boundless intellectual curiosity, a strong sense of self, and a wish for independence.

 Toddlers learn with their whole bodies—not just their heads. They learn more through their hands than they do through their ears. They learn by doing, not only by just thinking.... Toddlers solve problems on a physical level. "Me—mine!" indicates toddlers are beginning to see themselves as individuals with possessions. And of course, the "NO!" toddlers are so famous for is a further clue to their push for separateness and independence (Gonzalez-Mena, 1986, pp. 47–48). *"*

What Do Toddlers Do?

Figure 4-3 Toddlers will struggle to "do it myself"—though this is undeniably a messy process. *Courtesy Methodist Home Child Development Center.*

Toddlers walk, run, and move during all their waking hours—and frequently protest loudly when an adult suggests that it is time to stop moving and sleep. They have an insatiable desire to climb as high as they can manage. They rarely sit still for long, and when they do it is because some interesting thing to handle or manipulate has caught their attention. They use their full repertoire of manipulative abilities to discover the properties of anything they come in contact with. They enjoy dumping, dropping, banging, poking fingers in things, trying to pull things apart—all in the interest of pure research. They repeat and practice activities. They do a lot more undoing than doing, being able to pull socks and shoes off, pull diapers off, dump puzzle pieces out, or throw objects, long before they can put things back. (See Figure 4-2.) And as active as they are, toddlers also spend a good deal of time staring at things and people, and doing nothing much! Evidently this is yet another form of exploration (White, 1985).

Toddlers want to do most everything "*Myself!*," even if tasks are beyond their capability. They manipulate spoons and cups to feed themselves, albeit a messy process. (See Figure 4-3.) They prefer to wash faces and hands themselves. They try to dress themselves.

Toddlers spend only about 16 percent of their time in social activities (White, 1985), alternating between seeking physical contact and attention from adults, and resisting them. Yet, ambivalent as their social responses to loved adults are, toddlers resist and protest separation. Toddlers may show brief and transitory interest in peers, but other toddlers are used mainly as another vehicle for asserting self or conducting research. Toddlers may respond aggressively to others—biting, grabbing, hitting. While they are not yet very verbal, they manage to express strong emotions both physically and loudly.

 Neither infants nor preschoolers, toddlers are furiously becoming: increasingly mobile, autonomous, social, thoughtful creatures with language and insatiable urges to test and experiment. They embody contradictions: anarchist with an instinct to herd and cluster, assertive and independent now, passive and completely dependent moments later. These restless mobile characters have a drive to take apart the existing order and rearrange it, by force if necessary, to suit their own whimsically logical view of the universe. (Greenman, 1988, pp. 52–53) "

What Do Toddlers Need?

Figure 4-4 Toddlers need adults who can enjoy their exuberance. *Courtesy Methodist Home Child Development Center.*

Knowing what toddlers do, it becomes possible to consider what they need for development to be encouraged. Probably what toddlers need most is to be accepted for who they are. They suffer badly in comparison with older children, for they are by no means as capable of understanding or reasoning, self-control, or social learning as children a year or so older. They are accused of being clumsy, destructive, selfish, stubborn, and just plain "mean." None of this is fair.

Just because they can walk and talk, many adults feel that it is now appropriate to begin teaching lessons of self-control, and are visibly frustrated when toddlers do not respond. Using methods of teaching that are traditional with older preschoolers just doesn't work with toddlers, who are likely to wander out of circle time or resist adult-directed activities. Inappropriate expectations usually lead to a battle of wills between adults and toddlers, with the unhealthy possibility that toddlers end up feeling that they have failed to live up to the standards set by their adults.

More than anything else, toddlers need adults who can enjoy the exuberance and striving of the toddler to move to a sense of self. (See Figure 4-4.) They thrive when adults can find ways to nurture a sense of *autonomy*, (a sense of self as an independent being) as defined by Erikson, while recognizing the need to protect the toddler from the negative sense of shame and doubt that comes when the toddler is continually stopped or punished for natural physical or social testing. They need adults who can help them with the task of *separation* (being apart from those to whom the adult is attached). They need adults who can nourish a sense of the individual, while maintaining safety and rights for toddlers as members of a group. They need adults who can protect them from their immaturity and impulsiveness, yet safeguard their right to explore and learn while still in Piaget's *sensorimotor* stage (recall from Chapter 3 that this is the time of practical, physical intelligence, slowly constructed by taking in information from sensory and manipulative exploration), and slowly moving into the symbolic stage of the early *preoperational* years. (Preoperational cognitive functioning—basically a prelogical, intuitive approach—is described in detail in Chapter 13.)

As we remind ourselves of what toddlers are like, what they can do, and what they need to accomplish their developmental tasks, we can create a physical environment to enhance optimum development during toddlerhood. This environment will be unique, not one that is more appropriate for babies, nor a diluted preschool classroom.

How do you develop an environment that allows collecting, hauling, dumping, and painting (with the requisite tasting of the paint and experimenting with the logical primary canvas—themselves)? How do you allow the necessary robust, explosive, and occasionally motor learning with a group of amoral beings who are largely oblivious to the safety of others ... how do you accommodate to and support the wonderful, albeit erratic, *do it myself* desire and the equally developmentally important but often less wonderful assertion of "No!" and still accomplish anything in a reasonable time frame? ... Perhaps mission impossible may understate the situation. (Greenman, 1988, p. 53)

In designing physical environments for toddlers, it may be important first to consider several key components that must be present. There is a need for *safety*, as mobile, curious toddlers must be protected from their own impulsiveness and immaturity without frustrating them with unnecessary restriction. There is a need for *flexibility*, as the environment must keep in step with children's changing needs and provide spaces that must be used for several purposes, such as play as well as routine caregiving, new walkers, and relentless climbers. There is a need for *variety*, to provide for different toddlers doing different things and individual exploring, as well as for expanding the world beyond the confines of the four walls of a toddler room. There is a need for easily restorable *order*, since exploration becomes an untidy process; yet toddlers need the security of familiar objects being in familiar places. There is a need also for *organization*, so adults can help toddlers succeed at self-help, and so frustrating waits can be minimized. There is a need for *challenge*, as bored toddlers are more likely to get involved in undesirable behaviors. Adults need to keep these elements in mind as they evaluate the worlds they create for toddlers. In addition, adults need to consider the toddler developmental tasks they want to support. These include autonomy, separateness, movement ability, self-help skills, and sensorimotor exploration.

Figure 4-5 These older toddlers enjoy helping themselves to snacks and carrying them to the table. *Courtesy Avondale Children's Center.*

Environment to Support Autonomy

An environment for autonomy includes components that allow toddlers to achieve a measure of independence and sense of doing things for themselves. (See Figure 4-5.) Furniture and fittings need to be toddler-sized, so toddlers can sit comfortably with their feet touching the floor, and climb up to use sinks and toilets unaided. Coathooks and cubbies are within toddler reach, as are hooks for washcloths, etc. A mirror at toddler height encourages face washing. Feeling some control over the environment increases a sense of competence. For toddlers who have physical limitations and special needs, efforts to provide for autonomy need to be increased, so that lack of mobility or ability does not mean lack of opportunities to develop autonomy.

Toy shelves are open and accessible, and toys and materials are stored in the same places each day, so toddlers can find their favorites confidently. If everything has a place, clearly indicated with pictures, photos or other markers, it is

Figure 4-6 It is easier to restore order if materials are stored in basins clearly marked with pictures. *Courtesy Avondale Children's Center.*

easier to restore order. (See Figure 4-6.) Toddlers are encouraged to participate in meaningful responsibilities such as picking up toys, by storing items in basins or on trays, where toddlers can return them. Some toddler teachers have found that clean up time goes easier if each child has a personal bucket to pick up small toys to carry them to the shelves. Nearby sponges help toddlers mop up their own spills.

When the materials provided for toddler use can be used without adult assistance, toddlers can enjoy their own accomplishment. Open-ended materials that can be used in whatever way the toddler chooses nurture a sense of autonomy. (Read more about specific materials in Chapter 12.)

An environment for autonomy allows for toddlers to have some space that is just theirs, and does not have to be shared with others at the time. Toddlers love to have small nooks and crannies, hiding places into which they can retreat, especially when the demands of group life get to be too much. Removing the doors of low cupboards, throwing a blanket over a table, cutting a door into a large packing box—however it is done, toddlers enjoy a hiding place or time for quiet solitary play.

When the environment allows for toddler choice, autonomy is encouraged. A variety of materials and activities allows children the freedom to choose according to their interests and needs. Toddlers who do not have every movement controlled by the adult are more likely to accept the times adults do have to take the lead.

An environment for autonomy during toddlerhood includes the possibility to be free of most overt restrictions. Toddlers definitely need limits, but they respond less negatively if the limits are built into the environment, nonverbally showing them where they can go, what they can do. Burton White (1985) described the adult's role in providing a safe, interesting environment for toddlers as *designer of the child's world.* There are several parts to this.

Physical safety is an important factor to be planned for if the toddler is to explore and move about freely. Verbal prohibitions mean little to a curious toddler, and memory is quite shaky at best. Toddlers do not have the ability to look ahead to consequences or see the whole picture, so will have absolutely no judgment about what is potentially dangerous to them physically. This is borne out by the number of accidental poisonings and accidents that involve toddlers. Thus if the toddler is to be able to explore without frustrating restriction from adults, adults need to make the home or center safe for the child by:

- covering electrical outlets with safety plugs, and removing cords from reach
- keeping poisonous liquids, soaps, and medicines in locked cupboards or far beyond toddlers' climbing capacity
- locking drawers and cabinets that contain sharp utensils
- disposing of small objects or toy pieces that inquisitive toddlers might swallow or choke on
- removing unsteady pieces of furniture that children could climb on or pull over
- using gates and locks to prevent access to stairs, doors, dangerous areas, such as bathrooms, and cooking areas

Adults must assume that toddlers will have no good sense about what could harm them, and do all the protecting for them. Toddlers must never be left without supervision for any period of time, whether inside or out, whether the child is quiet or active, or even if adults assume the child is asleep.

Figure 4-7 Autonomy can flourish when arrangements allow toddlers to participate fully in self-help skills. *Courtesy NationsBank Child Care Center.*

The environment must not only be made safe for toddlers, but also safe *from* toddlers. Toddlers' overwhelming curiosity will impel them to explore everything, and with no concept of property rights, everything in the environment is fair game. Anything that adults value and want to keep intact needs to be removed during the toddler period, so the objects do not invite verbal battles of will. (Read more about what Burton White meant about this role of the designer of the child's world later in this chapter.)

By making the environment physically safe for toddler activity, adults must also make the environment emotionally safe, as a place where autonomy and good feelings about self can flourish, (See Figure 4-7) rather than be diminished by adult disapproval, prohibition, and frustration with toddler curiosity.

Make sure your environment for autonomy includes:

- toddler-sized furniture and access to areas that encourage self-help skills
- an easily recognizable arrangement for toddlers to get their own materials
- clues for toddlers to particpate in responsibilities, such as helping to restore order
- opportunities for toddlers to make some choices
- hiding places where toddlers may choose to play alone
- child-proof environments, so exploring need not be restricted

Environment for Separateness

One of the true challenges in caring for toddlers in a group situation is that autonomy, a sense of self, is best nurtured by being able to concentrate on and test out the abilities of the individual. It is only after toddlers have formed a basic self-concept that they are ready to move on to learn how to care about and interact with peers. It is only after they have truly learned what it is to possess things that they are able to understand the concept of sharing. And when several children are at the same time testing out the nature of self, the adults who care for them are obligated to find ways to encourage separate activity while slowly helping children to recognize others.

An environment that allows for separateness stimulates toddlers to choose from a variety of choices that suit particular moods or activity levels. Toddlers are not all expected to do the same thing at the same time; when toddlers clump, there will inevitably be infringements on one child's space or activity. It is helpful to partition the room off to define areas for many individual explorations, rather than a large, undefined space that will encourage toddlers to bunch up too closely to one another. Small work spaces that fit individuals, or at most two or three children, can encourage parallel kinds of play, yet still allow space for separateness. (See Figure 4-8.) Rethinking the traditional preschool classroom furnishings is a good idea for this. Rather than big tables that put too many toddlers together, use small, easily stacked and moved plastic Parson-type tables or plastic cubes that allow enough space for one toddler, or a rug on the floor that defines the space to play with the animals, or a hula hoop where the toddler sits with a stacking toy. Other ideas for creating small play spaces include small plastic wading pools, trays, boxes, large inner tubes, circles of hosing, changes in the flooring such as a carpet area, a mattress area, a pile of cushions, a sheet of plastic, or

Figure 4-8 These side-by-side chalkboards allow two toddlers to work beside each other, yet separately. *Courtesy NationsBank Child Care Center.*

Figure 4-9 Toddlers may enjoy coming together to sing for brief periods, as long as they don't have to sit and be still. *Courtesy NationsBank Child Care Center.*

Figure 4-10 Toddlers may come together as a small group for mealtimes. *Courtesy NationsBank Child Care Center.*

Figure 4-11 Toddler classrooms need clear travel patterns for toddlers constantly on the move. *Courtesy NationsBank Child Care Center.*

small raised platforms. Separation allows for clearer understandings between toddlers of what is "mine" and what is "yours."

Using every available space for interest or activity contributes to a classroom teacher's ability to "divide and conquer." Window ledges, under tables, corners, in cupboards—using the room flexibly may offer a suitable variety. Pictures or sensory materials on ends and backs of shelves make a talking or patting place; a sheet of paper with crayons attached with yarn taped to the side of the changing table makes a drawing nook; a sheet of Contac paper, sticky side out, taped to the wall, with a basket of collage stuff to stick to it on the floor beside it—all of these minicenters will help increase the number of available play spaces for separate play.

One morning a toddler teacher had set up: the small slide; some foam blocks in the block corner; cars and trucks with a ramp on the floor; some pots and dishes in the kitchen, two baby dolls in the bed, and a collection of hats and shoes for toddlers to try on; some fat crayons and paper on one small table; and a basin of beans and cups on another. The permanent quiet corner in a tent big enough for one was also available, as was a big pillow located near the book shelf. He looked around in delight to see all eight of his toddlers busy, involved, and exploring separately, except for the two who sat together using the crayons on a mural-sized paper that was taped to the table. Planning enough different materials and activities in areas clearly separated by the arrangement of furniture allows for separateness.

When activities to be done in a group are limited to a short informal singing or story time that children are not absolutely required to sit through (see Figure 4-9) or are limited to coming together for eating, (see Figure 4-10) toddlers can slowly experience being part of a group while being free most of the time to be separate.

When duplicates (triplicates, quadruplicates) of toys or equipment are available, toddlers are able to play separately while encouraging interest in similar kinds of play.

A task related to separateness is learning how to cope with separation from parents. Moving from dependence to independence involves some scariness and sadness. There is a good deal of ambivalence as toddlers swing between wanting to be quite separate and wanting to stay close to the adult as a source of security. In classroom environments teachers can help by having a toddler-eye-level display of each child's family photos and other pictures of home, for toddler reassurance. Some toddler teachers have found that a plastic picture cube allows toddlers to carry around their own personal collection of family photos—very comforting indeed! Pictures of the toddler him/herself facilitate the growing awareness of self; pictures on the cubby, for example, help toddlers identify their own separate space. Personal objects from home, including comfort objects and things that Mom or Dad may leave with the toddler as a reassuring symbol of promised return, may be kept in that private, separate space.

Make sure a toddler environment for separateness includes:

- clearly separated individual areas for play and exploration, created by rethinking traditional interest-center design

- varieties of materials for separate choices

- brief periods of group interaction for music, story, or eating

- several similar toys to allow for separate yet parallel play

- pictures of family, home, and self to encourage comfort with separation and feelings of self

Environment for Movement

Figure 4-12 Toddlers will carry objects as they're on the move, so the environment needs to be carefully designed to restore order from chaos. *Courtesy NationsBank Child Care Center.*

Figure 4-13 Safe climbing arrangements will satisfy toddlers' need to climb. *Courtesy Methodist Home Child Development Center.*

An environment for toddlers recognizes that these are people on the move. They move around the classroom, stopping when something interests them. Often they do not stop long enough to want to sit and settle in, as do older children. Toddlers much prefer to stand as they manipulate objects on the table, finger-paint, or pour sand from one bucket to another. They also squat to explore something interesting in their path, and then move on. An implication of this style is to streamline the environment for movement, removing chairs from the tables, placing basins with interesting sensory objects about the room to capture attention as the toddler travels. (Wallpaper water troughs or small basins work well for solitary explorers.) Clear travel patterns winding around furniture and play areas will help avoid collisions between other toddlers on the move. (See Figure 4-11.) When toddlers have special needs that require the use of walkers, braces, or wheelchairs, even more attention to travel patterns is necessary.

When toddlers are on the move, it is inevitable that they will carry toys or equipment from one area to another—this seems to be one of toddlers' pleasures, lugging objects about with them. It is only frustrating for both child and adult to try to restrict this carrying behavior. Better to put effort into systems to easily restore order when playtime is finished. (See Figure 4-12.)

Gross motor practice—movement—needs to be considered to be the main feature of curriculum for toddlers, both indoors and out. They *will* climb, so it is appropriate to provide safe space and equipment for them to do so. Adults who can realize this and support this movement will nurture feelings of confidence as well. Climbers, step arrangements, boxes to push and pull, riding toys, push and pull toys, tunnels, and wide balance beams all need to have ample space in toddler classroom design. (See Figure 4-13.)

Toddlers who are on the go wear themselves out long before they are ready to admit it, so an environment that provides an inviting cozy corner to flop down on a large beanbag chair or pillow with a stuffed animal, will indirectly guide children to alternate active and quiet periods.

Outdoor areas for toddlers provide additional possibilities for movement, under watchful eyes of adult supervisors. The equipment needs to reflect the development of toddlers: gently sloping ramps provide challenge; broad steps with sturdy low handrails; *low* climbing structures; sling swings or low-hung tire swings for toddlers to lean over and maneuver themselves through; various elevations; rocking and riding toys that children can propel themselves with; gently graded sliding boards that toddlers can go down head-first on; and open spaces for running and ball play. Opportunities for fine motor play and sensory exploration will be met by having sand and water available in warmer months, along with lots of things to fill and dump.

Areas designed specifically for toddler abilities and challenges and separated from older children and their equipment will provide for motor practice, as well as the freedom and good feelings of autonomy.

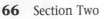

BUT WHAT ABOUT?

But what about my toddlers who insist on climbing? They climb on chairs, on tables, on the counter. The other day I found one trying to climb up on the toy shelf.

Yes, toddlers will, and in fact must, climb. Unless you recognize this and provide safe places to redirect their climbing, you and they will be extremely frustrated. You just can't stop it, so it is far better to figure out how you can provide climbing opportunities in your environment. One creative teacher, frustrated by continually removing toddlers from climbing on the toy shelves, took the toys off the shelves and turned the shelves on their back so toddlers could safely climb. Remember, you don't need a commercially designed climber; alternatives (depending on the toddlers' ages) may be piles of sofa cushions; arrangements of truck inner tubes; wooden boxes and cubes; and stools. You can't lick them, so join them!

As toddlers become increasingly mobile, the issue of their safety concerns adults. A specific danger to autonomy is conveying the sense that the toddler needs protection, that they are not competent to do things for themselves. Adults must guard against the tendency to overprotect; this is particularly an issue when children with special needs are part of the group. They can be comfortable as they prepare a toddler appropriate environment that allows for a balance of safety and challenge. Emphasizing the teaching and modeling of skills so children can manage their own environments gives adults something to focus on besides simple overprotection.

Provide an environment for movement by:

- streamlining the classroom furnishings and arrangement to provide for movement paths, and the toddlers' learning-on-the-move style of exploration
- providing space and equipment within the classroom for gross motor practice
- incorporating a cozy corner into the classroom arrangement to suggest quiet periods for toddlers
- designing outdoor play spaces suitable for toddler skills
- avoiding the tendency to overprotect by helping develop physical skills for toddler self-management

Environment for Self-Help Skills

Perhaps one of the best ways of nurturing good feelings about self is to encourage toddlers' already strong interest in doing things for themselves. Rather than seeing toddlers' desire to help as something to support, some caregivers impatiently try to rush through routine care, believing they can complete the tasks

Figure 4-14 Toddler mealtimes are smoother when children are given enough space at the table, chairs that allow feet to rest on the floor, and broad-based cups. *Courtesy NationsBank Child Care Center.*

Figure 4-15 Toddlers can learn to put on their coats "the magic way," flipping them over their heads. *Courtesy NationsBank Child Care Center.*

better and more quickly. Instead, when participation in self-care is considered important in toddler curriculum, the environment can support this.

Self-feeding is well within the ability of toddlers, especially when appropriate dishes and utensils are used. Short-handled spoons and forks allow for less spilling between dish and mouth. Broad-based bowls and cups, sometimes with lids, allow toddlers to do the job without adult hands involved. Bibs or complete cover-ups minimize changing of clothes afterward. The eating area should be on a washable floor, or a floor protected with a sheet of plastic. Enough space needs to be provided between toddlers to allow each child free movement. Seating arrangements that put feet right on the floor increase ability to sit. All of these suggestions allow toddlers to enjoy doing it for themselves at mealtime and adults to be able to restore order fairly quickly afterward. (See Figure 4-14.)

When toddler washcloths are available on hooks near the mirror, there is less resistance to cleaning faces and hands. Though toddlers undoubtedly need help with complete dressing, hair care, and tooth brushing, they can still participate when adults allow both opportunities and time for practice. Toddler participation is fostered when adults start a zipper on the track, for example, for a toddler to finish pulling up. Generations of two-year-olds have learned to put on their jackets "the magic way," after an adult has demonstrated how to place the jacket on the floor and flip it over the head. (See Figure 4-15.) Adult recognition of the importance of "doing it myself" for toddler autonomy encourages adults to find methods of including toddler participation.

One of the major self-help tasks of toddlerhood is learning toilet control. Besides toddlers learning to recognize physical cues for retention and release, toilet learning involves being able to remove clothing, to gain access to the toilet facility, and to carry out cleanliness routines following elimination. Toddlers are assisted when adults provide easily removed clothing with elastic waists, avoiding cumbersome belts, snaps, etc. Some experts feel that using a child-sized potty chair is not a good idea related to sanitation practices. Instead it is recommended that a stool up to the larger sized commode (fitted with a smaller seat) allows toddlers to get to the toilet when needed and feel confident in its use, with feet comfortably on a solid base. Removing doors from the bathroom area allows toddlers quick, independent access to the area, while allowing adults to keep an eye out for when assistance is needed. (Read more about toilet training in Chapter 8.)

An important component in the self-help environment is the adult's attitude that, even if it is messy or seems inefficient, it is time well spent to allow children time to practice developing abilities. A schedule that allows plenty of time for toddlers to try to do as much as they can will help; toddlers who are rushed become frustrated, uncooperative, and less able to function.

Ensure that your environment facilitates development of toddler self-help skills by including:

- sturdy, child-sized eating utensils, and an easily cleaned area

- stools to help with access to toilets, sinks, and mirrors

- time to allow toddlers to participate as fully as they want or are able

- a positive, supportive adult attitude

BUT WHAT ABOUT?

But what about parents who keep on feeding their toddlers? I know it isn't the tidiest process in the world, but I don't mind the mess at lunch time when toddlers feed themselves. Some of my parents keep on feeding, I guess because they hate the mess. A mother who I know still feeds her son at home came in during lunch the other day, and whisked her son off to the bathroom to scrub him before he was even finished eating.

You may have struck on a difference partly related to culture. In cultures where independence is not as valued as it is in your center, parents often go on feeding their toddlers, and it is not purely to avoid mess. Valuing cleanliness and not wasting food may also be culturally related, as well as tendencies to encourage or discourage attempts at independence (Gonzelez-Mena, 1993). It is certainly important to encourage parents to talk about their feelings on self-feeding, to expose potential areas of conflict with the caregiver and classroom practices. Caregivers will also want to explain their reasons for encouraging self-feeding and other self-help skills, related to the larger developmental tasks of toddlerhood, and point out their attempts to make the process easier, though not necessarily tidier, for the children. Parents may not have understood the important reasons why the caregiver felt the mess was worth it. It may be that parents will continue to control the spoon at home, but you may certainly allow the toddler the experience of attempting to feed himself while he or she is in your center.

Environment for Sensorimotor Exploration

Still very much sensorimotor creatures, toddlers learn most by muscle skill mastery and manipulative exploration. When they are allowed free access to a classroom or home that is filled with interesting things to handle, their needs for novelty and intellectual stimulation are met quite naturally, propelled by their deep curiosity. As Burton White put it, "The child spends a good deal of the time examining the various qualities of as many objects as he can get to in the course of a day" (White, 1985, p. 158).

Much of the natural learning style at this stage is quite experimental; that is, toddlers try out a variety of manipulative abilities on each object, evidently trying to see just what its limits are. They might: drop and throw objects; strike them against various surfaces; look at, feel, and more importantly mouth each object; stand objects up, then knock them down and replace them; put objects through openings; pour materials into and out of containers; hoard objects in pockets or containers, and drag them around the room; spin objects; or see if any part of the object can be made to move or come apart. Watch a toddler for a while to see what can be added to this exploratory manipulative repertoire.

Toddlers can be bored, when their desire for novelty goes unmet. Bored toddlers are naturally going to create their own interesting experiment, even if it is to see if the child who screamed when her hair was pulled the other day will scream just as loudly today! Part of the role of designer of the child's world is to ensure an interesting, unending supply of things to encounter and explore. Most of these will probably not be commercially bought toys, since the investment in toys means they are kept around far past the toddler's interest level, long after every attribute has been learned and figured out, and therefore contribute to toddler boredom. Commercial toys which have most value for toddler exploration include: balls of any size or shape, (since they hold endless possibilities for unpredictable results, and the delightful repetition of retrieval); some of the better busy boxes and busy bath toys (for use with water) that allow manipulation of various levers, knobs, latches, and buttons; small wagons for filling and pulling; large foam and cardboard blocks for stacking and knocking down, lugging about and climbing on. There are some manipulative materials that intrigue toddlers bent on mastery and repetition, and are uniquely suited for toddler style of grasp; pegboards with large pegs; stacking and nesting cups; snap/zipper/button boards; shape/sorting boxes; simple puzzles with knobs; bristle blocks and large-size Legos®. The advantage of most of these is that they are open-ended materials that suit any level of construction ability.

Many simple household objects and throwaways hold as much interest, and are easily replaced when their appeal is gone: all sizes of boxes or cartons; plastic bottles and containers of all sizes, sometimes filled with intriguing substances and tightly fastened tops, and sometimes just with tops to try to fit; funnels, tubes, sponges and strainers for water/sand play; locks, keys, fasteners, switches, hinges, chains, doorknobs, slide bolts, etc.; cigar boxes, metal adhesive bandage containers, castors, and anything else that can be made to move; baskets filled with scraps of intriguing textures, such as sandpaper, fur, satin, Brillo® pads, wigs, burlap, yarn, etc. Adults have to examine everything with an eye for safe exploration, and have to become creative in seeing exploration possibilities everywhere. Burton White suggests giving toddlers a small suitcase or bucket filled with thirty or forty small objects of different sizes and shapes to handle.

Natural objects also have great appeal. There is no shortage of large rocks, pinecones, big shells, gourds, large bones and other objects that will intrigue toddlers. Dishpans of water, sand, rice, dry oatmeal, grits, beans, macaroni, cornstarch, or ice chips, with spoons, shovels, and varieties of containers allow for endless sensory and manipulative exploration. Of course, all of these materials have to be used with careful supervision, so that exploring toddlers don't try unsafe experiments with them. (See Figure 4-16.)

In addition to sensorimotor exploration, toddlers are moving on to first stages of *symbolic* play. Interested in observing the world around them, they imitate the people and actions they have seen. Some simple props encourage imitative and beginning pretend play: recognizable household furniture such as a stove or bed; realistic looking baby dolls, representing the gender and racial diversity of the classroom and community; simple dress ups, easily used by toddlers such as scarves, ties, hats, purses, and shoes; pots and dishes; and empty food containers. Realistic looking small cars, trucks, or small figures will also stimulate imitative play. We'll talk more about appropriate materials in Chapter 12.

Because of the movement and sensorimotor nature of toddlers, the classroom environment for learning will not include the typical furniture and interest centers found in classrooms for older preschoolers. While it is important for tod-

Figure 4-16 Tubs of sand, with a variety of containers to fill, and shovels offer opportunities for sensory exploration. *Courtesy CPCC Child Care Training Center, Charlotte, NC.*

dlers' sense of order and confidence to separate the room into predictable areas for particular activities, these areas will be simplified beyond the traditional "art center," "blockcenter" orientation. It may be more useful to think of "a place for climbing, a place for pretending, a place for relaxing, a place for toys, a place for interesting textures," and so on (Miller, 1988, p. 52). Place for books, messy exploration, and manipulatives are other areas needed for toddlers. Cataldo refers to a creative corner for working with paint, crayons, and pasting; a music area; a construction center with blocks and cubes of various types; a curiosity corner, with natural objects to explore; an identity area, including mirrors and favorite photos; a social role area, with life-sized materials and also with miniature materials (people, cars, etc.); a problem-solving center; a gymnastics area; a sand table; and a play dough table (Cataldo, 1983).

Most of the materials mentioned for sensorimotor and imitative play allow for child-initiated, autonomous play and learning, in an environment carefully prepared by an adult. The adult's role as *consultant* (White, 1985) in learning is discussed in Chapter 12.

It is important to realize that the toddler's learning environment includes the whole world around him or her, not just the toys and materials added to a classroom. Toddlers thrive on being able to watch real people do real things, and to experience the way the world works. A toddler at home gets an opportunity to be in the kitchen while a parent cooks, or in the backyard while the parent cuts grass and gardens. Toddlers in centers need the same opportunity to watch the world go by. Access to the view out the window or door may be given by placing of a hollow block for a step, or a gate to look past. A walk down the hall may help a toddler figure out the noise coming from those machines in the office, or watch the delivery man wheeling in the cases of food from his truck.

Plan an environment for learning that:

- provides a changing variety of open-ended materials for sensorimotor exploration
- provides realistic toys and props for beginning imitative play
- simplifies the typical preschool environment, while dividing the space into appropriate centers for active learning
- offers real experiences with people and things to observe

Schedule and Transition Considerations

One thing that toddlers depend upon as they struggle with their own autonomy is a sense of predictability in the world about them—a secure base to return to. To have a dependable pattern to the way the day progresses gives the toddler security, and prevents struggles between adults and children because the built-in rhythm becomes habit not open to challenge.

The schedule in the toddler room may still need to allow for wide individual variations in need for rest. Carlos, a young toddler still needs a morning nap, while a short rest or quiet period may be enough for Antoine and Michelle, now eighteen-months-old. Toddlers who are giving up their morning nap may need lunch moved up earlier so they can fall asleep in the late morning instead of the traditional after lunch naptime. After two days of trying to keep Jonathan from falling asleep as he sat at the table, his caregiver arranged for lunch to be served at eleven o'clock. But for the sense of predictability, the major events of the day still occurred in reliable sequence: playtime, snacktime, outdoor play, clean up for quiet activities before lunch, etc. The adult may know she has shifted things forward an hour, but the toddler's sense of order has not been affected.

Because all toddlers would likely keep moving until they dropped from exhaustion (if no one stopped them first), it is necessary to provide for periods of relative quiet and inactivity as part of the built-in schedule. After a busy hour outdoors, Allison puts on a record of nursery rhymes, sits on the floor near the big cushions, and begins to sing. All the toddlers come and sit for a while with her. Later she'll put out some small cars and figures for them to play with while sitting on the carpet.

Providing nonverbal cues about what comes next helps toddlers feel they are in control. When Mary begins to sing the familiar clean-up song, Jessica recognizes it and importantly tells another toddler, "Clean-up time!" Another caregiver always puts on the same quiet classical music recording to signal the quiet period to lie on pillows while lunch is put on the table. Toddlers are creatures of habit and ritual, and this repetition provides soothing structure to the day. Because of their propensity to resist adult suggestions, transitions are helped by nonverbal rituals.

Transitions also go more smoothly when toddlers are given plenty of warning that change is coming. Toddlers definitely do not like to be interrupted, so they need plenty of preparation to get ready to give up their activity. When their important assistance is arranged for during transitions, they are more likely to go along with the caregiver. When Dana announces clean-up time, he gives each of the toddlers something each can do to help. Concentrating on their responsibilities, the toddlers eagerly begin to assist.

As discussed in the section on self help, toddler eating, dressing, and bathroom routines and hygiene take lots of time for practice of new skills and allowing toddlers to participate as fully as they are able. (See Figure 4-17.) Toddlers react with frustration to being hurried, so the schedule must allow ample time for satisfactory completion. If caregivers believe that this is truly an important part of the day, they will feel less compelled to rush toddlers on to other things.

When it is possible, transition times go more smoothly if toddlers are helped to move to a new activity individually, to minimize waiting time and to allow interaction with the adult, which encourages cooperation. Toddlers find it nearly impossible to wait, so should not be put in situations where they have to. If one caregiver is busy changing diapers, another can be singing songs with children as she sets the table, so there is no empty waiting time for hungry toddlers before lunch. Adult planning ahead will avoid waits during transition times.

Schedule considerations for toddlers include:

- a need for predictable order to the day, combined with a need for flexibility to accommodate individual physical needs

- built-in periods of quieter activities

- nonverbal clues that help toddlers recognize the schedule

- ample time for full toddler participation in routines and transitions

- transition times planned to eliminate need for toddlers to wait

Figure 4-17 It takes time to help toddlers participate as fully as they'd like during routines. *Courtesy CPCC Child Care Training Center.*

Things Not Seen in a Developmentally Appropriate Environment for Toddlers

The environment least helpful for toddlers' development of autonomy are those which are most restrictive. The presence of playpens or small play areas, where it is obvious from the ratio of table and chair space to open space that toddlers are not permitted much movement, are evidence that an environment is not suited to toddler needs. Items that would have to be forbidden from toddler exploration, such as teacher books, paint supplies, or materials that may only be used with adult supervision, have not been removed in inappropriate environments, and become sources of repeated contention.

A large group area will not be present in an appropriate environment for toddlers. Toddlers are not able to sustain attention for much formal group time activity. Moreover, the large area permits too many toddlers to congregate in one area, with likely friction from physical contact that is too close.

Also missing from a developmentally appropriate environment for toddlers is a large concentration of fine motor manipulative materials suited for older preschoolers. Knowing that toddlers will be unable to sit for the periods of concentration required, and knowing that finger dexterity lags behind large motor skill, adults will omit these items from the environment. Safety is a factor too, as small pieces would present a hazard to toddlers who explore all items orally. The natural toddler tendency to dump makes small pieces a frustrating item for caregivers.

A rigid schedule is not seen in an appropriate toddler environment. When sleepy toddlers are literally kept walking to avoid their falling asleep before the scheduled lunch or nap time, they get the feeling that their needs are not important.

SUMMARY

The physical environment for toddlers provides for opportunities to develop autonomy and a sense of self as a separate and unique individual. Attention to physical safety allows toddlers all the freedom they can safely use. Physical arrangements and time to encourage toddler self-help skills contribute to the sense of self. Teachers provide for the toddlers' desire for robust physical movement and practice of skills, as well as for their sensorimotor and imitative learning styles. The best environments allow toddlers within a group setting to move and explore individually. A predictable schedule helps toddlers move comfortably through the day, while allowing for the flexibility demanded by individual needs for food and rest. Transitions are managed without long waiting times. Within such a positive physical environment, toddlers are able to develop a positive sense of self.

THINK ABOUT IT

1. Examine the room you are presently in, in class, or where you are reading. How would it have to be modified to be able to allow toddlers to explore freely? What ordinary objects would toddlers be able to explore? What would have to be removed? If you had three or four toddlers in this same room, what changes would you make to encourage their freedom of movement?

2. Observe a toddler in any public place—a church, restaurant, bus, park. What does the toddler do? What draws the toddler's interest? What restrictions are made on the toddler? How does the toddler respond to the restrictions? What modifications could have been made in the environment to improve the situation from the toddler's point of view?

3. Be an observer in a toddler classroom in a child care center. See what evidence you can find that the environment nurtures (or does not nurture):

- a sense of autonomy
- a sense of separateness
- a curriculum of movement
- a curriculum of self-help skills

4. What materials do you see available for sensorimotor exploration? for imitative play? Visit the playground at the center. What are the modifications that have been made for toddler outdoor play? Discuss your observations with a small group of classmates who have also visited toddler classrooms and playgrounds.

5. If you could make changes in the physical environment you visited, what would they be, and why? Explain how your changes would improve the environment for toddlers. Share these ideas with students who have visited other centers.

QUESTIONS TO REVIEW OBJECTIVES

1. What are several of the developmental needs of toddlers that must be considered when planning the physical environment?

2. For each of the developmental needs listed above, describe several things that can be done in the environment to meet each need.

3. List appropriate materials to include in the toddler learning environment.

4. Discuss several considerations in planning appropriate schedules and transitions for toddlers.

5. Identify several components that would be omitted from a developmentally appropriate toddler physical environment.

REFERENCES AND SUGGESTIONS FOR READING

Cataldo, C. (1983). *Infant toddler caregiving*. Reading, MA: Addison-Wesley.

Gonzalez-Mena, J. (1986, November). Toddlers: What to expect. *Young Children, 41(1)*, 47–51.

Gonzalez-Mena, J. (1993). *Multicultural issues in child care*. Mountain View, CA: Mayfield Publishing Co.

Greenman, J. (1984, Summer). Worlds for infants and toddlers: New ideas. *Beginnings*, 21–25.

Greenman, J. (1988). *Caring spaces, learning places: Children's environments that work*. Redmond, WA: Exchange Press, Inc.

Leavitt, R. L., & Eheart, B. K. (1985). *Toddler day care: A guide to responsive caregiving*. Lexington, MA: Lexington Books.

Miller, K. (1988, August/September). A great place to be a toddler. *Pre-K Today*, 51–53.

NAEYC. (1989). *Developmentally appropriate practice in early childhood programs serving toddlers*. Pamphlet #508. Washington, DC: Author.

Stonehouse, A. (ed.). (1990). *Trusting toddlers: Planning for one- to three-year-olds in child care centers*. St. Paul, MN: Toys N Things Press.

Weiser, M. G. (1991). *Infant/toddler care and education* (2nd ed.). New York: Macmillan.

White, B. (1985). *The first three years of life* (rev. ed.). New York: Prentice Hall Press.

Wortham, S., & Marshal, R. (1992, Summer). Nurturing infant and toddler play outside. *Dimensions of Early Childhood*, 25–27.

Developmentally Appropriate Physical Environments:
For Preschoolers

*B*y around age three, the toddler evolves into the young child. If fortunate enough to have positive life experiences in infancy and toddlerhood, the next two or three years of childhood are approached with zest and enthusiasm. Preschoolers approach the world confidently and with a genuine desire to become part of it, to learn how it works, and how they can function within it. Now that they have a rudimentary concept of who they are, they are ready to learn how to interact with others; it is amazing to see how three-year-olds are eager to conform, after the resistance and "*me*-ness" of toddlerhood. Though still egocentric, preschoolers move toward experiences with peers. Learning to play with other children is not a skill that can be taught by words alone; it is through the day-to-day real experiences that young children discover firsthand how to modify their behavior to become more acceptable in childhood play groups. The issues of friendship preoccupy preschoolers; the greatest threat of all is to warn, "You're not my friend."

Preschoolers are talkers, excited to convey to others their perspective on experiences. Talk is powerful, and preschoolers slowly move toward self-control as they increase their understanding of reasons for behavior and alternate ways of behaving. And above all, play dominates the life and learning of preschoolers.

OBJECTIVES

After completing this chapter, students should be able to:

- describe the nature of preschoolers and what they do.
- identify needs of preschoolers to be supported by the physical environment.
- discuss components of an environment for initiative.
- discuss components of an environment for play, including outdoors.
- discuss components of an environment for self-control.
- identify characteristics of good schedules for preschoolers.
- discuss components of good transitions.
- identify components not found in developmentally appropriate physical environments for preschoolers.

What Are Preschoolers Like?

By the time they have lived three or four years, children have experienced such widely varying environments and experiences that the differences between children have become ever greater. It becomes difficult to generalize with much certainty about children; for every statement that is made, it is possible to find several examples of children who do not fit the characterization. Nevertheless, there are certain truths that seem evident for most three-, four-, and five-year-olds—at least much of the time.

What also becomes evident is the number of changes that occur during the much longer period of the early childhood years. Three-year-olds play, communicate, and understand the world very differently than do four-year-olds, who are themselves qualitatively different from most five-year-olds. This stage encompasses a longer period than the first two stages discussed, so it is understandable that development creates differences over a period of three years or so.

Having pointed out these cautions, let's consider some of what we can say about what preschoolers are like.

Preschoolers are physically active creatures. By the end of toddlerhood, they have achieved most of the large motor physical abilities they will have. But what they have not yet achieved is the coordination and agility that will be evident by the end of the preschool period. For example, two-year-olds can run and throw balls, but the quality of these movements is markedly different from the smooth skill of the five-year-old. The need for activity to increase coordination keeps preschoolers on the move, though lengthening attention spans allow them to stick with activities without the ceaseless movement of toddlers.

Preschoolers gradually become less dependent on attentions and constant assistance from adults, although they are still bound to them by affection, and thus a desire to please and be like them. It is this affectionate bond that motivates preschoolers to adopt adult standards of appropriate or inappropriate behaviors. But the process of developing a conscience and becoming more self-controlled is a long, slow process only begun during the preschool years. Children in these years struggle with egocentric perspectives against the dictates of limits for group behavior.

As they move from dependence on adults, other children become increasingly important to preschoolers. Children of this age are in search of friends, and are learning lessons about how one behaves as a friend.

The non-stop buzz of talk that is part of good preschool classrooms is a clear indication of the preoccupation of threes, fours, and fives with speech, in the form of monologues, dual monologues (when it looks like children are talking together, but in reality they are talking about what each wants to talk about), questions, comments, arguments, stories, and play discussion. Talk is the stuff of preschool learning about the world, self, and others.

What truly distinguishes preschoolers from younger children, though, is their ability to enter into increasingly complex forms of play. Preschoolers imagine and pretend, with wonderful fluency and fantasy, and gradually in cooperation

Developmentally Appropriate

This place looks lived-in
There were children here
I can tell by the markings
They are fresh and clear.
Walls covered in artifacts
And tables with books
The shelves somewhat misarranged
Like jackets on hooks.
The neatness is almost fragile
In its cluttered array
Anticipating the first student
Who'll return this day.
To this place of opportunities
Where a teacher seems to know
That there is much to be learned
As children continue to grow.
So she's harnessed their power
And captured the intensity of their play
By structuring intriguing possibilities
That they will meet along the way.
This place does look lived-in
There were excited children here
I can tell by the learned markings
They are fresh, intense, and clear.
The markings of hard work and delighted struggle,
The powerful learning comes through.
This is a place for children
Where no child needs to be dragged to.

Figure 5-1 A developmentally appropriate classroom for preschoolers is designed to meet their needs and interests. *Permission for use granted by author, Sigmund A. Boloz.*

with other children. Their play is focused, serious, and involves the whole child, nurturing physical, cognitive, social, emotional, and language development.

> Play enables children to create understandings of their world from their own experiences and exerts a strong influence on all aspects of their growth and development. Children become empowered in play to do things for themselves, to feel in control, to test and practice their skills, and to affirm confidence in themselves. Play is important for children's developing sense of competence (Isenberg and Jalongo, 1993, p. 32).

Preschool children play. They play alone, with others, inside, outside, always. (See Figure 5-1.)

What are preschoolers like? They are beautifully confident creatures who have tested themselves out in toddlerhood, and are now filled with enthusiasm to explore the world around them and the people in it. Hungry to learn how to live in this world, their awareness is moving from a strictly egocentric (that is, centered only on self) perspective to an outward perspective. They are like adventuring explorers, who have an insatiable need to know and do more in the world around them.

What Do Preschoolers Do?

If you have recently been in a room full of three- or four-year-old children, images probably crowd your mind when you read this question: What *don't* they do?

They hold up paintings for adults to view, after working painstakingly on them for fifteen minutes, busily talking with a friend about what they are creating on paper, and arguing about their ideas. They yell, they giggle, and they talk back to their friends and to adults. They build, they knock down, they argue over whose building was the tallest. They tease, they tattle, they exclude others from playing in housekeeping. They beg to help, they find reasons why they shouldn't have to clean up, they brag about their achievements. They defy adult restrictions, they smilingly agree to share, they demand turns. They wobble across the room in high heels, they work thirty-five piece puzzles, they tell long stories. They insist on an extra kiss good-bye, they leave their dad without a backward glance, they tell you everything their family did on the weekend. They lead a game of Simon Says, they insist it's their turn in Candyland, they invent a word to describe the bubbles floating in the wind: a "Bubblefly." They hit back at another child, they look guilty when they get caught, they go off to a corner to play for a while. They beg you to read the story again, they print their name carefully on their art paper, they demand that you watch them print. They find their own place at the table, they try determinedly to use the scissors again, they show you proudly they can button all the little buttons. They shriek with laughter at a good book, they ask question after question, they insist on being the baby when they play house. They hang upside down, they run down the hall, they tell you that you can (or can't) come to their birthday party.

You can add to this list. What they do and can do goes on and on. They are competent and confident about what their legs, fingers, and minds can do. Those preschoolers who are limited physically or mentally by special needs find their own ways of impacting the world with their initiative. They burst with ideas and energy and enthusiasm. Their excitement overflows on a daily basis, and often they get out of bounds and test the limits. But the difference is they now know there are limits, understand why there are limits, and sometimes even conform to the limits.

What Do Preschoolers Need?

Considering what preschoolers do is the first step in thinking about what preschoolers need for their development to be nurtured. They need an environment that can support all that active energy, and can challenge with experiences that introduce ever more of the world. A reminder of what some theorists have told us about these childhood years before formal school is also helpful. The psychosocial issue defined by Erikson for the preschool years is forming a *sense of initiative*, opposed to a sense of guilt. Initiative refers to a sense of self as a doer; competent, full of ideas, energy, and enthusiasm to explore the larger world. With the energy and ability of these years, children learn to initiate their own activities, enjoy their accomplishments, and become purposeful. If they are not allowed to follow their own initiative, they feel guilty for their attempts to become independent and competent. The curious preschooler needs a sense that he or she *can* do, *can* make, has good ideas.

Piaget helps us understand something of the young child's thinking and learning processes in his descriptions of *preoperational thought*. As we shall discuss more fully in Chapter 13, this cognitive perspective is mental activity that is not yet logical, but is more intuitive, based on limited perceptions; concrete, egocentric in being able to understand only one's own perspective, and limited in ability to focus and generalize logically. The implications are that learning experiences need to match these characteristics. Piaget defined play as the appropriate medium for learning by preoperational children.

Developmental tasks for this period include becoming socialized to norms of behavior; forming a sense of identity within the social context; beginning to form a conscience and develop self-control; and coming to understand one's position in the world. Continuing competency with language is critical to all these tasks. Adults planning developmentally appropriate environments for young children must focus on providing environments that encourage this learning, appropriate to the development of all preschoolers.

Environments encourage different kinds of experiences, depending on the physical arrangements of space and materials, of time, and of varying degrees of access to other people. Specific program goals may be affected by the behind-the-scenes decisions adults make that influence behavior. For example, in a classroom where cooperation and problem-solving skills are a major goal, a teacher might decide to put out limited numbers of materials deliberately, to stimulate dialogue and interaction about turn-taking and discussion among children (Ostrosky and Kaiser, 1991). In a program that emphasizes nurturing emerging literacy skills, a teacher might place many picture and word labels for common items at children's eye level. In programs that include many children with special needs, individualized plans and therapists help children develop optimally. Educational goals of any program will be reflected in the physical environment.

In addition, as teachers develop individual goals for individual children in the classroom, they use their environmental decisions to work toward these goals. A teacher who wants to promote lunch-table conversation in a quiet child might place the quiet child beside a more talkative one at the table. Another teacher, realizing that a particular child has a special need for help with screening out distractions, might create several small, protected work spaces, stocked with materials of particular interest to the child, and encourage him to choose a friend to explore the area.

Thus, the physical environment may encourage goals for both the developmental stage and for individuals, as well as specific program goals. In addition to creating an environment to promote specific goals, physical environments may also work to solve or prevent typical problem behaviors associated with individual or age-span development. There is much for adults to consider as they plan physical environments for preschoolers.

Figure 5-3 Sand is an example of a soft material, as well as an open material. *Courtesy NationsBank Child Care Center.*

Prescott's Dimensions of an Environment

1. Softness/Hardness
2. Open/Closed
3. Simple/Complex
4. Intrusion/Seclusion
5. High Mobility/Low Mobility
6. Risk/Safety
7. Large Group/Individual

Figure 5-2 Dimensions of an Environment. *Elizabeth Prescott, 1984.*

Dimensions of Environments

In a classic discussion on physical environments, Elizabeth Prescott described seven components—dimensions, to use her word—to consider in physical environments (Prescott, 1984). (See Figure 5-2.) As adults plan environments, they should consider where on the continuum their particular environment falls, and whether there are modifications that could benefit children. Prescott advocates a balance of the dimensions for an optimum environment for the kinds of play that enhance development.

Softness/Hardness

Softness in an environment is provided for by the presence of objects (finger paints, play dough/clay, couches, pillows, rugs, grass, water, sand, dirt, animals that can be held, swings, laps) that are soft, malleable, and responsive to touch, providing a variety of tactile sensory stimulation. Hardness (tiled floors, wooden furniture, asphalt playgrounds) gives a more unyielding environmental message, one that encourages children to shape themselves to the environment, inevitably tiring and stress-inducing for both children and adults. A balance means the environment is both responsive and resistant. (See Figure 5-3.)

Open/Closed

Figure 5-4 This writing center offers super complexity, with a variety of stencils, pencils, scissors and markers. *Courtesy CPCC Child Care Training Center.*

Openness in an environment is perceived by the presence of open equipment and materials; those that can be used in a variety of ways, with no one correct way of using them, and no arbitrary stopping point. Sand, blocks, collage, and other art materials are all open. Activity formats may also be open, based primarily on children choosing from a selection of activities planned and prepared by the teacher. The issue of openness is related to choices.

Closed materials can only be played with in one way; puzzles and various Montessori materials are closed. Program styles that utilize mostly teacher-directed group and individual activities are called closed, as are experiences that have a clear ending. While there are advantages to both open and closed materials and experiences, Prescott (1984) believes that it is especially important to have open materials and experiences for preschool children to experience success and a sense of initiative.

Simple/Complex

As children interact with materials, it becomes obvious that some materials have greater holding power than others. The simplest play unit has only one aspect, and one obvious use; there is nothing to improvise in its use. An example would be a swing or tricycle. More complex units combine two different kinds of materials; supercomplex units combine three different kinds of materials. Examples of complexity include adding shovels to make a sandpile complex, or rolling pins to lumps of play dough; supercomplex would add water or molds to the sandpile, or decorative elements to the play dough and rollers. A supercomplex dramatic play area adds cookbooks, pads and paper for grocery lists, and a shopping cart to the household utensils. Simplest arrangements usually do not hold attention as long as when complexity is added, thereby increasing the number of things that can be done in an area or activity. (See Figure 5-4.)

Intrusion/ Seclusion

An environment introduces the dimensions of intrusion and seclusion as it defines boundaries and provides opportunities for privacy and control over personal territory. Every classroom should have areas that must be shared by the group of children. It is also important that there are areas where children may withdraw to be alone, or apart from the total group, and to safeguard their personal property and interests.

Desirable intrusion also comes when the classroom makes connections with the larger world about, such as by windows that connect them to the world, and visitors that come to the classroom (Gonzalez-Mena, 1993).

High Mobility/ Low Mobility

This dimension of the environment concerns the freedom children have to move around. With high mobility, there is space and equipment to encourage gross motor, active movement, such as running, climbing, and tricycle riding. With low mobility, children are required to sit still for activities such as storytime, working puzzles, and other fine motor experiences. A balanced environment provides space and materials for both.

Risk/Safety

Prescott (1984) refers to the needs for both risk and safety within the environment. While children need to be protected from obvious dangers and taught safe practices, such as having fire drills and using utensils carefully, the environment must not overlook important opportunities for risk taking, such as opportunities to experiment with bodies in space: swinging, climbing, jumping off. She notes that there is a difference between providing for safety by teaching children how to do interesting and challenging things with care, rather than forbidding any kind of risk or innovation because it is unsafe.

Large Group/ Individual

Again there is a need for a balance in the social structure within the classroom, and not an overbalance or omission of either dimension. A large group experience is listening to a story at group time; an individual experience is being read to one to one. Both kinds of experiences are necessary and valuable.

The key to using these dimensions in considering the physical environment is not an either/or approach. Most appropriate environments include things from both ends of the spectrum. The important thing is to evaluate the environment for appropriate balances of experiences, matching developmental level and needs of individuals and programs. Attention to the dimensions is useful for problem solving.

Figure 5-5 Space speaks. What messages do children get when they see this is a classroom? *Courtesy NationsBank Child Care Center.*

Space speaks (See Figure 5-5): As children and adults enter a classroom, the arrangements of furniture and materials convey messages about expected activities and ways of behaving. For example, if most of the classroom space is filled with tables and chairs, it is evident that the teacher expects that the children will spend most of their time seated doing quiet sitting activities, implying a good deal of teacher direction. If, on the other hand, there are a number of different learning centers arranged throughout the room, it seems more likely that the children will be more actively involved with materials that they will choose. (See Figure 5-6.) The way that physical space is arranged implies an underlying philosophy that will have a definite impact on what children can and will do in learning activities.

Environment for Initiative

Figure 5-6 Children see clear choices in the learning environment arranged with a variety of learning centers. *Courtesy CPCC Child Care Training Center.*

With the development of a sense of initiative being an important task of the preschool years, children's active participation as decision makers is enhanced by an environment that encourages making choices and plans. Much of their time will be spent in active play of their choosing, rather than in teacher-directed lessons.

Choosing is helped by making clear what the choices are. Each activity needs to be set up in its own clearly defined zone, separated from other activities by space, furniture, and other distinct dividers. What this means is that the room is divided into many small play areas, appearing as a number of obvious choices, not one large area. Arrangement of shelves, cubbies, tables, carpet pieces, masking tape markers, and other creative kinds of dividers (e.g., hanging shoebags; lattice or pegboards with feet; rows of low hanging plants; walls of tree stumps; crates, cartons, or ice cream containers wired together; hanging curtains, sheets, or bamboo blinds) act to create visual boundaries, while still allowing for adult supervision. (See Greenman, 1988, and Miller, 1987, for more suggestions on dividers.)

Teachers decide what interest centers are appropriate to their particular group. Typical centers may include: a creative art area; a block area; a dramatic play area; a book area; a music area; a manipulative/math area; a science area; a gross motor area; a writing area; a woodworking area; a water/sand area. An extensive discussion of the rationale for arranging the environment in learning centers is included in Chapter 13. Centers are labeled so children can "read" what the choices are. Labels are at child eye level, and include both a picture representation and print.

Figure 5-7 Separate tables and shelves used as dividers indicate interest centers, with materials displayed openly on shelves. *Courtesy NationsBank Child Care Center.*

To further encourage child choice, teachers make sure that materials for use in each area are stored near the location where they will be used, displayed on low, open shelves where children can reach what they need. When classrooms include children with limited mobility, duplicate materials may be stored in several areas of the classroom. Containers are open or clear, for visibility, or distinctly marked with labels children can interpret, or feel, in the case of children with visual limitation. The arrangement of the materials on shelves serves to highlight the separate choices by surrounding each material with space. (See Figure 5-7.) Teachers create picture or shape markers on shelves, to make it obvious where materials will be returned to. As materials are readily available in predict-

Figure 5-8 These necklace hooks are methods to help children make conscious choices. *Courtesy Avondale Children's Center.*

Figure 5–9 This pictograph illustrates steps for children to follow in clean-up after painting.

able places, children learn to take responsibility for their environment, and develop a sense of initiative as learners.

> We also found that organized storage seems to produce more complex and longer lasting play. It seems that storage can help children to visualize relations and to plan future actions. Thus organized storage would appear to support initiative and imagination (Prescott, 1984, p. 48).

The environment subtly supports children's idea development. Centers that might logically be combined in children's play are positioned near one another; for example, the book center and the writing center are side by side. Having an area where children may choose to display personal work conveys the value for their ideas. This area may be: a clothesline to pin art near their name tag; a designated shelf space for completed items, such as a puzzle or manipulative creation, to show parents; an area for works in progress and projects to be protected over the time period of creation; a poster for each child's use. Most of the classroom decor is of children's creation and design. Children with initiative will want to see that they can impact their environment, that it is not purely the creation of adults. Many teachers feel that a key question in the preschool classroom is, Do the children feel a sense of ownership of the environment? (Humphrey, 1989).

Open-ended materials support and encourage creativity, decision making, and original thinking in all interest areas. Initiative and self-esteem as a learner are encouraged when many of the materials offered have no right or wrong uses, and are process rather than product oriented. Variation in individual abilities is provided for by open-ended materials; children may use such materials as they are able. We'll talk more about specific open-ended materials later.

Initiative is encouraged when children are able to decide which activity to participate in and when to terminate it. In order to encourage preschoolers' thoughtful choices about self-selected activities, some teachers find it helpful to institute systems for "signing up" for activities. Such systems may include planning boards with hooks or pockets for adding a child's name tag, or a number of necklaces hanging by an interest center to indicate whether there is space available to play there; putting on and removing the name tag or necklace helps children make conscious decisions, as well as indirectly controlling the numbers of children that can productively play in an area. (See Figure 5-8.)

An environment designed to maximize independence encourages feelings of initiative. Teachers use clues of placement and pictograph sequences to help guide preschoolers through the steps of using an area without direct teacher instruction. For example, in the art area, easily managed cover-ups hang nearby. A stack of fresh easel paper is right beside the easel. There are easily managed clips to fasten the paper to the easel, and a drying line with clothespins right behind it. The pictograph for the children in charge of cleaning the area after its use shows washing and drying brushes, and placing them on the shelf, dumping and washing the paint containers, and washing the table. (See Figure 5-9.) An important sense of accomplishment results when children can move independently through their chosen activities.

Initiative is encouraged when children are enabled to play meaningful and responsible roles in their classrooms. Preschool children thrive on doing impor-

Figure 5-10 This helper chart helps children see their responsibilities in the classroom. *Courtesy Avondale Children's Center.*

tant, real work. Teachers can capitalize on this desire by offering regular opportunities to contribute to classroom routines and maintenance. A helper chart allows children to rotate responsibilities. (See Figure 5-10.)

Be sure to provide preschoolers with an environment that develops initiative by:

- encouraging child choice of play opportunities in clearly defined and labeled activity centers
- displaying materials that children may get for themselves
- allowing children opportunities to display their work in the classroom
- offering open-ended materials that encourage creativity and use at varying levels of individual ability
- establishing systems that help children make conscious choices for play
- providing opportunities for independence and responsible participation in the classroom

Environment for Learning Through Play

A teacher's belief in and support for learning through play is conveyed by the careful preparation of the physical environment. In a classroom where teachers believe that children learn best through active involvement with materials, other children, and adults, the physical design of the classroom will offer well-designed places to play and materials to play with. The placement of centers and design of the classroom contributes to meaningful play experiences for children.

Most teachers do not have the luxury of designing a preschool classroom; some architect or builder has already done so. (For those fortunate enough to be involved in preliminary designs, the issues and questions raised in Greenman, 1988, are excellent.) When teachers get assigned to a particular classroom, however, they can begin the process of visualizing the learning environment, forgetting what they know about how the room has been used, and starting freshly. A plan for a physical environment, as Greenman says, grows out of "fixed space, inhabitants, program

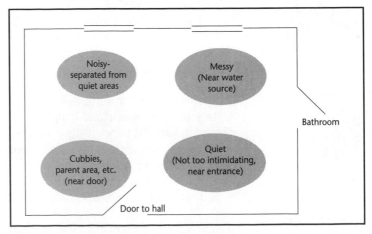

Figure 5-11 Preliminary placement sketch.

goals and philosophy, and resources." (Greenman, 1988, p. 135) It is no doubt relatively easy to set up the traditional classroom that emphasizes teacher instruction and individual study; but in the developmentally appropriate preschool classroom emphasizing "active, individualized learning, autonomy, and social interchange," (Greenman, 1988, p. 135) teachers are challenged to create a dynamic, inviting atmosphere. When programs last for a full day, the quality of living experiences that include eating, sleeping, privacy, adult ease and comfort must be examined.

In deciding how to set up the room, Greenman suggests beginning with the fixed space: doors, windows, sinks, bathrooms, electrical outlets. Think about the flow patterns of air and light, of people and supplies. List every activity that will take place in the room, big and small, from play to snack time, from dressing for outdoor play to teacher-parent conversations. Think about special physical accommodations needed by children with special needs. Decide on the activity centers that will be part of the classroom learning, and on the areas that will be used for more than one purpose—eating and table toys, for example.

Placement of centers will determine how well children can become involved in meaningful play. Teachers will want to think about separating messy and neat activities, noisy and quiet ones, activities that need to spread out, and those that can be contained, activities that need a table, and those that take place on the floor or in other nooks. See Figure 5-11 for a preliminary placement sketch.

As the designing continues, teachers need to consider pathways about the room, recognizing that straight, unbroken pathways encourage running, as do large, empty spaces that spend most of the day waiting for something, like group time, to happen. Pathways recognize the need to prevent intrusion on play; some activity centers, such as books and blocks, need to be protected from through traffic. The dividers for defining areas discussed earlier in the chapter will also be important as means of screening out distraction for children trying to concentrate on their own play. See Figure 5-12 for a sample diagram of a pre-

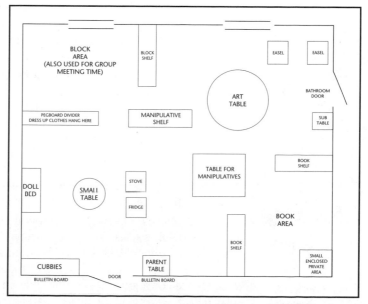

Figure 5-12 Sketch of preschool classroom arrangement.

Figure 5-13 This table already set is inviting to children as they arrive to play. *Courtesy Methodist Home Child Development Center.*

Figure 5-14 These block builders have clearly defined boundaries for their building. *Courtesy CPCC Child Care Training Center.*

school classroom. Notice the grouping of noisy areas for play (dramatic play, blocks, gross motor center). Notice also that the areas most likely to need frequent access to water are strategically placed. There is no dead space. Children's entrance into the classroom is inviting without being overwhelming with too many choices and too much activity.

As preschool children with special needs are included in the classroom setting, teachers will consciously modify arrangements so that children of all abilities are able to play. Wide pathways and entrances to interest centers, architectural modifications, and materials organized for accessibility and avoiding clutter will improve the classroom for all children.

While it is important for teachers to analyze their plans for areas carefully balanced to provide learning opportunities for all domains (gross motor, fine motor, self-help, language, cognitive, emotional, and social experiences) and for a variety of curriculum subject areas (art, reading, construction, manipulation, science, math, music, dramatic play, movement), it is equally important for them not to be drawn into thinking that learning is as clearly divided as the interest center areas would suggest. Boundaries are defined for children to think of their play opportunities, and to have meaningful play protected and sustained. Boundaries are not meant to suggest that a particular kind of learning only goes on in that one center, or that learning is one-dimensional; for example, dramatic play goes on all over the room, and the art area involves creative expression, scientific discovery, manipulative skills, cognitive concepts and planning, and language subject areas. Nor are boundaries meant to be inflexible ("The blocks need to stay in the block area," when a child takes one to housekeeping to use as a camera). One of the recommendations of emerging literacy programs (those that believe that children's interest in reading and writing develops as they are encouraged to practice these skills and are provided the materials for their play) is that books and writing materials be incorporated into every activity center, encouraging looking at books about science and writing signs on block constructions; such practices may help teachers move to less compartmentalization philosophically, while still keeping a room organized to encourage productive play.

The room arrangement is not meant to be permanent; as children's interests and play behavior expand, so the need for new or expanded centers may emerge.

Arrangement into separate interest centers is not the only consideration for physical environments to encourage play. The thoughtful selection and display of materials invites children's use. The scales and a box of rocks on a science table suggest an activity; the notepad and pencil arranged beside the telephone in the house corner suggest a beginning plot line. Today, the play dough table, with a dish of bright beads, invites sculpting, when last week the same table had a set of tiny dishes to suggest producing a "tea party" with the play dough. Careful arrangement of materials helps children begin their play without need for teachers telling the children what "we are going to do today." (See Figure 5-13.)

Play is often interactive. The physical environment supports social encounters by providing spaces designed for small groups, varying from two to five or six children. For children who are beginning social interaction, activity areas for just two support early social skills, with parallel kinds of play and chances for face-to-face conversation. A small table and two chairs may be the setting for play dough, writing, manipulatives, and for a good talk with a friend. Other centers may accommodate larger numbers of children, each with their own place.

Figure 5-15 The number of notepads at the writing table limit participation to two at a time. *Courtesy Methodist Home Child Development Center.*

Groups of four or five work well for preschoolers. Teachers are careful to provide clues about how many children may use the area at one time; four chairs surround the art table, and three smocks hang by the water table. Block builders find three large masking tape squares on the carpet to indicate building space for three (see Figure 5-14) and two pads at the writing table limit participation to two children (see Figure 5-15). The systems that support conscious choice also limit the numbers in areas to facilitate social play and interaction.

But all play is not social. There are times when children need and want to play alone, to read a book, or to concentrate on some challenging task. A room should have some small play spaces and an atmosphere that allows children to withdraw or define a space of separateness for play. If a child chooses to build alone, for example, he should be able to put a tape strip across the carpet to indicate his personal area for building. The individual carpets used in Montessori classrooms allow for such individual involvement. (See Figure 5-16.)

Involvement in play takes time. Teachers support the environment for play by providing blocks of time long enough for play to become established and embellished, without unnecessary intrusion. We'll talk more about this later in the chapter.

Adults are also an important part of the environment for play. Play that is not facilitated often goes undeveloped. The adult's role as facilitator will be discussed in Chapter 13.

Outdoor Play

Figure 5-16 A mat defines a play space for someone who chooses to play alone. Note also the carefully labelled storage bins. *Courtesy Avondale Children's Center.*

Outdoor experiences are considered a vital component of the environment for play. Developmentally appropriate preschool programs value the play and learning experiences for children both indoors and out, and consider both equally vital. Outdoor play is not thought of as just a time for children (and adults) to blow off steam, a sort of recess before going back indoors to get down to the serious business of learning. Rather, it is recognized that qualitatively different kinds of play experiences can be had outdoors, different in scale and scope and decibels.

Children need opportunities for physical challenge and risk on playgrounds. They need places for swinging, for sliding and rolling, for climbing and jumping, for running, throwing and kicking, for riding and transporting. For all these active pursuits, they need space and suitable equipment, and adults who supervise with encouragement and without overcautioning and restriction.

In addition to the physical challenges, outdoor environments for play must also support more contemplative pursuits: making discoveries in the environment, with digging, with planting, exploring with water and sand, finding a quiet spot to sit, maybe even to read a book. Creative opportunities exist, with outdoor art materials and construction materials, props for dramatic play—the curriculum goes outdoors. Teacher planning for materials and activity areas for outdoor play is essential.

Part of the planning is provision for safety, so that children may be permitted to play freely. Poor playground design and equipment selection, and lack of maintenance contribute to most playground accidents. Adequate pathways and space around equipment are essential to avoid crowding. Appropriate installation of fixed equipment, and continual monitoring of equipment is an impor-

---

Safety Outdoors

Outdoor safety includes:

- area enclosed by fence and locked gate
- assurance that all plantings are nonpoisonous
- a well drained play area
- protection from sun for hot days
- soft ground cover under climbing and sliding equipment, at least one-foot deep
- play equipment that is inspected daily for missing or broken parts, splinters, sharp edges, rust, flaking paint, frayed ropes
- play area that is inspected daily for trash, sharp debris, animal waste
- large pieces of equipment anchored firmly in the ground and sturdily constructed
- railings protect from falls on high equipment (slides and climbers)
- equipment spaced for safe movement between pieces and adequate supervision
- swings that are separate from riding or running areas
- groundskeeping and maintenance chemicals and tools that are locked away from play area
- equipment that is appropriate and stimulating for children's developmental abilities (infant, toddler, preschool, schoolage)

Figure 5-17 A checklist for safety monitoring of the outdoor environment. *Adapted from* Health, Safety, and Nutrition for the Young Child, *Third Edition, Marotz, Cross, and Rush, Delmar, 1993.*

tant adult responsibility (see Figure 5-17), as is teaching children responsibility for safety (see Figure 5-18).

Environments for play are provided when adults:

- arrange the classroom to suggest active play is the main vehicle for learning
- design the classroom in interest centers arranged to protect play and screen out distractions
- arrange materials to invite active participation
- plan area size to facilitate small group interactive play, as well as spaces for secluded play
- provide long time blocks for play
- function as facilitators of play
- plan outdoor play areas and materials as carefully as indoor play areas

Environment for Self-Control

Preschoolers who are learning to control their own behavior are helped when the environment provides a sense of stability, order, and predictability.

The arrangement of interest centers to convey clear guidelines about the activity expected in each area, places to use materials, and numbers of children in each area provides indirect guidance to make appropriate behavior become habitual. As children know what is defined as appropriate behavior, they are more able to behave in acceptable ways without direct instruction or control from adults.

Figure 5-18 Areas for children to swing are clearly separated from riding and running areas. *Courtesy Methodist Home Child Development Center.*

Other teacher decisions that indirectly influence behavior include: the kind of materials available for use, including materials that are neither too simple nor too difficult; the quantities of materials available for use; the predictability and balance of the time schedule; the presence and availability of adults. Such behind-the-scenes management of factors that can affect children's behavior prevents the kind of problems that often lead to classroom conflict: overcrowding; disputes over rights to use materials; distraction; boredom; over-stimulation and too much noise; too little supervision; and fatigue. Attention to the physical environment contributes to a positive social atmosphere.

Posters or signs that pictorially remind children of classroom behavior expectations are useful reminders for self-control. The chart on the wall behind the teacher at grouptime reminds: "We listen; we keep our hands to ourselves; we sit on our bottoms." Other clues for self-control may be added to the classroom. A child's name on the carpet helps him find his place to sit for story time, in a place the teacher knows he is least distracted, away from a talkative friend and close to the teacher. Outlines of two feet on the floor remind a child where to stand while waiting for his turn to brush teeth, to prevent crowding and waterplay in the bathroom. Preschoolers want to behave well, and clues are helpful reminders.

Within a group situation, the demanding rules of social interaction may be quite exhausting for young children. Adults need to provide private spaces for children to retreat to when they feel a little tired, unhappy, or out of control. A small, quiet, soft area should be provided, and its purpose clearly explained to children, so they learn that withdrawal is approved of, and may even be a necessary act to incorporate as children learn to exercise control over their feelings. Tentlike spaces may be created with arrangements of sheets or blankets, crates and barrels, spaces behind or under furniture. Private spaces do not take much room, and are important components of an environment for self-control. (See Figure 5-19.)

Preschoolers are helped in moving toward respecting rules of social interaction as they perceive that they personally are treated with respect. The physical environment conveys respect for each individual child by recognizing their needs for a sense of belonging. Each child needs a personal space in the classroom, a place to keep personal items of value to the child, such as a toy from home, a note a child wrote for Mom, a rock another found on the playground and wants to take home. This space, whether provided by a cubby or a small basket, needs to be labeled and accessible for the child, and declared off-limits for everyone else. Respect for individuals is also conveyed by the presence in the classroom of materials children personally identify with. Pictures, books, dolls, housekeeping props and clothing need to represent the ethnic and cultural diversity of the families of the classroom, including the various family structures children live in and the neighborhoods and work experiences they recognize. In Chapter 9 you will find a more detailed discussion of materials to include in the classroom that encourage self-acceptance and development of antibiased attitudes toward differences.

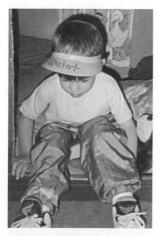

Figure 5-19 A quiet space is an important area to include in preschool classrooms. *Courtesy Avondale Children's Center.*

An environment for self-control may also offer materials and activities that can be used as outlets to redirect children for the physical release of emotion. Classrooms that have punching bags, pounding boards, tearing corners, closets designated for yelling, or outdoor space for stomping give tangible evidence that it is acceptable to do something physically to express strong feelings energetically. When a child comes to the teacher to say "I need to tear some papers to stuff in the pillow case," it means this child has learned to control impulses to hurt when angry, and to divert that strong energy into socially acceptable outlets.

Grace Mitchell talks about having "talk-it-over" chairs in classrooms: chairs drawn to the side, arranged so knees will touch (and therefore eyes will look into eyes) as children are encouraged to actively discuss problems to attempt to find mutual solutions (Mitchell, 1982). After teaching, modeling, and reminders from adults, children learn to move to their own negotiation, when the chairs and attitude are part of the physical environment for self-control.

Environments for self-control are available when adults:

- plan physical environments that prevent problems caused by boredom, frustration, over-crowding, and fatigue

- plan physical environments that clearly convey positive expectations for appropriate behavior

- use posters and other visual clues to remind children of classroom behavior

- provide private spaces for withdrawal

- use classroom materials that demonstrate respect for individual rights and differences

- offer materials for vigorous use as outlets for expressing emotion

- model opportunities for children to meet for problem solving

Schedules for Preschoolers

In an environment where initiative and self-control are important goals, and where active play is the dominant activity, a good schedule functions to give children large blocks of uninterrupted time, and to give them the security of knowing what comes next. It is important that schedules not work against these goals. When schedules function not as predictable sequences, but as rigid timetables, they intrude and disrupt, ignoring children's needs.

Elements of a Good Schedule

How is a schedule for preschoolers judged for developmental appropriateness? Every program will have to adapt its own schedule based on program goals, required sharing of space and facilities, length of the program day, and staffing patterns. Whatever the variations, certain features will be found in schedules that meet children's needs.

A good schedule is predictable. No matter what event comes first, second, and third, these events always follow each other. Children function with confidence when they recognize a pattern each day. They do not have to guess what their next action will be. There is an understood order and rhythm to the day, which is comforting to children and helpful to adults.

A good schedule is flexible. At first glance, this principle might seem to argue directly with the preceding one. But the two components can be held simultaneously by using an understanding of *time-blocks* (Hildebrand, 1989).

Activities	Flexibility
Arrival and Selection of Child-chosen Activities Indoors	*Shortened when:* • Children not involved in play • Field trips/visitors planned for later *Lengthened when:* • Children are deeply involved in play • Bad weather
Teacher-Guided Activities Indoors such as clean-up, snacks, group time	*Shortened when:* • Children are unusually active • More time needed for play in or out *Lengthened when:* • Special visitors/activities • Issues to be discussed
Child-Selected Choices Outdoors	*Shortened when:* • Weather is inclement (gross motor activity indoors is substituted) • Other time blocks have been lengthened *Lengthened when:* • Time is needed to go to particular outdoor environment • Projects on playground bring extra interest

Figure 5-20 A sample preschool schedule showing flexible time blocks.

(See Figure 5-20.) Rather than a strict by-the-clock system for deciding when an activity is over, teachers gauge children's involvement or restlessness to decide whether to shorten or lengthen a time-block. Thinking about blocks of time, rather than specific points on the clock, allows teachers to give children the time needed to get deeply involved in their play, without the interruptions necessary to keep on a strict timetable.

On Monday, Felicia's preschool class seemed unusually active. A number of the children looked tired, and wandered from activity to activity during free choice period. She decided to give the signal for picking up toys after about 45 minutes, and they then moved to the carpeted group area. She played some quiet music for them to move like butterflies for a while, and then shared two quiet stories. After snack time they moved outdoors. She added art materials and water play to the playground activities. The beautiful spring weather allowed them to enjoy over an hour of outdoor play. The next day, there was such complex block building and dramatic play interaction, she extended free play to about 75 minutes, and group time and outdoor play were a little shorter.

Flexible time-blocks also permit special events or adaptation for weather, without disturbing children's sense of the predictable sequence.

Figure 5-21 This group time might not have deteriorated into widespread children's disinterest if it had been scheduled earlier in the morning, when children were not hungry and tired. *NationsBank Child Care Center.*

Wednesday's group time included a visit from B.J.'s dad, who plays guitar in a band, and enjoys singing with the children. The event extended group time to almost 40 minutes; interest was high. On Thursday Felicia planned a spring walk through the neighborhood to talk to a couple of gardeners. She knew that the walk would take quite a bit of time, so after a song with the group, she used a few minutes to explain what they would do on their walk and remind the children of safety rules. After 5 minutes they were ready to leave group.

A good schedule balances child-initiated time-blocks with those that are teacher-initiated. For children to become truly involved in their play, they need unbroken periods when they may choose and carry out their plans. Teachers become involved in directing children's activities during the briefer periods when they need children to follow directions, such as clean-up time, or to become involved in a teacher-initiated group activity, such as meal time or storytime. Much of the day in a developmentally appropriate program for preschoolers is spent in blocks of child-initiated free choice activity, indoors and outdoors.

A good schedule balances active and passive, and indoor and outdoor, learning experiences. There is recognition that children need a variety of learning experiences, and that alternating active and passive experiences in the schedule prevents excessive fatigue, boredom, and loss of control. Activities that require concentration, such as large group time, should be scheduled early in the day before children become too fatigued. (See Figure 5-21.) Shorter, quietening group stories or music may be scheduled to help children relax before lunch, after a period of active outdoor play.

A good schedule provides for a reasonable pace for children's participation. Nothing diminishes self-confidence more than to be rushed through the day. The general feeling of being hurried destroys a positive learning environment; but, it is also disastrous to fill the day with times of "hurrying up to wait," which leads to boredom and social friction. A helpful schedule leaves enough time for children to complete tasks in a satisfying way, and allows for individual differences in ways that avoid empty waiting times. For example, children who have already finished with bathroom routines may gather for fingerplays on the carpet with one of the teachers. The younger the children, the more time needed for self-help transitions; more time is also needed for children with special needs.

A good schedule recognizes developmental differences in attention span. While most two-year-olds can benefit from only very brief large group experiences and need considerable choice and variety during free play periods to keep them occupied, preschoolers generally have a longer attention span. Many three-year-olds are able to sustain interest in self-initiated activities for 45 minutes or longer, and fours and fives may remain productively involved for longer than that. Group times for three-year-olds, or at the beginning of the year, might last 10–15 minutes, extending to 20 minutes or so for older or more experienced preschoolers.

Transitions

The times in the schedule that require the most thoughtful adult planning are the transitions, the times when children are asked to move from one activity to the next. If chaos is to be prevented, children need adult attention and guidance during these times. Unfortunately, much of the adult attention in too many transitions focuses on unpleasant interaction meant to help children keep under control. It is important to recognize that many of the problems that develop are related to developmentally inappropriate practices, such as having children wait for everyone to line up quietly before they walk out to the playground, or control their behavior with nothing to occupy their attention.

Developmentally appropriate transitions for preschoolers incorporate the following principles:

1. *Advance notice* is given that change will be forthcoming. Interrupting children abruptly and arbitrarily from their play suggests the unimportance of that play, and encourages resistance.

2. *Familiar cues*, such as clean-up songs, notes played on a piano, or a particular tape of music, help emphasize the repetition of a familiar pattern, encouraging children to notice and behave according to habitual experience. This also ensures getting children's attention. Clues may be environmental, such as the darkening of the room before nap time. Following consistent routines is beneficial to help children know what to expect from day to day.

3. *Understanding of what to do next* is improved when teachers are clear and specific in their directions. "Time to put toys back on their shelves," helps children more than "Time to clean up" (What? hands, tables, toys—what?). Adults establish eye contact or touch children to be sure they have their attention. Teachers use names to be sure children realize the instructions are meant for them personally. Teachers also limit the number of instructions given at one time in order to avoid confusion. After most of the toys are picked up, teachers may come back to remind children to use the bathroom before snack.

4. *Using an adult to begin the next activity* avoids empty waiting time. While one teacher is encouraging those still picking up toys and keeping an eye on the bathroom, another is having a conversation or leading a finger play with those already seated for snack. While one adult accompanies out to the playground the children who already have their coats on, the other assists those who need more help and time with zippers. When the next activity doesn't have to wait until everyone is ready, it provides incentive to children to move on, and does not penalize children who are either quicker or slower paced in their abilities. Teachers develop a repertoire of transition songs or games children can enjoy as they prepare to change activities.

5. *Chaos is minimized* when everyone doesn't move at once, and when they move purposefully because there is no doubt where they are going. For example, when group time is over, the teacher sings a song that dismisses three children at a time, to go to their cots and the books waiting for them there.

Figure 5-22 Children can help each other during transition times. *Courtesy Avondale Children's Center.*

6. *Giving children classroom responsibilities or opportunities to assist peers* provides purposeful experiences during transition times, as well as freeing teachers to give words of encouragement or instruction to children who need more assistance during transition.

Sarah has put her shoes on after nap and is ready to go outdoors to play. As she waits she helps Maria and Keisha with theirs. (See Figure 5-22.)

Developmentally appropriate preschool schedules incorporate:

- predictability
- flexible time blocks
- balance of child-initiated and teacher-directed activity
- balance of quiet/passive and indoor/outdoor experiences
- reasonable pace of participation
- recognition of developmental differences in attention span

Well-planned transitions support smooth changes throughout the day by:

- advance notice
- familiar cues
- clear, simple, personal directions
- adults beginning the next activity
- chaos minimized by not moving whole group at one time
- giving children responsibility during transitions

Things Not Seen in a Developmentally Appropriate Physical Environment for Preschoolers

Figure 5-23 These children are holding a "Magic rope" as they go for a neighborhood walk. *Courtesy NationsBank Child Care Center.*

1. *Physical arrangements that suggest direct teacher instruction:*

   For play to have the central place in the curriculum of a preschool classroom, physical arrangements must support an atmosphere of movement, interaction, and activity. When the physical space and furnishings allow only sitting, and when the teacher arranges tables or desks so they focus on his/her position in the classroom, the physical environment dictates passive learning experiences for children.

2. *A schedule dominated by teacher lesson time:*

   When teacher talk and structured lessons are valued more highly than child-initiated play experiences, the schedule will reflect only short free play periods, both inside and outside. Play is used here to "let the children be children" for brief breaks from the "real learning" that the teacher directs.

3. *Worksheets, ditto sheets, flashcards, and other abstract materials:*

   The predominance of these materials in a preschool classroom suggests a lack of recognition of preschoolers' concrete style of learning and thinking. The emphasis on developing particular skills represented by such structured materials reflects a narrow cognitive focus on learning in the classroom, rather than nurturing holistic child development.

BUT WHAT ABOUT?

The worst time of the day for me is getting the children ready to go out to the playground. My director insists that children walk quietly in straight lines, and it's agony for all of us to try to get them to wait for the line to be straight and quiet. What do I do?

Most likely your director is concerned that children be safe while walking down the hall. For a long time we've confused our desire for order and control with a perception that the only way to achieve it is for children to adopt semimilitary procedures of lining up and achieving perfect control under the adult's direction. While it is certainly desirable to keep children from mad dashes that would likely lead to someone getting hurt, there are more developmentally appropriate ways to keep children together, focused on safe behavior and quiet that respects the rights of others in the building. Some teachers who want to avoid the lines they feel are inappropriate for young children try more imaginative approaches, capitalizing on preschoolers' imagination and willingness for group participation. They might:

- play a quiet follow-the-leader down the hall, first patting their head, then crouching down, then raising their hands in the air, then waving first one hand, then the other. By the time they have reached this point, they have likely arrived at the door to the playground, without once having to remind the children to walk, so intent were they on the game.

- suggest a quiet thing to pretend to be, often creating a "mental bridge" from an earlier experience. After reading a story about the first snowfall, Deidre suggested they each be a quiet snowflake going down the hall: "Careful! Don't let anyone touch you or you'll melt!" Annie suggested her four-year-olds look for something red to tell her about when they get outside. Having a mental focus helps children maintain their control.

- using a "Magic rope." (See Figure 5-23.) A rope with a bead knotted at strategic intervals along the rope helps keep children together, yet spaced a bit to avoid crowding. A teacher whose director felt very strongly about "lines" found this to be a less directive way of keeping the children together.

The other reason some adults use for insisting that preschool children learn to walk in lines is that they will need this skill for later schooling. This is truly inappropriate, emphasizing "children's future development as more important that their current well-being" (Goffin, 1989, p.155). Spending early childhood preparing for future stages of growth ignores the understanding that childhood is a "meaningful time for development in its own right." (Goffin, 1989, p.155). A child who has developed self-confidence through respectful, appropriate responses and expectations is better able to conform to later guidelines than one who has failed to fit adults' inappropriate expectations and is thus less self-confident. There are some very good ideas on transition activities in an article by Betty Ruth Baker: "Transition Time: Make it a Time of Learning for Children." In *Day Care and Early Education.* Summer, 1986, pp. 36-38.

4. *A time-out chair:* The central position of a chair labeled for "time out" in the physical environment suggests adult reliance on teacher power and punishing techniques to control behavior. In Chapter 9, we will discuss appropriate guidance for preschoolers; at this point we will merely note that it is inappropriate to include "an unhappy place" in the preschool classroom.

SUMMARY

Developmentally appropriate physical environments for preschoolers include: well-defined separate interest centers for a variety of active play experiences; spaces large enough to encourage social interaction, as well as some spaces small enough to encourage solitary or pair play; private space to withdraw to, and personal space to feel a sense of belonging; carefully selected, open-ended materials arranged to invite exploration; a decor that reflects children's interest, identity, participation, and planning; an outdoor play area that provides for gross motor challenges, as well as space and materials for other choices; a predictable schedule that allows for adjusting to children's needs and interests; and transitions planned to avoid chaos, confusion, and empty waiting.

THINK ABOUT IT

1. Visit a preschool classroom. Consider each of Prescott's seven components for the physical environment. List specifics that you find for each of the components. Mark the places on the continuum of this classroom for each of the components then discuss your findings with classmates.

2. Sketch the arrangement of interest centers, indicating storage space, work areas, other dividers, pathways, and traffic patterns. Indicate the number of play spaces shown in each center.

Evaluate the room arrangement for:

- separation of noisy and quiet areas, clean and messy areas

- clear messages about where to use and store materials

- protection of play areas from traffic

- clear pathways and entrances to centers

- no empty dead space

- centers large enough for group play, and small enough for pairs and singles

Are there obvious ways this arrangement could be improved? If so, redesign them on paper.

3. List the cues you see that would help children know:

- where to return toys and clean up

- how to plan their play

- how many children may play in an area

- where their personal spaces are

- how to behave in particular activities

4. Evaluate the schedule for:

- flexibility allowed by time-blocks

- alternating active and quieter periods

- most of time spent in child-initiated time-blocks

- alternation with teacher-directed periods

5. Observe several transitions. Note evidence you see of:

- giving advanced warning

- using familiar songs and other clues

- ensuring that children understand what to do

- avoiding empty waiting time

- giving children real responsibility during transitions

QUESTIONS TO REVIEW OBJECTIVES

1. Describe what preschool children are like, what they do, and what they need.

2. Identify some of the considerations in creating an environment for initiative.

3. Identify some of the considerations in planning an environment for play.

4. Identify some of the considerations in planning an environment for self-control.

5. Discuss some of the characteristics of a good schedule for preschool classrooms.

6. Describe things teachers do to create smooth transitions in preschool classrooms.

REFERENCES AND SUGGESTIONS FOR READING

Crosser, S. (1992, January). Managing the early childhood classroom. *Young Children, 47(2)*, 23–29.

Goffin, S. G. (1989, Winter). How well do we respect the children in our care? *Childhood Education*, 68–74.

Gonzalez-Mena, J. (1993). *The child in the family and the community.* New York: Macmillan Publishing Co.

Greenman, J. (1988). *Caring spaces, learning places: Children's environments that work.* Redmond, WA: Exchange Press, Inc.

Harms, T., & Clifford, R. (1980). *Early childhood environment rating scale.* New York: Teachers College Press.

Hildebrand, V. (1989). *Guiding young children* (4th ed.). New York: Macmillan Publishing Co.

Humphrey, S. (1989, November). Becoming a better kindergarten teacher: The case of myself. *Young Children, 15(1)*, 16–22.

Isenberg, J.P. & Jalongo, M.R. (1993). *Creative expression and play in the early childhood curriculum.* NY: Merrill Press.

Miller, K. (1987, August/September). Room arrangement: Making it work for you and your kids. *Scholastic Pre-K Today*, 26–33.

Mitchell, G. (1982). *A very practical guide to discipline.* Chelsea, MA: Telshare Publishing Co.

Ostrosky, M. M., & Kaiser, A. P. (1991, Summer). Preschool language environments that promote communication. *Teaching Exceptional Children*, 6–10.

Prescott, E. (1984). The physical setting in day care. In Greenman, J., & Fuqua, R. (eds.), *Making day care better: Training, evaluation, and the process of change.* New York: Teachers College Press.

Schillmoeller, G. L., & Amundrud, P. The effect of furniture arrangement on movement, on-task behavior, and sound in an early childhood setting. *Child and Youth Care Quarterly, 16(1)*, 5–20.

Developmentally Appropriate Physical Environments:
For Primary-Aged

*O*ur society has created an arbitrarily chosen milestone in young children's lives: the entry into school, at age five or six. Although many children today have likely been attending educational/care programs for several years before this time, traditional thinking links entrance to "big" school with the beginning of the learning needed to equip children for their future lives. While the children themselves are aware of the importance the adults place on this symbolic event, no other decisive change has precipitated it. Five, six, seven, and eight-year-olds are not so very different in their learning styles and abilities from children a year or so younger. They are more comfortable away from their parents than younger children, but are still very eager for recognition and relationships with other important adults. They enjoy being with other children, and are still learning the skills that allow them to function as group members. They are still active creatures gaining control over their bodies, practicing both gross and fine motor skills. Their understandings of the world around them are still related to their concrete experiences; the errors in their judgments and logic are still governed by their preoperational mode of thinking. Much in the world around them is still very new and interesting to them. The one thing that has changed is that adults are expecting them to accomplish skills that the culture has deemed necessary. So the transition to school is likely to be accompanied by excitement and anticipation of a new experience, as well as anxiety and apprehension about succeeding in it.

This is a whole new environment for 6 or 7 hours a day in most cases; there are now very few part-day kindergarten programs in the public school systems. And for children whose working parents must find supplemental care for them before and after school and in vacation times, it often means still another environment for more hours each day. This is an environment not meant to be the same as the formal elementary school classroom, but so recent is its evolution that there are questions about what *should* be included.

In this chapter we will consider the physical environments of both the primary school classrooms and the after school care classrooms that are best suited to the developmental tasks of primary-aged children.

OBJECTIVES

After completing this chapter, students should be able to:

- describe what primary-aged children are like.

- describe what primary-aged children need for optimum development.
- describe elements of an environment that nurtures a sense of industry.
- describe elements of an environment for emergent literacy.
- identify elements of an environment that promote relationships.
- discuss considerations in developmentally appropriate schedules for primary children.
- identify components of appropriate after-school environments.
- describe elements not found in developmentally appropriate primary classrooms.

What Are Primary-Aged Children Like?

Figure 6-1 The desire for competence is a driving force of primary-aged children. *Courtesy Scarborough School Department.*

So much has already happened to children by the time they begin formal schooling at age five or six that there are millions of unique histories and developmental patterns. Within every kindergarten classroom, there are likely to be children whose lives have been blessed with secure love and attention from parents and families since birth, and others who have been abused, neglected, or ignored by adults unable to cope with the responsibilities of parenthood and their own lives. There are some who shout with glee when a funny story is read to them, and some who are puzzled by the very words and are unused to handling books. There are some who move comfortably into the new challenges and relationships in the classroom, and some who hang back, timid, fearful, and mistrusting. There are some who can read and print their names and are eager for more challenges, and some who don't recognize colors or comprehend what "biggest" means, and seem to expect not to succeed in this new world. There are some who climb, swing, run, and jump with zest, and some whose physical limitations or lack of experience make them unable to. There are children who are losing their first teeth and putting them hopefully under their pillows for the Tooth Fairy, and others who have already lost some due to poor nutrition and health, no dental care, or accidents. There are children whose out-of-school lives involve busy rounds of lessons, visits at friends' homes, and family activities, and some who spend much of their time watching a lot of mostly unsuitable television. There are differences influenced by culture, neighborhood, social and economic circumstances of their families, and by temperament and individual rates of development. There are enormous differences—and there are things they all have in common.

What they have in common is their entrance into a period of their lives where they are in enough control of their bodies and minds, and their emotions and communication abilities, that they have the potential of doing just about anything they want to do, things that have not before been possible. Perhaps the most outstanding characteristic of many primary-aged children is their thirst to know and to understand. A desire for competence is their driving force, and they are willing to spend time and energy at becoming competent at the things that interest them, and that seem important to their adults. (See Figure 6-1.) This is the age of creation, when children want to make things, to make them well, to be good at doing things. They are capable of becoming totally absorbed in passionate interests.

What they do with friends is one of those passionate interests. The friendships of the early school years tend to be somewhat longer lasting than the tempestuous first efforts of preschoolers. There are still episodes of pain and hurt feelings, but these friendships give primary-aged children important opportunities for exploring social relationships and becoming less egocentric. Interaction with peers gives children important feedback to incorporate into their personal identities.

Physical competence and skill is also an important component of self-concept for primary-aged children. Physical abilities often form the basis for common activity and entrance into games with others. Primary-aged children are great game players. The traditional games of childhood have been passed virtually unchanged from one generation to the next. Because their growth rate has slowed, their bodies change more slowly, giving them more time to "feel at home" inside their "skins." Their joy and skill with large muscle activity is reflected in their boundless energy and activity. Primary-aged children are still creatures who find it difficult to remain still for very long.

Time is still rather a vague concept for primary-aged children. They tell somewhat disjointed stories about experiences that happened sometime in the past or will happen in the future. They are instead creatures of the moment, enjoying the present to the fullest.

What Do Primary-Aged Children Do?

The most obvious answer to the question of what primary-aged children do is they spend long hours away from home and families, in formal, organized schooling, and in less formal, but often equally organized, recreational and after-school activities. In these settings they spend a lot of time listening, sitting, following instructions, and working at new skills. Depending on the classroom practices, they may spend a lot of time with pencils in hand, working on paper assignments. They may spend time waiting until their reading group is called, either working industriously at the list of assignments on the board, or trying to catch the eye of a friend and talk with him until the teacher asks them to be quiet. They may spend time waiting for everyone to line up to walk to the gym or the cafeteria or the playground. They may spend time sitting in time out, because they were unable to wait quietly.

Or they may spend their school day hours deep in involvement with reading with a friend, working on writing a story about a trip to the bakery, enjoying the big book read by their teacher, and then constructing a bakery in the block center. So very different are the experiences of school-aged children, based on what decisions have been made by teachers, administrators, and their individual communities.

After school they may be among the children who can go home to play in their yards or streets, enjoying the freedom that parents now give to this age of child: freedom to talk, to play games, to just hang around with friends. Or they may be among the children who are dropped off by bus or van at an after-school program or a family day care home arrangement, to wait several more hours until their parents are able to pick them up. They may engage in planned recreational activities, supervised homework sessions, or watch television. When they do go home, they will likely watch even more television—many school-aged children watch more hours of television each week than they spend in school. It is likely they spend less time with their parents than they did as younger children.

Whatever their after-school arrangement, and no matter what the classroom practices are, these children will actively seek to be with friends. They want to talk with them, play with them, do things together. Friends are the big new influence in their lives. What their friends do and say is what is important to them. Primary-aged children create separate worlds with their friends, worlds entered only by other children.

In addition, what they do is shaped by their family and individual culture. They may spend time helping to care for younger siblings, talking with grandparents, or helping a parent prepare tortillas or spring rolls for a family celebration. They may spend time helping with chores on the farm, or going to dance class, or accompanying a parent to the laundromat. They may spend time in classes to introduce them to the family's religious or cultural traditions, or watching the older boys in the neighborhood fight on the corner, or having individualized evaluation and therapy for special needs. Saturday mornings may be spent playing in Little League games or watching cartoons or getting ready for Dad to pick them up for a weekend visit.

What all of these different primary-aged children are doing involves becoming a member of their society, learning its ways, its customs, and its knowledge. More is expected of these school-aged children, and they are now ready to participate more fully in the world around them. They are ready to become competent, and ready to be seen as competent.

What Do Primary-Aged Children Need?

What these children need is a world in which they can experience competence. Erikson designated the psychosocial conflict for this period as developing a sense of industry vs. a sense of inferiority. By this he meant that children need to feel a measure of success in accomplishing the tasks designated by adults to be important learning for entrance into participation in the culture. They need to see themselves as succeeding as a worker in the culture, rather than feeling a sense of failure in measuring up to the expected standards. The environment, then, must nurture those feelings of competence by selecting tasks that are attainable and by supporting children in their accomplishment. Competence refers not only to the accomplishment of academic tasks, such as reading and writing, but also to other achievements that are deemed valuable. These may be as varied as learning to play baseball well, singing in the church choir, sweeping leaves from the driveway, or being able to make others laugh. An environment that promotes competence gives children time, space, materials, and opportunity to practice the skills they are learning. The environment also conveys acceptance and recognition of the diversity of ability, skill, and interest that is obvious in children's differing capacities, and of the diversity of cultural backgrounds that have shaped the children's individuality.

Primary-aged children need an environment that allows them to proceed at their own pace in developing skills, without being compared with the pace of someone else. An environment that recognizes that there are differences in development and readiness for learning is critical. They are helped when the practices in the environment support their development within an atmosphere of cooperation, rather than a spirit of competition.

Becoming socially accepted is an area where primary-aged children set their own tasks of accomplishment, and where it is important that they do not feel inferior. An environment that supports group participation and peer interaction is helpful to nurturing both the skills and the satisfaction of group membership. Primary-aged children need opportunities to select their peers, to spend time with them, and to have their friendships accepted as important and valuable.

Primary-aged children need opportunities to communicate and to develop their communication skills. This means they need an environment that supports talk as well as listening, and that links speech with the other methods of communication that are demanded by the culture. An environment that supports literacy is an environment that communicates the practical usages of reading and writing, and the pleasures involved.

As Piaget described the preoperational stage of children's thinking, he noted that the stage extends to age seven or so. This means that most primary-aged children still retain the learning style and limitations of thought associated with preoperational mental activity. The environment must recognize this fact and support learning through concrete methods, related to real experiences, allowing children to construct their own understandings of concepts. The active learning style of preschoolers does not change, since the mental abilities have not changed. Environments for preoperational thinkers allow for using materials that teach children in active learning experiences. Where the environment for primary-aged children does look different from that for younger children, it does so because of the intense curiosity and passionate interests in particular topics, and their developing skills related to literacy. The environment for school-aged children offers time and space to pursue their expanded interests and experience in the world.

What these eager entrants into their larger culture need is an environment that supports the development of a sense of industry, of learning about the world around, including use of literacy skills as learned by a mostly preoperational child, and of relationships, primarily with the peer group.

Differences in Physical Environments for Primary-Aged Children

Contrast the situations for these two six-year-olds. Joel is a first grader at Elm Heights Elementary School, and LaToya attends the Parkwood School first grade.

When Joel enters his classroom, he goes immediately to his desk. It is the third desk in the row by the door. He waves to his friend Rodney, who sits in the front desk of the row by the windows. He would like to go over to talk, but Mr. Jordan looks up from his desk to remind them to get out their reading books. This is the time to read silently the books they have brought back from the library. Joel found out yesterday that his is too hard, but it is the book he has for the week, so he sits looking at it until the bell goes. None of his good friends sit near him anyway; Mr. Jordan moved their seats all around after the first month of school, so nobody would be near their friends and tempted to talk.

The bell is the signal for everyone to put away their books. Mr. Jordan calls for a child to go to the front of the classroom to lead the Pledge. The flag hangs at the front of the classroom, along with a large calendar, and pictures of several early presidents. The teacher's desk is at the front of the classroom, along with his file cabinets and storage shelves. There are shelves at the back of the room for the children to store lunch boxes, and there are hooks for their coats. A bulletin board by the door has the schedule for the week posted. It doesn't change.

There are the usual questions about the day of the week, the month, and the year to complete the calendar discussion, and a discussion about the weather to fill in the weather chart. Then Mr. Jordan writes their assignments on the board, to work on while he does the reading groups. Joel is usually in the third reading group that is called, so he settles in to do his seat work. Turning to page 17 in his reading workbook, he answers some questions about yesterday's reading lesson that involved a small dog. He underlines the correct answers to the questions, but there is a word in the fourth question he can't figure out. He raises his hand, but Mr. Jordan says, "Just go on with your work. I'll help you later." He turns to the next of the board assignments, which is to complete Section 2 on pages 34 and 35 in his math workbook. He discovers this is the same kind of subtraction problems that Mr. Jordan showed them on the board yesterday. They were pretty easy for him, so he finishes them quickly. The third assignment was to read the next story for his reading group and write ten words for his spelling lesson.

Mr. Jordan was only calling the second reading group, and Joel was getting tired of sitting. He went to the pencil sharpener although his pencil really didn't need sharpening. On the way back to his seat, he took the long way so he could talk to Rodney about the ball game last night. When they started giggling, Mr. Jordan looked up from the reading group, and warned, "If you don't get your work done now, you can stay in at recess and finish it then." Joel went back to his seat and wrote some of his spelling words.

When his reading group was called, Mr. Jordan asked him to read first. He stumbled over a word in the second sentence. Mr. Jordan said, "That's *thing*, Joel. Sound it out. You should have been paying more attention to reading than talking with Rodney." Rodney repeated "thing" then had trouble with "light." Mr. Jordan interrupted the reading to speak to the others working in their seats, who were getting restless and a bit noisy. When everyone had had a turn to read, Mr. Jordan told them to read through the story again quietly at their seats, then finish their seat work. Joel could hardly wait for lunch time. After the short recess, they came back to their desks to listen to Mr. Jordan's math lesson.

Now switch to Parkwood School. When LaToya enters her classroom, she looks around to see where her best friend Joy is sitting. She spots her over on the carpet near the book shelves. She goes over and joins her. Together the two girls look at the book Joy had chosen, a favorite of theirs. In the book area are large posters and pictures from some of the selection of books on display, as well as a collection of hand puppets and a small stage. Other children select books from the shelves and go to various places to read—some in the loft, a couple in the individual nooks, some sitting together at a low table, some on the steps by the window. The teacher, Mrs. Guerrera, moves around to greet them. When everyone has arrived, she plays a chord on her autoharp, and the children move over to the large meeting area where the teacher is seated beside a big book on an easel. She reads the book, and the children join in, for it is a favorite—*Curious*

George at the Zoo. After the book there is discussion about some of the words that reminded the children of their visit to the zoo the week before. Mrs. Guerrera removes the book and places an easel pad for her to print the children's responses on the list. There is a lot of laughing and talking. When she finishes with the list, she posts it on the wall.

Then it is writing time. LaToya gets her notebook and pencil from her box and moves to one of the tables grouped together near the writing center. On the walls nearby are posted several of the group stories they have written recently with the teacher, as well as several individual stories children have posted to share. There are several posters with words, and one with alphabet letters on it. Several other children join her, and others take their work to the carpet area. Several more children choose the individual tables placed at the sides of the room. LaToya started her story yesterday. She is working on writing a story about a little girl going to the zoo. She decides to add a monkey to the things the little girl sees. She goes back to the reading area to find the big book so she can see how to spell *monkey*. She looks through the book until she thinks she has found it. She carries the book to Joy and they decide together that the word she found is really mischief. They keep looking till they find *monkey,* and LaToya writes it in her story. Mrs. Guerrera comes around to talk with the children about their stories, and admires the new sentence LaToya has written. She asks LaToya if she wants to be on the list of children who will read their stories to some other children. Mrs. Guerrera writes her name on a list taped to the wall. LaToya is pleased. She goes and gets Joy so Joy can hear it too.

After the story reading, Mrs. Guerrera announces it is time for children to choose their activity centers. LaToya takes her turn to go to the planning board on the wall in the meeting area and moves her nametag to one of the five spaces under the heading Block Area. A glance around the room shows other children busy in a number of other centers: Three children are working on a large papier-mâché dinosaur in the art area. Several children are gathered around a listening center with ear phones on, turning the pages of books, and making comments to one another. Several others are constructing with a variety of small manipulative toys, and another group is playing a game. Three children are working on a large floor puzzle in another corner. A group in housekeeping is playing an elaborate game of store.

LaToya wants to build a cage for the monkey. She signals Joy and another friend to plan to come to the blocks to work also. When they finish, they make a sign for their construction "CAJ. Dont tuch." After lunch they plan to play monkeys on the playground. They ask their teacher what they can use for cages. She suggests taking some of the large boxes out of the storage shed.

The profound differences in these physical environments for primary-aged children reflect deep variations in educational philosophies. The arrangements of time and space dictate the kinds of learning opportunities available for children, as well as the specifics about curriculum, teacher's style of interaction, and children's role as learners. In this discussion of developmentally appropriate physical environments for primary-aged children, it will be obvious that the traditional sit-in-rows-of-desks-and-work style of classroom with time broken up into small chunks for specific teacher-directed instruction must be questioned as to how well it matches the learning style and developmental needs of the children.

Environment for a Sense of Industry

Learning Centers

As primary-aged children begin their formal school learning experiences in kindergarten and the classrooms for the early grades, they need an environment that conveys a message about their active roles as learners. Classrooms need to be designed for children to learn in the ways that are natural to them, so that they experience feelings of success and comfortable competence. The traditional arrangement of children sitting in rows facing the teacher's desk and blackboard at the front of the room showed clearly just who was in charge of learning, and the very passive roles of children in that classroom. Not only is the traditional primary classroom designed to make the teacher the focus of attention, but any interaction among children is clearly discouraged by the separations and the assigned individual desks. In such physical arrangements, children quickly learn to let the teacher be in charge of all their learning, becoming dependent on teacher ideas and assessment for their personal evaluations of their success. When children who find such inactive and confined learning arrangements difficult receive negative feedback from teachers about their classroom failures, their self-esteem as learners is doubly threatened.

An environment that expects children to make some of the decisions about what work they will do and how and where they will do it, is an environment that allows children to develop positive feelings about their learning. For this reason developmentally appropriate kindergarten and primary classrooms offer children a range of choices throughout their day. One of these choices will be in deciding what their learning activities will be during a significant portion of the school day. This means that the classroom will offer a variety of learning centers, so that children may select from assortments of materials and media that teachers have planned to make available to them. Children with different interests, learning styles, and abilities may find work that is personally meaningful in learning center arrangements.

These learning centers will likely bear some similarity to learning centers found in preschool classrooms, but the individual stamp of primary-aged children's environments will be found in the size and complexity of the centers. For example, while blocks may be found in both preschool and primary classrooms, the block center for the older children will more than likely be larger and contain more blocks, recognizing their need for planning grander structures and working with a group on a common plan. Teachers may incorporate reading and writing in creating challenges for the builders. Challenge cards may invite: "Build something that reminds you of our trip last Monday" or "Find a friend or two to help you build a building with six sides." Some books displayed nearby may include *Mike Mulligan and His Steam Shovel* and a book showing buildings from countries around the world. Teachers will also likely include writing materials nearby for builders to label or describe their efforts. Extra space may be provided for ongoing projects to remain until completion.

In addition to complexity, other differences in the primary classroom include degrees of responsibility. Primary-aged children will be asked to assume complete responsibility under limited adult supervision, helping to prepare materials for centers, caring for them, and working independently (Barbour and Seefeldt, 1993). Space and materials are arranged to require increasing degrees of skill.

In addition to blocks, primary classrooms often include centers for creativity, for reading and writing, for math/manipulatives/games, for science, for dramatic play, and for listening. Occasional options may be cooking, woodworking, and playing with sand and water.

There are benefits to the learning center approach. One is that it allows for the kind of integrated curriculum suggested by the guidelines for developmentally appropriate practice.

> The curriculum is integrated so that children's learning in all traditional subject areas occurs primarily through projects and learning centers that teachers plan and that reflect children's interest and suggestions.... Many learning centers are available for children to choose from. Many centers include opportunities for writing and reading.... Objects children can manipulate and experiment with such as blocks, cards, games, woodworking tools, arts and crafts materials including paint and clay, and scientific equipment are readily accessible (Bredekamp, 1987, pp. 67–69).

Rather than chopping the day into separate periods for science, social studies, math, reading, etc., children busy in learning centers are actively involved in incorporating these various subjects within single activities. Learning centers allow for teachers to use intentional strategies and materials that they plan to further curricular goals. The children's learning is hands-on, experience-based, and individualized to meet particular needs, interests, styles, and abilities. When a considerable portion of program time is spent in learning center choices, teachers are free to spend time observing and interacting with individual children to assess their instructional needs and plan future strategies.

There are decisions for teachers to make as they move to planning curriculum through learning centers. They need to plan the physical arrangement of the learning centers to avoid distractions of noisy activities near quiet centers, to minimize traffic interference, and maximize storage and clean-up activities. (See Chapter 5 for additional points to consider.) They need to decide on mechanisms for encouraging children's careful planning of their activities, and limits on numbers of children that can constructively use a center at a time. They need to decide whether all learning centers will be available each day, and whether there will be time devoted to the centers each day.

Another decision is whether each child must use each center during a specified time frame, and whether they are free to leave a center when they choose or only when the teacher guides. Some teachers want to ensure that children get a balanced selection of learning opportunities, so they ask children to participate in a certain minimum number of activities each day or week. See Figure 6-2 for an example of the kind of planning contract that allows children to see the requirements for center participation. Additional ideas for monitoring children's use of centers include giving children numbers of colored tickets with their names on to deposit for admission to a center, with perhaps a particular color indicating required activity (Kostelnik, 1993), or asking children to stamp a color-coded card to leave in the teacher's basket (Myers and Maurer, 1987). Others feel that such a system inhibits children's learning to make significant independent choices, and may detract from their deep involvement in long-term projects and learning activities. They believe that any center can incorporate a

---

Sample Planning Contract

Put a ✔ in the appropriate box each time you use this subject in a week. You should have at least ten check marks by Friday, including at least 4 for reading, 3 for math and 3 for writing.

Reading	Math	Writing	Creative Art	Games	Special This Week

Science	Wood Working	Music	Blocks	Dramatic Play

Figure 6–2 Sample planning contract.

Figure 6-3 Children may choose places to work that are most comfortable for them. *Courtesy Scarborough School Department.*

wide variety of different learning opportunities. As has been mentioned earlier, teachers must make such decisions based on what they know of children's development, experiences, and needs, and based on other variables such as school system guidelines, parent and community preferences, and teacher comfort.

Teachers also differ in deciding whether all learning centers should be arranged so as to offer children unrestricted opportunities to direct their learning, or should suggest particular activities to be done in prescribed ways. Myers and Maurer (1987) make distinctions of three kinds of learning centers: self-directing/self-correcting; self-directing/open-ended; and teacher-instructed/exploratory. The first type allows teachers to set up activities for particular purposes, with the materials telling children whether they have been used correctly. An example of this would be a puzzle that matched numerals with numbers of objects, or pairs of picture cards to be matched by common beginning letter sounds. The self-directing/open-ended centers, on the other hand, offer materials that may produce varieties of learning, depending on individual children's abilities and interests. Blocks offered with no instruction or specific challenge suggestion would be an example of this. The third type of center offers opportunities for children to explore further concepts that have previously been introduced by teachers. An example of this might be using eye droppers to mix colors, or working with salt and other ingredients to explore melting ice, after teachers have led lessons on these subjects. Teachers may use different proportions of these kinds of centers at different times, depending on children's curriculum needs.

Figure 6-4 Central planning boards help children choose among available activities. *Courtesy Avondale Children's Center.*

Teachers who use learning centers as a primary instructional approach organize learning experiences for the children around common themes or projects. See more about this in Chapter 14.

The thoughtful selection of materials that will challenge curiosity and sustain complex investigation of topics is an important component of the physical environment. Teachers work diligently to create inviting displays of materials that are available for use and manipulation. The physically attractive classroom conveys the teacher's recognition that children need to be joyfully involved in their learning. As discussed earlier in this book, teachers are careful to select all materials to indicate their respect for the diversity of race and culture, physical ability, gender, and socioeconomic backgrounds represented in the classroom and in the community.

An advantage to arranging the classroom to accommodate a number of separate learning centers is that the arrangement provides for choices of where to work during other work periods. There simply is not space for both the traditional and inflexible desks-in-rows arrangement, and the tables, shelves, and other furniture needed to create the separated interest center zones. The small tables and the separate work areas for individuals and small groups will allow children to select the places that seem most comfortable for them to work, whether by themselves or with others; even the floor is not excluded. (See Figure 6-3.) Pillows and carpet make relaxing areas to work. "Tables are used for children to work alone or in small groups. A variety of work places and spaces is provided and flexibly used" (Bredekamp, 1987, p. 69). There is no explicit or implicit prohibition on movement. In such a room, there is no particular "front" to the classroom; something is happening everywhere, and both teacher and children are mobile rather than occupying a fixed position.

Children will probably feel that the school classroom is an alien environment when their physical comfort and natural inclinations are less important than the teacher's insistence that they remain seated in order to be recognized as working. Children are more likely to sense success or *industry* in the learning center atmosphere than to experience a sense of inferiority at not being able to learn the narrowly prescribed curriculum in the specifically defined ways and places.

Planning Boards

A sense of industry is also nurtured when children feel they are in charge of making important decisions related to their learning. Many primary teachers use various forms of planning boards to help children make conscious choices about their learning activities. A central planning board is suitable for five through eight-year-olds, to allow them to decide among all the possibilities, possibly in conjunction with the decisions of peers. (See Figure 6-4.) The children have individual name tags to slip into pockets or place on hooks, or places where they can write their own names.

The ability to plan and to organize individual activity to accomplish goals is an important skill for primary-aged children to develop. Moving beyond the basic decision about where to play, children may need help in formulating goals and thinking through the steps of complicated projects. Conversations with teachers and peers and writing the ideas down may be helpful. Talking about the successes and problems that occur in completing planned activities also helps children learn how to control their progress. Casey and Lippman (1991) suggest that such a discussion time could replace the traditional show-and-tell time, as children share their progress with others. The High/Scope method refers to this

BUT WHAT ABOUT?

A teacher who has always taught in a fairly traditional physical arrangement would like to move away from the desks-in-rows arrangement to allow for more small group work. "But won't the kids go crazy? It won't seem like I'm in control."

What's important in this question is the teacher's own thinking. Physical arrangements alone do not make classrooms more developmentally appropriate. What is really important are the teacher's beliefs and values about teaching and learning. When the teacher comes to a realization that children need to be actively involved in interaction with others for total learning, and that children need to be the ones who direct their actions within the learning setting, she may be ready to let go of the physical arrangement that puts her so clearly in charge of everything that happens in the classroom. Until that time better not to try to change the furniture until she is willing to trust children's abilities to initiate and control their behaviors.

When she is ready, an initial discussion about proposed changes in the classroom arrangement needs to be held with the children at a class meeting. The teacher should share what she has been thinking, and solicit ideas for possible arrangements. She may even want to share her concerns about changed behaviors, and encourage the children to consider how to approach this issue. She might be surprised by their responsiveness and responsibility when they are included in the discussion and planning. Children respond in very different ways when they are brought into discussions, as opposed to having things done to them.

technique as plan, do, review (Hohmann and Buckleleitner, 1992). Children learn to evaluate their own work and that of others, to offer each other suggestions, and to collaborate on complex projects.

Portfolios, etc.

A sense of industry is also achieved as children are able to see the progress they make in their self-assigned learning tasks. Teachers may devise systems that help children keep track of their development. One such kind of system is the development of a portfolio. Each child has individual file folders in which to keep various papers, such as stories they have written, drawings, words they have learned to read, photos or sketches of their projects and constructions, artwork, and other samples of work. Portfolios are for the benefit of the children, their parents, and their teachers. In Chapter 14, we'll talk about the use of portfolios for assessment; here it is important to note their uses for children in following their own progress. Other variations on the portfolio idea are all designed for children to have tangible evidence of their learning. One example is envelopes to hold the letters and numbers recognized by younger children or the envelopes described by Sylvia Ashton-Warner and Sydney Clemens for children to keep their words that they have chosen to read (Ashton-Warner, 1964; Clemens, 1983).

Figure 6-5 The classroom has a central area for portfolios, so children may make their own additions. *Courtesy Avondale Children's Center.*

A central and accessible place in the classroom is created for portfolios, so that children may make additions when they choose to. (See Figure 6-5.) The traditional primary classroom gives each child a desk to store individual work. The active learning-center–based classroom gives children individual storage areas of some kind, in addition to the general portfolio storage area.

Evidence of children's work and progress is also everywhere in the room. Teachers create a sense of common ownership in the room, so that children can feel comfortable displaying the things that are important to them. Lists of accomplishments and posters that celebrate achievements of all kinds attest to children's industry. Group accounts of projects may be written or created.

In primary classrooms, teachers help to nurture a sense of industry by:

- creating learning centers for children's active learning at their individual level of interest and ability
- using the thoughtful selection and display of concrete materials to stimulate curiosity and productivity
- designing an informal and flexible physical arrangement that allows children to work alone or in small groups
- using planning systems to help children learn to plan their activities
- using portfolios and other methods to help children measure their own progress and to have a personal storage area

Environment for Literacy

Classrooms for primary-aged children have the development of literacy and numeration skills as primary objectives. Current thinking about the emergence of literacy as development of whole language skills has implications for the physical environment.

The physical environment should be *print-rich*. Children need to see the functionality of reading and writing skills practiced in their environment daily. Everything in the environment is labeled (boxes for "scissors" and "scrap paper"; hooks for "hats"; "Bathroom—3 at a time"). Lists (of everything: songs we like; favorite foods; things we saw on the bus ride; things we need to make vegetable soup; words that sound funny) are made and displayed. Notes and schedules are posted. Signs and stories are everywhere (Morning News; Our Trip on the Bus). Books and posters are in every area of the classroom. Children see adults write things down and read them back. When the environment is print-rich, children discover the usefulness of reading and writing and are highly motivated to do these activities themselves.

There are two large and important learning centers related to literacy. The reading center and the writing center are located close to each other to suggest their linked function. The reading center may include: pillows and beanbag chairs to encourage comfort; open-face shelves to display books (face out) and shelves to store books; many types of books, including stories, information and concept books, poetry, alphabet and counting books, wordless picture books, books made by individual children; duplicates of favorite books, to encourage children to read the same book at the same time as their friend does; puppets, props, and flannel boards, to encourage children to play out stories they've read; posters and pictures about books; the teacher's stock of big books for the whole group to read aloud; perhaps a library system for checking books out for classroom and/or home use.

The writing center should contain small tables and chairs, and shelves to store an abundance of writing supplies: paper of various sizes, unlined and lined; pencils, pens, markers, and crayons; pencil sharpeners; file cards, pads, notebooks, and tablets; stationery and envelopes; chalkboard and chalk; magnetic letters; sand or salt trays for writing letters; a primary or regular typewriter. Some teachers add personal mailboxes for each child. Posters on the wall that include letters and print are appropriate. Children's portfolios for writing work may be kept in this center. As children progress in their literacy experiences, both of these centers will expand to accommodate changing needs; an example of an expansion would be adding construction paper, staplers, and other fasteners as children begin creating their own books.

Literacy materials should not be confined to these two centers, but added to all of the other learning centers. The creative center may have books of famous artworks, or books with beautiful pictures that may inspire; the block center may have books showing buildings and construction. Cookbooks, catalogues, and magazines may be added to dramatic play; science may be enhanced by additions of books related to the theme. Math has counting books, and so on. Materials to write with in each area also extend learning possibilities.

When children spend their school lives in classrooms filled with materials that they see used regularly for reading and writing, they begin to use them. Emerging literacy depends a great deal on the availability of materials in the physical environment, and on the regular opportunities to use these materials and see them used.

Another component of a whole language environment is opportunities for oral communication. We will note this here, and discuss methods of using physical space to encourage communication in the next section.

Provide an environment for encouraging emergent literacy by:

- creating a print-rich environment, where print is seen regularly as it is used
- creating large and attractive reading and writing areas
- adding literacy materials to all other learning centers
- providing for communication and conversation

Environment for Relationships

The growing importance of peers and friends in the five through eight year age groups means that teachers need to plan for environments and practices that nurture a sense of group membership and cooperation. While both explicit discussion and implicit example are important here, as is teacher planning to create group work situations, the physical environment plays a role as well. There are several considerations in the physical environment to nurture friendship and peer relationships.

In the traditional classroom, teachers who were trying to minimize conversations so as to concentrate attention on their own instruction were likely to deliberately separate friends. Children were also put into groups arbitrarily, based on common skill levels. In developmentally appropriate classrooms, teachers recognize that social and communication development are as valid as cognitive skills,

Figure 6-6 The classroom provides places for pairs to work alone. *Courtesy Scarborough School Department.*

and are inextricably linked with cognitive development. They realize also that insights, help, and ideas do not come only from the teacher, but from other children as well. For these reasons they allow children to make choices about where they will work, and with whom. The flexibility in physical arrangements allows children to select the location and group size that feels comfortable personally, and to move furniture when necessary to accommodate the needs of the group.

In those situations where children's choices interfere with their concentration and productivity, teachers help them learn the natural and logical consequences of those choices for future self-control. For example, Shawn and Rodney spent more time talking today about their Little League team than they did writing on their stories at writing time. The teacher reminds them that the group will be reading their stories aloud the next day, so she suggests they think about where they can best work to complete their stories. The following day they again sit together, but concentrate on their writing this time. Specific assignments of physical placement are not made usually, though teachers may encourage isolated children in social skill development by creating paired situations, occasionally.

The arrangement of tables or desks to allow for the formation of small groups encourages interaction and group work. Physical arrangements that permit children to converse face-to-face are important. Children in such arrangements learn to ask peers for help. There should also be spaces small enough to allow for individual children or pairs to work alone. (See Figure 6-6.) When children are able to move freely about the classroom, they may form new groupings or work in different areas as they choose. They may work in several different groups during the day, for different reasons. During the morning they may choose to sit near particular friends to write their stories. Later, a child may choose to join another group that is working on constructing an airplane model. Still later, the teacher may ask a child to join a group of children who have shown a common interest in a particular science experience. Both time and ideas encourage children to work together in groups.

Most of the day is spent in small group or individual activity. Primary-aged children are still shy enough that large groups are often intimidating. When children do come together for large group meetings, they feel more comfortable making their own choices about where they will sit.

Primary-aged children need to be able to regulate their own needs for food and rest, and to make these decisions along with their friends. Teachers can provide a small snack area that children may use during specified times, forming their own small snack groups. During specified quiet periods, children may find a common activity with friends.

The other relationships that are important in the primary classroom are the relationships between children and the teacher. Time and personal contact are key ingredients in nurturing these connections. The physical environment allows opportunities for children and teacher to converse and interact meaningfully. The informal arrangements of work areas and learning centers encourages conversation. The teacher's role as facilitator and observer rather than instructor puts him or her in immediate contact with children involved in their work and ideas. Opportunities for individual interaction are definitely enhanced by the physical arrangements of primary classrooms into less formal work areas. Space here sends the message that children have active roles to play, including communicating in partnership with teachers.

Encourage peer and teacher/child relationships by:

- allowing children to choose where and with whom they work and sit at large group meetings
- using flexible arrangements of tables and chairs to accommodate group needs
- providing spaces small enough for one or two children to work, as well as small groups
- providing spaces for children to have snack or rest with a small group

Schedule

The traditional school day schedule is divided and subdivided into short time segments, with teachers directing the separate lessons. For example, after taking out their notebooks for a 15 minute exercise in handwriting, Miss Stewart's first graders are directed to put those notebooks away and get out their social studies books for them to read and discuss the lesson on bridges. Not only is the day broken up into individual lessons, but other interruptions are frequent; time to go to the gym with the physical education teacher, to the library, for music and art class. Usually, the children are unable to keep up with the frequent changes in their day, so they follow the teacher's directions ("Time to put your social studies book away. We'll have to finish that later. It's time for us to go to the library now.") Often children are asked to follow a schedule that makes sense only from the point of view of the adult keeping order ("Sit quietly at your desk until everyone has finished their math pages, and then we'll begin our spelling lesson"). Because of the emphasis on whole-group instruction, the traditional schedule is filled with such meaningless periods.

The result of this fragmentation of primary classroom schedules seems to be that children's attention spans for task orientation actually decreases as they spend a year in such classrooms (Gareau and Kennedy, 1991). Frequently changed from one activity to another, children become dependent on adult direction of their learning, and less able to concentrate on and establish their own meaningful activities.

In the developmentally appropriate primary classroom, teachers attempt to manage the time so that children are able to have uninterrupted blocks of time to involve themselves fully in activities that demand their concentration. Blocks of time are essential when the curriculum is accomplished in an integrated way, so that children can have opportunities to think, reflect, and make connections. As children work together on long-term projects, time is needed for communication, planning, and carrying out the plan. With blocks of time, both teachers and children concentrate on the tasks to be planned and accomplished, rather than being ruled by the clock dictating what learning should be occurring at any given time. Children need to have blocks of time to have the experience of learning to manage their own time.

An appropriate schedule allows children to be able to proceed at their own unique pace. Individual needs are well served by the large-block approach to scheduling; children who work faster or slower, or whose learning style requires particular modifications or the help of instructional specialists, are not rushed, hindered, or segregated. Within the blocks of time, children may be involved in individual or small group activities; their activities may be independent or teacher-guided. Large group activities alternate between the longer blocks for child-initiated activity. A large proportion of the day's time is spent on child-planned and child-initiated activity.

Teachers minimize interruptions, allowing children to direct their own productivity within the time block. For example, if a snack table is made available for children from 9:30 to 10:30, children may choose the time when they want to take a break from their work or chat with a friend, or are hungry, without the teacher having to interrupt everyone from their work at the same time to announce they must clear the tables for the whole group to have a snack. See Figure 6-7 for a sample schedule from a primary classroom.

As far as is possible in practical terms, teachers schedule necessary breaks to avoid disruption, for times when children need a change of pace, such as later in the day or between large work time blocks. For example, the visit to the music teacher might be scheduled for mid-morning, after the children have spent an hour on their reading/writing projects, and before they have their learning center time. The standards of the National Association of Elementary School Principals suggests that programs or activities that pull children out of the classroom should be "minimal or nonexistent." This does not, of course, refer to the field trips out into the community that may be an important part of integrated theme study. It does mean the interruptions for specialized instruction that is routine in some schools. With an integrated curriculum, creative experiences are part of the classroom day.

Teachers establish reasonable routines that make sense to the children, so they can manage their day without having to wait for teacher instruction. For example, the children know that after the teacher has read to them in the morning, they will select their own reading books and read independently before they decide they are ready to begin work on writing their own stories. Transitions flow smoothly and are kept to a minimum when meaningful routines have been developed.

An appropriate schedule for a primary classroom is based on allowing children to become involved in their individual learning activities early in the day, when their interest and energy levels are high. Later in the day, whole group activities that are likely to interest most children can be scheduled (Gareau and Kennedy, 1991). For example, most of the morning is spent in reading/writing activities and in learning center projects. After lunch the teacher plans a whole group activity to introduce a new science experience to the children.

An appropriate schedule for primary classrooms includes:

- uninterrupted large blocks of time for children's learning

- provision for individual learning styles and paces

- minimizing of interruptions

- scheduling of necessary breaks

- establishing meaningful routines for children's self-direction

- whole group activities scheduled later in the day

Nongraded Primary Program—Sample Daily Schedule*

8:45 a.m.	Greetings, attendance, lunch count, opening
8:50 a.m.	MORNING MEETING
	WHOLE GROUP: (child and teacher directed)
	Includes morning message
	Date and number of days
	Whole language (chart, story, poem, or song)
	Review plans for day's activities
	SMALL GROUP/INDIVIDUAL ACTIVITIES (teacher directed)
	Letter work/phonics skill work
	Content work related to theme topic being studied
	Introduction of literature related to theme topic
9:30 a.m.	CENTERS
	Examples:
	Mathematics problem solving with manipulatives
	Creative writing
	Construction
	Listening
	Water
	Science
	Art
	Handwriting
10:15 a.m.	RECESS
10:30 a.m.	FORMAL MATH
	Skills groups
11:30 a.m.	MORNING CHILDREN GO HOME
	LUNCH AND RECESS FOR ALL-DAY CHILDREN
12:15 p.m.	AFTERNOON MEETING
	Story starter
	Teacher introduction related to theme topic
	Children share
12:30 p.m.	PERSONAL READING
	Teachers hold individual reading conferences
1:00 p.m.	SHARED READING/SHARED WRITING
	Teachers continue reading conferences
1:30 p.m.	MEETING (ON MONDAYS ONLY) TO INTRODUCE CENTERS
	CENTERS (continuation of a.m.)
	Students sharing of center work
	Students share books and creative writing
2:25 p.m.	END OF DAY JOURNALS
	Students write about their day's activities
2:45 p.m.	BUS TIME

*Components used by all teachers, but there may be variations in order depending upon individual teacher's interests and needs.

Figure 6-7 Sample daily schedule for an ungraded primary classroom. *Used with permission of Beth Bellemere, Scarborough School Department.*

BUT WHAT ABOUT?

But what about the homework issue? My director insists that children do their homework as soon as they arrive at the after-school program, to keep their parents happy. She says, "After all, they're the paying customers!"

Yes, they are, but that doesn't mean that practices that are not in children's best interests need to be followed so absolutely. In today's world many working parents have so many responsibilities that they would like, and need, community support in carrying out some of them. After discussions it may well be that it is important and helpful for children to complete their homework assignments during the after-school care period, leaving them free for later family time and/or responsibilities. However, the discussions also need to focus on children's needs, including a consideration of the stresses of the academic classrooms. Most likely a schedule can be arranged that allows for children's homework time to be after they have had opportunity to rest and relax following the day's rigors. A compromise seems to be in everyone's best interest here. Adults administering a child care program must never lose sight of the fact that one of their functions is to be an advocate for children's interests, educating parents and others.

After School Day Care

When the school day is over, many children still spend several hours in other care arrangements until their parents are finished working. This is important time.

> The time between 3 p.m. and 6 p.m. represents approximately 20% of a young school-child's waking hours; it is valuable time that can be used productively for enriching experiences, learning social skills, developing or pursuing special interests, or just being six years old, or seven, or eight (Alexander, 1986, p.7).

Children need opportunities for physical activities, for socialization with peers, and for creative expression through arts and crafts. And after six or seven hours already spent in an environment that was likely heavy on the academic and teacher-directed emphasis, the setting of after-school care probably needs to have more of the "flavor of a neighborhood" than yet another school.

What are some of the components that might add to this neighborhood feeling? One component is the creation of *mixed-age groupings*. A span of three or four years age range is similar to the natural play groupings that develop at home. Mixed-age groupings allow older children to develop initiative and responsibility, to demonstrate nurturing and cooperation. Younger children learn by imitating older ones. Read more about mixed-age groupings in Chapter 10.

Another component is a variety of *choices*. Out of the school environment, children need freedom to select the activities for after-school, even the freedom to choose to do nothing at all. Many choices should be available: outdoor play; arts and crafts; games; cooking and other self-help skills; exploring hobbies; dramatic play.

The environment must include *challenge*. Greenman (1988) comments that it is not uncommon to see five- to ten-year-olds in after-school settings that are primarily preschool settings, bored because the planners don't pay enough "attention to the developmental differences between school-age children and preschoolers." (Greenman, 1988, p. 173) They need an environment that acknowledges that they are bigger, more capable, with interest in doing real things in the world. They need physical challenge, like using real tools; intellectual challenge, like complex jigsaw puzzles and projects that can last over a period of time. Greenman suggests real world challenge in the world of machines—seeing how things work and are put together; in the world of commerce—producing, buying and selling; and in the world of communication—producing newsletters and plays. Challenge may also be derived from fulfilling the kind of responsibility necessary to maintain the environment for the program—real adult chores, assisting one another and the adults, always in reasonable doses, so that the responsibility is fun and not just more work. Care must be taken that the environment promotes a nonsexist approach to challenge and responsibility; both boys and girls should feel comfortable and invited to do all of the possible activities.

The environment must include provision for *privacy*. Having been in group situations all day long, children may want time to play alone or with one or two friends. Privacy should be an option. Older primary-aged children often create their own clubs and secret societies; they need to be granted space and privacy for this activity.

Gross motor activity is essential after the physical confinement of the typical school day. Primary-aged after-school care needs to offer time and space for children to run, jump, climb, yell, and generally have physical and emotional release from the restriction of the day. Cooperative games may be a part of this gross motor activity; leaving behind the competition of the school environment is a good idea.

For children who need to spend some time doing homework or studying, the after-school program needs to offer a *quiet work place* where children may do assignments. After-school programs need to support differing parent and child needs, but must be careful not to simply extend the academic day for more hours. If children need to spend a part of their time doing homework, they should first have opportunities to relax and refresh themselves after the day's work.

Television or not is an issue to be resolved by any after-school program. Those who argue for it point out that children would more than likely be watching it if they were at home, and that they like it and learn from it. Opponents point out that violent content is not helpful to children trying to sort out prosocial behaviors, and the passivity of viewing robs children of more constructive experiences. When programs do decide to include television viewing as part of the planned activities, teacher supervision and limits are necessary.

Schedule considerations are different for an after-school program. There are only several hours spent there, and fewer transitions. But the key transition is the beginning period, as children arrive from their full-day school program. They are liable to be tired and hungry, and in need of relaxing after the day's work. Plans to provide for these needs are important. It is often useful to have a period for snack and relaxed conversation, followed by opportunities for vigorous physical exercise, before the children are ready for the projects and activities of the later afternoon. Many families also benefit by providing a quiet period just before home-going, when both children and parents are weary.

Developmentally appropriate after-school care environments include:

- mixed-age groupings
- choices of many activities, with the option of doing nothing
- challenges in both the planned materials and activities, with projects that can be extended over time
- responsibilities in the program
- privacy for individuals, and support for clubs
- time and space for gross motor activity
- quiet study area
- television under supervision, if at all
- a schedule that balances needs for rest and activity, with attention to the beginning transition

Things Not Found in Developmentally Appropriate Primary Classrooms

The issues of developmental appropriateness can be seen perhaps most graphically when examining the variety of physical environments offered to primary-aged children. It is recognized that school system traditions are undergoing scrutiny and change in many parts of the country, and many classrooms are currently in transition. In some cases the speed of transition is dictated by school system budgets to support purchase of new furnishings and materials. Some classrooms in change are likely to exhibit mixtures and combinations of inappropriate and more appropriate components. Nevertheless, it is probably fair to list some elements of the use of space, physical arrangements, and time that are not considered appropriate for an optimum learning situation.

1. Curriculum is divided into separate subjects, primarily reading and math, with others covered if time permits.

2. Teacher-directed reading groups take up most of the morning, while children spend most of their time doing paper and pencil practice exercises.

3. Special learning projects, centers, and outdoor play are either absent or used as rewards for good learning behavior, or occasional treats.

4. Children work silently and alone most of the time, in assigned desks that are not moved.

5. Instruction is given mostly to the large group.

6. Children have few choices in activities or planning their work day, which is broken up into short periods for different instruction.

SUMMARY

Primary-aged children are interested in becoming competent. They need physical environments that assist them in developing a sense of industry by succeeding at learning tasks that match their mostly preoperational learning style. They need environments that allow them to assume active roles in planning and directing their learning. They need environments that allow them to interact and work with peers. They need environments that help their emerging interest and skills in literacy. The arrangements of space and time need to convey messages of children's active roles in their own learning. Both regular school day programs and after-school programs need to recognize primary-aged children's developmental needs.

THINK ABOUT IT

1. Sketch out your memories of what one or more of your primary classrooms looked like. Ask your classmates to share their memories of the physical environments they experienced in the early grades. Where did their friends sit? What did the teacher's desk look like? How did they spend their time? What do they recall about transitions? What provision was there for individual pace or style of learning?

   After this class discussion, list elements that seem appropriate from your reading in this chapter, and elements that seem less appropriate.

2. Where possible, visit primary classrooms in your community. (Visit in pairs where practical, to compile and compare your observations.) Sketch out and describe the physical arrangements you see. Identify elements that would seem to contribute to: an environment to form a sense of industry; an environment to promote emergent literacy; an environment to promote peer and teacher relationships.

3. If there are after-school day care programs in your community, find out what you can about their programs and schedules. Compare your findings with the discussion in this chapter.

QUESTIONS TO REVIEW OBJECTIVES

1. Describe what primary-aged children are like, and what they do.

2. Identify developmental needs the physical environment must respond to.

3. Discuss considerations in creating an environment to nurture a sense of industry.

4. Discuss elements present in an environment that promotes emergent literacy.

5. Describe environmental considerations for promoting the development of peer relationships.

6. Identify aspects of appropriate schedules.

7. Discuss considerations for appropriate after-school programs.

8. Identify elements not present in developmentally appropriate primary classrooms.

REFERENCES AND SUGGESTIONS FOR READING

Alexander, N. P. (1986, November). School-age child care: Concerns and challenges. *Young Children, 42(1),* 3–10.

Ashton-Warner, S. (1964). *Teacher.* New York: Bantam.

Barbour, N. H., & Seefeldt, C. (1993). *Developmental continuity across preschool and primary grades.* Wheaton, MD: ACEI.

Bredekamp, S. (ed.). (1987). *Developmentally appropriate practice in early childhood programs serving children from birth through age 8.* Washington, DC: NAEYC.

Casey, M. B., & Lippman, M. (1991, May). Learning to plan through play. *Young Children, 46(4),* 52–58.

Clemens, S. G. (1983). *The sun's not broken, a cloud's just in the way.* Mt. Rainier, MD: Gryphon House.

Gareau, M., & Kennedy, C. (1991, May). Structure time and space to promote pursuit of learning in the primary grades. *Young Children, 46(4)*, 46–51.

Greenman, J. (1988). *Caring spaces, learning places: Children's environments that work.* Redmond, WA: Exchange Press.

Hohmann, C., & Buckleleitner, W. (1992). *K-3 learning environment.* Ypsilanti, MI: High Scope Press.

Kostelnik, M., Soderman, A., & Whiren, A. (1993). *Developmentally appropriate programs in early childhood education.* New York: Macmillan.

Myers, B. K., & Maurer, K. (1987, July). Teaching with less talking. *Young Children, 41(5)*, 20–27.

National Association of Elementary School Principals. (1990). *Early childhood education and the elementary school principal: Standards for quality programs for young children.* Alexandria, VA: Author.

SECTION THREE

Guest Editorial by Caroline Pratt

But all the people in the world were children once, and for the origin of most good or bad ways of doing things we must go back to childhood—for the origins of social reactions, back to birth. One can almost predict, from the impact of a baby's first cry, whether his social relations are to be happy ones. How his mother receives his first vocal demand is a reasonably clear omen of his future. If he is unwanted, or wanted for the wrong reasons, he is already off to a bad start, and his way will be a hard one.

If his mother loves him, if she offers him the simple respect which one human being owes to another human being however small and helpless, he is a lucky child. For him the world will have a friendly face, because the one on whom he first depended has tried to understand him. A good mother need not be gifted, or beautiful, or even very clever; she is a good mother if she offers her child understanding.

But no child has gone far who has merely come to terms with his mother; there are many other relationships with which he must deal, and the good mother helps him by setting him gradually free among his equals. Unlike his mother, these small strangers are utterly uninterested in finding out what he wants; they care only about what they want, and how to get it. He learns to defend himself, to fight if necessary, but chiefly he learns how to get along with his contemporaries. This first step in his emancipation from the home is enormously important in the pre-school years. If he already has healthy relationships at home, and is allowed to make his way with his own kind outside the home, he is well on his way to becoming a happy citizen of the community.

Now comes school—and this happy little citizen, this naturally gregarious little individual, finds himself in a strange world where an entirely different kind of behavior is expected of him. He cannot make friends with his teacher, who has thirty or forty other children to look after.... He dare not pass the time of day with his neighbor; now suddenly this is bad behavior, and he will be punished. If he is not willing to be cowed, if he shows a spirit of curiosity or playfulness, he is "anti-social." Mere friendliness is a disturbance. Whatever else he may learn in a formal school, he will not learn to live with others, for the system enjoins him strictly to go his own way and mind his own business.

Fortunately he spends only six hours of his day in this curious confinement. There are still daylight hours when, if he is lucky, he can play with other children in the park or his backyard, or even in the street. But he is only comparatively lucky. Though he is free to play, there is no one to help him and his friends to get the most out of their play together, to show them ways of planning together for the good of the whole group, of settling disagreements, of understanding each other. All too often the bloody-nose method becomes the only way to end an argument.

I don't think I overstate the failure of the traditional schools in ignoring this part of a child's learning. Some of them are beginning to realize this responsibility, and to make tentative efforts toward a "socialized curriculum." With standardized systems and, above all, classes and schools that are always too large, it is uphill work.

Life in school is only another setting for life anywhere. If we were preparing our children to live under an autocratic regime I could understand the need for iron discipline, for suppression of playfulness and friendliness, of adventure or individualism wherever it raises its head. But we are preparing our children to be responsible citizens in a democracy, perhaps some day in a democratic world. Why then the screwed-down benches, the interdiction on speech, the marching through the halls in silent single-file, the injunction on the teacher to behave like a classroom Hitler (Pratt, 1940, pp. 165–167)?

Developmentally Appropriate Social/ Emotional Environments

INTRODUCTION

In this section we will examine the nature of the social and emotional environments that nurture development in most appropriate ways. The discussion of social/emotional environments will include: practices and interaction that encourage healthy emotional growth and relationships; appropriate guidance to move children toward self-esteem and self-control; adult behaviors that encourage development of prosocial awareness and socialization skills; and classroom planning considerations for teachers who want to encourage cooperation and group participation skills.

When speaking of the social/emotional environments for children, we are talking about the people and relationships made available in the environment. Who the adults are and how they respond to the children they care for is the determining quality of the social/emotional environment.

This section is also divided into four chapters focusing on social/emotional environments for infants, toddlers, preschoolers, and primary-aged children. It will be noted that certain aspects of the social/emotional domain are tasks distinct to each of these periods of development (for example, toddler biting in Chapter 8), while others are continuous, begun in one stage, and continuing on into the next, such as helping children with emotional development. Some topics, such as an anti-bias respect for diversity, discipline, and mixed-age groupings, are relevant to several stages, though they will only be discussed at length in one of the chapters(anti-bias and discipline in Chapter 9, mixed-age groupings in Chapter 10).

Developmentally Appropriate Social/Emotional Environments:
For Infants

*B*abies are born with a predisposition to notice, interact with, and attract the attention of the people around them. Even in the first hours of life, babies react to their social world, gazing into eyes and seriously staring at faces, responding to verbal sounds, and molding their bodies to fit into arms waiting to hold them. And this is important, because babies are totally dependent on others to provide the necessities for physical survival and to nurture development of all domains. From newborns who vary between states of peaceful calm and passionate generalized upset, the first year of life finds babies developing particular specific emotions. In addition, infants become adept at communicating with those about them, entering into a world of social relationships. A crucial developmental task of infancy is to form an attachment with one, or more likely several, key persons in the environment in which each baby lives. Indeed, it is nearly impossible to overemphasize the importance of becoming attached during the first months of life to healthy development in infancy, and to optimum development in later periods.

Every infant will have a unique environment, depending on circumstances of family structure and roles played by the adults, cultural and community custom, and care supplemental to the family. Those who respond to the baby's needs may be related by birth or profession. But whoever the adults are who share the care of the infant, certain behaviors and characteristics will contribute to healthy social and emotional environments for babies.

OBJECTIVES

Upon completion of this chapter, students should be able to:

- discuss several social/emotional issues of infancy.
- describe characteristics of developmentally appropriate interaction.
- discuss positive implications for caregivers.
- list practices to avoid.

Social/Emotional Issues in Infancy

It is important to first consider the issues raised by various theorists and the social/emotional tasks of infancy as a base for the following, more detailed discussion about adult behaviors.

Attachment

There have long been debates about how babies become attached to their mothers. ("Mothers" is used to indicate primary caregivers, noting that today babies are increasingly cared for by other important adults to whom strong attachments are formed, including fathers, child caregivers, and other surrogates.) When Harlow discovered that his baby monkeys clung to the terry cloth "mother," even when the wire "mother" held the feeding bottle, it seemed to indicate that feeding or satisfaction of physical needs alone was not the source of attachment (Harlow, 1958). The later work of Bowlby and Ainsworth focused on specifics of styles of parenting and quality of parent-child relationship as most important in promoting secure and mutual attachments, and everything that such attachments mean in terms of security, personality, future relationships, and approach to life. Specifically, it seemed that secure attachments were the result of mothers who responded with sensitivity to what their babies communicated that they needed, and were warmly and physically responsive to their babies' signals for socialization. Mothers of anxiously attached infants had been observed to be inconsistent, unresponsive, or rejecting. (Bowlby, 1988; Ainsworth et al., 1978.) A good discussion of the influence of both Bowlby and Ainsworth on current attachment theory is found in Karen (1990). Studies also indicate the importance of recognizing differing temperaments in children (and in parents), and the influence on attachment (Chess and Thomas, 1977 and 1982). Later studies have found that there are correlations between preschoolers' approaches to problem-solving situations, peers, curiosity, persistence, and self-reliance, and the earlier formation of a secure attachment between parent and child. Given the strong evidence that attachment is so globally important to optimum development, there are implications from attachment theory as we begin to consider developmentally appropriate social/emotional environments for infants.

Trust

As Erik Erikson described the stages of psychosocial development, he placed emphasis on the first, the stage of infancy, where the infant had the potential of forming a basic sense of trust or a sense of mistrust, as a result of the way the infant's social environment (caregivers) responded to communication of needs. When needs are met consistently, with appropriate messages of caring, babies come to feel that the world is a good place to be, and by extension, the people in it are good, interesting, and caring. With less fortunate experiences, babies may find the world less friendly and people less helpful and available; such an attitude will truly shadow and influence later relationships with others (Erikson, 1963).

There is an obvious connection between the development of the primary attachments and the baby's capacity to trust. As there is a loving relationship with adults who respond warmly and positively to the baby as he or she communicates need, the baby learns to see these people as dependable, trustworthy. It is the responses of others that allow the baby to first learn trust.

Separation and Stranger Anxiety

Sometime in the latter months of the first year, infant behavior indicates that milestones in the attachment process have been reached. After even a few months, the baby indicates a clear recognition and preference for the mother or primary caregiver, saving the biggest smiles, most emphatic gurgling sounds, and most insistent attempts to attract attention for that special person. At around eight months or so, babies begin to protest desperately when mother leaves for even a brief absence. This first separation anxiety gives indication that true attachment has occurred, and the baby feels anxiety about losing mother's presence. At about the same time, many babies become very wary of people who are not familiar to them. Often misinterpreted by adults as the baby suddenly becoming "shy," stranger anxiety is another positive indication that the baby absolutely recognizes the special, trustworthy people in the social environment. Mahler refers to the process of separation individuation, as children emerge from a symbiotic relationship with their mothers (Mahler, 1979). Both of these social responses need to be recognized and accepted as part of the attachment process, and babies need to be supported as they slowly learn to trust that loved ones will reliably return and that new faces can also be accepted.

There are obvious practical implications for timing of separation and/or new experiences with caregivers, if parents have the luxury of choice. Entry into a child care situation either before or after the acute period of separation anxiety might help both baby and parent avoid some of that early pain. Maintaining staff stability in caregivers in infant rooms seems critical in helping babies develop comfort with familiar faces.

Emotional Responsiveness

The fear of strangers and anxiety when out of the comforting presence of a loved adult are examples of the developing emotional repertoire of infancy. Very young infants have vaguely defined emotional responses, seeming to feel either relatively calm or in an uproar. By the end of infancy, however, it is possible to differentiate the various feelings of fear, anger, frustration, pleasure, love, pride, or jealousy. Cognitive capacities of memory and increased understanding have a role in this differentiation. The critical factor in the appearance of emotion seems to be the first experience of love. Babies who have been unable to be involved in that close, secure attachment seem to remain emotionally flat, indifferent to what goes on in their lives (Fraiberg, 1973). It is important that babies be cared for by adults who can recognize that infant feelings are real and strong. Appropriate adult responses include respecting the feeling, neither teasing nor distracting the child away from the feeling, and helpful support in dealing with the cause of the feeling.

Spoiling

While no theorist has formally dealt with the topic of "spoiling" babies, every parent and caregiver has opinions on the subject, thus making it a social/emotional issue of infancy. In fact, before you read any further, find a sheet of paper and write down a brief response to these questions: Do you believe babies under the age of six or seven months can be spoiled? What is your evidence for your belief? Why do you believe this? Keep this response handy to refer to at later points in the chapters on infants.

What most adults mean by spoiling is teaching babies to believe that they can get what they want by crying or other methods of voicing demands. Such teaching, so goes the argument, is done when adults pick up babies when they cry.

Behavioral theory asserts that this practice reinforces the crying, thus producing a child who has learned to cry to get what is wanted (Skinner, 1938).

Actually, the attachment studies seem to refute this notion, as do studies that find that babies who have been responded to promptly during the first six months of infancy actually cry less and are more self-sufficient in later infancy (Ainsworth, 1982).

// Some people worry that if we make life too easy for babies they will be spoiled. A secure start, being given to, having needs met quickly and sensitively nourishes a much later capacity in the child to give, to wait, to share. In other words, it ensures against what is commonly termed "the spoiled child" (Stonehouse, 1982, p. 41). *//*

Nevertheless, popular thinking about spoiling, rather than developmental research, influences the practice and interaction of many parents and infant caregivers, who have strong feelings about the way "babies are *supposed* to be taken care of" (Gonalez-Mena, 1992, p. 4). Our consideration will recognize these strong feelings, while focusing on the critical need for responding to babies' signals.

Child Care for Infants

Figure 7-1 Many infants today spend hours being cared for by others in group care. *Courtesy Methodist Home Child Development Center.*

Today, fully one-third of women who give birth have returned to work by the time the baby is two-months-old, and about half are back to work by the baby's first birthday. Thus, it is obvious that many families have had to include caregivers outside the family in the baby's social/emotional environment.

While many families have always had others to supplement parenting efforts, the numbers of babies cared for full-time by nonfamily members today raises questions about the effects of this on attachment and relationships. (See Figure 7-1.)

There is certainly no clear agreement among researchers about whether infant child care is harmful or not. Jay Belsky was one of the first researchers who pointed to a finding that there are increased numbers of insecurely attached infants among children who are enrolled in child care during the first year of life for more than 20 hours each week (Belsky, 1988). While other researchers raised questions about how quality of care and family characteristics might influence such negative conclusions (Phillips, 1987; Clarke-Stewart, 1989; Hoffman, 1989), the controversy continues. (For a good overview of the opinions of many recognized child developmental specialists, see Chapter 3 in Greenberg, 1991.) This is clearly an issue that will continue to be researched and discussed in the light of developmentally appropriate practices for social/emotional health of infants (Honig, 1993). The one fact that seems obvious is that the quality of interaction either at home or in a child care center is of great importance.

Developmentally Appropriate Interaction Practices

Developmentally appropriate interaction behaviors match what is known about the issues of social and emotional development just discussed. Warm responsive attention from adults is necessary for babies to form the first important relationships from which so much comes. It is necessary to consider the various components of warm responsiveness that lead to the development of trust, attachment, and emotional responsiveness in infants.

Warm responsiveness comes with respect, sensitive responses, close physical contact, repetition and consistency in patterns of caregiving, and recognition of infant limitations in social relationships.

Respect

Caregivers must respect infants' needs as real and important. Babies are treated with an appropriate degree of seriousness. Despite their inability to talk and their real dependence on adults, babies are not simply helpless dolls, ready to have things done to them at the whim of adults. Once this respect is present, adults will try harder to discover what infants are trying to convey.

A lack of respect is shown when Candace shrugs to her co-worker, "I just changed her, and her bottle's not due for more than an hour so she's crying for no reason at all." A more respectful approach occurs when Robin comments, "Well, she's dry and fed, so that can't be it, so I'll have to figure out what else she's trying to tell me."

Respect is the key word in Magda Gerber's philosophy (Read more about this in Gerber, 1991). Respect implies that infants are not treated as passive recipients of whatever adults decide to do for them, but can actively participate and communicate in a care partnership. (See also Stern, 1986; for further discussion on adult-infant partnerships of mutuality.)

Implication for Caregiving

Babies need an active voice in decisions about their lives. This means:

- Following babies' self-demand schedules for feeding, sleeping, playing. The attitude of respect does not assume that adults know what is best for babies, and attempt to make them conform to the adults' timetables. Each of the babies is cared for as physical and social needs are interpreted, without any preconceived adult ideas about what the appropriate timing should be. Needs and decisions of individual families are also respected. Example:

   Jill is ready for her bottle about 9 a.m. Ebonee has been sleeping for an hour, and will likely sleep until about 10 a.m. Jasmine finished her nap about 8:30, and is on the floor playing with foam blocks. Their caregiver respects their varying needs, and responds accordingly.

- Assuming that crying babies have real needs, so responding promptly with some effort to let babies know their message is heard. Responding does not necessarily always mean, as some misinterpret, to pick the baby up, but may mean speaking, making eye contact, changing the baby's position or viewpoint, or offering a new activity. Responding means letting the infant know that the message has been received. Example:

   Michelle talks softly as she begins to warm Andrea's bottle, "I hear you, I know you're hungry. It will take just a minute." Andrea quiets as she hears the gentle voice.

Figure 7-2 Infants need the support of familiar caregivers as they encounter new situations. *Courtesy Methodist Home Child Development Center.*

- Allowing babies to take the lead and trying to interpret their communication. Respectful adults assume that babies *will* have their own nonverbal methods of communicating. Example:

  "I think you want to get moved over by the window. I see you watching the curtains move."

- Waiting to see if infants can solve a problem, soothe themselves, find something interesting to do, before adults step in. This is known as practicing "selective intervention" (Gerber, 1991). There are times to help and times not to, and only waiting to give the baby the first chance will help adults decide which time this is. Example:

  Charlotte watches Alexandro, whining softly, crawl around the floor toward the musical ball. She continues to watch as he stops whining and sits to grab at the ball. Problem solved—and by Alexandro.

- Giving babies cues and watching for their readiness to respond before proceeding with care. Respectful interaction assumes that babies will be active participants in the routines that involve them; adults talk and explain coming events as if babies could comprehend. Example:

  Stephan is dressing Myra and tells her it's time to put her shirt on. He waits patiently for Myra to stretch out her arm.

- Respecting infant preferences for certain people and obvious discomfort in contact with others. Particularly when babies have reached the landmark of stranger anxiety, caregivers allow infants to withdraw from those people they object to. They support babies positively as they encounter new situations and allow them to set the pace in becoming accustomed to new people and places. (See Figure 7-2.) Example:

  Charlotte holds Alexandro and allows him to bury his face in her shoulder when a visitor comes too close. She explains, "No, he's not shy, he just doesn't know you yet. If you sit over there and let him get used to you, he'll probably get comfortable soon. Let him come to you, instead of you going to him."

- Treating infants' emotions seriously, as they begin to demonstrate specific feelings. Adults support the child to find methods of coping, and acknowledge feelings. Example:

  "You're pretty unhappy this morning aren't you? There you go—good idea. I think your blankie will help you feel better."

Caregivers should not:

- ignore babies' crying, responses, or initiatives

- interrupt their play without words when adults want to do routine caregiving tasks

- force the attention of strangers on unwilling babies

- dismiss the feeling, distracting the baby from the feeling, or ignoring the feeling

Sensitivity of Responsiveness

Relationships grow as individuals learn to interpret the messages from the other. Even very young babies have their own temperamental style and tempo, their moods and feelings. Attachment is a two-way mutual process between adult and infant. Each partner must learn to attend to the individual signals and style of the other. Such discriminating sensitivity is linked to secure or insecure attachments.

> Ainsworth showed that mothers of babies who later are avoidant hold their babies as much as mothers of babies who later are secure. So if you just measure frequency of holding you get no difference. But there's one circumstance in which mothers of babies who are later avoidant do not hold them, and that's when the baby signals that it wants to be held (Karen, 1990).

As adults learn to read the messages from individual babies, they are able to modify their behaviors to match the real differences in need and temperament.

Juan, a slow-to-warm-up infant, may need an adult who stays close by, silently indicating her warm interest in his exploration; the same caregiver responds with loud, delighted laughter when Demetria, an extremely active baby, takes the initiative in patty-cake.

Implications for Caregivers

Sensitive responsiveness comes when adults:

- Take time to observe and tune into individual real differences and tolerances for sound, change, and activity, and do not simply respond to their own concept of what the baby might like or be like. Example:

   "It's been interesting what I've learned in the three months since the twins were born," says Allison. "Sam fits right in with what I expected my baby to be like—sociable, easy to please, ready to cuddle. But Will—he's another story. He can't stand loud noises, and gets downright irritable when anybody talks to him too loudly. I've really had to learn when he wants to play and when he just wants to be left alone."

Figure 7-3 Caregivers provide for infants' learning about reciprocal interaction by observing their responses, and pacing accordingly. *Courtesy Avondale Children's Center.*

- Learn from others in babies' lives about infant style and experiences. Communication between parents and caregivers is important to enhance overall awareness of individual infants' personalities.

   The twins' mother, who has cared for her babies for the past three months, has already learned much about the babies that the caregiver in the infant room can tap into.

- Realize that responsiveness implies reciprocal interaction. Caregivers have to practice turn-taking behavior, taking time in play and caregiving interaction to pause and allow the baby to participate and respond. A pause will also allow a sensitive caregiver to learn how the baby is reacting, and to pace or adapt accordingly. (See Figure 7-3.) Example:

   Belinda places the rings in front of the baby's hands and waits to see if the baby wants to reach out for them. She does not just shake the rings to entertain the baby or just put them into the baby's hand. Her turn is to offer the toy; the baby's turn is to decide what to do with the toy.

Caregivers should not:

- impose adult ideas of play and interaction on babies

- frighten babies with a style that does not match theirs

- overwhelm babies by not giving them opportunities to "take turns" in interaction

- neglect to form supportive and informative partnerships with parents

Close Physical Contact

Figure 7-4 Caregivers who can freely supply warm, physical intimacy are needed for healthy attachment. *Courtesy NationsBank Child Care Center.*

Touching, fondling, and skin contact are all necessary for attachment to take place. Alice Honig once expressed it as the infant "having absolute dominion over an adult's body," meaning being able to be in physical contact on demand. (She also said this means that a ratio of four infants to one adult is the maximum, with two arms and two legs able to supply that holding closeness!) The holding, nuzzling, and belly kisses that are a part of warm caregiving interaction are as crucial as the physical elements of food and sleep to healthy growth. Another important component of close physical contact is the eye-to-eye gaze that connects adult and baby, with a face filled with delight focused on the baby. Adults who care for babies must be able to be freely demonstrative of physical tenderness. (See Figure 7-4.)

Babies are born with attributes that promote this physical closeness the helpless cry designed to attract attention; the softness of their skin, and the way they grasp onto the fingers of the person holding them; the way they look right back into eyes, and of course, those first wide toothless grins of social delight. Selma Fraiberg wrote that babies have the rudiments of a love language: "There is the language of the smile, the language of vocal sound-making, the language of the embrace. It's the essential vocabulary of love before we can yet speak of love" (Fraiberg, 1973, p. 2). There are some babies who are less responsive temperamentally, and with them caregivers have to reach out to promote attachment, knowing how critical it is to find ways to reach babies who seem to be passive or indifferent to physical contact.

Implications for Caregivers

Opportunities for close physical contact are a crucial part of good practices for infants. Such opportunities are found by:

- Employing only adults who can be freely physically demonstrative with babies, and who can reach out to those babies who do not participate as actively as others in responsive physical contact. Example:

  The director at Alice's center observed her interaction with the babies for a morning before she was convinced that Alice was the right person for the position. Alice obviously was comfortable holding, touching, and nuzzling babies with genuine pleasure. Alice noticed right away that Jeremy squirmed when she held him closely, so she put him in an infant seat beside her, and continued to talk gently with him, looking into his eyes.

- Allowing time, space, and opportunity for relaxed caregiving interaction, as described in Chapter 3. Example:

  The director recently included a comfortable couch as part of the infant room furnishings. She schedules a part-time caregiver to work for several hours in the late mornings, so that the two full-time staff members do not have to rush hurriedly through routines with the babies.

- Including warm physical interaction in every encounter. Routines are seen not just as tasks to be completed, but opportunities for physical closeness. With this philosophy, babies are always held closely as they are fed, stroked as they are bathed and changed. Example:

  When Lee feeds Sandra in the infant room, he holds her closely, uses his free hand to stroke her face and forearm gently, looks directly into her eyes as she stares at him, and smiles. He murmurs quietly to her, and generally appears to be completely enjoying this close time with her. Example:

Caregivers should not:

- leave babies for long periods without adult attention or contact
- Accomplish routines quickly without interaction or involvement of the infant
- treat babies with cold indifference or impersonal, brusque handling

Repetition and Consistency

No one has yet told us how many hundreds or thousands of contacts between adult and infant are needed before attachment takes place. The stages of attachment indicate that it takes much of the first year spent in intimate, repeated, mutually satisfying experiences before attachment is evident. Studies of prolonged separation and disrupted relationship during this period show that attachments become anxious and difficult. But even without the drastic disruption of a mother's prolonged hospitalization or a series of different caregiving arrangements, there can be patterns of inconsistent responses. Imagine the dilemma of the mother who is torn between conflicting advice about spoiling from her mother and her doctor, or one who is exhausted by the demands of returning to full-time work outside the home and the care of other children, and just feels she must get the baby to fit the family schedule. In both of these cases, parents may not respond consistently to babies each time they make their needs known.

Implications for Caregivers

Practices that allow babies to develop a sense of predictability in their care are critical. Consistency is helped by:

- Communication between all adults involved in a baby's care, in order to coordinate responses as much as possible. Example:

  Both Alice and the twins' parents regularly write notes to one another in the log book on top of the twins' cubbies. This afternoon Alice wrote that she noticed Will had been quite relaxed today, and had not resisted being rocked before sleeping. His mother decided she would try rocking that night also.

- Education of parents and caregivers about infant development, needs, and the importance of attachment practices, to dispel myths about babies learning to manipulate others, and "spoiling." Using information to help adults become less fearful to respond to babies is one way to ensure predictable responses. Example:

  When the twins' mother worried out loud regarding her mother's advice about too much attention for the babies, Alice reassured her with some information about attachment formation.

- Employment of only those who are committed to being stable figures in infants' lives in child care settings. The smallest possible adult-child ratios and establishment of practices such as primary caregiving (see Chapter 3) all support consistency. Example:

  In the infant room, Alice cares for Sam, Will, Julio, and MeiMei. Her co-worker is the primary caregiver for Alexandro, Sandra, Vincent, and Demetria.

- Support of business, government, and community initiatives to assist families in the first months of babies' lives, thus promoting opportunities for families to provide the majority of caregiving contact, and to eliminate some of the stresses that interfere with the ability to respond to babies. Example:

  Three of the local businesses have begun to offer part-time employment to mothers returning from maternity leave. This means that the twins' mother is able to pick them up in early afternoon most days.

Caregivers should not:

- ignore babies' signals, to teach them to behave or schedule themselves as adults wish

- respond unpredictably

- behave "as if children are a bother" (NAEYC, 1989, p. 9).

Recognition of Limitations

Delightful and engaging as infants are in their first social relationships, it is important that the adults who care for them recognize their limitations socially and emotionally. These limitations are actually part of the developmental status of cognitive abilities and language. Caught up in the circle of attachment relationships, babies do not yet have a clear sense of themselves as individuals, or even of the concept that there is a clear delineation between themselves and others. The idea of others having needs, feelings, or rights is developmentally far beyond them. Babies are beginning to understand communication and language, but they are not yet controlled by language. In fact, the beginnings of control over feelings or behavior are still far from infants' abilities.

A caregiver who didn't recognize babies' limitations reacted with anger when Randy pulled Samantha's hair after he crawled over to where she was playing on the floor. SunLi, who realized this was the innocent exploration of a curious baby, patted both Randy's and Samantha's heads gently, saying "Gently, gently, Randy." Then she took Randy's own hand to help him pat gently.

Implications for Caregivers

These limitations on understanding and control of behavior point to some clear implications for guidance and discipline. Adults are most helpful to babies in first social/emotional situations when they:

- Accept that infants do not intentionally hurt other babies, and have no sense of property rights. They will help babies learn to touch others gently, and provide plenty of space and toys for each child. They recognize that preventing problems is more appropriate than trying to teach different behaviors. (See Figure 7-5.) Example:

  "Gently, Will, gently," says Alice, as she pats Will's head gently, and his brother's too. "Here, I think it is better if you play over here a bit," moving him away for more free floor space, and away from his brother's head.

Figure 7-5 Caregivers recognize that infants cannot control their own behavior, so keep a watchful eye on a situation like this when infants get close to each other. *Courtesy Methodist Home Child Development Center.*

- Expect that babies can't control their behavior by verbal direction, so rely on distraction, redirection, and removal of temptation to change the situation, rather than trying to change infant behavior directly. It is the adult's responsibility to provide the control; expecting babies to stop themselves is very inappropriate developmentally. Example:

  "Here, Will, I think you might like this rattle to shake," as she quickly removes Will from the hair he seems drawn to pull.

- Avoid frustration for babies as much as possible, by planning to shorten waiting times and restrictions. Recognizing that babies cannot wait and cannot control their emotional outbursts when frustrated is important. Example:

  When Alice hears the kitchen cart coming down the hall, she tells Andrea it's time for lunch now, and gets her bib ready. She has learned that if she puts the bib on before the lunch is imminent, Andrea quickly loses patience with waiting.

- Recognize that the basis for later teaching about others' needs and rights is laid in infancy, as babies are treated with tender respect. This is the true beginning of discipline, though not the kinds of discipline that most adults associate with the term.

  Caregivers should not

- expect more social/emotional control of infants than they are capable of
- punish or scold babies for assumed "naughtiness."

SUMMARY

Developmentally appropriate social/emotional environments for infants offer:

- adults who engage in warm, reciprocal interaction, tuning into individual infants' temperaments
- opportunities for one-to-one communication and play, along with lots of physical cuddling with primary caregivers

- consistent, prompt attention when babies indicate needs
- recognition that babies need adult help in distraction and redirection in situations of conflict or frustration
- child care practices in staffing, etc., that support these essential social encounters and emotional predictability

BUT WHAT ABOUT?

But what about the parents who seem horrified when I show them our discipline philosophy in the infant room, as we are required to do? One of my mothers said, "But aren't they much too young for discipline?"

Here the problem is probably based on semantics, on different understandings of the word "discipline." The center has no doubt formulated its philosophy to help parents understand their view on guidance suited to infant development. The parent is likely interpreting discipline to mean punishment, perhaps even physical punishment; the word "guidance" may help parents understand the difference.

A developmentally appropriate philosophy in the infant room stresses a demonstration of respect for infant needs and abilities. There is an understanding that babies need to have their needs respected and responded to in an atmosphere of sincere caring before they will come to be able to recognize and respect needs of others later in childhood. The atmosphere of loving care lays the base for good feelings about the world and the people in it, and eventually about self. A positive self-concept will help children want to behave in positive ways, and to please those who care for them.

It is recognized that babies will not be able to see dangers or problems in their behavior, and will need an adult to help direct their attention to positive actions. They will not be guided effectively by words alone, but by the actions of patient adults, who remove them from certain situations and direct their attention elsewhere. Recognizing their limitations, caregivers will keep the atmosphere as positive as possible, preventing stressful situations such as overcrowding or waiting.

When this view of discipline is explained to parents as a preliminary to the later teaching when children are able to understand, parents may begin to broaden their definitions of "discipline" from a narrower, more negative focus. Guidance toward self-control is a long and gradual process extending throughout childhood, and positive social interaction in infancy lays a solid foundation.

Floortime encourages adults to spend time one-on-one with babies and young children, physically at their level, observing the individual child, to tune in to her emotional cues, and respond in supportive ways. As adults share the child's emotion, they establish a sense of engagement that empowers the child with comfort and confidence, as she perceives the adult's supportive response. Good infant caregivers learn and practice the skills of "Floortime" to convey sensitive responsiveness.

THINK ABOUT IT

1. Discuss with several of your classmates your statement about "spoiling." How would your opinions affect practices appropriate for infant social/emotional development?

2. Watch an infant with his or her primary caregiver, at home or at a center. What signs of attachment do you see? What interaction and communication do you see that suggests developmentally appropriate practice to you?

3. With a small group, devise an educational plan to introduce a group of new parents who are considering child care options to important ideas of what to look for in developmentally appropriate social/emotional environments for infants.

QUESTIONS TO REVIEW OBJECTIVES

1. What are several of the social/emotional issues of infancy? Discuss each of them briefly, including ideas about how each issue affects decisions about practices that are developmentally appropriate.

2. Identify five characteristics of appropriate adult interaction with infants.

3. Discuss as many as you can recall of the practical, concrete things adults do and say that are part of appropriate interaction.

4. List several of the practices discussed in this chapter that are inappropriate to nurture healthy social/emotional development for infants.

REFERENCES AND SUGGESTIONS FOR READING

Ainsworth, M. D., et al. (1978). *Patterns of attachment.* Hillsdale, NJ: Lawrence Erlbaum.

Ainsworth, M. D., et al. (1982). Attachment: Retrospect and prospect. In Parkes, C. M., & Stevenson-Hinde, J. (Eds.), *The place of attachment in human behavior.* New York: Basic Books.

Belsky, J. Infant day care and socioemotional development: The United States. *Journal of Child Psychology and Psychiatry. 29(4),* 397–406.

Bowlby, J. (1988). *A secure base: Parent-child attachment and healthy human development.* New York: Basic Books.

Brazelton, T. B. (1981). *On becoming a family: The growth of attachment.* New York: Dell Publishing .

Chess, S., & Thomas, A. (1977). Temperamental individuality from childhood to adolescence. *Journal of Child Psychology and Psychiatry, 16,* 218–226.

Chess, S., & Thomas, A. (1982). Infant bonding: Mystique and reality. *American Journal of Orthopsychiatry, 52,* 213–221.

Clarke-Stewart, K. A. (1989). Infant daycare: Maligned or malignant? Special issue: Children and their development: Knowledge base, research agenda, and social policy application. *American Psychology, 44(2),* 266–273.

Erikson, E. (1963). *Childhood and society.* New York: Norton.

Fraiberg, S. (1973). How a baby learns to love. *Readings in Human Development,* 73–74.

Gerber, M. (eds.). (1991). *Resources For infant educarers.* Los Angeles: RIE.

Gonzalez-Mena, J. (1992, January). Taking a culturally sensitive approach in infant-toddler programs. *Young Children, 47(2),* 4–9.

Greenberg, P. (1991). *Character development: Encouraging self-esteem and self-discipline in infants, toddlers, and two-year-olds.* Washington, DC: NAEYC.

Harlow, H. (1958). The nature of love. *American Psychologist, 13,* 673–685.

Hoffman, L. (1989). Effects of maternal employment in the two-parent family: A review of the research. *American Psychology, 44(2),* 283–292.

Honig, A. S. (1983, January). Meeting the needs of infants. *Dimensions,* 4–7.

Honig, A. S. (1993, March). Mental health for babies: What do theory and research teach us? *Young Children, 48(3),* 69–76.

Karen, R. (1990, February). Becoming attached. *The Atlantic Monthly,* 35–70.

Mahler, M. (1979). *Separation-individuation* (vol. 2). London: Jason Aronson.

NAEYC. (1989). *Developmentally appropriate practice in early childhood programs serving infants.* Washington, DC: Author.

Phillips, D. (1987, November). Infants and child care: The new controversy. *Child Care Information Exchange,* 19–22.

Pratt, C. (1940). *I learn from children.* New York: Harper Collins Publishers, Inc, 165–167.

Skinner, B. F. (1938). *The behavior of organisms: An experimental analysis.* New York: Appleton-Century-Crofts.

Stern, D. (1986, October 21). Mother and child crucial interaction. *New York Times Magazine.*

Stonehouse, A. W. (1982). Discipline. In Lurie, R., & Neugebauer, R. (Eds.), *Caring for infants and toddlers: What works, what doesn't* (vol. 2). Redmond, WA: Child Care Information Exchange.

Weissbourd, B., & Musick, J. (eds.). (1991). *Infants: Their social environments.* Washington, DC: NAEYC.

White, B. L. (1981, November). Should you stay home with your baby? *Young Children, 37(1),* 11–17.

CHAPTER

8

Developmentally Appropriate Social/ Emotional Environments:
For Toddlers

A surprising transformation occurs about the end of the first year of life. From a docile, agreeable creature, the infant evolves into an individual with strong opinions about what she or he would like to do, much of which is contrary to what others wish. It seems as if the new power of control that comes with mobility causes the child to see a new independent self, and most of life thereafter is devoted to a new single-minded testing out of this idea. Forming a sense of self dominates much of personality development and social interaction during toddlerhood. But being one's own person is somewhat frightening, so toddlers vacillate between independence and dependence, maturity and immaturity. Adults who care for them are never sure which swing of the pendulum will show itself on any given day. (In dealing with the child about ten years or so later, adults will face similar unpredictability with the later thrust for independence in early adolescence.) Together with a lack of self-control, limited ability to communicate and understand, and only the most rudimentary social skills, happy coexistence with toddlers is a challenge for adults and other children. But the development of a positive sense of self is a critical task of toddlerhood, dependent on a social/emotional environment of appropriate guidance and interaction.

OBJECTIVES

After completing this chapter, students should be able to:

- discuss several social/emotional issues of toddlerhood.
- describe helpful adult behaviors for each of these social/emotional issues.
- discuss appropriate guidance techniques for toddlers.
- identify inappropriate adult responses to toddler social/emotional behavior.

Social/Emotional Issues of Toddlerhood

It should be emphasized at the outset that it is too easy to interpret a discussion of social/emotional issues in toddlerhood as a litany of negatives. Indeed, if we measure toddlers against the development of older children, it sounds as if there is a lot lacking. But having lived only a dozen or so months, toddlers are just emerging from the insulated cocoon of parent-child attachment and discovering what it means to live independently, and with others. Toddlers need to be respected for who they are at this moment, and not compared unfavorably to later phases of development. After a brief discussion of social/emotional issues and developmental tasks, we will return to the practical implications of each issue.

Autonomy

When Erik Erikson (1963) talks about the second stage of psychosocial development, he describes the importance to healthy personality development of forming a sense of autonomy vs. the negative components of shame and doubt. Autonomy means seeing oneself as a separate, capable individual, able to function independently. Autonomy implies a self-confidence, a belief in one's competence. Less positive responses from individuals in the toddler's environment lead the child to conclude that he or she is incapable of functioning independently in ways that adults approve of.

Toddlers seem to have a built-in desire to test out their own abilities, so it is important that the adults who care for them find ways to demonstrate their approval and support of these first steps toward independence. An optimum social/emotional environment supports the development of a positive sense of self.

Negativism and Resistance

One of the ways toddlers prove autonomy is in their resistance and testing directed to the adults around them. Separateness is shown by defining differences from others, and toddlers are quite sure that they must be on the opposite side of the hypothetical fence on every conceivable issue. If it is the idea of another person, it's definitely not a good idea. Toddlers are sometimes so bent on resistance for the sake of resistance that they will loudly proclaim "NO" even when it's an issue they actually approve of, as in "Do you want a cookie?" "NO," with hand outstretched.

It is often quite disconcerting for adults to find such vehement resistance in one so small, to say nothing of in one who so recently gave strong evidence of wholehearted approval of literally everything this same adult did. Resistance touches adult feelings about being in control. If caregivers do not understand the positive developmental purpose that drives the negativism, it is too easy to try to nip it in the bud. Instead, the inevitability and importance of these behaviors must be accepted. Adults who want to nurture positive feelings about self use their skills to avoid head-on confrontations, and find opportunities for toddlers to win some battles.

Separation

Paradoxical as it may sound after a discussion of resistance and negativism, one of the most difficult things for toddlers is separation from the adults who are important to them. Still in the attachment process (that lasts about two years), toddlers feel most secure when their adults are nearby, and protest heartily when they are left behind. Learning that loved adults will return, and that one can cope in their absence, is a crucial task of toddlerhood (Mahler, 1979). How adults help children handle separation is extremely important, and will have implications for future social relationships and emotional well-being.

Egocentric Behavior with Peers

As toddlers focus on testing out concepts of self, interest in other people as people, with their own needs and wants, is not yet an understandable concept. Although there is fleeting interest in others, this interest seems to be no deeper than in other objects in the world around, whose properties can be explored before moving on to something else of interest. The *Toddler's Creed* (Figure 8-1) states succinctly how toddlers view the world—through the perspective of their needs and wants only. Again, it should be noted that no amount of talking, teaching, or scolding can change this toddler perspective. Only after a sense of self is formed can a child begin to care about others; only when objects have been truly possessed is there a possibility for sharing those objects. When there is a group of equally egocentric toddlers, the potential for social/emotional friction is enormous; only alert and creative caregivers can protect the rights of all.

Importance of Social Learning

Burton White makes the statement that "to begin to look at a child's educational development when he is two years of age is already much too late, *particularly in the area of social skills and attitudes*" (White, 1985, p. 108). His list of social abilities developing during toddlerhood include:

- getting and holding the attention of adults
- using adults as resources after first determining that a job is too difficult
- expressing affection to adults
- expressing mild annoyance to adults
- leading peers
- following peers
- expressing affection to peers
- expressing mild annoyance to peers
- competing with peers
- showing pride in personal accomplishment
- engaging in role play or make-believe activities

Toddler's Creed

If I want it, it's mine.
If I give it to you and change my mind later, it's mine.
If I can take it away from you, it's mine.
If I had it a little while ago, it's mine.
If it's mine, it will never belong to anybody else, no matter what.
If we are building something together, all the pieces are mine.
If it looks just like mine, it's mine.

Figure 8-1 A toddler's creed.

The socially complicated toddler, trying to keep in balance his interest in the world around, in his primary caregivers, and in his own independence, is developing abilities that will become habitual patterns of behaving, and developing these through "hundreds of interchanges with the primary caretaker" (White, 1985, p. 152).

Emotional Responsiveness

Toddlers who have been involved in caring relationships with others give evidence of a wide range of feelings, from pleasure, joy, satisfaction, love and affection to anger, frustration, jealousy, and fear. On close inspection this appears to be nearly the spectrum of human emotions, but one or two are conspicuously missing from this list.

Figure 8-2 These toddlers are likely more concerned with the adult's firm words than feeling empathy for the toddler who got hurt. *Courtesy NationsBank Child Care Center.*

Because of the cognitive inability to mentally put themselves in another's place, most toddlers are not yet likely to give evidence of feeling much sympathy, empathy, or compassion for others. Occasionally some particularly sensitive toddlers may show brief appearances of being upset when someone else is upset, though this may come from the unfamiliar tone of the other's voice or expression, more alarming to the toddler than an occasion for empathy. Sometimes adults cite examples of toddlers who try to comfort others who are hurt as evidence of sympathy, but this may be just learned behavior, imitated from adults in similar situations and deferred. For example, a toddler may pat a child who is crying when her doll has been taken away, but then promptly take another toy away from the same child—certainly not seeming to be truly caring about the other's feelings. The toddlers in Figure 8-2 appear distressed by the sound of one of their peers crying, but a closer examination reveals that they are most intrigued in watching the adult's face as she disapproves of the biting. Obviously, emotional responses vary from one child to another, depending largely on how their emotions have been responded to, but the immature cognitive processes of the toddler make it likely that these emotions are not yet strongly present.

One emotion that is not unique to toddlers, but does appear in some unusual ways, is the emotion of fear. Toddlers learn to fear some things by associating something unpleasant, such as the toddler who has learned to fear the doctor's office because of the pain experienced there, or to fear a neighbor's yard because of the large barking dog that appears there suddenly. But some toddler fears appear not to have a connection with real unpleasantness, but rather the illogical assumption the toddler makes that the object threatens his or her person. An example of this is the bathtub drain. Many toddlers who have been quite happy sitting and playing in the bathtub during infancy suddenly scream at the thought of a bath. It seems that the sight of water disappearing down the hole suggests possible danger to the toddler. (Toilets and vacuums present similar frightening possibilities.) Some toddler fears do not seem understandable to adults, but toddler fears are real and need respectful responses.

What toddlers have, then, is most emotions, strong and real. What they do *not* have is control of immediate expression over these feelings and methods to express feelings other than by purely physical means. The result, in its most notorious form, is the classic toddler temper tantrum. A healthy social/emotional environment for toddlers avoids exacerbating negative emotional responses and guides children in these earliest stages, while conveying acceptance of emotionality.

Positive Guidance for Toddlers

Immature and impulsive as they are, there is no question that toddlers need limits. Burton White (1985) defines one of the roles for toddler caregivers as *authority.* Toddlers, so frequently out of control themselves, need the certainty of knowing they can depend on the adults around them for limits. But the issue is, What kind of limits? and How to convey them? Developmentally appropriate guidance takes into account the toddler's limitations on language, understanding, and world view, as well as the all-important developing sense of self.

Developmentally Appropriate Interaction with Toddlers

Having looked at the important social/emotional issues of toddlerhood, it is time to consider developmentally appropriate interaction.

Fostering Autonomy

Adults foster a sense of autonomy when they:

- Provide necessary support for toddlers to complete their self-defined tasks, allowing children to do everything they are capable of, and assisting gently with tasks beyond their abilities. Sometimes this means patiently allowing the longer time needed for the toddler "to do it myself"; other times it means unobtrusively offering a helping hand or a start on the task for toddlers to complete. Example:

  LeToya sat beside Robert, struggling to put on his shoes. She busied herself with folding some laundry, occasionally smiling at him or commenting on his hard work. Across the room, Gary realizes that SooHa is not yet able to put her coat on by herself, so he steps in to help her put her arms in, telling her he'll need her help to zip up.

- Recognize and appreciate children's accomplishments with genuine admiration and specific comments. Examples:

  "You put your dishes back in the tray all by yourself, Randy. Good job."

  "Look at you ready to slide down, Melissa. You climbed up all those steps!"

- Offer real choices in areas of toddler life they can control. Adults will make decisions on big issues related to what needs to be done, allowing toddlers to feel they have some control over *how* it is done. Examples:

  "Lunch time, Sheila. Do you want the blue cup or the red one today?" "Do you want to sing a song after we wash hands or before?" "Bananas for snack today, Sharon. Do you want a whole big one, or two pieces?"

- Encourage independent play of exploration and mastery. As children feel there is much they are allowed to do on their own, autonomy grows. Example:

  Vanessa sets up a fill and dump center for her toddlers with sturdy big boxes and lots of smaller objects they can put in and out. As they push the boxes around, she smiles in approval and comments how hard they work to push the big boxes.

- Help children with concepts of self by using names frequently. Adults also play body awareness games with toddlers ("Where's your neck? Show me your knee"), and use mirrors, photographs, and songs to help toddlers increase their self-identification. Example:

  Michael added a self-identity corner to his toddler room recently. He included a full-length mirror and several small unbreakable hand mirrors for toddlers to use. On the walls are photos of every toddler, along with pictures of family and home. When he gathers the tod-

Figure 8-3 Autonomy grows when caregivers do not overprotect toddlers, and allow them to solve some of their own problems. *Courtesy Methodist Home Child Development Center.*

dlers for singing, he sings each child's name. They don't sing much, but they beam when they hear their name.

- Provide all the freedom toddlers can safely use. Adults who avoid hovering or restricting over-protectively encourage self-confidence. Does the toddler in Figure 8-3 look as if he needs help? He has squirmed inside the narrow hole to try to get the ball, and is getting himself out just fine. An alert caregiver stands by and lets him do his own problem solving and confident learning. Example:

   Annie has arranged the toddler play area so there is literally nothing she has to say "no" to. She asked her director to have the parent volunteers make a sturdy, 6-inch high climbing shelf that she doesn't feel she has to warn the toddlers to be careful on.

- Make available toddler-sized materials, utensils, and equipment that toddlers can use with little or no assistance. Example:

   Tammy's toddlers have smaller chairs than those found in the preschool classroom, so the children can seat themselves without having to climb up awkwardly into them. She asked the kitchen staff to substitute special short handled utensils for the usual forks and spoons. The result has been toddlers who really can confidently look after themselves at mealtime.

- Observe toddlers for signs of readiness for toilet training, and then gently and without pressure introduce toddlers to toilet use. Adults assume that time will be spent in the process, and positively reinforce toddler attempts. Example:

   Maria-Theresa smiles when Robert climbs off the potty chair and proudly displays the results. This was the first day that he told her before the fact.

- Examine their own attitudes to the changing relationship with toddlers. Adults need to be able to respond to the push for autonomy with genuine delight at the emergence of unique personhood, rather than thwart attempts at independence because of their own needs. Sometimes toddlers push on faster than their adults, who need to consciously modify their style of interaction. Toddlers no longer need adults who actively fill all needs, but rather those who stand back to support the new challenges. Example:

   Susan grins and shakes her head, laughing at her toddler son, eager to try to comb his own hair. "It felt so strange at first," she admits. "I kind of liked being the one he always turned to. But I've gotten used to the idea that it's best for him to give him some freedom to move out on his own a bit. He still needs me—just in a different way."

Things to avoid. Shame and doubt are the unfortunate results when adults:

- overprotect toddlers, making them feel inadequate
- expect them to comply with all adult demands, offering them no choice in their daily lives;
- expect too much or too little of toddlers

- do things for toddlers that they could do for themselves, given time, appropriate equipment, and support

- impose toilet training, ready or not, and punish or shame children for toileting accidents

- are clearly impatient with toddler exuberance, movement, learning style, or limitations

Responding to Resistance and Negativism

When resistance and negativism are recognized as methods of striving for autonomy, adults can be more effective in working with these toddler behaviors. Adults find it helps when they:

- Realize that toddlers need control, and decide which are the few important issues regarding health or safety that need absolute adult authority. Example:

  > Rick says," The one "no" I have to stick to is him holding my hand when we walk in the parking lot. He squirms and clearly doesn't like it, but I just can't trust his judgment or control around sudden cars."

- Understand toddler resistance for what it is—another method of testing self—and accept the concept of the child's need to say "no," without feeling threatened about losing control.

  > Another toddler parent: "I used to feel I had to tell him he couldn't tell me 'no.' I was afraid that if I let this slip past, in no time he'd take over the whole show. But I've learned that some of those 'no's' I can ignore, and some I can change by giving him a bit of control. It's not that big a deal—I still know I'm in charge, and he needs to find out he is somebody with a bit of power too."

- Avoid power struggles that produce winners and losers. It is not emotionally healthy for toddlers to discover they have been able to manipulate adults into a losing position; they need to know somebody is in charge. Nor is it possible for a healthy sense of an autonomous self to develop when toddlers always lose.

  > "I'm trying more to find a way to let him save face, so he doesn't feel he has to resist me quite so hard to prove he is somebody."

- Give toddlers choices within absolutes to allow them to avoid resistance. Adults make the big choices, toddlers make the small ones. Example:

  > Nancy knows naptime is inevitable, but says, "A song or a story, Kenyetta—tell me which one you want." Harder for Kenyetta to resist totally when she still retains a measure of control. She'll be so busy deciding that she'll forget to resist the main issue—at least, most of the time!

- Use statements when things need to be done, rather than questions that give the toddler the opportunity to resist. Example:

  > "Let's pick up toys" rather than "Are you ready to clean up now?" "Time to get in our chairs" rather than "Would you like to come to the table?"

Figure 8-4 Toddler decisions about the amount of food they can eat should be respected, to avoid future meal time problems. *Courtesy Methodist Home Child Development Center.*

- Follow predictable patterns for the day and give clues of predictability during transitions with songs, etc. Toddlers are less likely to resist when life follows a secure rhythm. Example:

  "This is the way we pick up our toys," sings Denise, and the toddlers fall comfortably in to help.

- Help toddlers develop rituals for those times of day that often meet resistance. (A word of caution here: Know that toddlers become quite rigid and unchanging, so don't start anything you don't want to repeat several thousand times!) Example:

  If Jason knows that Mommy always gives Bear a kiss on each cheek, then gives Jason the same, then says, "Goodnight snugglebunny," he can "control" her ("Kiss Bear first!") to do this, and forget the resistance.

- Allow toddlers to do as much for themselves as they can. No's decrease when toddlers have already experienced a measure of autonomy. Example:

  "Here Thomas, you can carry the waste basket over to the table for the kids to throw in their trash."

- Accept the fact that toddlers can resist physically if biological matters become matters of adult pressure and toddler resistance. Allow toddlers to indicate decisions about the amounts of food they can handle or readiness for toilet training, and realize that it might be appropriate sometimes to back off and wait. (See Figure 8-4.) Example:

  Carolyn quietly removes Andrew's plate when it becomes obvious he isn't interested in eating any more. She has discovered that pressure from her to eat more only seems to make him more determined not to do so, and she certainly doesn't want to turn mealtime into the kind of battle where she pushed food into his closed mouth or bribes him into eating more with a game of "here comes the train—open wide!"

- Avoid the use of the word "no", as much as possible, saving it for only important occasions where safety is involved. Toddlers are likely to imitate much of the negativism from the adults around them, so adults help when they word requests positively. Example:

  "Climb on the slide, Julia" instead of "No climbing on the chair."

- Keep a sense of humor ("This too shall pass!"), and work around the resistance by involving the toddler in interesting things that distract from the negativism. Example:

  Lisa, responding with a resounding "no" to getting her face washed, laughed and started singing along when her caregiver made a funny face and started singing "NO, I don't want to get my face washed, NO, NO, NO," getting quieter each time she sang NO, all the while helping Lisa move into the bathroom. Adults are bigger and supposedly smarter, so let's use our creativity instead of anger and power.

Things to avoid. All-out warfare that makes toddlerhood very unpleasant for all concerned is increased when adults:

- do not accept toddler's assertions of self, responding either with anger or mockery

- punish children for resistance or saying "no" ("No child of mine is going to say no to me!")
- fear losing power, and involve themselves in power struggles over matters large and small
- make all choices themselves
- lose patience with toddler need for repetition and ritual
- turn mealtimes and bathroom times into times of pressure and conflict for what adults have decided about the amount of food to be eaten or the timing of toilet control

Helping with Separation

It is painful for toddlers and parents to give up what Berry Brazelton once called the love affair of the first year.

With the realization of independence and the ability to "leave" comes an overwhelming feeling of dependence. The trusting sense that the mother is available gives him the necessary capacity to make such a choice for independence. Ambivalence is at the root of this choice, and the experience of it, the mastery of it, are at the base of the child's ability to become a really independent person (Brazelton, 1974, pp. 14–15).

The experience of dealing with separation and increasing independence has lifelong impact. Adults can help toddlers most by:

- Accepting the evidence of fear, sadness, or anger that toddlers may show when experiencing separation. This is a time that toddlers (and their parents) need sensitivity and support. Example:

  Laverne, holding a sobbing Rosalind after her dad has just left, murmurs, "You wish your daddy didn't have to go to work, don't you? It makes you sad to see him go. I'll take care of you till he comes back."

- Allowing time to prepare toddlers for new situations, with simple words, visits, and chances to meet caregivers before the separation. Example:

  Rosalind came by with her parents for two short visits in the toddler classroom before her first day. She got to talk to her teacher, and at home her mom talked about going soon to play in Laverne's room.

- Recognizing that toddlers use their parents as a secure base from which to venture out as they become comfortable. Caregivers help parents understand the necessity (whenever possible) for parents remaining in the room as the toddler explores new people and surroundings. Example:

  After Laverne explained how it would help Rosalind for one of her family to stay with her as she got used to the room, her mom took time off to stay the first day.

- Creating separation policies in centers and classrooms that allow for gradual easing in and becoming familiar in a new situation. It is a good idea to shorten the time toddlers are expected to be separate from parents during the initial adjustment phase.

  Rosalind's dad arranged time from his job to pick her up before lunch every day for the first week.

Figure 8-5 Staying physically close and available may help toddlers deal with separation feelings. *Courtesy NationsBank Child Care Center.*

- Helping parents and toddlers say good-bye to one another, even when crying, and helping toddlers watch their parents leave. Trust slowly comes as toddlers experience both the leaving and the returning. Example:

  "I'll hold her while she says good-bye to you, Mr. Phillips. She'll cry, but we'll handle it. We'll see you after snacktime."

- Greeting toddlers and their parents warmly and helping toddlers get involved with a good deal of attention at the beginning of the day. Example:

  "Hi Rosalind. I'm glad you've come to play today. Look at the big boxes we've got to fill up. Mr. Phillips, it looks like we're all getting used to this morning routine, doesn't it?"

- Staying physically close to toddlers so they can hold or touch adults when they want to, or at least know adults are available to them. (See Figure 8-5.) Adults who move gradually, slowly, and gently convey a nonverbal impression of calm. When they speak, they talk quietly with toddlers, using both tone and words to convey understanding and acceptance of feelings. Example:

  Laverne speaks quietly and stoops to be near Rosalind as she talks. "It's hard, I know," she says. "Daddy will come back."

- Recognizing that mealtimes and naptimes may be particularly difficult for toddlers, and paying extra attention during these periods (Balaban, 1985). Example:

  "Rosalind, I've got a place for you right here beside me."

- Ignoring as many of the behaviors that may accompany the pain of separation as they can. Toddlers may test, withdraw, become aggressive, cling, or revert to earlier behaviors. The more accepting adults can be, the sooner toddlers will trust the environment as caring for them. Example:

  Laverne and Rosalind's parents have decided not to discuss her increased thumb-sucking, assuming it will drop away as she becomes more comfortable.

- Encouraging toddlers to bring favorite toys, blankets or other security objects, or something that belongs to their parents, and not removing these objects from them (Jalongo, 1987). When toddlers feel ready to play, safe cubbies are ready for toddlers to keep their precious bit of home safe. Example:

  Rosalind brings her blankie that she likes to hold most of the day.

- Surrounding toddlers with pictures and taped messages of parents, giving them the chance to talk about them and hear them as often as they need comfort. Example:

  Rosalind frequently walks over to the wall to pat the pictures of her mom and dad.

- Encouraging parents and toddlers to develop plans and rituals for leaving one another (Gestwicki, 1992). Example:

  Every day now, Rosalind's dad comes in to read her one story over in the book corner, then brings her to Laverne to help her say good-bye.

Figure 8-6 When each toddler has her own paint jar and space to work, there is no need to squabble over possessions. *Courtesy Methodist Home Child Development Center.*

Working with Egocentric Behavior with Peers

- Expecting that each toddler will have an individual timetable for developing trust and coming to accept separation.

  It seems to be getting a bit easier for Rosalind now after about four weeks.

Things to avoid. Toddlers' sense of themselves as persons competent to deal with the feelings engendered by separation is not helped when adults:

- show impatience and no understanding of the effort separation involves

- prove untrustworthy at times of separation. Parents sneak out or do not appear after snacktime, as they said they would, or caregivers ignore pain and are not available to help toddlers in parents' absence

- try to stop the tears with shame: "You're too big to cry"; with bribes: "Don't cry and Mommy will take you for ice cream"; or with impatient anger: "Now stop that! I'm tired of all this crying"

- treat the feelings with cold indifference. Toddler feelings are valid, and need recognition and support

When toddlers are cared for in group situations, caregivers spend much of their time safeguarding the rights and safety of each child. Helpful adult interaction includes:

- Recognizing that toddlers first have to be autonomous individuals before they can learn group membership rules, and accepting the role of gently guiding social behavior, in the recognition of toddlers' lack of self control.

- Preventing aggressive interaction by careful preparation of the environment to allow for separate play spaces and sufficient numbers and kinds of materials to avoid possessive squabbles. (See Figure 8-6.)

- Providing materials that toddlers can share easily, which usually means big, stationary things, "too large to be dragged away by one child and large enough so both children can act on the material at the same time" (Lauter-Klatell, 1986, p. 24). Examples would be large boxes with two openings, climbing structures, and stairs.

- Planning for brief cooperative experiences. A mural-sized paper taped to the table allows two toddlers to crayon together without any infringement on the other. (See Figure 8-7.) Example:

  "Sarah, DeJuan needs a friend to help hold the side of the blanket so we can bounce the ball. Oh, isn't this fun?"

- Helping toddlers become aware of each other positively:

  "Rachel, you and Alex are both swinging high, aren't you?"

- Playing with toddlers to model social behaviors of cooperation.

  "I'm going to play with my blocks right here beside you. Would you like some of my blocks?"

- Playing with toddlers, which gives adults the opportunity to model verbal communication of needs. Example:

  "DeJuan, I think Sarah wants to tell you she doesn't want you to take her truck. Sarah, you can tell DeJuan 'no.' Say 'I want it now.'"

Figure 8-7 Everybody can have a piece of the parachute and enjoy it together. *Courtesy Methodist Home Child Development Center.*

- Reinforcing any progress toward prosocial behavior:

    "Good words, Sarah. You told DeJuan 'no.' DeJuan, listen to Sarah please. She's telling you something important."

    "You waited till he was finished, Timmy. I like to see that."

- Redirecting toddlers before frustration levels grow into aggressive outbursts:

    "DeJuan, Sarah is really busy with that truck now. Let's go find you the big dump truck to load until she's finished."

- Pausing before intervening in confrontations between toddlers. This may allow the toddlers experience in settling the matter themselves or allow the adult to see whether the interaction is really aggressive or just incidental exploration. Example:

    Jeannie watched as Antonio bumped into Derrick as they climbed the slide. Derrick pushed him back, but both toddlers proceeded with their activity, apparently not bothered.

- Firmly protecting children and preventing physical aggression. Where necessary, firmly and gently holding a child's hands, feet, or jaws before hurting can occur. Children need a clear message that adults will protect and control:

    "DeJuan, I can't let you hit Sarah. Hitting hurts. No hitting."

- Disapproving with strong and controlled emotion when toddlers have hurt others.

    Say, "No! DeJuan, no biting! Biting hurts!" with a facial expression that matches the firm words, but does not convey a frightening loss of adult control.

- Eliminating references to sharing that are beyond toddler comprehension ability. Adults will wait for this important teaching until it is developmentally appropriate. Meanwhile, they will be responsible for safeguarding individual rights:

    "DeJuan needs a turn when you're finished with that, Sarah."

Biting

Biting is such a common occurrence in toddler group situations that it earns particular mention here. Aggression because of frustration with others is not the only reason by any means that biting occurs. Other reasons include: teething discomfort; stage of oral exploration; imitative behavior; cause and effect exploration; overcrowding; or a need for attention. As caregivers try to puzzle out the cause for an episode of biting, they are more able to respond appropriately.

A child who bites for teething discomfort might be helped by using a teething ring or chewing on a clean, soft towel that has been placed in the freezer. Frozen bread sticks or hard biscuits might also relieve. Rubbing the toddler's gums with clean hands might help, and some doctors recommend medications that numb the gums.

A child who bites as part of oral exploration may need a variety of clean, soft objects that can be used for redirection for chewing experiences. Plastic rings, soft toys, celery sticks—all can be used when adults want to say, "You can't bite Sarah, that hurts her. Here's a ring you can bite on if you want to bite."

Toddlers who bite as investigation of cause and effect ("What will happen when I push the book off the table? What about when I bite Suzie?") need toys

Figure 8-8 When teachers show their serious disapproval of hurting others by biting, the message comes across. *Courtesy NationsBank Child Care Center.*

and experiences to nurture that drive to discover. Cause and effect toys, such as busy boxes and jack-in-the-boxes, and open-ended materials, like sand, water, or blocks that can do lots of different things, give positive opportunities to explore.

Toddlers who bite when they get physically crowded need adults who can manage the available space to protect an area for each child.

Toddlers who bite from frustration may need help with simple words to express themselves, or a recognition for what they seem to feel, if language is impossible. "You can tell him 'no,' Joel," or "I think Joel wants to tell you he doesn't want you to touch his bear right now."

A child who bites in imitation of another toddler who has been observed biting needs to discover that this is not the best way to get attention. Any child who seems to be biting for attention needs to be receiving positive attention, lots of it, for times when she or he is involved in busy, appropriate behaviors. Adult response when biting does occur must be careful to pay most attention to the child who has been bitten, and only brief, disapproving attention to the biter.

If caregivers observe when biting occurs, and try to explore what the reason for biting might be, they are more likely able to try the most appropriate solution (Ward, 1990).

When biting has occurred, adult reaction needs to be swift and clear. Turning to the victim, the adult gives her appropriate attention, including washing the area and holding ice on it. The biter needs to be quickly removed from the victim, while the adult shows with voice and facial expression that it is absolutely unacceptable to bite. Speaking very firmly, looking into the child's eyes, holding him firmly, the caregiver says, "I don't like it when you bite people. Look at her. She's crying. You hurt her." (See Figure 8-8.) When possible, the biter can help the adult hold the ice on the hurt child, since this brings him face to face with the consequences of his actions. However, if the biter resists, it's inappropriate to give him more attention at this point. When order has been quickly restored, or while comforting the hurt child, the adult can state alternate behaviors to the biter: "If you want something you can tell her," or "If you want to bite something, you can use the plastic ring."

If a child bites frequently, it is worth the staff time to assign one caregiver to shadow this child closely, watching for potentially frustrating situations, and being available to redirect the child before complete loss of control occurs.

Communication with parents to coordinate responses to biting and learn of possible stresses on the toddler is vital. All parents of toddlers in a toddler room need information about biting: that it is developmental and normal, why it occurs, and what caregivers are doing to protect and help children. If this information is given as a matter of course *before* an incident occurs, parents may be less alarmed. Communication is also important so all adults involved with the toddler can behave in similar ways when biting occurs. In most cases toddler biting will not last a very long time, especially if dealt with consistently, using a logical consequence solution. In cases where it does persist, adults involved in the child's care may need to discuss other care alternatives, with fewer children or more one-on-one adult attention.

Things to avoid. Toddlers are unlikely to progress in social relations with peers when adults:

- expect toddlers to learn to share or take turns, and punish when they fail to do so

BUT WHAT ABOUT?

But what about the parent who is just plain furious with me because his child was bitten twice last week? He practically accused me of not doing my job!

It is often frustrating for toddler caregivers to be on the receiving end of parental anger when their child is the bitee, and parent blame if their child is the biter. While biting is certainly a topic that raises vehement and protective impulses in adults, it is important to cool everyone down enough for some communication.

Offering parents articles and information about toddler biting is one way of helping them realize how widespread the problem is. Let parents observe as much as they can, to see firsthand how vigilant the adults in the classroom are in trying to create an environment that prevents some of the conditions that may lead to biting. Share the notes and observations that indicate your attempts to figure out the problem. Share your puzzling process, and use them to get as much information as you need to understand their particular child.

Actively listen to indicate your empathy for their distress at their child's hurt, and share your own distress when a child in your care is hurt. Don't become defensive; such a stance will only cause more problems. Instead, emphasize an attitude of working together to solve the problem.

Read in Polly Greenberg's fine book, *Character Development: Encouraging Self-Esteem and Self-Discipline in Infants, Toddlers, and Two-Year-Olds*, for interesting samples of comments to toddlers about biting.

- show no understanding of the modeling and prevention value of their play involvement with toddlers, and think it silly or boring to play with them

- punish or control aggressive toddlers in ways that "escalate the hostility" (NAEYC, 1989, p. 11)

- attempt to teach toddlers "how it feels to bite" (or hit or pull hair, or anything else the toddler has done), by doing it back to the child

Fostering Emotional Development

The kinds of gentle guidance toward prosocial awareness that we have just discussed are the appropriate methods to help toddlers toward the eventual capacity of feeling sympathy and compassion. The sensitive responses of adults who respond to toddler feelings of separation help toddlers learn to master those feelings eventually, while learning that feelings of sadness and fear are valid and can be expressed.

A developmentally appropriate social/emotional environment helps toddlers learn that their feelings are respected and that there are ways that feelings may be expressed and dealt with. Adults foster emotional development when they:

- Invest themselves emotionally in the children. Rich relationships permit toddlers to experience the power of a warm emotional climate firsthand.

- Are authentic in their own expression of emotion and modeling of coping skills. Toddlers learn most by watching and listening to those around them. When adults accept their own feelings and express them constructively, toddlers have a positive model. Example:

- "I'm so glad to see you today Yvette," conveys love a young child can perceive.

- "I really don't like it when you hurt Antoine. It makes me angry."

- Accept both the feelings people enjoy and those that are more painful.

- Recognize that although toddlers have strong feelings, they lack both the language to express emotions verbally and the ability to delay immediate expression of these feelings. Together, these facts mean that toddler expression of emotion is largely through nonverbal, physical means.

- Let's look at a common emotional issue of toddlerhood.

Temper Tantrums

Along with resistance and negativism, toddler temper tantrums are what have given the toddler period the cliché characterization, "terrible." Given the strong feelings, the lack of other than physical means of expression, and the amount of frustration met by many toddlers as they try to investigate their world, it is nearly inevitable that some emotional outbursts may occur.

> Tantrums spring from inner forces in the child over which he is seeking control. . . a reflection of the inner turmoil of decision-making that one is faced with when decisions become one's own, and are no longer made by a parent. In all likelihood the tantrums are necessary and are private expressions of such turmoil. They are appropriate at this age (Brazelton, 1974, pp. 20–21). "

Although tantrums are appropriate in toddlerhood, they are certainly not at later stages when other methods of expression and coping can be developed. The frequently strong responses of adults to toddler temper tantrums probably result from a fear that this undesirable behavior might linger on if not quelled permanently. It is more appropriate, however, for adults to focus on what is most helpful right at the present:

Figure 8-9 A quiet period is scheduled mid-morning to prevent toddler loss of control through fatigue. *Courtesy CPCC Child Care Training Center.*

- Realize that many outbursts can be prevented by adults who ensure that toddlers not get too tired or hungry. Managing the toddler's schedule to allow for sufficient rest and food can help increase toddler tolerance. (See Figure 8-9.)

- Avoid frustrating incidents by keeping expectations and situations appropriate for immature toddlers. For example, a wait at a restaurant, doctor's office, snack table, etc., when there is nothing to occupy toddler attention and adults repeatedly ask for more tolerance than children are capable of, is extremely frustrating for toddlers and should be avoided. While prevention is not the only answer for temper tantrums, it certainly deserves thoughtful consideration as the one component that is under adult control.

- Respond to toddler temper tantrums with calm control. When children have lost control, it is important to realize that they can count on adults for secure boundaries.

- Prevent toddlers from hurting themselves or others when they are out of control. Sometimes removing the child from the scene of the frustration is helpful. The toddler throwing herself on the floor in the supermarket will benefit from being taken outside or to the car. The purpose is not isolation, but removal from the stimulus.

- Verbalize quiet understanding of the toddler's frustration, to let the toddler know his feeling is understood, to model other methods of expression, and to calm with gentle sounds, as in "It really made you mad when the puzzle pieces didn't fit."

- Pick the child up to love and comfort after the tantrum has subsided, and help to change the subject. Now is the time for diversion—diversion during the tantrum is quite futile, as well as sending the negative message of ignoring the strength of the feelings.

- Avoid any behaviors that would reinforce temper tantrums as a method of getting something.

Things to avoid. Adults contribute to unhealthy emotional development when they respond to toddler temper tantrums by either attempting to suppress them, or by responding to them in ways that actually reinforce and strengthen the behavior.

Sometimes adults try to suppress the behavior by:

- Punishing the tantrum, with isolation or with angry outbursts of their own: "Now stop that, do you hear me? I don't want to hear any more of that screaming. I'll give you something to *really* scream about!" There is something quite incongruous about an adult having a temper tantrum of her own, while trying to stop that of a toddler.

- Ignoring the child and his emotion altogether. Since this is the only method of expression available to the toddler, the implicit message is that the feeling is not valid or important. Toddlers are unable to understand that adults are disapproving of the *method* of expressing anger rather than the feeling itself, and simply learn that if they want to retain adult approval, they'd better hide any evidence of feeling. Suppressed feelings are both unhealthy and dangerous.

- Laughing at or mocking the toddler's outburst also trivializes the feelings, to say nothing of compounding the emotional response by adding anger or more frustration. It certainly shows lack of respect for toddlers (as well as a lack of understanding of cognitive ability) to see an adult down on the floor pretending to cry loudly, then saying, "Now doesn't that look silly?"

Sometimes adults actually reinforce the likelihood of temper tantrums recurring and lingering on long after developmental abilities to express in other ways appear. Tantrums are reinforced when adults:

- Give into the tantrum. Rather than be embarrassed or confronted with an out-of-control child, adults who want peace at any price are quite frequently willing to pay the short-term price, not weighing in the long-term cost. This is the caregiver who gives the toy to the toddler flinging herself on the floor after the adult had already told her she couldn't have it, or the parent who buys the candy in the supermarket after the screams have gotten so loud they're attracting attention. Once adults have set the boundaries, they need to stick to them, or toddlers learn that tantrums are a powerful tool to use to get what they can't get otherwise.

- Pay attention that is beyond acknowledging the feeling and ensuring the child will not cause harm. Attention can be just as rewarding as the concrete object the child was fussing over in the first place. As Brazelton says, the "ultimate goal will be for him to incorporate his own limit." (Brazelton, 1974, p. 20) This means that children need to feel they are supported as they try to regain their own control. Too much adult attention may prevent the child from learning how to stop herself.

Brazelton's words help us sort out the appropriate response from the inappropriate:

> I feel that a parent's role at this time is to comfort and sort out the sides of the struggle. Certainly, retreating completely for fear of setting them off, or getting so involved that one ends up having a tantrum too, is no help to the baby. Picking him up to love and comfort him afterward, and realizing the fact that boundaries are necessary whether the baby must respond with a tantrum or not, may be the best roles a parent can play (Brazelton, 1974, p. 21).

Developmentally Appropriate Guidance

There is so much for toddlers to learn as they grow. Learning what pleases and displeases adults and beginning to learn how to control impulses is one of the most challenging tasks for toddlers, and it is equally challenging for the adults who want to help toddlers in this process.

Burton White defines the third necessary role for adults (after designer of the child's world and consultant) as *authority*. He states that from his studies, when toddlers develop well, they live in environments run with a "loving but firm hand," where the toddlers "rarely have any question about who is the final authority." He has found that toddlers do not do very well in situations where "there is often ambiguity with respect to the setting of limits and the determination of who is going to have the final say on disagreements" (White, 1985, p. 140). It stands to reason that, with toddlers being the bewildered new visitors to the planet, it helps them to believe that somebody knows what should be going on, since they themselves are so unsure.

But firmness should not be confused with an atmosphere of adults concentrating on winning over toddlers' losing. Rather, the adult should keep two goals in mind: first, helping the child learn from the experience, and second, allowing the child to "save face," "get out of the situation without feeling stupid, ashamed or embarrassed" (Stonehouse, 1982, p. 45).

Building toward a positive self concept is the important goal of toddlerhood, and methods of discipline used should build up rather than tear down good feelings in children.

Developmentally appropriate guidance focuses on:

- Having age-appropriate expectations for behavior and control.

- Changing the environment where possible instead of trying to get the child to change behavior. Examples of this are things like adding duplicates of toys to prevent fighting; removing objects rather than having to verbally restrict their use; moving up the lunch schedule so tired toddlers do not have to wait.

- Using both actions and words to guide toddlers. It is frustrating for adults to observe that toddlers seem to recognize words, yet not be controlled by them. Toddlers need someone to help them physically to stop or leave the situation. Examples:

> "Climb over here," says Debbie as she lifts Patrick down from the table.

> "That's Akwanza's, he needs it back," says Michael, as he helps Elizabeth hand back a toy, then leads her to find another.

- Redirecting children positively to desirable behavior. "Climb over here" tells Patrick what he may do, rather than just stopping him with "Don't climb" or "Stop climbing on the table."

- Changing the child's direction of thinking is less frustrating for both toddler and adult than attempting to stop him altogether. Positive guidance feels less restrictive and contributes more to a toddler's sense of what is acceptable.

- Recognizing and accepting reasons children are doing things, while still pointing out the "buts." Slowly toddlers need to recognize that others have needs too. Examples:

> "You want to play with the doll, but Lindsay is using it now."

> "You like to climb, but this is not a safe place."

- Offering solutions. For every "no," offer two acceptable choices (Greenberg, 1991). Examples:

> "You could play with the bear while you wait or come with me while I set the table."

> "You could climb on the pillows or jump off the step."

- Relying heavily on techniques such as distraction, substitution, and redirection which allows adults to set limits while avoiding having toddlers "lose." Burton White found that most of the effective caregivers of children from a year to a year and a half relied heavily on distraction and physical removal of either the child or the object; after one and a half, they used distraction, physical distance, and firm words. Examples:

> When Leah is grabbing the doll from Jonathan, Cindy tells her that's Jonathan's right now, and says," Here's a doll for you to hold, Leah. Now you and Jonathan both have your babies."

> "Sand in the table," reminds Darlene when Hope throws sand on the floor.

Such guidance helps children keep within the limits of acceptable behavior.

- Following through consistently on a very few limits to help toddlers come to understand what is expected of them. Limits are selected for toddler protection, and the reasons are explained briefly, even as adults realize that toddlers are not likely to understand fully. Example:

> Because of the danger of children slipping, the "sand in the sand table" limit is kept each time the toddlers test it, till eventually they test it no longer. (See Figure 8-10.)

- Displaying a calm, authoritative approach, recognizing the necessity for adults to provide secure limits while toddlers cannot yet control themselves.

Figure 8-10 "Sand in the sand table" is a limit that is consistently maintained. *Courtesy NationsBank Child Care Center.*

BUT WHAT ABOUT?

But what about the mother in my room who insists that her doctor told her time-out is the only way to discipline her toddler?

Sometimes developmentally inappropriate advice is passed along by professionals, and parents are confused when one professional seems not to be following the prescription of another. Toddlers are often so bewildering for parents that they are eager to get specific advice from others on how to handle behaviors. Suggest that there are clear areas of agreement between classroom practice and the doctor's perspective: Both agree on a definite need for limits for toddlers, and in helping them in ways that don't depend on physical punishment to control. In your conversations with the mother, remind her of what she and you both notice about the toddler's ability to reason, remember, and control his own actions, and how these abilities relate to any effectiveness of a guidance technique. Remind the mother of some alternative techniques that seem to better match developmental ability. Describe your responses to particular behaviors. Continue the dialogue.

Remember that your goal is not to prove the doctor wrong, but to allow the parent to try to make guidance decisions based on development. Support her as she tries out new ideas and encourage her to talk about her discoveries. In all matters of guidance, it is important to help parents realize that there is no one correct method, but that some methods are better suited to particular levels of development, as well as particular temperaments..

Things to avoid. Most of the developmentally inappropriate guidance of toddlers results from the error of assuming that toddlers can understand and control themselves much better than they actually can. As a result adults become impatient and angry with what they interpret as toddlers being "mean," "stubborn," or "bad," and punish them accordingly.

For example, when a toddler is told repeatedly not to touch others' belongings and she continues to do so, the adult may respond angrily with "I've told you three times to stay away from that. Now you go in time-out until you decide you're going to listen to me." There are several things about this which do not match what we know about toddler development. First, words alone will not control the toddler, and the adult has not helped her comprehend and control actions by giving physical assistance with follow-through. Second, the concept of time-out as a time to think about one's actions and change according to one's recognition of what is right or wrong action is beyond toddler mental capability. Third, the struggle has been framed as a power struggle that the adult must win, by having the toddler realize she is the wrong one and must give in to the powerful adult—certainly not helpful for the development of positive self-concept.

Does this mean that time-out is generally a developmentally inappropriate guidance method to use with toddlers? Based on what we know about developmental abilities and understanding, the answer is *yes*: Generally it is inappropriate. If you have seen or used time-out frequently with toddlers, this is the time to rethink it.

Developmentally inappropriate guidance sometimes neglects to consider that toddlers learn much about behavior from imitating the actions of those around them; when adults behave in ways opposite to what they want toddlers to do, their actions speak much louder than the words they might have thought explained their actions. "I told you not to touch that," shouts the adult, popping the toddler's hand to underline the prohibition. The same adult is angry a little later when that toddler hits at a friend when she is trying to emphasize her point with the peer. Many adults say that they must use physical contact as a means of "getting through" to toddlers who "just don't understand words," by which the adult means the toddler's actions are not controlled by words. Realizing the negative lesson taught by the aggressive physical contact may help some adults rethink using physical force as toddler guidance.

In general, developmentally inappropriate guidance does not recognize the limitations on toddler understanding and control, nor does it model the respect for needs and feelings of others that will be necessary for true prosocial development.

Fostering Positive Self-Esteem

The critical formation of self-esteem during toddlerhood means that caregivers must view their actions and interactions with toddlers through the filter of considering the effect on self-esteem. Self-esteem has several sources: feeling we can positively affect others; feeling lovable; feeling capable; and feeling listened to and accepted (Greenberg, 1991).

Adults foster positive toddler self-esteem when they:

- are promptly responsive to toddler needs, requests, and communication
- ask toddler opinions and take their advice ("Do you think we should make our play dough blue or green today?")
- snuggle, stroke, play with toddlers briefly
- structure situations so toddlers can succeed
- call attention to toddler success ("Look what Jamal can do. He flipped his coat on the magic way!")
- offer just the right amount of help for success
- pay close attention, and make every effort to understand toddler communication

It is from such daily occurrences that positive self-esteem grows.

SUMMARY

Toddlers thrive in relationships with adults who recognize their need for proving autonomy and support their attempts at independence. They gain self-confidence as they function separately from their important adults and learn to master their sadness. They grow as adults protect them from their lack of impulse control with peers, slowly helping them become aware of the needs and rights of others in the environment. They need adults who can accept their expressions of strong emotions until they develop other capabilities to express them. They respond to respectful, firm, positive guidance based on a knowledge of their inability to stop themselves.

This is a long chapter, not because the social/emotional development of toddlers is more difficult than other topics, but because it is definitely a period not well understood by many adults. It is unfortunately in the toddler room that the most inappropriate social/emotional environments are likely to be found. It is vital that adults who care for toddlers realize their limitations and their struggles for independence, and learn how best to strengthen self-esteem during the time which is trying for child and adult alike. The formation of a healthy sense of self is too critical to later development to risk inappropriate interaction during toddlerhood.

THINK ABOUT IT

1. Talk to several parents and/or caregivers of toddlers. Ask them to describe several of the most difficult times they've had with their toddlers recently. Share these with your classmates. Try to identify which toddler social/emotional issues discussed in this chapter are at work in the situations.

2. Watch a toddler in a home or center. What evidence do you see of self-assertion? of resistance?

3. Where possible, observe a toddler classroom in a child care center. Note examples of guidance you feel are appropriate for toddlers, and any examples you see that are less appropriate. Discuss them with your classmates. What principles of learning are at work in each example?

4. Try to imagine a day from the perspective of a toddler. What experiences might have a positive or a negative impact on the development of a sense of self?

QUESTIONS TO REVIEW OBJECTIVES

1. Describe the major social/emotional issues of toddlerhood.

2. For each of these issues, discuss several kinds of adult interaction that contribute positively to its outcome. Give examples to illustrate.

3. For each of the issues, discuss several kinds of adult interaction that contribute negatively to its outcome. Give examples to illustrate.

REFERENCES AND SUGGESTIONS FOR READING

Balaban, N. (1985). *Starting school: From separation to independence.* New York: Teachers College Press.

Balaban, N. (1992, July). The role of the child care professional in caring for infants, toddlers, and their families. *Young Children, 47(5),* 66–71.

Brazelton, T. B. (1974). *Toddlers and parents: A declaration of independence.* New York: Delacorte Press/Seymour Lawrence.

Erikson, E. (1963). *Childhood and society.* New York: Norton.

Gestwicki, C. (1992, June). It's OK to cry when you say goodbye: Dealing with the tears and fears of separation. *Growing Parent, 20(6),* 1–2.

Gottschall, S. (1989, September). Understanding and accepting separation feelings. *Young Children, 44(6),* 11–16.

Greenberg, P. (1991). *Character development: Encouraging self-esteem and self-discipline in infants, toddlers, and two-year-olds.* Washington, DC: NAEYC.

Jalongo, M. R. (1987, March). Do security blankets belong in preschool? *Young Children, 42(3),* 3–8.

Lauter-Klatell, N. (1986). Supporting social interaction between toddlers. In Palmer Wolf, D. (ed.), *Connecting: Friendship in the lives of young children and their teachers.* Redmond, WA: Exchange Press Inc.

Lauter-Klatell, N. (1991). How do I say 'let's play'? Social interaction between toddlers. In *Readings in child development.* Mountain View, CA: Mayfield Publishing Co.

Leavitt, R. L., & Eheart, B. K. (1985). *Toddler day care: A guide to responsive caregiving.* Lexington, MA: Lexington Books.

Leipzig, J. (1986). Fostering prosocial development in infants and toddlers. In Palmer Wolf, D. (ed.), *Connecting: Friendship in the lives of young children and their teachers.* Redmond, WA: Exchange Press Inc.

Mahler, M. (1979). *Separation-individuation* (vol. 2). London: Jason Aronson.

NAEYC. (1989). Developmentally appropriate practice in early childhood programs serving toddlers. *Brochure #508.* Washington, DC: Author.

Stonehouse, A. W. (1982). Discipline. In Lurie, R., & Neugebauer, R. (eds.), *Caring for infants and toddlers: What works, what doesn't.* Redmond, WA.: Child Care Information Exchange.

Ward, C. (1990, March). What to do when toddlers bite. *Pre-K Today, 4(5),* 51–52.

White, B. L. (1985). *The first three years of life* (rev. ed.). Englewood Cliffs, NJ: Prentice-Hall.

CHAPTER

9

Developmentally Appropriate Social/Emotional Environments: For Preschoolers

*A*s the preschooler emerges from the isolated cocoon of the attachment relationship and the insistent separateness of autonomy, interest in the world of people blossoms. For many children this is the time of moving beyond the confines of home and parents to begin spending time in group situations with other preschoolers and other adults. There are new expectations from parents and teachers about children's abilities to conform to social standards and limits. While new social situations offer opportunities for developing new interpersonal skills, this learning is complex, and much time in the preschool years is devoted to coming to an understanding of just how to fit into the larger world of people. There are rules that must be learned and controls that must be developed. There are behaviors that must be modified to be accepted as a friend in the play of childhood. There are messages and teachings from the surrounding culture that must be incorporated into a personal understanding of identity.

Along with the social experiences and learning, young children are coping with their emotions and learning just what constitutes acceptable expression of feelings. None of this learning comes without the guidance of caring adults, who demonstrate, explain, and teach alternative behaviors within the context of their teaching and/or parenting relationships.

OBJECTIVES

After completing this chapter, students should be able to:

- identify several social/emotional issues of the preschool years.
- discuss implications for teachers for nurturing positive identity.
- identify classroom practices that foster gender identity.
- identify classroom practices that foster racial/cultural identity.
- describe ways teachers can promote social skills for friendship.
- identify ways to nurture prosocial awareness.
- discuss ten positive guidance techniques to move preschoolers toward self-control.
- identify ten components of emotional environments that encourage developmentally appropriate learning about feelings.

161

Social/Emotional Issues of the Preschool Years

Identification

As children move beyond the infant and toddler years where attachment is the key issue in social/emotional development, they enter a time when the process of *identification* plays a key role in their relationships and social development. From wanting to be *near,* children move to wanting to be *like* the important adults in their lives. Through the psychological process of identification, children seek to look, act, feel, and be like significant people in their social environments. Thus identification is a key force in personality and social development in the early childhood years. There are variations in theoretical perspectives on how identifications form, but the perspectives include: observation and imitation; general conceptual and cognitive growth; and affectionate affiliation. Much of the identification process is on an individual and personal basis, though the larger culture certainly influences messages about valuing certain identifications.

The identification process is related to issues of acquiring a gender or sex-role identity, a cultural or racial identity, internalizing adult standards for behavior, and feelings of self-confidence, all important issues of early childhood. Developmentally appropriate social/emotional environments recognize the importance of identification as a mechanism for personality and social learning.

Gender Identity

Gender identity consists of two components. One is the sexual identity, determined by biology; the other is sex-role behavior, determined by culture. Preschool children actively seek to understand gender identity. By questions and observations, they go beyond their first knowledge of being able to label themselves as a boy or girl, to trying to figure out just exactly what it is that makes them a boy or a girl.

"Children's comfortable acceptance of their gender anatomy is the cornerstone of constructing a healthy sexual identity and frees children to go beyond stereotypic gender role constraints" (Derman-Sparks, 1989, p. 50).

Beyond biology, preschool children are clearly developing a conceptual grasp of sex-role behavior defined by the culture. In the beginning of the preschool period, boys and girls play house in about the same way; costumes and behaviors representing male and female roles are casually exchanged (Paley, 1984), and children pay little attention to the gender of their play companions. But by age four, boys are less comfortable playing in the housekeeping corner, and by age five girls have taken over the domestic calm, while boys occasionally raid, disguised as Superheroes or "bad guys" (Paley, 1984). Four- and five-year-olds actively look for friends like themselves, and emphatically exclude (almost always) children of a different gender. Gender specific forms of play are common, moving boys and girls into such different directions in their fantasy play that they simply do not know the script in order to be able to join each other at play (Pitcher and Schultz, 1983). Also by age four, children clearly distinguish between "boy toys" and "girl toys." Naturalistic studies tell us that this happens, but do not explain why. Some experimental studies indicate that parental behaviors shape children's concepts and behaviors; in addition, social norms may override children's firsthand experience at home or in the classroom, as children struggle with powerful cultural messages (Weisner and Wilson-Mitchell, 1990).

Cultural and Racial Identity

In addition to personal identification, preschool children identify themselves as members of families and their larger culture. Over time children not only conceptualize their membership in a particular group, through experience with their bodies and their social environments, but also show signs of being influenced by societal norms and attitudes toward the group of which they are members. Research indicates that children are aware of their racial/cultural identity by the age of four, and have absorbed attitudes toward their own and others' racial identity (Katz, 1982). Early studies were interpreted as evidence that young African American children expressed negative feelings about their identification with their racial group (Clark and Clark, 1939); more recent studies indicate that their attitude toward their own and other peoples' ethnicity "depends on the attitudes of adult caregivers, and on the perceptions of the power and wealth of their own group in relation to others" (Cole and Cole, 1993, p. 369). Clearly this is a social/emotional issue that deserves attention.

Initiative

A component of a healthy sense of self in the preschool years, as defined by Erikson's (1968) psychosocial theory of personality development, is a sense of *initiative*. As children learn to initiate their own activities, enjoy their accomplishments, and feel valued for their purposeful actions, they become confident in their own actions and abilities. If they are not allowed to follow their own initiative, they feel guilty for their attempts to do so. Certainly it is obvious that there is a close connection here with identification; as children want to be like significant adults in their lives, they want also to please them. When they perceive that their ideas and accomplishments are supported by parents and teachers, both initiative and identity are strengthened.

 Nothing I say or do arouses the same intense interest Mollie has in her classmates. After many years of teaching I must admit that mine is not the primary voice in the classroom (Paley, 1986, p. 107). *"*

Friendship

Preschoolers are distinguished from younger children by their interest in spending time with peers. The questions: "Are you my friend?" and "Who will I play with?" loom large in the awareness of three-, four-, and five-year-olds. From toddlerhood children move through stages of play that indicate their increasing interest and skill in social interaction. After *parallel play*, in which children engage in similar kinds of play near each other without interaction or evident recognition between them, preschoolers move to *associative group play*. Here children are held together in brief episodes of play by their interest in a common activity, but the particular membership of the group is loose and not particularly selected. *Cooperative play* represents more complex social interaction, where children choose their playmates and work out plans for their play. Children at this stage are likely to define "best friends," individuals particularly selected for companionship, though the friendships may not be of lasting duration and may be characterized by much friction (Parten, 1932; Smith, 1982). Research has been done to identify behavior patterns of popular and unpopular children (Dodge, 1983; Kemple, 1991; Hazen et al., 1984). Many of the behaviors can be taught and/or modeled by helpful teachers. Friendship, and learning the skills of friendship, are important social/emotional issues of early childhood, and issues that need support in developmentally appropriate classrooms. In Chapter 13 we will examine reasons for defining play as the appropriate curriculum for cognitive development; here let us note that play is the essential medium for

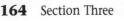

allowing children to experience opportunities to develop skills for friendship and cooperation.

Prosocial Behavior vs. Aggression

The increased aggressiveness that was associated with the distinctive sense of self of toddlerhood is one of the behaviors that adults expect preschool children to begin to control. New verbal abilities allow children to learn to defend their rights with methods other than physical aggression. Preschoolers can be helped to move slowly beyond totally encompassing egocentrism to some awareness of the needs and rights of others. Here again the process of identification is an important teaching mechanism, combined with modeling, direct instruction, and experience. Adult interaction is essential in helping preschoolers with these new abilities and understandings.

An issue related to aggression and prosocial behavior is emotional control and appropriate, constructive expression of feelings. Adult guidance is also necessary here.

Self-Control

The long, slow process of developing the ability to regulate individual behavior becomes a social/emotional issue of early childhood. The preschool child's expanded abilities for language and understanding permit comprehension of standards of conduct taught by adults. The process of forming a conscience— "an inner voice of self-observation, self-guidance, and self-punishment" (Erikson, 1968 p. 119)—is the goal of appropriate guidance for preschoolers. (Selma Fraiberg's discussion of conscience formation is classic. See Fraiberg, 1959.) A discussion of discipline vs. punishment is part of this social/emotional issue of helping move children toward self-control.

Developmentally Appropriate Social/Emotional Interaction

With so many important social/emotional issues to consider, it is vital that teachers of preschoolers realize that curriculum in their classrooms involves far move than narrowly defined skills, such as learning colors, numbers, or cutting skills. Curriculum very appropriately grows out of relationships and experiences that are important to children. Learning how to fit into the world about them is at the heart of the concerns of three-, four-, and five-year-olds. It must also be recalled that nurturing individual children's needs gives them the strength to accept the difficult challenges of adapting to group demands.

Forming personal relationships with young children is the necessary first step in the process of identification; children only want to be like adults they care for, and who they sense care for them. The interaction that comes from warm adult-child relationships is the vehicle for the crucial social/emotional guidance from adults.

Nurturing Individual Identity

One of the most developmentally inappropriate aspects of any preschool environment is the tendency to treat children as if they were *only* members of a group, restricting attention only to group identity ("our friends") and group standards for behavior ("our rules"). While group membership is certainly important, developmental appropriateness involves consideration of unique characteristics and needs of each child, and efforts to ensure messages of acceptance of that uniqueness.

In this section we will consider implications for nurturing individual identity, looking also specifically at nurturing positive gender and racial/cultural identity.

Implications for Teachers

Positive individual identity is nurtured when teachers:

- Use words and nonverbal actions to show affection for children and sincere interest in them. Teachers greet each child individually on arrival, and take time to help them become involved in activities of personal interest. Their personal comments throughout the day indicate they are aware of what each child has done or cares about. Examples:

  "You look ready to play today, Dominique. We've got the clay out again—I remember how much you liked that last week."

  "Antonio, you've been working really hard on that puzzle. I see you like the ones with lots of pieces."

- Make opportunities to spend time talking individually with each child each day. Routine times, such as bathroom time, getting coats on, walking to the playground, waiting for other children to gather for group time, are used as occasions for adult-child conversation. As teachers move among children busy at self-selected activities throughout the day, they are free to initiate conversation. They listen attentively to what each child has to say and are courteous in their interaction. Examples:

  "Tell me more about your visit with your grandparents, LaPorcha. It sounds like you had lots of fun."

  "I liked watching you climb on the bars, Rickie. I was remembering when you were too little to do that. Do you remember how you learned?"

- Create a classroom atmosphere that encourages and values individuality. Teachers call children's attention to each other's accomplishments, not to foster a spirit of competition, but to show children they value their competence. They recognize differences and strengths in all domains of development. "Giving children concrete examples of past successes is another way to build their feelings of confidence" (Berne, 1988, p. 35). Important for all children, this respect for individual strength and accomplishment is especially important for children with disabilities, to feel truly included and competent in their own right. As a component of an anti-bias classroom, nondisabled children are helped to interact comfortably and knowledgeably with those who have special needs, as their real accomplishments are pointed out. Examples:

  "Look, Jasmine, Anna had a good idea about using the funnel. Anna likes to figure out her own way of doing things."

  "Christopher likes to make pictures of airplanes, have you noticed, Jeremy? I can always tell when it's a picture Christopher made." (Christopher is in a wheelchair.)

  "I'm making a list of what we're all good at, to put on the wall. Would you like to help me? I already got Susannah for tying her shoes and Jason for fast running. Oh, you're right—Christopher can go really fast! What about Leah for remembering things? She was good at that last week

when we wrote our story about our trip to the farm." (Leah is hearing-impaired.)

- Respond with sensitivity to children's individuality. Adults support and encourage individual styles of making decisions, choices, preferences for certain activity, people, and interaction. They try to learn each child's characteristics, rather than viewing evidence of individuality as interfering with adults' plans, or as problem behavior or weakness in personality. Examples:

  "Sally would rather watch you sing than take a turn to sing by herself. Sally, do you want to sit with me while we watch them?"

  "Julio finds it hard to relax with a book at naptime, so I let him take his favorite little cars on the cot."

> Good teaching implies being comfortable making exceptions for people when they need them. It is the opposite of that killer phrase my teachers used to use: "If I do it for you, I'll have to do it for everybody." This was untrue and unfair (Clemens, 1983, p. 25).

- Convey respect also for individual parents' styles and needs, and use parental knowledge of their own children as a primary source for getting to know individuality. Example:

  "Jeremy's mom is a single parent with three children, so I realize she doesn't have much time to spend in the classroom. I call her every now and then to let her know what we've been doing, and to have a chance for her to tell me how he's doing at home."

- Provide opportunities, materials, and encouragement for children to initiate activities that have meaning and interest for them personally. As children experience a reasonable number of successful, positive play experiences in their classroom life, they will continue to take initiative. The child-centered curriculum of choice contributes to positive self-identity. Examples:

  "Hey, look what I did," exclaims Victor as he displays his carefully balanced box construction.

  "I *thought* you could walk that balance beam," comments the teacher, smiling; Jeremy grins broadly, agreeing. "It's pretty hard, and I can do it."

- Incorporate concepts related to personal identity into learning activities. In some classrooms teachers plan a week's unit on the theme "I'm Me, I'm Special." Rather than paying cursory attention once a year to this theme, in developmentally appropriate classrooms teachers plan unit topics that are meaningful to children's experiences and lives, and regularly help children see connections with their own experiences. Examples:

  "There's a big grocery truck like the one Danny's daddy drives," notes the teacher as they walk down the street.

  "You were just as little as LaPorcha's baby sister a long time ago, and your mommy gave you a bottle when you were hungry, just like that. Your mommy took good care of you." Danny is curious about the visiting baby.

Things Caregivers Should Not Do

A social/emotional environment does not contribute to positive feelings of identity when adults:

- are too busy or involved with other activities to acknowledge children's presence
- use names as synonyms for "no," "don't," or "stop," as in "Tony!" (Kostelnik et al., 1988)
- fail to maintain eye contact or be available physically for conversation
- pay superficial attention to what children have to say or actively discourage children from talking with them
- speak to the whole group most of the time, only speaking to individual children to admonish or discipline them
- create an atmosphere that fosters competition to meet the adult standard of behavior and evaluates children by narrowly defined standards, focused on children's intellectual development
- criticize or belittle typical child-like behaviors, as in "Why can't you sit still and do something quiet for a change?"
- use judgmental vocabulary (often within children's hearing) to describe individual children's behavior, style, or interests, as in "He's the shyest child I've ever met"
- judge parents by their own standards of what "good" parents do
- fail to communicate with parents respectfully as a necessary source of information to understand children's individuality
- use highly structured, teacher-directed lessons without many opportunities for children to initiate their own ideas or make connections with their own lives

Gender Identity

In developmentally appropriate classrooms, teachers recognize that forming a healthy gender identity is a preschool developmental task. They help children in this by enabling them to clarify answers to biological questions, and by promoting participation in activities for equality of development for both genders. Teachers facilitate healthy gender identity when they:

- Accept children's right to be curious about their bodies, and the need for simple, factual responses when they demonstrate that curiosity. Where needed, teachers find resources that help explain answers to preschoolers' questions in ways matching their cognitive abilities. *What is a Girl? What is a Boy?* by Stephanie Waxman is helpful. Examples:

  "Roberto stands up when he uses the toilet because he is a boy. Boys' and girls' bodies are made differently. It's more convenient for girls to sit on the toilet seat."

  "Some girls prefer to wear pants, but wearing pants doesn't make you a boy. The difference between girls and boys is not what they wear, but the way their bodies are made. Boys have a penis, girls have a vagina."

Figures 9-1, 9-2 Teachers encourage girls (and boys) to participate in activities that challenge narrow, stereotypical views of gender behavior. *Courtesy Methodist Home Child Development Center.*

- Offer experiences that challenge narrow, stereotypical views of gender behavior. (See Figures 9-1 and 9-2.) Use parents and others in the community to help children understand the breadth of choices available to both genders. It is important for children to see males and females respecting one another as individuals. Examples:

  "Roberto's father is visiting us today. He works as a nurse at the hospital."

  "Yes, that's right. We did see two women firefighters when we visited the fire station, Jennifer. Firefighters can be men or women; they have to be strong and trained in how to fight fires."

- Reorganize the play environment to encourage more cross-gender play choices. Suggestions include expanding the dramatic play area to include props from other rooms in the house: woodworking and tools; materials for a "study"; work dress-up props (tool chest, lunch box, hard hat, barber tools) (Derman-Sparks, 1989).

- Examine pictures and books in the classroom to make sure diversity in work and home roles is portrayed. Anatomically correct dolls are available for children to play with.

- Involve children in new activities. Derman-Sparks suggests teachers consider occasional teacher-initiated activities to counteract the limited choices children may make for play, based on children's perceptions of cultural definition of appropriateness. Having an "everybody plays with blocks day" or "boys only" art day may encourage children to experience new choices until they become comfortable enough to select them on their own initiative.

- Communicate with parents about goals and classroom practices to support healthy gender identity. Teachers need to recognize that ethnic and cultural backgrounds influence parents' feelings about nontraditional gender behavior or responses to children's interest in sexuality. There may be tension about differences between home and classroom approaches. Communication that conveys respect for diversity of opinion is essential as parents and teachers resolve areas of disagreement. Read comments in Gonzalez-Mena, 1993, as you think about this important topic.

- Examine personal feelings about gender-free activities, comments, and attitudes.

Cultural and Racial Identity

Teachers are helpful in promoting positive attitudes toward racial and cultural identity for all children when they work to create an anti-bias environment that conveys a true respect for diversity in all its forms. It is important that teachers become personally aware of the ways that prejudices have influenced their own development, and of ways that messages of bias are passed on to children. Reading the NAEYC publication *Anti-Bias Curriculum: Tools for Empowering Young Children* is a good place to start. See additional suggestions at the end of the chapter: York, 1991; Clark et al., 1992; Derman-Sparks, 1990; Byrnes and Kiger, 1992. In their own classrooms, teachers can do the following.

Figure 9-3 Classrooms include materials that show diversity of the population, including racial composition and non-stereotypical occupations. *Courtesy CPCC Child Care Training Center.*

- Examine all pictures and books to ensure a realistic representation of the diversity of the individual classroom, community, and the total U.S. population, with respect to racial composition, nonstereotypical gender representations, different abilities, ages, classes, family structures and lifestyles. Such diversity is important whether the classroom population is primarily homogeneous or diverse. The Council on Interracial Books for Children analyzes children's books and other learning materials for racism and sexism. A free catalog is available from them at 1941 Broadway, New York, NY 10023.

- Provide toys and materials in every interest center that children can identify with, representing the families in the classroom, and the major groups in the community and in the nation. Art materials, manipulative objects, music, dolls and dramatic play props, and circle time activities should regularly celebrate diversity. See ideas in Derman-Sparks 1989 and 1990, and York, 1991.

❝ The teacher must become an active pluralist, who will imbue every aspect of the classroom with cultural and racial diversity. The classroom should become a microcosm of the pluralistic society the children do and will continue to live in, always emphasizing the similarities among people more than the differences.

The teacher should focus on the people in the child's world of today, not a historical world. The goal with preschoolers is not to teach history, but to inoculate them against racism (Clark et al., 1992, p. 8). ❞

Teachers who actively create an anti-bias environment are helping children of all racial and cultural backgrounds form healthy identity and attitudes. (See Figures 9-3 and 9-4.)

Things Caregivers Should Not Do

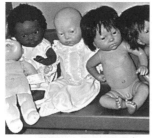

Figure 9-4 Dolls that represent diversity of race and gender should be available for children's play. *Courtesy Avondale Children's Center.*

Healthy gender identity is not nurtured by teachers who:

- respond differently to boys and girls
- reinforce stereotypes by their comments or expectations
- shame or punish children's curiosity about biological differences

Healthy cultural/racial identity is not nurtured by teachers who:

- respond with discomfort to children and families whose racial/cultural backgrounds or family structure are different from their own
- fail to challenge, and help children challenge, biased remarks or actions in the classroom
- provide stereotypical materials that do not convey respect for diversity
- offer a "tourist approach" (Derman-Sparks, 1989) that treats other cultural groups as if they were exotic and actually emphasizes differences

Friendship

Preschoolers are exploring the beginnings of friendship. Through language ("I'll be your friend"; "Are you my friend?") and action, they are experimenting with the social skills that lead to friendship. Some children, through temperament or helpful life experiences, seem to move into friendship more easily than others. But all children can benefit as adults assist them in identifying effective ways to communicate with peers. Adults foster beginning friendships when they:

Figure 9-5 Small group areas encourage the interaction that is important to developing friendships. *Courtesy CPCC Child Care Training Center.*

- Offer space and time for the face-to-face conversations that are essential for developing social understandings. Small group areas, (see Figure 9-5) such as the water or play dough table and dramatic play or block center, encourage social interaction. Unstructured, uninterrupted time is necessary for conversation.

- Pairing particular children occasionally for a common activity may be helpful, especially in the case of shy or overlooked children (Kemple, 1991). Examples:

   "Alberto, would you choose a friend to help you be our block area clean-up crew?"

   "Jennifer and Jasmine, our baby dolls need washing this morning. Here's a washcloth for each of you."

- Help children clarify their needs by asking them what they would like to play, or with whom. Preschoolers are so preoccupied with their own needs that they mistakenly assume others want what they want. Example:

   "Would you like to play in the grocery store this morning? Or did you want to play with Alex? He's in the block area this morning."

- Help children develop effective skills for entering play. Young children sometimes alienate others by focusing on their own needs in the play ("Can I play?"), or by using bizarre methods not easily recognized by other children as overtures (knocking down the block structure as a way of saying "I'd like to play too"). Examples:

   "If you want to play with Jennifer go over and say 'Jennifer, do you want to play blocks? We can make a bed for the dolls.'"

   "You could ask Erika if you can go to the store with her."

- Help children practice effective communication skills such as using names, talking directly to others, and maintaining eye contact. This is reinforced by the teacher's own example.

   "I don't think Jeremy knew you were talking to him, Sam. Look at him, and say his name when you're talking with him."

   "Nancy didn't look like she heard you when you asked for a turn. Say it again, and louder."

- Give children information to help them recognize friendly overtures of others (Kostelnik et al., 1993). Preschoolers generally have a difficult time grasping others' intentions. Examples:

   "I hear Sam asking you to play with him, Jeremy. You could have two steam shovel drivers."

"It looks to me as if Jennifer would like to go to the store with you, Erika. You can get more groceries with two people to carry them."

- Help children understand how their behavior affects the response of others. Some children do not see connections between their actions and others' feelings or responses. Teachers can help them understand the connection, in order to modify their behavior for the desired response. Examples:

  "When you knocked down the blocks, it made the other boys angry, so that's why they said they didn't want you to play. If you want to play blocks with them, you need to ask what you can do to help."

  "Jasmine really enjoyed working on washing the dolls with you. You gave her turns, and that was a friendly thing to do."

- Model social skills with children to help less skilled children learn ways of entering the play, while supporting them emotionally. When teachers accompany children to help them become participants in play, they supply a suggested role and demonstrate how to do it. Example:

  "Catherine and I are going to be the passengers buying a ticket for your train. How much is the ticket? Where do we sit?"

- Recognize that preschool friendships may be short-lived, and support children as they experience feelings of frustration or anger, or a desire to withdraw temporarily from social interaction. Examples:

  "It upset you when Jeremy said he didn't want to be your friend. Maybe he'll feel differently later on."

  "I think Jennifer would rather play by herself for a while. You could ask her again later."

- Explore ideas of friendship and social skills with children. Teachers may read books, talk about pictures, or use puppets to demonstrate skills.

A list of good books for preschoolers on friendship appears in Figure 9-6.

Books about Friendship for Preschoolers

Artis, V. *Pajama Walking*

Carle, E. *Do You Want to Be My Friend?*

Carlson, N. *Loudmouth George and the New Neighbors*

Cohen, M. *Jim Meets the Things*

Delton, J. *New Girl at School*

Ets, M. *Play with Me, E. Me and Neesie*

Hoban, R. *Best Friends for Frances*

Lobel, A. *Frog and Toad are Friends*

Maestro, B. *Where Is My Friend?*

Marshall, J. *George and Martha* (several in series)

Vincent, G. *Ernest and Celestine's Picnic* (several in series)

Viorst, J. *Rosie and Michael*

Wells, R. *Timothy Goes to School*

Zolotow, Charlotte. *Hold My Hand; My Friend John*

Figure 9-6 Good books for preschoolers about friendship.

Things Caregivers Should Not Do

Adults are not helpful in nurturing beginning friendships for preschool children when they:

- insist that everyone in the class are "friends," rather than helping children learn to distinguish friendly behaviors

- insist that everyone in the class like one another, rather than accepting children's real preferences in playmates

- dictate children's play partners constantly

- require children to do activities together, or share toys

- intervene too quickly or too constantly to manage social situations, preventing children from getting direct experience in managing interaction with peers

Teaching Prosocial Behavior

Beyond the social skills that encourage preschoolers to develop friendships, teachers recognize that preschoolers are developmentally ready for encouraging the development of prosocial behaviors. These are behaviors that are the opposite of antisocial, aggressive behaviors, such as helping, cooperating, empathizing, sharing, and displaying friendly and generous behavior in group situations. It will be well into the school years before most prosocial behaviors are established, but the preschool years are the time to be aware of early opportunities for learning and teaching. There are several things teachers can do to nurture prosocial behaviors.

Providing Materials

Materials that encourage playing together and cooperation on a task are helpful in increasing opportunities for preschoolers to share or support one another. Wagons, vehicles with two seats, simple board games, and mural art are all examples of things that just don't work without the assistance of another child. Timers can be introduced to help children regulate their own turn-taking. Some teachers have found that by not providing an abundance of many toys, they create the need and likelihood of sharing.

Providing Activities

When teachers plan activities to be done in pairs, such as creative movements or imitative games, they encourage children to learn how to support and enjoy participating with one another. Planning group activities, such as writing group stories or making cards to send to the sick sister of one child, encourages both turn-taking and opportunities to experience positive results of cooperation. Assigning responsibilities in pairs also encourages mutual cooperation. Example:

"Rosario, you and Luther are our table setters for today."

Encouraging Assistance

In every group there will be children who have different abilities or unique talents. Encourage children to ask one another for assistance. Example:

"Thomas can tie shoes very well now. You could ask him to please help you with yours."

Considering Prosocial Actions

Teachers actively guide children toward awareness of others' needs and feelings. Such guidance is necessary for the egocentric preschooler, who needs help in recognizing signals from others. Examples:

"Darius is looking very unhappy because he has had to wait so long for a turn. What could we do to help him feel better?"

"Anna hurt herself on the slide and she doesn't feel like playing now. What could we do to help her feel like joining us?"

Helping Children Recognize Prosocial Behavior

Sometimes children are so caught up with their own interests that they fail to recognize the positive motivations of others. Teachers can point out when other children are attempting to show concern or helpfulness. Example:

"Rob was worried that you were hurt, Anna. He wanted you not to feel all alone, sitting over here. That was a friendly thing to do, to come to stay by you."

Reinforcing Prosocial Behavior

Teachers pay attention to instances when children play together cooperatively, share, and help one another. They make sure these occasions do not go unnoticed. They reward such behaviors nonverbally by smiles, touch, and attention. They also specifically point out the prosocial behavior and its positive results. Examples:

> "It's good to see you helping Sarah with her shoes, Thomas. Now she'll be ready to play with you."

> "Thanks for sharing your play dough with Tina, Katherine. Now you'll each be able to work together." (See Figure 9-7.)

Modeling Prosocial Behavior

Once again teachers' actions speak louder than demands for caring behaviors. When teachers demonstrate and verbally explain helpfulness and cooperation, they show children the importance of behaving in prosocial ways. Examples:

> "Tina's Mom is coming to help us on our field trip today. I appreciate her taking the time, so we can have a special time."

> "Let me share some of our new books with you," spoken to the teacher in the next room.

Limiting Aggression and Antisocial Behavior

Vivian Paley has recently suggested that there is one cardinal rule that is used in her classroom. That rule is, "You can't say you can't play." (Paley, 1992). While she recognizes that rejection is one way children have always dealt with the difficulties of learning to be friends, this new rule protects everyone from exclusion in the classroom.

Figure 9-7 Teachers reinforce prosocial behavior, such as sharing play dough. *Courtesy CPCC Child Care Training*

> Paley believes that school should be a child's first experience of life in a democratic society. She likens the child's right to play to the adult's right to participate in society (Heller, 1993, p. 27).
>
> Is it fair for children *in school* to keep another child out of play? After all this classroom belongs to all of us. It is not a private place, like our homes (Paley, 1992, p. 16).
>
> In general, the approach has been to help the outsiders develop the characteristics that will make them more acceptable to the insiders. I am suggesting something different: The *group* must change its attitudes and expectations toward those who, for whatever reason, are not yet part of the system (Paley, 1992, p. 33).

It is worth considering further this notion of creating an absolute model of prosocial behavior for children to experience. Certainly as teachers limit aggression as a method of social interaction, they direct children to more positive forms of contact.

Helping Develop Empathy

When teachers verbalize others' feelings, and their concern for them, children are gradually led toward an understanding of how others feel, and what appropriate responses are to those feelings. This ability to "put yourself in another's place" comes more easily with school-aged children, but teachers can certainly begin the awareness now. Example:

> "I'll bet Sarah is feeling pretty sad today, because her dad has left for a long trip. I think I'll see if she would like to sit with me to read a story."

Opportunities for Kindness

Teachers help promote prosocial awareness and learning when they deliberately devise opportunities for children to participate in situations that foster kindness. Older children are encouraged to help and protect younger children.

Special needs are pointed out, and there is discussion about how to meet those special needs. Example:

"Sarah, since Lisa can't hear our words, could you show her the pictures carefully, so she'll know what we're talking about and not feel left out?"

Things Caregivers Should Not Do

Inappropriate guidance from adults regarding prosocial behavior includes:

- expecting too much in the area of sharing and cooperation
- insisting on children exhibiting insincere prosocial behavior
- forcing adult solutions for conflict

Guidance Toward Self-Control

Preschool children are developmentally ready to begin learning to control their impulses and behavior to conform to the demands of adult teaching and limits. They have the language required to understand basic explanations and to express their needs and wants to others. They have the interest in interacting with others and in being socially accepted in their world. However, their judgment about what is right or wrong is still limited by preoperational thought processes, which center on just one aspect of a situation rather than the whole situation. They perceive behavior as "good" or "bad," based arbitrarily on rewards and punishments. Preoperational thought also limits preschoolers' abilities to take another's perspective and to accurately reason out cause and effect. Preoperational thought is concrete, based on understanding of real experiences; abstractions such as requests for "nice" behavior are too far from their own reality. Adults who guide preschool children must take these developmental characteristics into account as they choose effective techniques to teach appropriate behavior.

In general, developmentally appropriate guidance is:

- positive, focusing on helping children learn what they should do, rather than emphasizing what they did wrong
- teaching-oriented, focusing on thoughtful selection of techniques that help children experience the sense in acting in more appropriate ways. As Katz said, "a trained teacher would ask: 'What can I be teaching the children in this situation?'" (Katz, 1984)
- collaborative, with adults and children working together to correct situations

Things Caregivers Should Not Do

Developmentally appropriate guidance for preschoolers does not:

- emphasize coercion and adult power to enforce rules or resolve disputes
- rely on punishing unacceptable behavior
- focus on retaliation
- stop behavior without teaching alternatives
- display adult anger with children's limitations in self-control

Ten positive guidance techniques that are developmentally appropriate include: modeling; positive statements; reinforcement, noticing, and strokes; redirection; setting limits; choices for control; natural and logical consequences; discussion for problem solving; I-messages; and renewal time.

Modeling

Adults teach very important lessons by living the behaviors they want children to adopt. Through the process of *identification,* children are influenced to want to be like their beloved adults, and to do things that will please them. Actions truly do speak louder than any number of words. Examples:

> "I'm very sorry your feelings got hurt," says the teacher to an upset child. "I can see that bothered you a lot. What could I do to help you feel better?" Her face echoes her compassion. None of this is lost on the children watching nearby.

> "Hmm, let's see, we both want to take our classes to the gym. What can we do about that? How would it be if we went after snack time for a half hour, and let you know when we get back? Would that give you time to go after your story time?"

> As teachers work out problems aloud, children get a chance to see the process of negotiation and problem solving that demonstrates respect for others' needs.

Positive Statements

Teachers recognize that preschoolers have much to learn about how to behave in the world, so they don't clutter the learning process by telling them what not to do. Instead, they focus on letting children know clearly, specifically, and briefly what is acceptable behavior. Some of the positive statements are mostly informational, and some are brief reminders. Cherry suggests using action verbs formed as gerunds (sitting, whispering, remembering) as respectful, quick, positive reminders (Cherry, 1983). With such brief and positive statements, adults convey the confident belief that children will control their behavior in the light of the information, instead of having to be harangued. When adults imply that children will want to do right, children rise to the expectation. Examples:

> "Puzzles stay on the table."

> "Keep hands away from other peoples' work, please."

> "Walking!"

Reinforcement, Noticing, and Strokes

Positive attention is a powerful reinforcer. Teachers discover that time is well spent when children are "caught being good," and given appropriate and authentic notice for that desirable behavior. When adults are specific in giving positive feedback, children will come to understand exactly what behavior it is that earns them positive recognition. As adults dwell minimally on the mistaken behaviors they see, ignoring them when possible, and focus instead on the behaviors they would like to see repeated, both self-esteem and self-control in children are enhanced. When teachers pay attention to desirable behaviors, children quickly learn they don't have to misbehave to get the teacher's attention. Examples:

> "I liked hearing you tell Mario he could have a turn on the swing, DeJuan. Those are friendly words."

> "Good walking, Timmy. Thanks for remembering."

> "I'm happy to see that Katie is all ready to listen. She's sitting very quietly and her eyes are looking at me." Several children who were not so ready quickly copy Katie's behavior.

Redirection

When teachers step in with suggestions of more acceptable activities, children are able to change direction before their behavior gets out of bounds. Suggestions related to children's interest and/or activity level are most likely to be effective. Redirection helps avoid negative situations, and hence, negative feedback, which is damaging to self-esteem.

Redirection requires that teachers be alert to situations that could deteriorate into conflict or rule-breaking. It is much less effective to wait until a problem has occurred and then move in, since then time and attention have to go to restoring order and discussing the problem, before redirection is used to change the mood. Examples:

"Let's see how deep a hole you can dig with that shovel," to a child who looked dangerously as if he were about to throw the sand.

"Blocks are for building with, Jennifer. How about using the Nerf ball for throwing? See if you can get it in the box."

Setting Limits

When children understand that there are certain behaviors that are not permitted, they are relieved of a good deal of need to test the parameters of behavior. Effective adults stop behaviors that are unsafe for the child or others, that are destructive, or that infringe on others' rights. They know that in order for limits to be incorporated into children's systems of self-control, they must be understood and make sense to children. This means that reasons are part of every limit. Reasons must be stated in words that children can understand from their personal experiences, and in ways that suggest large principles of behavior that children may apply themselves in subsequent situations. In addition to reasons, children are reminded of more desirable behavior. Examples:

"When you talk at story time, your friends who want to hear the story get interrupted. Please wait until later."

"Hitting hurts, and people are sad when they get hurt. Please talk to him instead."

Choices for Control

Authoritative adults help children follow through on expected behavior, but in doing so, they want children to retain as much control of their behavior as they can, as well as preserving their self-esteem. By offering children a choice of how they will respond to a limit, adults share power with children. The adult has the power of deciding and defining the limit; the child has the power of controlling individual participation within the limit. Examples:

"It's clean up time now. You may pick up the blocks by yourself, or ask a friend to help you."

"It's clean up time now. You may pick up the small blocks or the large ones—which would you prefer?"

"It's clean up time now. You can work when we do, or you can work when we're starting our music."

In any case, the child is expected to do his share of picking up blocks, but a "face-saving" choice is his to make.

A contrasting and confusing situation occurs when adult words make it sound as if children have choices when in fact they do not. Example:

"Would you like to help pick up blocks now?" sounds as if the child has the option of refusing. This is not likely the adult's true intention.

Natural and Logical Consequences

Recognizing that preschoolers learn best from concrete experience and not so well from abstract words that have little real meaning for them, teachers use consequences to help young children experience the reality of their behavior. With natural consequences teachers have to do little more than help children see the connection between their actions and the results. With logical consequences, teachers have to select an obvious follow-up action to help children experience the effect of their behavior. Consequences help children understand and accept their responsibility for their actions. Examples:

"When you forgot to put the paint smock on, you got paint on your shirt." —Natural

"Running in the hall made you slip."—Natural

"Tavarius wanted to play with you because you gave him a turn on the swing."—Natural

"Please get the mop to dry the floor where you splashed the water. Someone could fall."—Logical

"Look at Keisha's face. She is very sad because you took her truck. What can you do to make her feel better?"—Logical

"Please go back and walk down the hall, to remember our rule."—Logical

Discussion for Problem Solving

Children need a lot of help with learning how to resolve conflicts with one another. Teachers want to encourage the development of negotiation skills, so that children become increasingly able to work out interpersonal differences themselves, and less likely to try to involve adults in solving their problems with peers. In encouraging negotiation adults function best as facilitators, drawing children into direct discussion with one another, while keeping themselves removed from taking over active solution of the problem. Examples:

Adults help children define the problem: "Hey, what's going on here? What seems to be the difficulty?" "Looks to me like two people both want to use the doll buggy."

They encourage children to talk directly with one another, and to listen to what others have to say: "This is something for you and Danny to work out. Please talk with him." "Danny, Sophia's saying something important you need to listen to."

They make sure that children have opportunities to suggest their own solutions, knowing that their decisions will be respected. They check with children, to be sure they have understood and agreed to a solution: "I think we should park the buggy until you two have a chance to talk about how you can agree to use it. When you've decided, let me know."

"You've decided Danny can have a turn first for six minutes. Is that OK with you, Sophia?"

Moving beyond one's own egocentric perspective to take someone else's needs and wants into account is a slow and difficult process. Efforts at discussing differences rather than fighting about them need to be supported and applauded: "I thought you two could come up with a good idea. Shall I tell you when six minutes is up, Danny?"

While it is much quicker for adults to solve the problem themselves ("You'll each have to take a turn; who had it first? I'll just put it away if there is going to be fighting about it"), children need adults who can help mediate or encourage problem solving on their own. This is the only way to build skills and confidence in one's ability to communicate with others.

Supporting children to solve problems for themselves sometimes means outlining a script for them, to give them specific ideas on how they may assert their ideas positively with peers. Example:

To Jamie, who has complained to the teacher that a playmate pushed him, "It doesn't sound as if you liked it when Sabrina pushed you. You could go and tell her 'I don't want to be pushed.'" Or, "How could you tell her you don't like that?"

I-Messages

Adults give children powerful motivation to change undesirable behaviors when they express their personal emotional response to children's actions. Because of the affectionate relationship and the desire to please the adult, a child pays attention and responds when an adult lets him or her know the effects of behavior on the adult. The expression is straightforward and honest, not manipulative, and does not directly attack the child with judgment or shame. Instead, the child is helped to understand the reason for the adult's feeling. The burden is on the child to modify behaviors in response to the adult's message:

> "When you hit your brother, I get angry, because I know hitting hurts him."

> "I'm disappointed that we had to stop our music time because some children were too noisy to hear the record."

Renewal Time

Figure 9-8 Playing alone may help a child regain control. *Courtesy CPCC Child Care Training Center.*

As Clare Cherry (1983) points out, there are times in every child's life when the demands of group life and the need to keep social rules become overwhelming. Whatever the reason—perhaps stress from changes at home, fatigue, personality conflict, frustration with developmental abilities—there are times when a child needs a chance to withdraw from the situation, calm down, and get prepared to re-enter the usual routine. It may mean leaving the area or the room where an upset has occurred; it may also mean participating in a solitary, quiet activity that allows a child time and opportunity to recover equilibrium. (See Figure 9-8.) It may mean the necessary presence of an adult to comfort or quiet. When considered this way, renewal time is a positive technique to help children control their feelings and behavior, not the negative, punishing "time-out" that is so frequently used. Helping children learn that withdrawing from a situation allows them to come back with a different frame of mind or renewed energies is teaching them self-control for the future. Examples:

> "I think you need to do something quiet over here for a while. When you're feeling better, you can go back to your playing."

> "It seems like things are bothering you a lot today. I'd like you to play by yourself until you feel more relaxed."

Developmentally appropriate guidance recognizes children's limitations on impulse control and the need for firm, positive guidance that protects their self-esteem while moving them gradually toward self-control.

Helping Preschoolers with Emotional Control

The topic of emotions is inextricably linked with concepts of self and socialization. Learning to adapt one's behavior to social expectation can be stressful for children and frustrating for those who are guiding them. Developmentally, preschool children have the verbal capacity to learn the vocabulary to be able to express their range of emotion, and some of the cognitive capacity needed to identify particular feelings. However, the limitations of preoperational thought mean they are restricted to recognizing only one emotion at a time, and have trouble recognizing another's feelings, relying primarily on facial clues. They need support in the task of learning to channel their emotional expressions into

BUT WHAT ABOUT?

A lot of the parents at our preschool are concerned that there is no longer any discipline in the schools. They believe in strong discipline, and want to know what we're going to do about it, since there is no corporal punishment allowed in our state.

Developmentally appropriate practice affirms that discipline is an important part of the learning necessary for young children. However, what it sounds like most of your parents are talking about is punishment. It is important to realize that discipline and punishment are not two words that can be used interchangeably. Discipline has two long-term goals: to teach children what they need to know so that eventually they will be able to control their own behavior, and to teach in such a way that children's positive sense of self and relationship with others is maintained. Punishment, on the other hand, is usually focused on more short-term goals, such as stopping misbehavior and exerting adult power over children.

It is the large subject of goals that needs to be discussed with parents first. As they focus on teaching for the future, it is also necessary to talk about preschool children's developmental abilities and cognitive limitations. Lessons that are taught in ways that don't make sense to young children, or that expect more than children are capable of will work against a strong discipline plan.

Parents who bemoan the absence of discipline from a school (by which they often mean the absence of corporal punishment) are usually reassured when they discover that schools and teachers have precise discipline philosophies and firm strategies they put into practice. Share your school's discipline philosophy with parents and discuss the views both school and parents share. Invite parents to spend time in the classroom, so they can observe for themselves as teachers firmly and kindly help young children learn skills of acceptable social interaction and self-control. Remember that the whole subject of discipline has emotional connotations for most adults, and don't force instant agreement. When teachers themselves believe in the effectiveness of positive guidance toward eventual self-control, they can be powerful spokespersons.

constructive verbal methods, rather than nonverbal aggressive, socially destructive means.

A healthy emotional environment offers the security, example, and teaching necessary to nurture emotional control. In the following discussion you will find ten components of emotional environments that encourage developmentally appropriate learning about feelings for preschoolers.

Security   Classroom environments provide security when there is the predictability of unchanging sequences and repeated routines. Security is nurtured by the trustworthy meeting of physical and emotional needs as expressed by children. There is security when teachers encourage a sense of each belonging to a community that supports individual growth, as well as valuing individual variations in temperament and ability. There is security when materials are planned to provide experience of successful mastery and where activities do not invite comparisons and competition. There is security when teachers and parents communicate in an atmosphere of mutual respect for one another's contribution, to share information that will ensure continuity for children's care. In emotionally secure environments, children feel comfortable in revealing their feelings and trust that adults will help them in gaining control.

Warm Relationships

A responsive, affectionate environment contributes to children's emotional health by promoting positive relationships as the major means of teaching reciprocal caring and emotional responsiveness. When the teacher actively demonstrates genuine feelings of concern for others, there is a positive classroom climate that is based on warm relationships. Children can only learn in the context of warm, positive relationships. Teachers recognize that creating such a classroom atmosphere is an important part of their teaching role. They do not become so busy with details of routine or organization that they lose sight of taking the time for individual responsiveness. They comfort children when they cry and reassure them when they are fearful. Generally, they provide "emotional bolstering" (NAEYC, 1992, #516).

Acceptance

When adults recognize and accept children's emotional responses as normal parts of their being, children's self-awareness of feelings is positive. Feelings are recognized and respected when teachers talk about feelings, giving them names and concreteness. When there is regular classroom discussion about feelings, when there are activities and books read that help children begin to recognize the breadth of emotional experience and the commonality of the feelings they experience with others, acceptance is conveyed. There is no limitation on feelings; every feeling is respected as valid and important. No one is told what they do or don't feel ("That doesn't hurt, it's only a scratch." "You don't hate her, she's your friend.") No one is told what they should or should not feel ("You shouldn't feel jealous of her." "You should love your sister.") The only restrictions adults make is on the *methods of expressing* the feelings. They are extremely careful to make this distinction clear to children, always first expressing recognition of the feeling without any judgment on whether the feeling is good or bad, or legitimate, in their opinion. Children are not shamed or made to feel guilty for having the feeling. The adult's attitude conveys the firm message that feelings are real and are accepted as an indivisible part of the person.

In order to be able to honestly accept feelings of others, teachers have to examine their own attitudes toward emotions. Usually this means recalling early teaching and experiences with ways their feelings were dealt with as children, since such examples often have long-lasting significance. Adults who are unable to accept their own range of emotional responses are unlikely to be able to convey acceptance to children. Example:

> "You seem very angry with me because you think I let Carlos have a longer turn than you. When you're angry, I can't let you hit me. You can tell me in words just how mad you are."

This example conveys calm and nonjudgmental acceptance of the feeling, while defining a limit on expression and suggesting a more productive method of expression.

Active Listening

The previous example showed the adult reflecting back to the child a perception of what the child was experiencing. This is known as active listening (Briggs, 1970; Gordon, 1975). It is a technique that identifies feelings that are expressed verbally and/or nonverbally, and reflects that understanding back to the individual. In identifying the feeling, adults often make "educated guesses," using all the clues from the individual child, as well as all the information they have about particular situations, to become sensitive to what the emotion might be. When they reflect the feeling back, they restate the child's feeling tentatively, for confirmation: "It seems to me that you...." "Sounds to me like you feel...." By labeling the feeling, the young child may realize just how to refer to this emotion, or may need to correct the adult's misperception: "No, I feel...." In either case, the way has been indicated to continue to discuss the emotional experience, releasing the feeling in words, and leading to possible problem-solving formulations.

The following examples illustrate these steps to helping children become aware of their feelings, aware of ways they can talk about them, and aware of steps they can take in dealing with feelings.

Example 1. The teacher has watched Sabrina playing listlessly by herself since her grandmother left her at the center this morning. Her grandfather had a heart attack last week and has been hospitalized. While the doctor is optimistic, it has been a stressful week. Sabrina lives with her grandparents.

Teacher:	"Sabrina, you seem pretty sad today. Would you like to talk about it?"
Sabrina:	"Yeah, I want to see my Paw-Paw."
Teacher:	"Sounds like you're missing him."
Sabrina:	"Yeah, they won't let kids into the hospital."
Teacher:	"You'd really like to see him—it's kind of scary when you know he's sick and you can't see him."
Sabrina:	"My Grandma cried last night."
Teacher:	"I guess that made you feel sad? And maybe worried too?"
Sabrina:	(with a sigh, but relaxing:) "Yeah."
Teacher:	"We do worry when the people we love are sick and away from us. I wonder if there's something that would help you feel better about this? What about writing a note to your Paw-Paw? Then he'd know you were close by, even if you couldn't come to see him. And maybe a special picture would help Grandma not feel so sad?"
Sabrina:	"Yeah. Will you write the words for me?"

It is enormously reassuring to know that someone understands and accepts the way we feel, and emotionally healthful to be able to release some of those feelings and feel control over them.

Imagine the opposite effect if the teacher had dealt with the situation by ignoring the feeling.

"Sabrina, it's time you got busy and found something to do this morning."

Another frequent response of adults who do not recognize the importance of helping preschoolers learn to express feelings is to deny the child's feeling.

"Your grandma says your grandpa is going to be just fine, and she certainly doesn't need to see you walking around with a long face."

Sabrina would not feel that her feelings had importance or validity with such responses.

Example 2. The teacher watches a conflict between two boys on the playground, and notices Jesse sitting by himself afterward. She approaches and sees that he's crying.

Teacher: "Jesse, I'm sorry to see you're sad."

Jesse: (He says nothing, and continues to cry.)

Teacher: "It looks to me like you'd like to figure out a way to play with Seth."

Jesse: (angrily) "I don't want to play with that stupid-head. He's not my friend."

Teacher: "Oh, I misunderstood. You sound pretty mad at him."

Jesse: "I am mad. He said I couldn't ride the tricycle with him any more."

Teacher: "And that hurt your feelings?"

Jesse: "No, it's not fair, it was my idea to be policemen, and now he's just policemen with Kenny."

Teacher: "You're angry because it was your idea in the first place?"

Jesse: "Yeah."

Teacher: "Well, is there a way you could tell Seth how you feel about that? Maybe there's something you two could work out."

Jesse goes off to talk to Seth. The opportunity to talk about feelings has helped him clarify his experience, and helps him approach Seth with more control and focus.

A teacher who did not use active listening skills might try to handle the situation with a logical solution that does not touch the feeling:

"Well, you could play with somebody else until they're tired of being silly."

Other teachers are tempted to deliver lectures on behavior, again ignoring the feeling at the heart of the matter.

"All the children in the class are our friends, and you need to learn to play nicely together."

Active listening allows adults to facilitate children's expression of feelings so that they understand more of their own emotions, and more about how they can express them to others. Complete acceptance of feelings is part of active listening.

Limits on Expression

While adults are emphatic in their expression of acceptance of children's rights to feel, they are equally emphatic in the limits on methods of expression they permit. The same limits discussed earlier are the guidelines: Children may not hurt themselves or others, they may not destroy property, and they may not infringe on others' rights in the expression of their emotions. This means that children may not throw toys when they are angry about having to share, they may not attack others aggressively when experiencing frustration, they may not scream or yell hurtful things. These limits need to be firmly maintained, and the reasons given repeatedly. It is not a safe feeling for children to perceive that no caring adult is strong enough to help them control their own impulses. Example:

> "I won't let you hit David when you're upset with him. You can be mad at him, but you have to let him know some other way than with your hands. Hitting hurts."

Outlets   Recognizing that strong feelings often need strong release, and that just putting the feeling in words may not be enough for complete relief, adults suggest and provide outlets for emotional release and calming effects. They explain carefully to children just how and why to use the outlet, so that children may internalize these concepts for future self-control. The goal is to help children learn methods of coping with and channeling their feelings. Emotionally healthy classrooms have materials available for such outlets. Materials might include clay, play dough, pillows, or a punching bag for pounding, paper for tearing, a ball for kicking, a place for yelling or running. Some children benefit from the suggestion of a quiet retreat: a soft pile of pillows to lie on, a basin of water to play in, a lap to sit on. Examples:

> "You can come and pound on the clay to let all those angry feelings out. When you're feeling calmer, we can talk about your problem with David."
>
> "Playing in the water may help your sad feelings."

Modeling Behavior   Teachers know their example will help children learn many important lessons about feelings, such as acceptance of one's own feelings as an integral part of the self, constructive verbal expression of feelings, and self-control. They are honest about their feelings and don't try to hide them from children. Adults seldom succeed in disguising feelings, and attempts to do so leave children bothered by confusing messages, like the teacher saying they will have fun today, and looking anything but! Many teachers mistakenly believe they should always be above emotional responses in the classroom, but this would rob children of important opportunities to experience what it means to be human and to respond to others' emotions. Besides, a teacher who has struggled to hold emotion in through a stressful day is somewhat like a smoldering volcano; an eruption is imminent, and no one knows exactly when or how it will occur. This is not a secure place for children to be! While teachers should give themselves permission to express emotion in the classroom, the importance of a positive adult example must be recalled. Adults do not have permission to behave in destructive ways; there is nothing more alarming than to see an adult having an uncontrolled temper tantrum! Examples:

> "I'm sad today because children in my classroom have destroyed the sand structure the three-year-olds built on the playground," says Diane to her group of four-year-olds. "I'm not feeling much like playing with you right now. I think I'll sit over here for a while and you can decide what you might do to help the three's."
>
> "I'm getting annoyed by so many children coming to me with complaints about other children. I'm going to go wash the paint brushes and maybe then I'll feel more like talking with you."

Such expressions allow children to experience responsibility for their behaviors, in understanding their effect on others' feelings.

Materials for Expression   Healthy emotional environments recognize that children express and deal with feelings and stressful situations through play. Provision of materials that are meaningful for young children encourages playing out of many feelings. Dolls and other house corner props and puppets may encourage dramatization of emotions. Alert teachers may provide specific props based on what they know of children's immediate situations. A teacher who knew that several of her preschoolers were coming to terms with emotions following the birth of siblings added lots of baby paraphernalia such as diapers, bottles, and pacifiers. When one of the young "mothers" reacted with anger to that "darn baby crying again," she was able to help the child express some of her very mixed feelings about the new baby at home. Another teacher, aware of the stress in a particular family that included a job change and moving to a new residence, added suitcases and packing boxes to allow the child to deal with the fearful unknowns of moving. Various art media may help other children express feelings through creative expression. (See Figure 9-9.) Supporting children's meaningful play is a very developmentally appropriate way of helping preschoolers deal with feelings.

Learning about Feelings

Preschoolers need help in understanding some of the cognitive concepts related to feelings. Teachers plan activities that help introduce children to common emotional responses, situations and behaviors that may trigger feelings, and possible courses of action in response to feelings. Both planned group activities and informal discussions allow children to sort out more of the information that they need for emotional control and expression. (See Figure 9-10.) Examples:

> "Look at this picture. What do you think is happening here? How do you think the girl feels? Why do you think she feels that way? What could she do to let her friend know about how she feels?" and so on.

> "Can you find the picture where someone looks worried? Show me how you look when you're worried. When have you felt worried?"

A list of books for preschoolers that encourage conversation about particular feelings appears in Figure 9-11.

Vocabulary to Express Feelings

Not only do children need acceptance of their feelings and support to express them, they also need direct instruction on ways of expressing them to others. An overused cliché in classrooms for young children is, "Use your words!" While the intention is commendable, it is not so simple for young children to use language unless an adult has helped them learn the kinds of words that can be effective. Adults ask children questions to help them describe how they feel. They can then suggest words that children can use with others; depending on the child's cognitive and verbal skills, they may suggest alternative approaches and longer sentences.

After children have had some experience with using adults' words to describe their feelings to others, teachers may encourage children to think of their own. Examples:

> "How did you feel when Sarah called you that name? Well, you could tell her, 'Sarah, I don't like it when you call me names.' She doesn't know that's how you're feeling."

> "You're upset with Sarah. How could you let her know that?"

Learning to express feelings in language is a gradual developmental process. Children need encouragement and reminders to do so, and reinforcement when they do. Example:

> "I like the words you used to tell David you needed a turn. Good talking."

Helping preschoolers learn to control and express emotional reactions is a very important role for the teacher, one that is integrated into each classroom day and every encounter.

Things Caregivers Should Not Do

Inappropriate responses from teachers hinder healthy emotional development. Such responses include:

- ignoring, distracting, mocking, shaming, or "cheering children up"
- showing anger with children's lack of emotional control
- forcing children to express feelings they do not feel, as in a very unintended "I'm sorry"

SUMMARY

The complexity of learning patterns of social behavior and rules, and of achieving control over emotional expression and behaviors necessitates much positive adult guidance. Adults recognize that the learning begun during the preschool years will continue into later periods of development, so they maintain realistic developmental expectations. They recognize that positive issues of identity formation and positive relationships with adults help children learn acceptable behavior.

THINK ABOUT IT

1. Bring a selection of picture books for preschoolers. In small groups, students should analyze the books for positive or negative messages about acceptance of diversity in gender behavior, racial/cultural identity, family structures, etc. Are there messages about friendship, prosocial behavior, emotions?

2. Share examples of guidance techniques students have observed, used, or experienced in adult-child relations. How do they compare with the examples of positive guidance techniques discussed in this chapter?

3. Visit a preschool classroom that you have not visited before. After observing for an hour, write a report that includes specifics you noticed about:

   - provisions to encourage a personal sense of identity
   - overt acceptance of diversity
   - active adult guidance for self-control, for developing friendship skills and prosocial

   awareness, for emotional control and constructive expression of feelings
   - the overall social/emotional climate, and your sense of how it was created

4. For the following situations, role-play the responses of a teacher who is trying to guide children in developmentally appropriate ways to positive emotional and social behavior.

   A child comes to you crying to complain that another child has taken her trike.

   A child hits another child who called him a name.

   A child tells another he can't play in the block area.

   A child cries quietly in the corner after her mother leaves.

   A child won't play in the block area, saying that's for boys.

   For additional suggestions, brainstorm other social/emotional situations you've encountered with preschool children.

QUESTIONS TO REVIEW OBJECTIVES

1. Describe some of the important social/emotional developmental tasks of the preschool years.

2. Discuss ways that adults can nurture positive feelings about identity.

3. Identify classroom practices that nurture positive gender identity.

4. Identify classroom practices that nurture positive racial/cultural identity.

5. Describe ways teachers can help children develop social skills for friendship.

6. Discuss methods of nurturing prosocial development in the classroom.

Figure 9-9 Art media may be used to encourage a child to express her feelings. *Courtesy Avondale Children's Center.*

Books That Help Young Children Know It's All Right To Feel ...

Allington, Richard. *Feelings*
Berger, Terry. *I Have Feelings*
Brenner, Barbara. *Faces, Faces, Faces*
Hazen, Barbara. *Happy, Sad, Silly, Mad*
Lalli, Judy. *Feelings Alphabet*
McGovern, Ann. *Feeling Mad, Feeling Sad, Feeling Bad, Feeling Glad*
Simon, Norma. *How Do I Feel?*
Wittels, Harriet. *Things I Hate!*
Yudell, Lynn. *Make A Face*

Angry

Alexander, Martha. *And My Mean Old Mother Will Be Sorry*
DuBois, William. *Bear Party*
Erickson, Karen. *I Was So Mad*
Hapgood, Miranda. *Martha's Mad Day*
Sharmat, Marjorie. *I'm Not Oscar's Friend Any More*
Viorst, Judith. *Alexander and the Terrible, Horrible, No Good, Very Bad Day*
Watson, Jane. *Sometimes I Get Angry*
Zolotow, Charlotte. *The Quarreling Book*

Jealous

Alexander, Martha. *Nobody Asked Me if I Wanted a Baby Sister*
Asch, Frank. *Bear's Bargain*
Hoban, Russell. *A Baby Sister for Frances; A Birthday for Frances*
Kraus, Robert. *Big Brother*
Mayer, Mercer. *One Frog Too Many*
Weber, Bernard. *Lyle and the Birthday Party*
Zolotow, Charlotte. *It's Not Fair*

Embarrassed

Carlson, Nancy. *Loudmouth George and the Big Race*
Cooney, Nancy. *Donald Says Thumbs Down*

Lexau, Joan. *I Should Have Stayed in Bed*
Townsend, Kenneth. *Felix, the Bald-Headed Lion*

Afraid

Alexander, Martha. *Maybe a Monster*
Carlson, Nancy. *Harriet's Recital*
Cohen, Miriam. *Jim Meets the Thing*
Kraus, Robert. *Noel the Coward*
Mayer, Mercer. *There's a Nightmare in My Closet*
Turkle, Brinton. *It's Only Arnold*
Viorst, Judith. *My Mama Says There Aren't Any Zombies, Ghosts, Vampires, Creatures, Demons, Monsters, Fiends, Goblins, or Things*

Lonely

Battles, Edith. *One to Teeter-Totter*
Coontz, Otto. *The Quiet House*
Fujikawa, Gyo. *Shags Finds a Kitten*
Gag, Wanda. *Nothing at All*
Keats, Ezra Jack. *The Trip*
Stevenson, James. *The Bear Who Had No Place to Go*
Sugita, Yutaka. *Helena, the Unhappy Hippopotamus*
Yashima, Taro. *Crow Boy*

Sadness

Allen, Frances. *Little Hippo*
Baker, Betty. *Rat Is Dead and Ant Is Sad*
Clifton, Lucille. *Everett Anderson's Goodbye*
DePaolo, Tomie. *Nana Upstairs and Nana Downstairs*
Kaldhol, Marit. *Goodbye Rune*
Low, Joseph. *The Christmas Grump*
Viorst, Judith. *The Tenth Good Thing About Barney*
Zolotow, Charlotte. *Janey*

Figure 9-10 Activities and stories help children understand the feelings of themselves and others. *Courtesy NationsBank Child Care Center.*

Figure 9-11 Books that help young children know it's all right to feel.

7. Identify several of the ten positive guidance techniques discussed in this chapter.

8. Identify several of the ten positive components of an emotionally appropriate environment for preschoolers.

REFERENCES AND SUGGESTIONS FOR READING

Berne, P. H. (1988, August/September). Nurturing success. *Pre-K Today*, 33–37.

Briggs, D. C. (1970). *Your child's self-esteem.* Garden City, NY: Doubleday and Co.

Buzzelli, C. A., & File, N. (1989, March). Building trust in friends. *Young Children, 44(3)*, 70–74.

Byrnes, D., & Kiger, G. (eds.). (1992). *Common bonds: Anti-bias teaching in a diverse society.* Wheaton, MD: Association for Childhood Education International.

Cherry, C. (1983). *Please don't sit on the kids: Alternatives to punitive discipline.* Belmont, CA: Pitman Learning Inc.

Clark, K., & Clark, M. (1939). The development of consciousness of self and the emergence of racial identity in Negro pre-school schoolchildren. *Journal of Social Psychology, 10*, 591–599.

Clark, L., DeWolf, S., & Clark, C. (1992, July). Teaching teachers to avoid having culturally assaultive classrooms. *Young Children, 47(5)*, 4–9.

Clemens, S. G. (1983). *The sun's not broke, a cloud's just in the way.* Mt. Rainier, MD: Gryphon House.

Cole, M., & Cole, S. R. (1993). *The development of children* (2nd ed.). New York: W.H. Freeman and Co.

Derman-Sparks, L. et al. (1989). *Anti-bias curriculum.* Washington, DC: NAEYC.

Derman-Sparks, L. et al. (1990, November/December). Understanding diversity: What young children want and need to know. *Pre-K Today*, 44–53.

Dodge, K. A. (1983). Behavioral antecedents of peer social status. *Child Development, 54*, 1386–1399.

Erikson, E. (1968). *Identity: Youth and crisis.* New York: W.H. Norton.

Fraiberg, S. (1959). *The magic years.* New York: Charles Scribner's Sons.

Goffin, S. G. (1989, Winter). How well do we respect the children in our care? *Childhood Education*, 68–74.

Gonzalez-Mena, J. (1993). *Multicultural issues in child care.* Mountain View, CA: Mayfield Publishing Co.

Gordon, T. (1975). *Parent effectiveness training.* New York: Wyden.

Hall, N. & Rhomberg, V. (1995). *Affective curriculum: Teaching the anti-bias approach to young children.* Toronto: Nelson.

Hazen, N. L., Black, B., & Fleming-Johnson, F. (1984, September). Social acceptance: Strategies children use and how teachers can help children learn them. *Young Children, 39(6)*, 26–36.

Heller, C. (1993, Spring). Equal play. *Teaching Tolerance*, 24–28.

Katz, L. (1984, July). The professional early childhood teacher. *Young Children, 39(5)*, 3–10.

Katz, P. (1982). Development of children's racial awareness and intergroup attitudes. In Katz, L. (ed.), *Current topics in early childhood education.* Norwood, NJ: Ablex.

Kemple, K. M. (1991, July). Preschool children's peer acceptance and social interaction. *Young Children, 46(5)*, 47–53.

Kostelnik, M., et al. (1993). *Guiding children's social development* (2nd ed.). Albany, NY: Delmar Publishers Inc.

Kostelnik, M., Stein, L. C., & Whiren, A. P. (1988, Fall). Children's self-esteem: The verbal environment. *Childhood Education*, 29–32.

NAEYC. (1992). *Developmentally appropriate practice in early childhood programs serving younger preschoolers (vol. 516).* Washington, DC: Author.

Paley, V. G. (1984). *Boys and girls.* Chicago: University of Chicago Press.

Paley, V. G. (1986). *Mollie is three.* Chicago, IL: University of Chicago Press.

Paley, V. G. (1992). *You can't say you can't play.* Cambridge, MA: Harvard University Press.

Parten, M. (1932). Social participation among preschool children. *Journal of Abnormal and Social Psychology, 27 (2)*, 243–269.

Pitcher, E. G., & Schultz, L. H. (1983). *Boys and girls at play.* New York: Praeger Press.

Smith, C. A. (1982). *Promoting the social development of young children: Strategies and activities.* Palo Alto, CA: Mayfield Publishing Co.

Waxman, S. (1976). *What is a girl? What is a boy?* Los Angeles: Peace Press.

Weisner, T. S., & Wilson-Mitchell, J. (1990). Nonconventional family life-styles and sex typing in six-year-olds. *Child Development, 62*, 1915–1933.

Wolf, D. P. (ed.). (1986). *Connecting: Friendship in the lives of young children and their teachers.* Redmond, WA: Exchange Press.

York, S. L. (1991). *Roots and wings: Affirming culture in early childhood settings.* St. Paul, MN: Redleaf Press.

Developmentally Appropriate Social/Emotional Environments: For Primary-Aged

*L*eah is spending the night with her best friend Joanna, who is also six.

Julio plays on a Little League team that practices twice a week and plays games on Saturday mornings.

Jasmine has joined the Brownies.

Eddie and his friend Will have recently begun a collection of rocks. They spend hours every week talking about it.

Marty had a bad dream after he watched a scary television program last week, but he didn't call out for his parents, because he didn't want them to know he was scared.

Jamar watches the children on the playground, but doesn't join in the chase game.

Michelle draws a picture with a face covered with tears, and tells her mother, "This is how I feel when Daddy brings me home after the weekend."

A sign on the backyard gate proclaims "Secret Club—No girls get in—this means you, Rachel."

The expanding world of the primary-aged child is a world that includes increasing skill in interpersonal relationships, as is evidenced by the preceeding list. The influence of peers becomes a major force in shaping children's behavior, and adding new information to their self-concepts. Increasing control and communication abilities allow five- through eight-year-olds to deal with their emotions in more mature ways. Moving slowly to less egocentric perspectives, they become increasingly able to take another's viewpoint.

Yet there is much to learn. Learning group skills, developing a sense of moral judgment, discovering how to resolve conflicts without adult intervention, and maintaining friendships are important tasks for this age group. This chapter will examine the social/emotional issues for primary-aged children and consider the most helpful social/emotional environments for them.

OBJECTIVES

After completing this chapter, students should be able to:

- identify social/emotional issues of the primary years.

- discuss the implications of teacher responses for developing peer group participation skills.

- discuss the implications of teacher responses for self-esteem and a sense of industry.

- describe considerations about cooperation vs. competition.

- describe the benefits of mixed age groupings.

- identify strategies to nurture moral development.

- discuss teacher behaviors for optimum emotional development.

Social/Emotional Issues for the Primary Years

Self-Esteem

The development of self-esteem in the primary years is closely bound to developing a *sense of industry*, defined by Erikson as the core conflict of the school years. This sense is influenced by both cognitive and social accomplishments. As children learn the cognitive skills expected in their early schooling, they either see themselves as capable learners or not. Socially, as children spend more time away from family members, the sense of self they acquired in their families is challenged; they add new information to their self-concepts, based on their perceptions of peer response to them. Moving outside of the protection of home and family, primary-aged children get new opportunities to see how they measure up to the standards of others. The school has its standards of accomplishment, as do other adults: Cub Scout leaders, Sunday school teachers, coaches, dance teachers. The process of *social comparison* gives children new information to incorporate into their developing self-concepts: Am I as fast a runner? Do I learn as quickly? Do I have as many friends? Success is defined in relation to comparative assessment with the child's social group.

Relationships with other adults and within the peer group are not the only influences on self-esteem during this period. Self-esteem has also been linked with patterns of child rearing and interaction with parents. Parental responses that convey acceptance of their children, respect for their individuality, and clearly defined limits are linked with high self-esteem in school-aged children (Cole and Cole, 1993). Appropriate guidance for the primary years is crucial for continuing development of self-control as well as positive self-esteem.

Peer Relationships and Group Skills

Increasingly, the lives of primary-aged children become bound with their interest in spending time with friends at school and at home. It is estimated that from the age of six, most American children spend over 40 percent of their waking hours in the company of peers (Cole and Cole, 1993). They play together, they talk together, they do "nothing" together. Much of the time they spend with peers is unstructured, although the increasing number of organized recreational or alternate child care arrangements affects the amount of adult supervision over peer activities.

> *"* The increased time that children spend among their peers is both a cause and an effect of their development during middle childhood. Adults begin to allow their children to spend extensive time with friends because they recognize the children's greater ability to think and act for themselves. At the same time, the new experiences with peers challenge children to master new cognitive and social skills (Cole and Cole, 1993, p. 517). *"*

There are four basic developmental functions of friendships:

1. Friendships are the source of learning basic social skills such as communication, cooperation, and the ability to enter an existing group.

2. Friendships help children learn about themselves, others, and the larger world.

3. Friendships offer fun, emotional support, and relief from stress.

4. Friendships help children begin to learn about intimate relationships (adapted from Cole and Cole, 1993).

Learning the skills to fit into a peer group is an important task for the primary years.

Teachers who have narrowly constrained views of both curriculum and teaching strategies appropriate for the five- through eight-year-olds often overlook their crucial roles in helping these children develop the social skills necessary for group membership. But recent research indicates clearly that children who do not develop the skills to maintain friendships in childhood are at risk for poor achievement in school, a greater likelihood of dropping out of school, higher incidences of juvenile delinquency, and poor mental health as adults (Schickedanz et al., 1993). Research also indicates that adult intervention and coaching can help children develop better peer relationships (Burton, 1987). This underlines the importance of teachers in developmentally appropriate primary classrooms recognizing their function in the social/emotional domain.

Games and Rules, Competition vs. Cooperation

One of the ways primary-aged children attempt to regulate their social relations by themselves is by basing their play in games with explicit rules. Rules determine what roles children play, and what they can and cannot do in their play together. Not only is the ability to engage in rule-based games related to cognitive development, but the games themselves are also a vehicle for developing skills of negotiation, settling disagreements, and learning to cooperate. Games with rules offer children standards for their conduct that enable them to measure up to criteria set by others. Rules allow primary-aged children to play together for longer periods and in more complex ways. However, for young primary-aged children, rules tend to be treated inflexibly; listening to them at play, one hears many references to "being fair" and "not cheating." Developing skills of communication and conflict resolution are important social tasks of the primary years.

One of the social/emotional issues to be resolved in developmentally appropriate environments for primary-aged children is the extent to which competition among children is healthy or stressful, and the need for a balance with learning cooperation as a skill of group membership. Critics of organized sports, like Little League, point out that the pressure to win from parents and coaches may put unhealthy stress on children, and rob them of opportunities to engage in spontaneous activity with their peers. Classroom practices often pit children against one another ("Let's see who can finish their math problems first!" "Who got the most A's?") rather than encourage them to support and help one another. Adults must consider the effects of competition vs. cooperation when evaluating social/emotional environments.

Mixed Age Groupings

One of the ways some programs have dealt with the issues of competition vs. cooperation is to create mixed age groupings in classrooms and care settings. There are advantages noted for both younger and older children in settings with a span of chronological ages. The advantages are not only social, since the mixed age grouping allows for the normal uneven cognitive development of individuals, the individual pacing and style of learning, without any diminishing of self-esteem. Socially, older children in mixed age groupings have opportunities to exhibit leadership skills with less threatening younger children, and exhibit an enhanced sense of responsibility. Older children also seem to improve in self-regulation of their behavior. On the other hand, younger children benefit by participating in the more complex forms of play developed by the older children, and by imitating the behaviors of older children. Mixed age interaction may also offer therapeutic effects. Older children who are socially isolated may feel comfortable playing with younger children, thereby gaining opportunities to practice and refine their social skills (Katz et al., 1991). The benefits of mixed age groupings need to be considered in positive social/emotional environments. (See Figure 10-1.)

Moral Development

Primary-aged children are becoming increasingly able to make judgments about the rightness or wrongness of actions, based upon what they understand about the intentions of actions. Younger primary-aged children, according to Piaget, are in the state of *moral realism* in which rules are regarded as unchangeable, absolute, and imposed by an external authority (Piaget, 1965). Kohlberg refers to this same moral period as the *preconventional level of morality* in which moral reasoning is influenced by a concern for obedience and punishment and for satisfying personal needs (Kohlberg, 1976). Slowly, school-aged children shift into the *conventional level* of moral reasoning, where they become more concerned with appearing "good" and "fair" and look to others to approve their moral acts. Primary-aged children need opportunities to consider the basis for socially responsible actions, and need guidance from adults as they move toward being able to regulate their behavior.

Emotional Development and Stress

The image of carefree children at play may be true of some school-aged children, at least some of the time. But for many children, the early school years and the recognition of some of the realities of their lives bring stress. Considering how to create less stressful situations for primary-aged children is important, as is helping children learn how to deal with their own stress. Learning how to cope with feelings continues to be a developmental task of primary-aged children to be considered in planning social/emotional environments.

Having considered the major social/emotional issues of the early school years, it is time to think about appropriate implications and responses.

Multi-Age Grouping

Features	Benefits
Two- or three-year age range of students	Access to wide range of interests, thinking, skills, and modeling
Heterogeneous grouping	Positive self-image; natural interactions; receptive to special needs
More than one year with classmates	Supportive "family" environment
Multiple years with same teacher	Secure stable child/family/teacher relationship
Child-centered learning activities	Learning experiences consistent with how children learn
Two- or three-year skills continuum	Flexibility for children to progress at own rate
Integrated curriculum	Develop concepts that connect learning; deeper thinking
Individualized expectations	Develop independent learners; match curriculum with children's needs
Performance-based assessments	Match types of assessment with types of learning
Extended time for learning	Teacher-student familiarity allows teaching from first school day
Potential cost effectiveness	Smaller quantities per learning resource; fewer consumables; class assignment flexibility
Parental choice program	Provides option for parents

Figure 10-1 There are real advantages to multi-age groupings. *Used with permission of Beth Bellemere, Scarborough School Department.*

Implications for Teachers Planning Social/Emotional Environments

Skills for Group Participation

Teachers trying to help children develop peer group skills will:

- Become aware, through careful ongoing observation and note-taking, of children's style of interaction, preferences in companions, and ease or diffi-

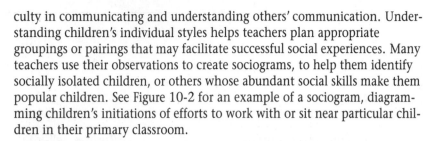

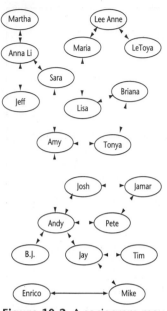

Figure 10-2 A sociogram may show teachers patterns of social interaction and isolation in a classroom.

Figure 10–3 Teachers may create work pairings based on what they know of children's interests and communication styles.

culty in communicating and understanding others' communication. Understanding children's individual styles helps teachers plan appropriate groupings or pairings that may facilitate successful social experiences. Many teachers use their observations to create sociograms, to help them identify socially isolated children, or others whose abundant social skills make them popular children. See Figure 10-2 for an example of a sociogram, diagramming children's initiations of efforts to work with or sit near particular children in their primary classroom.

- Create informal physical arrangements that allow children to choose to work with particular people and allow for small group interaction and conversation. Timid children tend to get lost in larger groups, but may be able to find their own place of comfort in smaller groupings. When the physical environment supports children's working and talking together, there are opportunities for them to have firsthand social experience, and not simply learn by having adults tell them what they "should" do or say in theoretical situations. As discussed in Chapter 6, the physical arrangements that include opportunities for group interaction are work tables and other small, informal areas, rather than the traditional rows of desks; blocks of time in which children plan and carry out joint projects; and interest centers for common activity. Example:

  Ms. Hoban has a variety of work areas in her first-grade classroom; one area is big enough for five children, one for four, four areas for three children, three areas for two, and five areas for individual work.

- Create specific pairings to work on particular projects, using what they know of children's interests and communications styles (Gamberg et al., 1988). Children become friends when they have things they can do together (Cole and Cole, 1993). As teachers design common activities, they help children experience a sense of cooperation for mutual benefit. (See Figure 10-3.) Example:

  Ms. Hoban arranged for the children to work in pairs as they planned their project on "Houses Around the World." She paired Stephen and Antonio, counting on Stephen's communication and social skills to help him respond to Antonio's quieter style.

- Teach social skills directly. Less popular children tend to be unable to initiate contact successfully with other children, and in fact alienate others with unprovoked hostility, whining, silliness, and other unattractive or disruptive behaviors. Such patterns of social style tend to become stable in the early primary years, so direct and early adult intervention is necessary to prevent lack of skills from becoming a permanent handicap. Teachers can help by calling attention to behaviors that work and those that don't, and by encouraging children to recognize and identify their own behaviors.

Social skills that can be taught directly include:

1. Giving attention to others
2. Becoming aware of others' perspectives and wishes
3. Learning to take turns
4. Initiating conversation
5. Listening and talking appropriately

6. Being assertive rather than aggressive

7. Looking at and being supportive to other children

8. Learning to enjoy being with others

> Miss Hoban said to Antonio: "You could ask Stephen what his ideas for the project would be. Be sure you look at him as he tells you."
>
> Later she said, "Did you tell Stephen what you would like to build for your house? He needs to hear your good ideas too."

- Coach children by encouraging them to consider the most appropriate behaviors with peers, and providing feedback on their attempts at socialization and group work.

> Miss Hoban asked Antonio, "What do you think would be the best way to let Stephen know you want to try your idea for building the house with wood? If you just say 'No, my idea,' it will likely make him mad."
>
> Later she said, "You know, Stephen really listened to you when you explained your idea clearly to him. Nobody can know what is in your mind until you tell them."

- Mediate, and teach children negotiation skills. Skills of conflict resolution are vital learning for primary-aged children, who spend so much more time without adults available to them. Teachers help children learn to express their views and needs, and then to keep talking until they come up with a solution all participants can live with. Helping children become aware of their own abilities to solve difficulties without resorting to violence is important learning for children who have been exposed to so much media and real-life violence (Carlsson-Paige and Levin, 1990).

> There seems to be an impasse. Antonio and Stephen look genuinely disturbed, and angry words are flying. Miss Hoban takes them aside. "I see that you have a problem. Let's talk about it. Stephen, please listen while Antonio tells you what he wants, and then he'll listen to you."

- Support children as they learn to take a social perspective. Teachers may plan classroom activities and discussions to help children understand others' feelings and viewpoints. Books that present particular responses and feelings in situations may be read and discussed. Skits presented at large group meeting time may help children see social skills and others' feelings enacted. (See Drew, 1987, for activity ideas.) Example:

> Miss Hoban noticed that several of the pairings were having difficulty with arguments and disagreements. At the morning group meeting, she asked two children to pretend to be partners disagreeing about how to build their house. Then she asked the whole group to brainstorm what would be better ways to handle the differences so they could handle it better the next time a problem occurred.

- Plan groupwork activities, so that curriculum and daily time is designed for cooperative learning experiences. As children discover how much pleasure and benefit can be derived from working with others as a team, they are motivated to develop group participation skills. Children with socialization problems have many more opportunities to practice when classroom plans

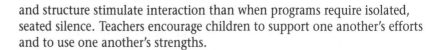

Figure 10–4 Teachers help children learn social skills needed to succeed in group work. *Courtesy Scarborough School Department.*

and structure stimulate interaction than when programs require isolated, seated silence. Teachers encourage children to support one another's efforts and to use one another's strengths.

Positive groupwork experiences do not just happen. Teachers must carefully lay the foundations for positive interdependence. They help children define mutual goals and perceive their responsibility for one another's learning and success, while stressing the individual's accountability to the group (Johnson et al., 1984). Teachers stress a focus on social as well as academic goals for group activities, giving direct instruction in social skills necessary for performing successfully in groups (Watson et al., 1988). (See Figure 10-4.) Example:

> Miss Hoban plans regular times each day when the teams work together on their theme projects. Now that the teams have completed their brainstorming, they are proceeding to do the background reading for their buildings. Stephen discovers that Antonio is a good reader, able to help his partner understand some words Stephen couldn't figure out for himself.

- Create a classroom atmosphere that will not tolerate exclusion or unkindness to its members. Primary-aged children can be cruel to one another, and need teachers who convey respect for diversity of race and culture, of gender role behaviors, or different physical abilities, and who challenge all exclusionary behaviors. Teachers regularly help children see that each member of the classroom community has a different and valuable contribution to make.

" Look for daily and weekly opportunities for each individual to contribute appropriately and significantly to the group. Who has super humor—the class comedian?... Who has special abilities, such as the ability to get around in a wheelchair, the ability to speak sign language, the ability to dance, the ability to teach others?... Who enjoys working cooperatively?... Who is musically, aesthetically, artistically, athletically, theatrically, etc. talented? (Greenberg, 1992, p. 11). "

> Miss Hoban asked Antonio to teach the other children some words in Spanish, since he knew two languages. Now the other children occasionally ask him to tell them what a word is in Spanish.

- Create a sense of a "caring community" (Schaps and Solomon, 1990). As children are helped to engage in empathetic activities and consider others' perspectives, they are helped to develop prosocial skills of considerateness, concern, and kindness. They learn to balance their own needs with a consideration of others. They are encouraged to ask others for help, and to help others. (See Figure 10-5.) Example:

Figure 10–5 Children are encouraged to ask peers for help. *Courtesy Scarborough School Department.*

> Recently, when the teacher heard some boys teasing Antonio about his accent, she called a class meeting to talk about differences, and about comments that hurt feelings. She wants the children to feel comfortable enough to defend themselves against unfair comments and treatment, so she encourages assertiveness.

Things Caregivers Should Not Do

Teachers do not support development of peer group participation skills when they:

- maintain classrooms where children learn mostly in silent, individual work, or in large, teacher-directed groups

- avoid using social issues as direct teaching opportunities, either ignoring problems or intervening to solve disputes directly, without using opportunities for discussion and problem solving

- allow unfair practices to occur without challenge and discussion

- concentrate on narrow definitions of curriculum as cognitive skills and facts, rather than seeing the development of social skills as an ongoing, integrated, and important part of the curriculum

Self-Esteem

Primary-aged children continue to grow in self-esteem when teachers create environments where:

- Children are able to succeed, because the adults have chosen learning tasks and methods that are appropriate to their developmental level. School-aged children are powerfully motivated to become competent at the knowledge and skills recognized by our culture as important. Teachers who individualize plans and materials allow children to learn at their own level without fear of failing. Example:

  > Mr. Rodriguez encourages his kindergartners to select books that are simple, repetitive, and predictable. He teaches strategies such as reading to get context clues about what happens next and then rereading difficult parts, or substituting one or more words to get the basic idea. He encourages the children to collaborate on their figuring out techniques. (See Figure 10-6.) His kindergartners love to read.

- Primary-aged children begin to use *social comparison* as a method of defining themselves. Being aware of this, teachers attempt to broaden the scope of activities where children see themselves involved with others, beyond just the acquisition of cognitive skills. They recognize achievement in interpersonal relations and communication, in athletic and artistic abilities, in mechanical and constructive talents. They make sure that every child can recognize their own areas of strength, as well as areas to work on.

  > Mr. Rodriguez keeps charts in the classroom that recognize many fields of accomplishment, including Jamar as the big fish catcher—Jamar wears a leg brace and knows he cannot keep up with other boys in running games at recess.

- Children perceive that teachers expect and believe they are capable of learning, no matter what their social class, ethnic background, or gender. Children are treated with equal and positive respect and responsiveness. The classroom mirrors this concept of respect with multicultural and nonsexist materials carefully chosen to enhance individual self-esteem by conveying acceptance of the diversity represented in the classroom, the community, and the nation. Teachers remember that the way others respond to children

Figure 10–6 Children are encouraged to collaborate on figuring out solutions in reading and writing. *Courtesy Scarborough School Department.*

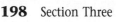

BUT WHAT ABOUT?

But what about a child who prefers to play alone? I have a boy in my after-school program who never wants to join in games or play with other children. Should I be doing something about this?

As with so many situations, it is impossible to give a definitive answer to this. The answer begins with, "it depends." You will need to observe this child carefully, and to find out other information from parents and teachers at school. For example, does this child seem contented playing by himself, or frustrated and unhappy to be left out? Does the child make overtures to other children that are rejected, reject the overtures of others, or simply find his own independent entertainments? How does he spend his play time? Is he deeply engrossed in his own activity or simply watching the other children? What does the child like to do, and are these interests different from others? Has the child had the opportunity to develop the skills used by the other children in their play? Are his language skills comparable to those of the other children? Is there any physical impairment that is interfering with his ability to relate to other children? Most importantly, have adults given the child the opportunity to talk about his reasons for playing alone, and his feelings about doing so?

Family information that might be helpful includes: the family's cultural and ethnic background; living conditions and neighborhood experiences; factors in the family that might cause the child to prefer solitary play; typical past responses in group situations; and the child's temperament and patterns in relationships.

Putting together this kind of information should help you decide whether this is a situation that would benefit by intervention, or whether this is a child whose temperament and interests make him contented in solitary play. Individual temperament must be respected; every child does not need to be the popular center of a group of friends. But every child does deserve the opportunity to develop the social skills that will help him ease into group situations. Teachers can ensure that children are not totally isolated from group situations by providing activities to do in pairs, and some fun group activities to encourage everyone to join in for short periods. A goal is to ensure that everyone has the opportunity to experience the benefits of social interaction, without forcing children to change their temperamental style.

helps form their self-concept; children will behave according to the image of themselves they perceive that others hold (Rosenthal, 1987). Examples:

> Mr. Rodriguez's class is working on the theme of "Work." Every parent in the classroom has been asked to come to talk about his or her work. There are three single mothers who do not work, and two parents who have been recently laid off from their jobs. These parents came to talk about their work at home. The children understand that there are all kinds of important work, both inside and outside of the home.

Miss Hoban recently attended a workshop on increasing awareness of gender-free responses to children, aimed at decreasing teacher differentiation in their responses and expectations of girls and boys.

- Children are encouraged to be independent and self-reliant, to rely on their own thinking, answers, choices, and solutions. Teachers intervene, demonstrate, and suggest solutions only to the extent necessary for children to succeed. Children are given meaningful responsibilities within the classroom community, and are recognized for their contributions.

  Mr. Rodgriguez says frequently, "You decide!" or "Why not ask a friend what he thinks about that?" or "I'll bet you'll have a good idea about that." The job list has twenty-five tasks on it, one for each child to do; the responsibilities rotate each week. One of the jobs is to remind anyone who has forgotten to do their job!

- Teachers plan games and classroom activities designed to enhance self-esteem and self-awareness. See Borba, 1984, for ideas about activities for self-awareness.

- Children participate in "developmental discipline" (Schaps and Solomon, 1990). They are encouraged to take an active role in classroom regulation, including participating with the teacher in developing positive classroom rules and in problem solving for solutions. Beginning principles of participation in a democratic society are taught in this way (Greenberg, 1992). Teachers are positive in their expectations and treat children with respect. When self-control slips, they redirect children or take them aside for individual discussion and problem solving.

  Mr. Rodriguez has planned a meeting to discuss the rough play on the playground that concerns him. The meeting leader (a designated weekly job) will ask for solutions. Mr. Rodgriquez will make sure children have opportunities to discuss the situation fully, so they understand the problem and know what is expected. He believes that children who know and understand the limits want to do what's right.

Things Caregivers Should Not Do

Self-esteem in primary-aged children is damaged when teachers:

- select learning tasks that are too difficult for children, and teaching methods that ignore their natural learning style

- expect too much or too little of children, and convey an attitude of differential responsiveness, as for example, having reading groups for the poorest readers that imply these children are less capable

- ignore cultural and other differences, or treat these children as if they are expected to learn less

- rely heavily on reward and punishment systems of discipline in the classroom, assuming a position of powerful judge and rule enforcer

Thoughts about Games with Rules, and Competition vs. Cooperation in Developmentally Appropriate Classrooms

Since the play of primary-aged children is primarily based on their games with rules, teachers need to consider their role in supporting children in this play, and in helping children balance cooperative skills with competitive attitudes. Many early childhood educators feel that organized games are only developmentally appropriate when adults recognize and "positively confront the competitive element" (Isenberg and Jalongo, 1993, p. 236). Some helpful practices include:

- Providing materials, games, and time for children to organize their own games. The skills of leadership, communication, problem solving, and cooperation develop through games, so this is time well spent.

- Teaching children skills necessary to succeed at playing games. Children who are neglected or rejected by their peers are often those who cannot properly join in the games. Helping children develop gross motor skills of throwing, catching, hitting, running, jumping, etc., as well as giving them practice with the turn-taking and reasoning needed for board games, may help children be included in the game playing. Varieties of games and materials are necessary to include all children, no matter what their physical or cognitive limitations.

- Letting children manage their games and rules without adult interference. The valuable learning may be lost when adults intervene too frequently with admonitions about playing properly, or advice (or pressure) on how to win. If children choose to modify the rules for their games during play, their creative thinking should be encouraged and allowed. Children's competitive standards will be high enough, without the addition of adult standards. Children's games should be left to children.

- Planning cooperative games for classroom and after school programs. These are games that emphasize pure enjoyment, rather than being first, or winners and losers. Although the American philosophy emphasizes individual achievement and a competitive spirit, young children probably don't need this philosophy overemphasized. For examples of cooperative games that can be used with primary children, see Orlick 1978 and 1985; Rowen, 1988; Sobell, 1988; and Figure 10-7.

- Taking competition out of the classroom. Children's motivation for learning should come from the intrinsic satisfactions of making sense out of the world and acquiring competence. This kind of motivation is subverted when there is too much emphasis on success and competition. When children chronically experience failure in competitive learning situations, they suffer a loss of self-esteem. They also become primarily oriented toward avoiding more failure, thus inhibiting them from attempting tasks on which they will be evaluated competitively (Johnson and Johnson, 1975). Competitive practices such as acquiring stickers, letter grades, gold stars, candy, or extra privileges, or singling children out for extraordinary praise, are not only contrary to the idea of setting personal challenges for achievement, but are

Feathers Up

The object of this game is to keep the feathers in the air by blowing.

Lips Are Sealed

Children play whatever they like best in silence—no talking. Just watch the other ways they find to communicate.

Pretzels

Give the children directions to get into an odd position, holding it as they try a second move. Like, "Put your finger on someone's back. Now put your elbow on the floor." Keep it up until you run out of ideas—or they fall over.

Bang Bang!

The first player gives a nail a bang into a board with a hammer. Each player hits the nail once until it's all the way into the board. See how many hits it takes, then start over again.

Figure 10-7 Games that encourage cooperation—everybody wins! *Adapted from Everybody Wins, Sobell, 1988.*

also divisive in peer relations, and are frequently damaging to the self-esteem of children who receive fewer rewards.

Research shows that competition and cooperation are partly a factor of the socialization patterns in a culture (Madsen and Shapira, 1970), but can also be heavily influenced by the social organization of the environment (Sherif and Sherif, 1953). Teachers need to examine the social/emotional environments of their classrooms with this in mind.

Thoughts about Mixed Age Groupings

One way to avoid competition is to include obviously unequal children in classroom groupings. A multi-age classroom is multidimensional, legitimizing and extending the wide variations in ability and activity that will be found in any classroom. Mixed age groupings have been used successfully with young children both in the United States and abroad (e.g., England, Sweden, and Italy). This is certainly not a new idea in education, but merits rethinking as developmentally appropriate practice asks teachers to concentrate on individual appropriateness.

There are benefits to mixed-age classroom groupings in the preschool and primary years:

1. Family and neighborhood settings have always offered mixed age environments for children's socialization and education. In times when children now spend little time in either family or neighborhood settings, they do not benefit from those kinds of interage contact. It has been said humans are not usually born in litters, but we now educate them in litters, keeping them strictly with age-mates.

2. In mixed aged groupings, social development is enhanced as leadership and prosocial behaviors have been observed to increase. Mixed age groupings

give all children the chance to be the oldest and most mature at some point in their school experiences.

3. Research on cooperative learning and peer tutoring suggests that interaction between children with greater and lesser abilities benefits all, both academically and socially.

4. Rigid curricula with age-graded expectations must be relaxed in a mixed age grouping. This benefits all children, shielding them from dangers of competition and failure, and allowing for children's uneven development.

5. Children whose knowledge is similar but different stimulate one another's mental growth and thinking (Adapted from Katz et al., 1991).

Teachers who work with mixed aged groupings are enthusiastic (Nachbar, 1989), recognizing that deeper relationships among teachers and children can develop when they are together for more than one year. It must be recognized that a change to a mixed age grouping involves work and adjustment for teachers, but the benefits may outweigh such initial disadvantages.

The following strategies may deserve special emphasis:

• Suggesting that older children assist younger children, and that younger ones request assistance from older one such as, "I think you could help Sarah and Felicia figure out how to share the trike." Children of all ages can be encouraged to give and accept emotional comfort from one another.

• Encouraging older children to assume responsibility for younger ones such as helping them feel at home in a new classroom.

• Discouraging stereotyping or expectations strictly by age, such as challenging a statement like, "He can't do that, he's not old enough."

• Helping children understand and accept their current limitations ("I think you'll be able to climb that ladder too, when you're a bit bigger,") and helping older children appreciate their own progress, as in, "Wow, I can remember when that ladder was hard for you too."

• Helping children focus on peers' needs, feelings, and interests: "Jamie would like to play with you. What do you think you two could enjoy doing together?"

• Encouraging older children to read to younger ones, and all children to contribute their skills to appropriate projects: "Maybe Jamie could hold the dinosaur steady for you while you outline his head."

Children in mixed age classrooms are likely to become more dependent on one another, and less dependent on the teacher, if such strategies are used.

Helping Primary-Aged Children with Moral Development

During the primary years, children are slowly moving to internalize the social constraints of behavior they have been taught by their parents and teachers—the beginnings of conscience formation. Moral development is a complex process that involves both cognitive and social/emotional development. The ultimate goal of moral development is to supply children with both the information and the controls they will need to be able to take over on regulating their own decisions and actions. It is likely that they are not truly able to reach the level of moral development that allows them to make their own correct moral judgments, since the ability to reason logically and to take the perspectives of others is not reached until age seven or eight.

Progress toward moral development as the ultimate self-control is helped when teachers:

- Design activities and use informal experience to help children develop perspective-taking abilities. The ability to understand the different viewpoints of others in any situation can be helped through discussion with others. Example:

  > Ms. An Hoc planned a group time where she told the children a story about two boys who had a disagreement about who could use a computer in a classroom. Tom had had a turn the day before, but had a small part of his project yet to finish; Eric had not had a turn, and felt he should have a turn today. As the children discuss who should, in their opinion, get the turn, the teacher helps them clarify issues of fairness and justice.

  > When an argument erupts in the block corner, the teacher discovers that the problem is that Anna Maria had accidentally knocked down the structure built by Dennis and DeJuan, when she joined them to help build. The teacher brings the builders together to discuss intentions of helpfulness vs. deliberate destructiveness.

These teachers are helping children toward becoming able to make independent decisions about correct actions.

- Help children to make more logical decisions for actions, which is part of the teacher's role in moral development. Teachers can do this by leading group discussions about the actions children chose, the reasons, and the results. Through guided discussion children may be able to help one another see alternative actions and better choices. Such discussions will help children in their future actions. Meeting times in the child-centered classrooms become opportunities to discuss issues that teachers believe will help children understand issues of social actions of general importance to everyone. They are not allowed to deteriorate into "public humiliation sessions" (Gamberg et al., 1988). Example:

  > Mr. Hammons asked his kindergartners to think with him about what to do about the problem of children being disruptive on the school bus. The children thought through the consequences of the present behaviors, and decided on what they believed to be the right actions for teachers and bus drivers to take with the children in question.

- Get young children to find their own answers and solutions in interpersonal situations. Teachers do not provide solutions or ready-made moralizing, but instead ask serious and pertinent questions to help children arrive at a more autonomous morality, not dependent on the adult's presence or prescriptions.

  > As he guides the discussion, Mr. Hammons asks, "What do you think the problem is here? What could happen if people continue to behave

in this way? What are the important ideas to consider here? Whose rights should we think about? What do you think is the right way to control this—who should do that? Why?"

- Use authoritative guidance systems, rather than authoritarian or permissive styles in limit-setting and discipline. The differences in the three styles create corresponding differences in children's ability to govern their own behaviors. Permissive and authoritarian styles are at opposite ends of a spectrum, in that permissive teachers and parents exert few demands on children's behavior, and authoritarians exert too many arbitrary demands for obedience to behavior standards. Nevertheless, the effects of these two styles are quite similar, in that children fail to develop the feelings of empathy and mental understandings of their actions needed to internalize a code of ethical standards for behavior. Both groups remain dependent on adults to guide their behavior.

Adults who are authoritative in their guidance, on the other hand, respond to children's needs with warmth while establishing clear behavioral boundaries. They teach children how to behave, and help them understand the reasons that lie behind the required actions with a variety of direct teaching strategies such as suggestions, demonstrations, explanations, and considering the impact of their behavior on others. Authoritative styles of guidance have been found to be most effective in helping develop internal behavior controls in children. Children know what is expected of them and understand how to make their own decisions fit in with the needs and rights of others. Authoritative teachers offer children reasons for why certain behaviors are appropriate, knowing that personal morality must be built upon cognitive foundations. They remind of rules frequently, and help children experience the consequence of their decisions. They understand the gradual process of building moral understanding and control, and use every classroom opportunity that presents itself to help children work on questions of justice and social harmony. Example:

> Mr. Hammons draws Luisa aside when he sees her hit a friend. He tells her he will not allow her to hurt others, as he will protect her right not to be hurt. They discuss the situation, and alternatives of action. He supports her in later attempts to consider a friend's point of view and reach a fair solution.

- Present issues of responsibility and morality that affect the larger community beyond the classroom. Primary-aged children are ready to consider a larger perspective.

> Mr. Hammons has initiated a classroom recycling project. The children have investigated the town's recycling efforts, talking with an environmental group and working with the collection group in their neighborhoods. At the last class meeting, the children talked of ways their efforts would benefit others.

Things Caregivers Should Not Do

Teachers are not helpful in nurturing primary-aged children's moral development when they:

- manage behavior themselves, solving problems and ignoring opportunities to help children understand the moral issues involved in their actions

- talk about moral practices without demonstrating the principles in their own actions

- expect more sophisticated moral judgment than the children's cognitive level allows

- use either authoritarian or permissive styles of guidance, either setting no limits or too many harsh and arbitrary limits

- maintain a narrowed perspective on cognitive learning that leaves moral issues out of the curriculum

Helping Primary-Aged Children with Emotional Growth

During the preschool years, children began to learn skills necessary to control and express their emotions in socially acceptable ways. Moving into the primary years brings increasing cognitive ability to identify feelings in oneself and in others, recognizing emotions as factors to be reckoned with in relationships and behavior. New situations, such as school and peer relationships and increasing awareness of the surrounding world as well as family circumstances, may cause stress and anxieties not found in younger children. Teachers of primary-aged children can be instrumental in helping children with both of these aspects when they:

- Provide opportunities for children to learn to identify feelings in themselves and others. Young school-aged children begin to understand that people can hold more than one emotion at a time, but still do not recognize that people can hold contrasting emotions about the same event, such as being both excited and frightened at the prospect of a new classroom.

One way that teachers can help children identify feelings is by talking about emotional responses. Time for individual conversations is important, especially when children are involved in problem solving. Teachers can facilitate identification of feelings by asking questions. Examples:

> "How did you feel when he said that to you? Did you feel anything else?"

> "What do you think she was feeling when that happened?"

- Plan group discussions and activities that help children focus on understanding feelings and their influences on peoples' actions. Reading stories that portray emotional responses stimulates discussion for furthering understanding. Example:

> Miss Alfred read her kindergartners *A Chair for My Mother* by Vera Williams, the story of a little girl whose hard-working family loses everything they have in a fire. In the discussion that followed, Roberto said, "They were scared when they came home and saw the fire, and they were scared that something had happened to the Grandma. They felt happy when they found her, but they were still upset that they had lost all their stuff. That's why it was so important to save the new chair."

- Provide materials and supportive encouragement for children to express their emotions in positive, constructive ways. Primary-aged children can be helped to represent their feelings in creative arts, such as drawing, painting, sculpting, or creative movement, and in writing, such as in a journal or story.

Teachers may make direct suggestions to stimulate such activity: "I wonder if you would feel better about that if you wrote it all down." "Lots of great artists paint out their feelings like that—what about trying to show how you feel?"

- Create a low-stress classroom. In her book, *Think of Something Quiet: A Guide for Achieving Serenity in Early Childhood Classrooms,* Clare Cherry (1981) describes fundamentals of a low-stress program. These include: relationships among children and teacher-child relationships that are based on respect, trust, and caring; stressing self-awareness and self-expression; classrooms that permit movement; a predictable schedule; reductions of visual and auditory stimulation; balancing of quiet and active experiences and comfortable pacing; developmentally appropriate activities for success; a sense of humor; incorporation of fantasy and creative movement into classroom activities. When children feel physically and emotionally at ease in their classrooms, stress and anxiety often associated with school is diminished. When teachers actively teach strategies to reduce stress, children learn skills to help in their future emotional health.

- Promote children's sense of self-worth. As children feel accepted for themselves in classrooms, stress is lowered. All children should feel valued and included as worthwhile members of their classroom communities. Teachers should take care to ensure that each child has positive experiences each day. Their awareness of diversity helps them monitor classroom materials and representations for inclusion of the racial and ethnic backgrounds, the differences in ability, and the particular interests of their individual children. Issues of self-esteem have enormous impact on children's overall emotional health. Example:

  > Brandon has been quite unhappy lately. His teacher presumes his feelings could be related to the family stress with his father's layoff from his job. One of her strategies to help is to make sure that he has opportunities to help one or two peers with math each day; Brandon has superior skills in math, and this seems to contribute to his positive feelings about himself.

- Develop partnerships with parents to facilitate continuous home-school communication. When teachers and parents share information, they are often able to help with emotional stress children may experience in either setting. Teachers can help parents with easing children's transitions to classrooms and more advanced academic work, and with understanding educational practices so that parents are less likely to pressure their children for academic achievement. Parents can help teachers understand the particular circumstances of children's home lives that may be emotionally upsetting or need individual attention.

  > The teacher talks regularly with Brandon's parents, so she understands the home situation, thus they are aware of his emotional re-

sponses exhibited at school and she makes herself available as a friendly support during the family's difficult time.

- Recognize signs of excessive stress and emotional distress in young children. David Elkind refers to the stresses of hurried children, whose lives are complicated by family stress, premature advancement in lessons and accomplishments, and heavy expectations for mature behavior (Elkind, 1981). Teachers are often in a position to be able to identify signs of unhealthy stress and emotional unhealth in the children in their classrooms. Sometimes these stresses can be alleviated by home-school collaboration, and sometimes they need attention by other professionals. In either case, as teachers care for all aspects in children's lives, stress is something that must be recognized.

- Monitor primary-aged children's exposure and reactions to frightening and disturbing real and fantasy events such as media exposure to real-life disasters or movie and television violence. Although they are now able to distinguish between reality and fantasy, primary-aged children can become disturbed or preoccupied by frightening events. Teachers help children with this by recognizing signs of overstimulation, and helping children deal with and express their feelings. Teachers and parents need to share information, so all will be sensitive to children's needs for protection from potentially overstimulating situations. For example, a recent very popular movie about dinosaurs has been marketed as if it were for young children, and is actually quite terrifying to them.

> The first-grade teachers at Oakwood School realized that a large downtown fire the week before was preoccupying the attention of many of their children. They planned group discussions to try to help the children understand what had happened, held individual conversations with the children who appeared most frightened, and provided lots of art materials for expression. Later in the week, they planned a lesson on safety techniques in an emergency, so children could feel more confident of their own knowledge.

Things Caregivers Should Not Do

Teaching practices that are unsupportive of healthy emotional development in primary-aged children include:

- omitting discussion of feelings from curriculum or informal conversations

- providing no materials, opportunities, or encouragement for children to express or identify feelings

- a classroom environment that produces stress through its restrictions and expectations, and provides no opportunities to relieve stress or teach children skills to reduce their own stress

- poor communication between teachers and parents, so teachers are often unaware of emotionally upsetting factors in the child's environment

- lack of awareness of the need to monitor children's exposure to potentially frightening situations

SUMMARY

Primary-aged children move on in development when adults plan for social/emotional environments that:

- help children develop skills for peer group acceptance

- nurture positive self-esteem

- encourage moral development

- allow for emotional development and the decrease of stress

Developmentally appropriate social/emotional environments consider a balance between competition and cooperation, and may provide mixed age groupings.

THINK ABOUT IT

1. Find out if there are any mixed age groupings in your local schools and after-school programs. If possible, visit. What activities do you see younger and older children cooperating on? What do you notice about the social interaction of the younger and older children? Talk to the teachers involved about their perceptions of how the system works.

2. Observe children at play on a school playground or after school. How are the games being organized? What references to rules and fairness of play do you hear?

3. In discussions with your classmates, recall the games of your childhood. What were the games and who were the players, the leaders, the rejected? How does the issue of competition relate to your memories? What competitive practices initiated by the teacher do you recall from your early classrooms?

4. If you have opportunities to observe or work with primary-aged children, draw a sociogram based on your observations of children's preferences in play and work partners. What are the peer-group skills displayed by the most popular children? by the least popular? Are there specific skills that you see could be directly taught and coached?

5. Tell Kohlberg's famous story for evaluating stages of moral development to several five- and six-year-olds, and then to older primary-aged children. Do their responses suggest that the younger children are still tied to arbitrary moral judgments based on egocentric perspectives?

   " A woman was dying from cancer. Only one drug might have saved her, a form of radium that a druggist in the same town had recently discovered. The druggist was charging $2,000.00, ten times what the drug cost him to make. The sick woman's husband, Heinz, tried to borrow money from everyone he knew, but could only raise about half the cost. He told the druggist his wife was dying, and asked him to sell it cheaper or let him pay later. When the druggist said no, the husband got desperate and broke into the man's store to steal the drug for his wife. Should the husband have done that? Why? (Adapted from Kohlberg, 1969). *"*

6. Plan a classroom activity to help children grow in their ability to take the emotional and social perspectives of others. Carry out and discuss the activity with your classmates.

QUESTIONS TO REVIEW OBJECTIVES

1. Discuss several social/emotional issues of the primary years.

2. Identify ways teachers can help children develop social skills for peer group acceptance.

3. Describe practices for enhancing self-esteem.

4. Discuss considerations related to children's games with rules, related to competition vs. cooperation.

5. Discuss positive aspects of mixed age groupings for young children.

6. Identify ways teachers can nurture moral development in primary-aged children.

7. Describe teachers' contributions to emotional development and stress reduction in primary-aged children.

REFERENCES AND SUGGESTIONS FOR READING

Borba, M., & Borba, C. (1984). *Self-esteem: A classroom affair* (vols. 1 and 2). Nashville, TN: School Age Notes.

Bredekamp, S. (ed.). (1987). *Developmentally appropriate practice in early childhood programs serving children from birth through age 8.* Washington, DC: NAEYC.

Bullock, J. R. (1992, Winter). Children without friends. Who are they and how can teachers help? *Childhood Education, 69(2),* 92–96.

Burton, C. B. (1987). Children's peer relationships. In *Children's social development: Information for teachers and parents.* Urbana, IL: ERIC Clearinghouse on Elementary and Early Childhood Education.

Carlsson-Paige, N., & Levin, D. (1990). *Who's calling the shots?* Philadelphia: New Society Publishers.

Cherry, C. (1981). *Think of something quiet: A guide for achieving serenity in early childhood classrooms.* Belmont, CA: Pitman Learning Inc.

Cole, M., & Cole, S. R. (1993). *The development of children* (2d ed.). New York: W.H. Freeman and Co.

Drew, N. (1987). *Learning the skills of peacemaking: An activity guide for elementary-aged children on communicating, cooperating, resolving conflict.* Rolling Hills Estates, CA: Jalmar Press.

Elkind, D. (1981). *The hurried child: Growing up too fast too soon.* Reading, MA: Addison-Wesley Publishing Co.

Gamberg, R., et al. (1988). *Learning and loving it: Theme studies in the classroom.* Portsmouth, NH: Heinemann Educational Books Inc.

Greenberg, P. (1992, July). How to institute some simple democratic practices pertaining to respect, rights, roots, and responsibilities in any classroom (without losing your leadership position). *Young Children, 47(5),* 10–17.

Isenberg, J., & Jalongo, M. R. (1993). *Creative expression and play in the early childhood curriculum.* New York: Macmillan Publishing Co.

Johnson, D. W., & Johnson, R. T. (1975). *Learning together and alone: Cooperation, competition and individuality.* Englewood Cliffs NJ: Prentice-Hall Inc.

Johnson, D. W., et al. (1984). *Circles of learning: Cooperation in the classroom.* Alexandria, VA: Association for Supervision and Curriculum Development.

Katz, L. G., Evangelou, D., & Hartman, J. (1991). *The case for mixed-age grouping in early education.* Washington, DC: NAEYC.

Kohlberg, L. (1976). Moral stages and moralization: The cognitive-developmental approach. In Lickona, J. (ed.), *Moral development behavior: Theory, research, and social issues.* New York: Holt, Rinehart, and Winston.

Kohlberg, L., & Kramer, R. (1969). Continuities and discontinuities in childhood and adult moral development. *Human Development, 12,* 93–120.

Madsen, M., & Shapira, A. (1970). Cooperative and competitive behavior of urban Afro-American, Anglo-American, Mexican-American, and Mexican village children. *Developmental Psychology, 3,* 3, 16–20.

Nachbar, R. (1989, July). A K/1 class can work—wonderfully. *Young Children, 44(5),* 67–71.

Orlick, T. (1978). *The cooperative sports and games book: Challenge without competition.* New York: Pantheon Press.

Orlick, T. (1985). *The second cooperative sports and games book.* New York: Pantheon Press.

Piaget, J. (1965). *The moral judgment of the child.* New York: Free Press.

Rosenthal, R. (1987). Pygmalion effects: Existence, magnitude, and social importance. *Educational Researcher, 16(9),* 37–41.

Rowen, L. (1988). *Beyond winning: Sports and games all kids want to play.* St. Paul, MN: Toys N Things Press.

Schaps, E., & Solomon, D. (1990, November). Schools and classrooms as caring communities. *Educational Leadership, 48(3),* 38–42.

Schickedanz, J., et al. (1993). *Understanding children* (2d ed.). Mountain View, CA: Mayfield Publishing Co.

Sherif, M., & Sherif, C. (1953). *Groups in harmony and tension.* New York: Harper and Row.

Sobell, J. (1988). *Everybody wins.* St Paul, MN: Toys N Things Press.

Watson, M., Hildebrandt, C., & Solomon, D. (1988). Cooperative learning as a means of promoting prosocial development among kindergarten and early primary grade children. *International Journal of Social Education, 3(2),* 34–47.

SECTION FOUR

Guest Editorial by John Holt

Let me sum up what I have been trying to say about the natural learning style of young children. The child is curious. He wants to make sense out of things, find out how things work, gain competence and control over himself and his environment, do what he can see other people doing. He is open, receptive, and perceptive. He does not shut himself off from the strange, confused, complicated world around him. He observes it closely and sharply, tries to take it all in. He is experimental. He does not merely observe the world around him, but tastes it, touches it, hefts it, bends it, breaks it. To find out how reality works, he works on it. He is bold. He is not afraid of making mistakes. And he is patient. He can tolerate an extraordinary amount of uncertainty, confusion, ignorance, and suspense. He does not have to have instant meaning in any new situation. He is willing and able to wait for meaning to come to him—even if it comes very slowly, which it usually does....

Children do much of their learning in great bursts of passion and enthusiasm. Except for those physical skills which can't be learned any other way, children rarely learn on the slow, steady schedules that schools make for them. They are more likely to be insatiably curious for a while about some particular interest, and to read, write, talk, and ask questions about it for hours a day and for days on end. Then suddenly they may drop that interest and turn to something completely different, or even for a while seem to have no interests at all. This usually means that for the time being they have all the information on the subjects that they can digest, and

need to explore the world in a different way, or perhaps simply get a firmer grip on what they already know.... Children's need to make sense of the world and to be skillful in it is as deep and strong as their need for food or rest or sleep....

What is essential is to realize that children learn independently, not in bunches; that they learn out of interest and curiosity, not to please or appease the adults in power; and that they ought to be in control of their own learning, deciding for themselves what they want to learn and how they want to learn it....

In my mind's ear I can hear the anxious voices of a hundred teachers asking me, "How can you tell, how can you be sure what the children are learning, or even that they are learning anything?" The answer is simple. We can't tell. We can't be sure. What I am trying to say about education rests on a belief that, though there is much evidence to support it, I cannot prove, and that may never be proved. Call it a faith. This faith is that man is by nature a learning animal. Birds fly, fish swim; man thinks and learns. Therefore we do not need to "motivate" children into learning, by wheedling, bribing, or bullying. We do not need to keep picking away at their minds to make sure they are learning. What we need to do, and all we need to do, is bring as much of the world as we can into the school and the classroom; give children as much help and guidance as they need and ask for; listen respectfully when they feel like talking; and then get out of the way. We can trust them to do the rest (Holt, 1983, pp. 287–293).

Developmentally Appropriate Cognitive/ Language Environments

Introduction

In this section we will examine the nature of the cognitive and language environments most appropriate for various stages. The discussion of cognitive/language environments will include: appropriate materials, curriculum ideas and planning methods; teaching practices and interaction to facilitate optimum cognitive and language learning; special issues in the cognitive/language domain. Some topics that are common throughout the stages, like the importance of play (Chapter 13), or assessment (Chapter 14) will be dealt with at length in only one chapter.

CHAPTER 11

Developmentally Appropriate Cognitive/Language Environments: For Infants

Newborns are born with the ability to cry. During the year that follows, they move through stages that allow them to make increasing varieties of sounds: cooing, babbling, laughing, advanced babbling—complete with inflections, and finally a real word or two. They also become increasingly able to decipher the meanings of the language used in their environment. At the same time that they are learning to make sense of words, they are learning also to figure out how the world around them works, and how they can act on the world.

Babies demonstrate more clearly than at later stages the complex intertwining of all aspects of development, for it is only on paper that we can separate out learning into distinct and separate domains. "Perhaps the most salient finding of the past decade's infancy research is that *loving and learning are intrinsic and intertwined for infant flourishing*" (Honig, 1991, p. 39). In reality it is through the same social relationships that introduce infants to the emotions of love and trust, and to the behavior of people in their environment, that babies learn language as part of the complex system of communication they will use throughout their lives. It is through their physical abilities to manipulate objects and move through space to come into contact with ever more objects that infants explore and discover, developing their first very practical understanding of the world around them. Before children acquire language, they have learned something about their world. They have rudimentary concepts, waiting for words to name those concepts. When they learn language, there is possibility for even greater understanding of the world, as they can more directly communicate their need for knowledge, and for labels to put on things, people, experiences, and eventually concepts. Without learning there is no need for language; without language there is no way to organize learning. With understanding comes the need to communicate. Cognitive and language learning are inseparable.

One of the most difficult concepts for adults not trained in child development to grasp is the idea that cognitive development is nurtured in infancy, even though traditional school-type learning activities are not seen. In recent decades the concept of "building better and brighter babies" has been promoted, usually by entrepreneurs who want to capitalize on parents' desire to give their children the best start in education as soon as possible. To counter those forces who proclaim the need for "infant stimulation" programs, complete with flashcards, it is important to become quite familiar with the concepts and substages of sensorimotor learning. Adults who want to provide the most developmentally appropriate cognitive/language environments for infants begin by recognizing innate abilities and unfolding patterns that need appropriate responses and support from adults.

OBJECTIVES

Upon completion of this chapter, students should be able to:

- discuss an understanding of the infant substages in sensorimotor learning.
- discuss typical patterns of infant language development.
- identify ten principles to guide adults facilitating sensorimotor learning.
- identify ten appropriate practices for adults nurturing language development.
- identify inappropriate practices in the cognitive/language environment.

Understanding Sensorimotor Intelligence

According to Piaget, infants are born with no initial ability to "think," but with a selection of reflexive behaviors that allow them to begin acting physically on objects to gain sensory information (assimilating) and adapting to their environment (accommodating). Thus they begin to actively create their own intelligence. The name he gave to this first stage of cognition in infants and toddlers is the *sensorimotor period,* because physical development and intellectual growth are so closely intertwined at the beginning. Babies begin to learn about the world through their senses and muscle movements of their bodies. This information is organized mentally for later use. (Students have probably learned more detail on Piaget's theory in basic child development courses. For a good, brief summary of sensorimotor learning, see White, 1988.) The sensorimotor stage extends from birth to about age two and consists of six substages. The first four substages occur in the first year of life.

Substage 1—Babies begin by using simple reflexes to take in information and act on the world right after birth. They suck, they grasp, they cry. Much of what happens at first is accidental, caused by random movements. They use their abilities one at a time; a baby will grasp a rattle placed in his fist, but not look at it.

Substage 2—After about a month of this behavior, infants gain a measure of control over their bodies, thus they are able to combine their behaviors. With repetition and practice comes increased ability, and ability to act more purposefully. For example, they learn to bring their hands to their mouths to suck on them. Babies' discoveries of being attached to their hands (a wonderful event for observant adults to watch) help move them past purely random behaviors to events and behaviors they can control on their own body.

Substage 3—Sometime after four months, babies take a more active interest in the world around them. With increasing manipulative and maneuvering abilities, they discover they can make rather interesting things happen outside themselves, and they want to make them happen repeatedly. In this shift to making consequences happen, it is evident that the first primitive understanding of cause and effect emerges, although at first repeating an event is more an accidental occurrence.

Substage 4—As babies enter the fourth substage around eight months, a new level of understanding is evident. For the first time, they demonstrate intentional behavior. Experience has helped them develop an understanding of cause and effect; thus, they are able to coordinate actions to solve problems in a more sophisticated way. The baby discovers that she can get her ball out of the corner where it is stuck by poking it with her broom handle, or lifts the blanket to find a toy underneath. This is primitive planning: to look ahead to see, "What will happen if I do this."

Imitation also becomes a factor in learning during this fourth substage.

This is about as far as the infant goes in the first four substages of sensorimotor development; the last two substages will be accomplished during toddlerhood. However, one more momentous cognitive occurrence takes place in later infancy: the development of *object permanence* at around eight to ten months of age.

Object permanence refers to the concept that babies gradually come to realize that objects and indeed people still exist even though they are not physically present. The development of object permanence represents infant ability to mentally call back the object they have experienced. This is the first real evidence of memory, of stored mental concepts. A lot of physical experience has gone into development of this cognitive concept.

Language Development

Children acquire much of their language in the first three years of life. The amazing accomplishments of infancy alone are worth noting. It is important to realize that language involves both listening and deciphering skills, and sound production. Babies appear to be born with innate capacities to begin with each of these.

Babies are born with a reflex to cry, and can quickly communicate different needs with different sounding cries. Within a month or two they begin to make cooing, open vowel sounds. The universally similar babbling of all possible sound combinations for all possible languages begins a month or so later. In late infancy babies begin to produce two syllable combinations of sounds they hear around them (Da-Da; Ba-Ba), and at around their first birthday they usually produce a word or two that is attached to real meaning. Language that is produced by the child is called *expressive language,* and it always lags behind language that is understood by the child, or *receptive language*. The first words are understood at around eight or nine months.

Babies react to sound from the beginning, startling when they hear a loud one, quieting when they hear a familiar voice, turning their heads to seek the source of sounds. After a few months they respond with differential attention to the voice of a loved caregiver, beginning to smile even when that person is still out of view. Babies get a lot of pleasure out of listening to their own vocal play and practice. Their listening is evidenced by the inflections of speech they add to their own babblings, and by their receptive understanding after eight months or so. "Time for your bottle" says Mary, and Joshua looks expectantly toward the fridge. "Come here," says Grandma, and the baby crawls rapidly toward her.

There is as of yet no exact understanding of how babies learn language. While the beginning stages of sound production appear to be innately patterned, the controversy over later sound production divides itself between those who believe that language is a product of environmental teaching and reinforcement (B.F. Skinner for one) and those who believe that children learn language because they were born with a capacity to do so, with what has been called a language acquisition device programmed into the brain (Chomsky). What is evident is that neither theory seems to completely answer all the evidence. Therefore adults promoting language development will want to consider their roles in responding to infants' sounds and communicating as language teaching and modeling. (For more detail on the development of language, see Anisfield, 1984.)

After this brief review of what is known about development of infant cognition and language, it is time to consider adult roles in nurturing this development.

Principles for Cognitive Development

As infants actively construct their knowledge of the world around them and learn to communicate, there are developmentally appropriate behaviors in caregivers to be considered. These ten principles provide useful guidelines.

Principle 1— Relationships Come First

Figure 11–1 Much of infant learning takes place as a result of solitary exploration. *Courtesy NationsBank Child Care Center.*

Caregivers promote social/emotional security and attachment relationships as a prerequisite to the comfort needed for infants to put energy into active exploration of the environment. Securely attached infants will trust enough to move away for independent exploration. They use the caregiver as a secure base from which to move out, their "refueling station" (Honig, 1993), when infants need affirming from adults. From exploration comes understanding, but relationships come first. "The security of attachments early in infancy predicts competence and autonomous explorations later on" (Honig, 1991, p. 18). Example:

> Watch eight-month-old Melinda playing on the carpet. She glances over at Kim, the infant teacher, and when she catches her eye, she sends a wide grin. Minutes later she has crawled to the far corner of the room, and is busily engaged in trying to fit two containers together, without another glance at Kim.

Putting attachment first prevents caregivers from inappropriate emphasis on cognitive "teaching." A baby propped up in her swing for long periods to (supposedly) watch *Sesame Street* is missing out on the important human contact that is a prerequisite for interest in the world and all that it contains, including alphabet letters and big birds.

Principle 2— Learning Comes Through Interaction

Caregivers recognize that the basis for cognitive development is interaction with objects and people. Babies play an active role in creating their own understanding of the world. Sometimes they need to play with toys and other simple objects. At other times conversation or simple games with adults introduce new ideas and extend language and practice at reciprocal interaction for infants, as well as strengthening the relationship. Adults observe babies carefully to know when babies are ready and responsive to adult interaction, and when it is time for solitary exploration. (See Figure 11-1.) In either case they recognize that infants absorb their learning through interaction. (See Vygotsky, 1978, regarding how adults help children develop through recognizing the *zone of proximal development*.) Example:

> Melinda is finished with the nesting toys. Kim hears her begin to whine and interprets it as a signal that the baby is ready for some one-

on-one interaction. Soon the two are enjoying a game of "Where's the Baby?" with Kim putting a scarf on Melinda's head and waiting for Melinda to pull it away, chortling.

Principle 3— Learning Is Sensorimotor

Caregivers recognize physical play and exploration as an indivisible part of cognitive development. They do not feel pressure to stop the play and teach the babies something, because they realize infants who are exploring are actively constructing their own intelligence and understanding. Caregivers become familiar enough with Piaget's stages that they can enjoy perceiving the cognitive component that is the invisible element behind the physical activity they see.

> As Kim and Melinda play the hiding game, Kim is very aware that just a few weeks ago this would have been beyond Melinda's cognitive capacity. But now that she is developing object permanence, it is great fun for something to be hidden and then found.

Principle 4— Learning Is Playful

Although important learning takes place in infancy, it is in the context of joyful, spontaneous play. There is pleasure as babies maneuver their bodies and manipulate objects. There is pleasure as they use all of their senses. There is pleasure as adults watch infants absorbed in their learning. Most importantly there is mutual pleasure as babies and adults come together for brief learning partnerships. Adults introduce babies to games (involving language, imitation, and turn-taking) that have been played for time immeasurable; games like patty-cake, peek-a-boo, hide-the-doggy, and where's-the-baby. These games have in fact profound meaning for infants who are working on serious cognitive concepts like object permanence, and physical abilities like midline hand coordination. But their greatest value comes in the joyous mix of play, interaction, language, and participation. This is not forced learning, but learning at its best. Example:

> Kim is not acutely conscious of her role as teacher as she plays with Melinda, but loses herself in the pleasure of the moment, laughing as Melinda squeals again in anticipation. She is teaching, but the mutual pleasure is the main thing.

Principle 5— Learning Involves Repetition

Caregivers support the need for infants to practice and repeat physical actions and abilities. "Children cannot push themselves on until they have done very thoroughly what it is they need to do" (Gonzalez-Mena, 1993, p. 70). Lots of time and space to move and explore repeatedly is provided to babies as necessary for physical, and thus cognitive, growth. (See Figure 11-2.)

This is very different from the forced repetition of adult-directed learning assignments for babies, as when adults try to show the infant how to fit the correct shape into the hole on the container over and over again until they believe the lesson has been learned. Adult-directed repetition quickly exhausts and frustrates infants. This is shown by the fretful baby, who rubs her eyes, and keeps looking away from the "lesson."

Figure 11–2 Infants need time and space to move and explore, over and over again. *Courtesy Avondale Children's Center.*

> When four-month-old Daniel wakes up from his morning nap, Kim puts him on the exercise mat on the floor under a cradle gym with interesting things to reach for. He seems more confident in his reaching skills now. There is none of the hesitation there was not long ago as he struggled to coordinate his eye and hand movements. Repetition makes his moves less tentative each time.

Principle 6— Learning Follows a Sequence

Caregivers recognize that physical development moves through predictable sequences of events, so they are aware of which forthcoming behaviors to watch for, and support with appropriate positioning, space, or materials. Similarly, they are aware of the pattern of cognitive stages. This does not mean that caregivers push babies on to the next stage; rather, they are able to be more sensitive to cues babies offer that they are moving on, and respond accordingly. Because they accept the idea that babies will do what they can when they are ready, they do not put babies into positions that they could not assume themselves. Trying to hold a position for which muscles are not yet ready is uncomfortable and exhausting.

> Daniel has been rolling from his stomach to his back for about a week now. Sometimes when Kim lays him on the mat she puts him on his back, so he can work with the muscles he'll use for his next turning, from his back to his side.

Principle 7— Learning Is Unique to the Learner

Caregivers learn the individual timetable and learning style of each infant in their care; thus, they are able to provide the best possible learning experiences for each child. Alice Honig (1991) calls this "matchmaking": individualizing the learning situation for each baby. Such individualizing is only possible when adults observe and get to know the temperament, characteristic style of behavior, pace, and interest of each infant, as well as where he or she is in the predictable sequence. Example:

> Daniel is a very active baby, reacting with apparent frustration when he is unable to inch forward on his stomach as he frantically tries to do. Kim recognizes this frustration, and soon moves him over to the reaching area where he seems more comfortable with his mastery. Alicia is about Daniel's age, but seems quite content to lie on her back, busy with a soft toy to handle. She rarely moves her body in the same frantic ways Daniel does, though she allows Kim to change her position from time to time. Seth, six months now, is contented playing in a lying position, while Francisco protests loudly until he's propped into a sitting position. Each baby needs a different approach and response from the adult.

Principle 8— Infants Take the Lead

Caregivers recognize that the motivation and choices for learning rest with babies. No one has to teach a baby to want to explore, assuming normal physical capabilities and nervous system are functioning. (The only infants for whom it is appropriate to discuss "infant stimulation" are those who have special needs.) But this does not mean that adult caregivers have no role to play. Sometimes this responsibility includes watching to see babies' cues for when to become involved or when involvement might be interference. Other times adult responsibilities include planning to provide activities and materials that challenge and reinforce developing skills, providing a balance between what is already accomplished and a new situation. In other words adults recognize that the responsibility for learning and moving on is the infant's, while it is the adult's task to provide appropriate choices and opportunities.

Caregivers follow the lead of infants, rather than intruding on their exploration and play interests. They recognize that their role is that of supporter, offering attention and encouragement as babies proceed with their self-imposed tasks. Example:

> Kim perceives Daniel's frustration with being unable to creep forward, so the next time he is on his belly she lies on the floor beside him, making admiring comments as he tries again. She places a favorite stuffed animal just out of reach in front of him, and reacts with verbal pleasure and physical excitement when he inches toward it.

Principle 9— Caregivers Provide the World

If infants are to learn by means of their own free exploration of the world around them, it is a primary responsibility of adults to provide a world in which it is safe and interesting to discover. Caregivers realize that an environment rich in sensory experiences and safe, interesting objects to manipulate invites exploration, with eyes, fingers, and mouth. The specifics in the world are not left to chance, but are provided by caregivers who have thought carefully about what will be appropriate. Example:

> Kim carefully inspects the room each day to make sure there are no items that are potentially dangerous as her babies become increasingly mobile. She is eager to watch Daniel's reaction this morning. The day before she filled a small clear plastic plumber's tube with beads and colored water and glued corks securely in each end. Just big enough to grasp securely, she thinks it might make attractive responses if Daniel can give it a push as he maneuvers. She opens the window slightly so the breeze can sway the pastel streamers that hang down near the mat for Alicia to enjoy. It will be a good morning to take the older infants out in the big wagon. There will be new things to explore today, as well as some of the old favorites.

Principle 10— Learning Demands Communication

As infants make discoveries or get stuck in their exploring, they want to share their discoveries with their beloved adults. At first much of this sharing is nonverbal on the infant's part: smiles, bouncing pleasure, pointing, holding toys out to caregivers, frustrated howls. Helpful play partners verbalize what the baby is doing and discovering. As babies learn more about the world around them, they rely on alert caregivers to supply the labels and language so they can communicate more verbally. Thus we see the inseparable union between the learning process and language. (See Figure 11-3.) Examples:

> "Daniel, you're working hard. You want to go, don't you? Pretty soon, I'll bet."

> "Yea, Melinda, you got those two cups apart. Problem solved!" The babies respond bright-eyed to the sound of encouragement, though the exact meaning may still be beyond them.

Figure 11–3 Learning demands communication. *Courtesy Avondale Children's Center.*

The ten principles of cognitive development will guide adults to provide for the most appropriate cognitive environments and responses.

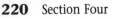

BUT WHAT ABOUT?

One of your parents brings a brochure she's received about a week-long institute to teach techniques to teach babies to read. She's excited, and suggests she'll use her vacation time to go, since it will so obviously benefit her baby.

There are any number of programs that have sprung up around the country, promising advanced learning results for parents who want to expose their infants to reading, foreign language, physical training, and so on. Unfortunately, both the results and the methods of such programs are questioned by most developmental professionals (White, 1988). "As yet no substantial knowledge on how to bring about giftedness exists" (White, 1988, 140).

The concern is about programs that require lengthy drills to induce learning at a fast pace and in great quantity during the early years. The potential disadvantages lie in the hours of daily teaching sessions for parents and children. Children's spontaneous interest and pleasure in learning are likely to be at risk.

> If large portions of time are spent in any narrowly focused direction... the child will probably have to pay a significant price in other developmental areas as well as in motivation to learn. If a child comes to be valued too much for what she has achieved... rather than for what she is.... that could be a serious negative factor in any young child's life... Any program that promises precocity ultimately has to be evaluated in the light of how it may subtract from other important, even crucial learning times; (White, 1988, 297-298).

It is important to help parents consider the overall effects of such a program, and help them see the importance of balanced development in all areas, rather than the purely cognitive.

Materials Appropriate at Various Stages

One of the important roles for adults wanting to nurture cognitive development is to provide developmentally appropriate materials.

Early Infancy: For Visual Reaching

In the first month or so, it won't be necessary to worry too much about enriching the environment. Much of the time will be spent sleeping, and infants' adjusting nervous systems do not need bombardment from too many stimuli. As they have longer wakeful periods during the next couple of months, they are interested in looking about them. Caregivers provide interesting things to look at. First and foremost will be the face of the caregiver, by far the most fascinating item a baby can have access to. A loving grown-up has been called the ideal first play thing for a baby.

> It moves (no switches, buttons, batteries, or windup keys required).
>
> It talks, makes music, plays back baby's first coos and calls.
>
> It's cuddly (provides security and hours of pleasure).
>
> It's highly educational.
>
> It's entertaining; encourages curiosities.
>
> It's composed of resilient, flexible, nontoxic, 100 percent natural materials.
>
> It's a unique toy, crafted to meet an individual child's needs.
>
> It's available only through private distribution.
>
> (From Oppenheim, 1984, quoted in Weiser, 1991)

In addition to infants' human companions, mobiles placed within the 8–24 in. distance of baby's visual capability become useful in the second and third months. Mobiles need to be chosen or created that are interesting from the baby's viewpoint, looking up. Some commercially produced mobiles are still primarily designed to be attractive to adults, not infants. Interesting mobiles can be devised from things like paper plates with colorful designs facing down, or colored tennis balls.

Strategically placed mirrors may be intriguing at this time, and will continue to be through infancy.

An occasional change of scenery, by changing the baby's location or position, may be another stimulus to interest in the world around.

Toward the end of this period, as babies discover their hands, they become ready to physically reach and grasp, so fragile mobiles should be replaced with cradle gyms, as reaching devices are called. (Recall from our discussion in Chapter 3 that babies ready for play are on the floor, so the "cradle gym" is suspended in a play area.) Sturdy arrangements using dowels or broomsticks can be created, so that a changing array of objects can be suspended with semirigid materials, such as plastic wire or pieces of old electrical cord (to avoid the frustration of having the object escape the infant's first tentative grasp) within range for visually directed reaching. Reaching devices are used when infants are on their backs or in an infant seat.

During the times of play on the abdomen, babies are positioned on brightly patterned surfaces with a variety of textures, and small toys are placed within view.

Materials for Infants Who Use a Palmar Grasp

As babies roll, play on their bellies, and sit to explore, they need an assortment of objects on the floor. Up until about eight months, infants use a palmar grasp, using the thumb and fingers as if the fingers were in a mitten. For this scooping grasp, babies need large, soft items that are easily attained. Examples of this include stuffed animals, foam blocks, large rings, teething toys, bead necklaces, soft balls, objects about 4–5 in. in diameter. Because they are also in the sensorimotor stage where babies try to repeat interesting sensory events, toys that make sounds are fascinating: squeeze toys, sound toys with bells or chimes, large rattles.

Materials for Infants Who Use a Pincer Grasp

After about eight months or so, babies are able to manage more complicated grasping, using a pincer grasp, which allows them to use thumb and forefinger together. They are also able, soon after, to bring both hands together to hold things in the midline. This improved manipulative ability allows the exploration of things that fit into one another, or move in some way. Examples of this type of material include nesting toys (bought or made), stacking objects, toys with parts that move, such as knobs, the sturdy board books that are also present as part of the language environment, and hinged objects, which may include household discards like cigar boxes or boxes for wooden matches. Added to this increased physical dexterity is the cognitive stage of investigating simple cause and effect; caregivers realize this is the time for toys where the infant becomes the active agent. Some of the simpler busy boxes that allow for gross hand movement are intriguing. Although they can't manage themselves, infants love Jack-in-the-boxes at this stage. Balls continue to have great exploring possibilities, never behaving quite the same way when the infant pushes or drops them. Ordinary kitchen items like pots and pans are interesting, with the banging possibilities. Many throwaways have lots of exploring possibilities: empty detergent bottles, where air squeezes out the opening; diaper wipe containers with their hinged tops, as well as space for filling; a selection of sizes of plastic containers with lids; old purses that can be stuffed with safe noisemakers. (Walk around your house to see if you can think of more.)

Also interesting to the older infant are simple, realistic looking cars, trucks, and small dolls. (See Gonzalez-Mena, 1993, and White, 1988, for lists of suggestions of appropriate materials.)

Part of creating the environment for exploration requires positioning items where they will encourage movement toward them by newly mobile infants.

Again it should be said that all of these objects will be thoroughly mouthed and handled, so size (nothing smaller than about 2 in. to prevent accidental choking) is important, as is sturdy quality.

When these objects are combined with abundant floor space for free movement, with rails or low furniture when babies are ready to stand and move about, the cognitive environment is almost complete. The only thing missing is the adult, available to indicate supportive interest and appreciation of infants' self-directed exploration and movement.

Appropriate Adult Roles to Nurture Cognitive Growth

Although infants set their own goals, do their own exploring, and create their own understanding of the world, adults have several roles in nurturing cognitive growth.

Caregivers create the physical environment for exploration. Safe areas, large enough for movement, with abundant interesting materials and strategically placed and available adults are part of the physical environment.

Caregivers create the social/emotional environment for exploration. The evident interest and support of infants, the interaction to sustain interest, the praise for their accomplishments: All of this adult interaction strengthens infants' desire to continue in their efforts and to succeed. Adults stay available for social interaction even while infants are playing by themselves.

Name	Gross Motor	Reach and Grasp	Language/ Cognitive	Social/ Emotional
Brianna (4 months)	Time on back under cradle gym	Change objects on cradle gym (chore girl, circle of beads and bells)	Nursery rhyme songs	Tummy tickles
Trenarie (6 months)	Prop to sit with support	Give objects to hold in both hands	Name body parts when dressing	Sit to play in front of mirror
Danielle (6 months)	Encourage rolling over by placing favorite lamb just out of reach	New shaker bottles	Picture book of objects	Pat-a-cake
Jehan (9 months)	Playing catch me (on all fours)	Stacking two big blocks	Hiding objects	Encouraging him to show affection

Figure 11-4 Caregivers plan for individual babies, according to specific goals and development level.

Caregivers create the cognitive match. As caregivers learn physical and cognitive development stages of infancy, they are able to know where each infant is and what are appropriate materials and activities for each infant. The cognitive environment is not left to chance or instinct. Caregivers deliberately plan materials and experiences that they believe will interest babies—activities that they are ready for. Planning for sensorimotor events is part of the caregiver's responsibility in creating the cognitive match.

See the sample planning sheet in Figure 11-4 to see how a caregiver has planned materials and strategies for individual children. Planning in the infant classroom is done on an individual basis. Planning allows for the happening of cognitive experiences that are suited to the infant's level. Because the brief exploratory episodes fit into the baby's day among the baby-run rhythm of other curriculum encounters of feeding, diapering, cuddling, etc., the caregiver plans ahead so that she can be prepared for the spontaneous games or play; that is, materials or activities are preplanned, but not scheduled. The caregiver has thought of what the next learning game will be, for when the opportunity arises. This is not the "10:30 a.m.: language lesson" kind of planning!

For ideas of games and activities appropriate for each stage of infancy, see Sparling and Lewis, 1984, and Cryer and Harms, 1987, and Figure 11-5.

Creating the cognitive match requires infant caregivers to be constant observers and recorders who are able to find out where the baby is at a given time on the developmental ladder. Effective caregivers observe throughout the day, making brief notes as babies explore on their own.

You will have noticed the overlapping of adult's cognitive and language roles. Let's look more closely at language practices.

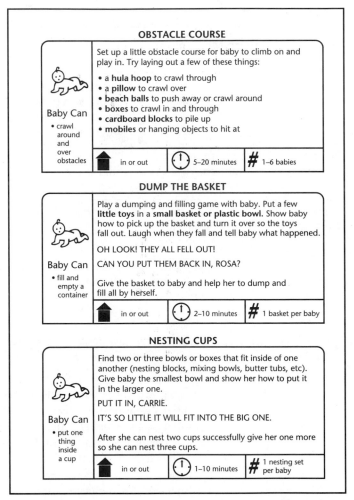

Figure 11-5 Caregivers plan materials and interaction that offer opportunities for playful learning. *Used with permission; from* Active Learning for Infants *by Cryer, D., Harms, T. and Bourland, B., Menlo Park, CA: Addison-Wesley Publishing Co., 1986.*

Nurturing Language Development

Infants require language partners if they are to grow in their knowledge of the communication process. They need to discover that speech sounds have value and meaning as a method of communicating between persons. Many linguists believe that children probably learn language by processes that include imitation and reinforcement, but also include an increasing sensitization to interpreting the meaning of a partner in communication (Bruner, 1977). (See Figure 11-6.) This understanding has real implications for adults who will be involved in helping infants "finetune" their language learning.

Language Is Acquired

By Inborn Mechanism?	By Environmental Teaching?
All children acquire language about the same time, in the same ways.	Children always acquire the language heard in the environment.
Deaf babies cry, laugh, coo, babble.	Deaf babies imitate sign language formed by parents' hands.
Children invent original structures, words, and expressions they could not possibly have heard.	Sounds and words that are reinforced are more dominant in childrens' speech.
Adults rarely "teach" language or grammar.	Hearing infants born to nonhearing/speaking parents learn to speak by exposure to other language sources.
Neither explanation accounts for all language development.	

Figure 11-6   The mechanisms of language development are not completely understood, but undoubtedly interaction with others is important.

Infant language is nurtured by adults paying attention to the ten ideas that follow.

1. Adults speak directly (face-to-face), with babies from the beginning, regularly, during every caregiving encounter, throughout every day. Long before adults think babies are understanding, they speak as though they believe babies *can* understand. Their speech is in a natural tone, clearly enunciated and "following ordinary polite rules for adult dialogue" (Bruner, 1978, p. 284). There is no "baby talk," meaning adult words being mispronounced—"weally"— or turned into diminutive forms, such as "fishy-wishy."

   "You're having a really good time with that ball, aren't you," Angela says to five-month-old Roger.

   "It's almost time for your bath. I'm going to put your pink fish in," says Enrico to his three-month-old daughter.

2. Recognizing that language is taught as conversation, adults demonstrate turn-taking skills of communication. After they speak they pause and look to infants for a response, which will be nonverbal. They look infants in the eye, and direct words to them physically.

   Angela's silence and physical indicators of expectation show Roger it's his turn to talk. "Woo-wa-ooo," he replies.

3. Adults reinforce infants' first cooing and babbling sounds. Sometimes they respond to them with words as if the infant were really speaking; other times they repeat back what they heard. In either case, they respond and continue the dialogue, adding nonverbal methods of communication such as gestures and intonation for additional clues.

   "Ma-ma-ma-ma," says six-month-old Jennifer. Her caregiver smiles at her and moves her face toward her. "Ma-ma-ma-ma," she repeats.

Jennifer grins with delight. "Ga-ga-ga-guh-ooo." Her air of expectancy indicates she knows it's the adult's turn. "Aah-ma-bababa." This time the caregiver says, "Yes, I know you like that ring. You can really chew on it."

4. Caregivers tie their monologues into objects and actions that are present in the environment. This kind of descriptive commentary provides the names for things that babies will learn first, as part of their daily life. Forming the habit of commenting about what they are doing will both encourage adults to talk before the baby can talk back, and also strengthen adult awareness of respectfully involving children in the actions that concern them. As infants explore and handle objects, sometimes adults provide commentary on their learning activity as well. Relating words directly to concrete objects and experiences is a helpful language teaching technique.

> "I'm going to put your socks on now. First one sock on this foot, there, now the other sock on your other foot. There we are, two clean socks. Two feet, two socks. Are you ready for your shoes now? Here comes shoe number one."

> "Look at you. You've got a cup in both hands. Bang, bang, bang. They make a good noise, don't they?"

5. With infants who have begun to babble, adults occasionally simplify speech, frequently using one word labels, repeating them, and linking them by physical indication to the object referred to. Adults also isolate and stress key words to make it easier for infants to understand (Fowler, 1991). These modifications of speech help infants focus on the single words.

> "Bottle, Sarah, bottle. Here's your *bottle*," spoken while holding out the bottle for Sarah to see.

6. Adults sing and recite rhymes to infants. This singing and reciting is not just for entertainment value. "One of the first and most important conclusions is that the mother tongue is most rapidly mastered when situated in playful activity" (Bruner, 1991, p. 79). With songs and rhymes, the playful quality of the speech patterns involves the babies in a different kind of listening and responding. When action and gesture are tied in with the words, infant understanding is enhanced. Engaging infant attention directly in language and physical activity helps them focus on the language. Adults can make up songs too, using the babies' names for recognition.

> "Where's my Sarah, where's my Sarah, there she is, there she is. Going to come and get her, going to come and get her, Big, big kiss; big, big kiss." Seven-month-old Sarah grins happily; this song her mother made up is becoming familiar.

7. Reading books with infants should be a regular activity from the beginning. This leads partly to the positive associations of books and reading with pleasure, as does being held closely while listening to the soft rhythms of a loved adult's voice. In addition, language acquisition is nurtured by hearing the words, watching the adult point to large, clear pictures, going back through the same book and hearing the same words, making the same visual connections. Story time probably won't last long for infants, and will be a one-to-one experience, rather than the small group of older toddlers. But research

Figure 11–7 Infants need early opportunities to look at and handle books. *Courtesy Avondale Children's Center.*

has shown that reading to infants stimulates all areas of development (Carew, 1976). (See Figure 11-7.)

> Kim has selected several new books for her infant room. They include *Pat the Bunny,* which she likes for its short sentences and things for babies to touch, a collection of Mother Goose rhymes, which gives her a large selection of "mini-stories" just long enough for the babies, and several well-illustrated alphabet books, which she uses to be able to talk about the large single objects on each page. She has a selection of heavy board books the babies can manipulate by themselves, and she points out the objects on each page. She has also made books, with large pictures from magazines laminated on cardboard, fastened together by rings.

8. Adults who want to encourage words in older infants give them experiences and objects to label. Language is learned in particular context. Caregivers create patterns of repeated activity that can be labelled the same way each time. As caregivers respond to infant clues for communication—the pointed finger to indicate an object they want—they supply the words asked for by the infant. Examples:

> There are bright pictures of familiar objects around the room to talk about. "Let's go look at the bunny. Oh here's the bunny. Do you see the bunny?" And finally, "Where's the bunny?"

> "Time for Daddy to go," says Kim. "Let's go to the window and wave bye-bye. Bye-bye," she gestures, and encourages the infant to wave also.

9. Caregivers recognize that many infants are exposed to the sounds of different languages in the home and the center, or even more than one language in the home. They need to respect the choices parents make regarding the language relationship they will have with their child. Caregivers working with infants who have already begun to understand one language have to adapt and emphasize nonverbal clues if they speak in a second language to the infant. Supporting bilingual ability for infants is supporting the cultural choices their parents make (Gonzalez-Mena, 1993).

> "Ball," says Kim to Francisco as she holds out the ball to him. She has heard his parents call it "pelota," but they have agreed for her to use English words when he is in the center, to help develop both English and his parents' native Spanish, which they speak to him at home.

10. Adults who endeavor to figure out what the infant is interested in are more likely to provide meaningful language. What this probably means is that effective language partners will not always be talking, but will frequently be silently observing the infant.

Unsupportive Cognitive/Language Environments

The cognitive and language development of infants is not helped by the following behaviors, which are unfortunately too common.

Restricting the Physical Movements of Infants

This restriction might include confining them to equipment such as cribs, infant seats, swings, or playpens, where babies cannot take the initiative in exploring. It might be by removing them frequently from interesting areas or activities. Restricting movement prevents the natural emergence of locomotor abilities, frustrates infants, and turns them into passive observers, rather than active learners.

Restricting the Sensory Exploration of Infants

This happens when adults do not recognize the necessity for infants to handle and mouth the objects they are in contact with, and infants are continually thwarted when they try to do so (Ooh, nasty! no!). It also happens when adults do not recognize the cognitive activity behind physical exploration, and provide limited or unchanged selections of inappropriate toys and materials. Infants must touch and manipulate objects to take in the sensory information that will lay the base for cognitive concepts. Infants explore less and less when objects do not catch their interest or ability.

Super Stimulation and Teaching Beyond Infant Ability

The programs that have developed around the country to attempt to induce precocious advanced learning involve practices and interaction contrary to the active, self-directed learning style advocated by developmentally appropriate practice. Most of these programs also concentrate almost exclusively on the cognitive aspect, failing to recognize that all aspects of development are interrelated and necessary.

Absence of Play Partners

Adults who do not play active roles interacting with infants who are busy at play miss opportunities to reinforce and sustain learning experiences, and to introduce new ideas or games to the play.

Noisy Environments

Noise hinders the ability of infants to tune in to the speech they need to hear for language development. Too many people in one space create noise: another argument for small adult-child ratios. But other noise comes when adults fill the room with too much adult-to-adult speech, which does not involve the infant in the dialogue, or when adults constantly play music or television to create chronic noise clutter.

Silent Environments

Silence hinders language development, as well as the important developmental task of forming attachment. Caregivers must speak frequently, comfortably, warmly, and reciprocally with infants.

SUMMARY

Developmentally appropriate cognitive/language environments allow infants to proceed at their own rate of development by allowing freedom for sensorimotor exploration. Adults observe babies to learn their stages of physical and cognitive development, so they can provide the most appropriate materials and activities to match the child's abilities. They encourage and support infants who are actively involved in learning. When appropriate, they talk with babies as they play and initiate simple games. Language is used in the context of daily life. Infant communication is imitated and responded to. Learning and language both grow out of the context of joyful, responsive relationships.

THINK ABOUT IT

1. Make a collection of interesting, durable and safe household throwaways that would encourage infant exploration. Bring them to class. As you show your collection in small groups, differentiate the items most suitable for infants who grasp with the palmar grasp, and those more suitable for babies who can manipulate objects more completely.

2. Go to the library and check out four books that would be suitable for reading one-to-one with infants. Explain your choices.

3. Create a mobile designed from the baby's viewpoint.

4. Observe for a half hour in an infant room. Record examples you see of: reinforcing babbling; talking about activity and objects surrounding the infants; and simplifying speech to emphasize and label words.

QUESTIONS TO REVIEW OBJECTIVES

1. Explain what is meant by sensorimotor learning. Describe behaviors infants use to explore during the four substages of infancy. Identify the term *object permanence*.

2. Describe the normal sequence of language development during infancy.

3. Discuss ten principles of learning that influence adult behavior in the cognitive environment.

4. Discuss ten things adults do to support infant language development.

5. Identify six practices that are inappropriate to find in infant cognitive/language environments.

REFERENCES AND SUGGESTIONS FOR READING

Anisfield, M. (1984). *Language development for birth to three.* Hillsdale, NJ: Lawrence Erlbaum.

Bruner, J. (1977). Early social interaction and language acquisition. In Schaffer, H. R. (ed.), *Studies in mother-infant interactions.* London: Academic Press.

Bruner, J. (1978, September). Learning the mother tongue. *Human Nature Magazine,* 283–288.

Bruner, J. (1991). Play, thought, and language. In Lauter-Klatell, N. (ed.), *Readings in child development.* Mountain View, CA: Mayfield Publishing Co.

Carew, J. V., Chan, I., & Halfar, C. (1976). *Observing intelligence in young children.* Englewood Cliffs, NJ: Prentice-Hall.

Caruso, D. (1984, November). Infants' exploratory play. *Young Children, 40(1),* 27–30.

Cataldo, C. (1982, January/February). Very early education for infants and toddlers. *Childhood Education,* 149–154.

Cryer, D., & Harms, T. (1987). *Active learning for infants.* Reading, Ma: Addison-Wesley.

Dombro, A., & Wallach, L. (1988). *The ordinary is extraordinary: How children under three learn.* New York: Simon and Schuster.

Fowler, W. (1991). *Talking from infancy: How to nurture and cultivate early language development.* Cambridge, MA: Brookline Books.

Gonzalez-Mena, J. (1993). *Infants, toddlers, and caregivers* (3d ed.). Mountain View, CA: Mayfield Publishing Co.

Honig, A. S. (1991). Recent infancy research. In Weissbourd, B., & Musick, J. (eds.), *Infants: Their social environments.* Washington, DC: NAEYC.

Honig, A. S. (1993, March). Mental health for babies: What do theory and research teach us? *Young Children, 43,* 69–76.

Sparling, J., & Lewis, I. (1984). *Learning games for the first three years.* New York: Walker and Co.

Vygotsky, L. S. (1978). *Mind in society.* Cambridge, MA: Harvard University Press.

Weiser, M. G. (1991). *Infant toddler care and education* (2nd ed.). New York: Macmillan.

What is curriculum for infants in family day care (or elsewhere)? (1987, July). *Young Children, 42(5),* 58–62.

White, B. (1988). *Educating the infant and toddler.* Lexington, MA: Lexington Books.

Wilson, L. C. (1995). *Infants and toddlers: Curriculum and teaching* (3rd ed.). Albany, NY: Delmar Publishers Inc.

Developmentally Appropriate Cognitive/Language Environments:
For Toddlers

*I*t has been said that the peak of curiosity occurs in toddlerhood. Just watch the tireless exploration of children between ages one and three years, and you will be convinced that toddlers are indeed driven to learn, and are actively coming to terms with the way the world around them operates. Around the middle of toddlerhood, an explosion of language allows toddlers to interact more verbally, thereby giving us clearer insights into their perceptions and learning.

Once adults become aware of this absorbent mind, many are tempted to begin with earnest attempts to "teach" toddlers. Indeed, it seems rather rare to find many two-year-olds who have not been taught the "Alphabet Song," being able to sing "ellemenohpea" (L, M, N, O, P) with the best of them, and blissfully unaware that these nonsense syllables have the profound meaning that adults assume they are teaching with such essential learning. If such direct instruction is not in line with what we know of toddler development, what then is the adult's role in providing a cognitive/language environment that will nurture optimum toddler learning? That is the question we will explore in this chapter.

OBJECTIVES

After completing this chapter, students should be able to:

- discuss an understanding of toddler cognitive development.

- describe typical patterns of toddler language development.

- list three roles identified by Burton White for toddler education.

- discuss behaviors of an adult acting as consultant.

- discuss principles for teaching toddlers.

- list appropriate materials for toddler interest center.

- describe principles for teaching language.

- describe inappropriate cognitive/language practices.

Understanding Toddler Cognitive Development

You will recall from Chapter 11 that infants and toddlers are defined by Piaget as being in the stage of sensorimotor intelligence, meaning that they use senses and manipulative abilities to gain a practical understanding of the world around them. The first four substages of the sensorimotor period occur in infancy, and the last two substages describe the cognitive abilities of children from age one to about two. We will consider these two substages here, and then, look in detail at the preoperational stage in Chapter 13, into which older toddlers are moving.

Substage 5 of Sensorimotor Development

From about twelve to eighteen months of age, toddlers are in the fifth substage of sensorimotor development. Now much more adept at getting around and using their hands, the possibilities for exploration are increased greatly. But there is a new twist to this exploration: No longer content to just repeat actions that have been interesting or pleasurable, toddlers use their increasing repertoire of physical skills to attempt to make new things happen. This is the scientific researcher at the purest form: With no predetermined hypothesis of what will happen as the result of certain actions, toddlers systematically try to see what will happen "if."

Insights into toddler cognitive working of typical stage five exploration might go something like this: "If I drop the ball, what will happen?" After enjoying that discovery, a new question occurs: "If I climb up to the chair and drop it from there, what will happen? Oh, my—interesting. Now let me see, what else could I drop? Hmm—here's something (a tomato left on the counter to ripen). Not very interesting—no noise, just a splat. Oh, looks to me as if that bowl of sugar might make an interesting effect when it falls." Not only achieving a very satisfying crash and lots of action, that experiment produces an interesting response from Mom.

What most long-suffering and bewildered adults do not realize is that there is truly no aforethought malice here; the trial-and-error style of attempting to produce a novel effect produces absolutely unlooked-for consequences. Because the toddler has not looked ahead and known what would happen, he can't be accused of deliberately making a mess or breaking the sugar bowl. He was simply caught up in the "here-and-now" desire to create a new event. And all this experimentation is not just for the sake of entertainment. With each new strategy, toddlers learn more about the relationship between their actions and the result.

Incidentally, in just the same style of conducting research on what new event can be created, toddlers investigate the changing properties of human responses. If Mom got all upset when I dropped the sugar bowl, wonder what she'll look and sound like when I touch this, or drop that, or climb up here? If Stephen screamed when I grabbed his toy, wonder if I can make that happen again, or even louder? Some of the toddler "aggression" that we discussed in Chapter 8 may have begun as an innocent accident, such as stumbling over another child as the first toddler was intent on moving over to something she wanted. Many adults will attest to the observation that the toddler who caused the first child to scream gets a very interested look on her face, and goes back, the second time quite deliberately, to see what else can be produced. Many adults find it a little more difficult to see this as innocent exploration in the name of trial-and-error research, but this is most likely a product of stage five sensorimotor cognitive development.

This ability to go beyond merely repeating or using old methods of exploring that have worked before indicates a new understanding of the distinction between the toddler himself and the world about him. Being able consciously to vary earlier familiar ways of acting, shows the increasing flexibility of learning toddlers are capable of in the first half of their second year. But they are not yet able to mentally imagine actions and their probable consequences; they are limited to making physical discoveries in their physical environment.

(There are obvious safety implications for caregivers here; because toddlers can not look ahead to consequences, and are so powerfully motivated to explore everything in their environment, they must be protected from the results of limitless curiosity.)

Substage 6 of Sensorimotor Development

Around eighteen months toddlers begin to show evidence of increasing mental activity—true thinking at last. It becomes evident that toddlers have retained memory of various actions and situations by their *deferred imitation* (Piaget's term) of behaviors they have seen at another time or place (Piaget, 1951).

Piaget described the scene that his daughter witnessed, of another toddler having a strong, screaming and kicking temper outburst. Never having witnessed such a scene before, she reproduced it exactly in her own behavior in a similar situation a day or so later. The memory of one's own or another's actions allows toddlers to find solutions mentally, rather than only by physical trial and error. This representation allows toddlers to take all they have learned from past experiences in different situations, to test the possibilities mentally, and to choose the most appropriate response. Adults say they can literally see the "wheels going around"; toddlers pause and appraise the problem before acting with some certainty. In earlier stages they would have simply rushed in to try a variety of methods of solving the problem physically. For example, in playing with a shape-sorting toy, a toddler in the sixth substage would most likely look at each hole the cube could go in, and decide mentally where it will fit. A younger toddler would have to actually try each different hole, to try to physically figure out the answer.

Other behaviors that seem to be evidence for this new ability for representational thought include the ability to think about the relation between objects when not literally physically present. A toddler was seen to lift an elbow-shaped noodle to his ear and say "Hello." He was able to associate the similarity of shape of the tiny macaroni and the telephone receiver, which was not actually in the room. This ability to make the symbolic connections, as well as the memory of earlier scenes, allows toddlers to begin pretend play, another evidence of representational thought. Bobby takes a block and pushes it along the floor, making car sounds. His thinking transforms the block into a car to pretend with. The emerging use of language is also tied to representational thought, as the word stands for the object, person, or event. "Ba," says Julia, looking for the ball she likes to play with. The ball is in her mind, and symbolized by her word.

Having actually achieved representational ability and true thought, the end of sensorimotor development shows us how much has been achieved in infancy and toddlerhood. However, this is thinking at its most primitive level, and it will take several more years of interaction and refinement before the child's thinking even remotely resembles that of an older child or adult. This statement should have serious implications for caregivers interested in developmentally appropriate guidance and learning activities for toddlers.

Around age two, toddlers move into the next phase of cognitive development, called by Piaget the *preoperational period*. The entire preoperational period actually extends from ages two through seven, and will be discussed extensively in Chapter 13.

Language Development

Near the beginning of toddlerhood, the first real words in a child's expressive vocabulary appear. These are usually naming words that are in some way related to toddlers' actions and experiences; again we see the intertwining of cognitive (sensorimotor) development and language. For example, Rosa's first word was "ca-ca" for "cracker"; Benjamin's was "woo-woo" for "blanket." From these examples it can be seen that first words may approximate adult pronunciation, or be an unconventional sound combination that the toddler chooses to apply to an object.

Single words, or *holophrases,* continue to be used for six months or so, with toddlers conveying quite a bit of meaning with one word, depending on inflection, context, and lots of adult interpretation to fill in the rest of the meaning. So "woo-woo?" means Benjamin is looking for his blanket; "woo-woo!" indicates he wants it now!

When toddlers begin to combine words as they get close to two years, it is in two and three word combinations, leaving out the less important words in a message, thus called *telegraphic messages*. An older Rosa says "Cracker allgone"; an older Benjamin says "Where woo-woo?"

Expressive vocabulary increases dramatically between eighteen and twenty-four months. During this time a commonly used phrase is "Whattzat?" (What's that?) It is as if, toward the end of the sensorimotor stage, toddlers are hungry to have labels to apply to the categories of experience and information now stored in memory (that cognitive/language connection again!).

The second year is a critical period for language development, and success is dependent on available adult language partners. Shortly, we will examine recommended practices to nurture toddler language development.

Developmentally Appropriate Cognitive Environments

Having briefly reviewed the cognitive abilities and learning interests of toddlers, we are now ready to consider the adult's role in providing the most suitable environment for nurturing optimum development.

Burton White on Toddler Education

Some of the most extensive research on optimum development of infants and toddlers has been done by Dr. Burton White in the Harvard Preschool Project, The Brookline Early Education Project, and the New Parents as Teachers programs. (See White, 1985 and 1988.) His findings bear serious consideration for caregivers wanting to provide the most appropriate experiences for toddlers. His research finds that there are few obvious differences before age eight months, yet *"relatively few families, perhaps no more than ten percent, manage to get their children through the eight- to thirty-six month age period as well educated and developed as they can and should be"* (White, 1985, p. 106). White goes on to say that groups of children who underachieve in elementary grades never look particularly weak at one year of age, but begin to lag behind sometime toward the end of the second year. Optimum cognitive development in toddlerhood is related to language development, the development of curiosity, social development, and the roots of intelligence; what he refers to as learning-to-learn, "laying the substructure of sensorimotor exploration upon which higher levels of intelligence are built" (White, 1985, p. 113). The abilities related to intellectual competence that White pinpoints as crucial to develop in toddlerhood include:

- good language development

- the ability to notice small details or discrepancies

- the ability to anticipate consequences

- the ability to deal with abstractions

- the ability to put oneself in the place of another person

- the ability to make interesting associations

- the ability to plan and carry out complicated activities

- the ability to use resources effectively

- the ability to maintain concentration on a task while simultaneously keeping track of what is going on around one in a fairly busy situation (dual focusing) (White, 1985, p. 173).

White finds specific differences in rearing conditions to be responsible for later variations in children's abilities to flourish in cognitive settings. He makes specific recommendations for helpful practices for adults interested in nurturing these specific abilities. They include three roles for adult caregivers: *designer of the child's world* (see Chapter 4); *consultant* (specifics to be discussed below); and *authority* (see Chapter 8).

The Adult As Consultant

In Burton White's research, he discovered that the real differences between caregivers who produced children with the intellectual, language, and social competencies listed earlier and those who did not, were measurable in terms of availability as a resource person, or consultant. Having created a safe, interesting environment with plenty of intriguing things to manipulate, the adults left it to the natural curiosity of toddlers to propel themselves into a variety of explorations. Effective adults were found to be tolerant of messes, accidents, and natural curiosity. The adults remain "on call," available for brief interaction when toddler exploration leads them into situations where they experience excitement with discoveries, frustration, puzzlement, or pain.

Characteristics of Effective Consultants

When toddlers come to adults in excitement or puzzlement, effective adults are available to *respond to them as soon as possible*. They do not keep the children waiting or fail to recognize the teaching opportunity. Even if they have to say, "You will have to wait a minute while I finish helping Sally," they give toddlers the sense that they care about their discoveries or concerns.

Figure 12–1 Open-ended materials, such as the potting soil in this basin, allow toddlers to explore according to interest and ability. *Courtesy Avondale Children's Center.*

Figure 12–2 Adults observe while interacting and assisting. *Courtesy NationsBank Child Care Center.*

The important learning for toddlers in this is that their excitement and curiosity are valued, and that others can be used as resources in situations they cannot handle for themselves.

Having responded, effective caregivers pause to see what it is toddlers are interested in. They identify the subject, then *provide whatever is appropriate to the situation.* It is here that adults need to exercise judgment. There are subtle differences between providing assistance when children cannot completely handle the task themselves, and doing so when toddlers have learned that adult help is the fastest way to accomplish something or get attention. Adults find ways of helping toddlers succeed by providing suggestions, demonstration, or realistic understanding of task limitations, with the least possible interference.

In cases where toddlers ask for assistance, they are learning something about completing tasks for satisfaction, and discovering that they can do things for themselves with only slight assistance.

As adults interact with toddlers, *they express an idea related to the child's interest or discovery.* To a child holding out a play dough ball, an adult might say, "You made a ball, didn't you? Can you pat the ball and make it flat?" or "You've got a little ball. A little ball in a little hand. Now I'm holding it in my *big* hand." The adult has referred to the topic that interested the child, and connected it with something else the child is familiar with and can understand concretely.

The toddler's intellectual world is broadened by such brief cognitive connections.

The brief interaction also allows adults to *provide a few words related to the topic,* whether it is answering a question or interpreting the child's discovery. They use language at or slightly above toddlers' own levels. "A ball. You rolled it round and round."

The toddler gets a language lesson, because the adult is providing language that makes sense with its relevance to the situation.

The *interaction is brief,* (White estimated that no more than 10 percent of adult time was spent deliberately interacting with toddlers in a home setting), and the toddlers break away when ready, sometimes stimulated by adults' suggestions, sometimes ready to repeat the exciting accomplishment. Effective adults, says White, do not bore toddlers. Most encounters such as these might last 20 or 30 seconds—truly teaching "on the fly."

In this description of effective adults as consultants, it is obvious what is missing. There is no push to teach lessons adults have decided toddlers are ready for. Nor is there a good deal of restriction to make toddlers available for formal instruction. The toddlers are directing the pace and style of learning. From this description of characteristics of consultants, we can formulate six principles for toddler teaching.

Principles of Teaching Toddlers

Principle 1— Environment Is Everything

Perhaps this is a slight overstatement, but it is important to realize just how important are the decisions teachers make regarding the materials arranged in the classroom. The physical arrangement of play spaces allows adults to be available to toddlers, while allowing the children freedom to work on their own. Emphasizing the importance of environment helps teachers move from assuming the dominant role in teaching to a focus on toddlers as dominant in directing their learning.

Principle 2— Curriculum Is Materials

The choice of materials that are interesting, novel, and challenging is a key to extending the toddlers' sensorimotor investigations. Teachers have a major role in selecting items that are not so simple as to cause toddlers to lose interest quickly, nor so difficult as to frustrate attempts to use. In many cases the solution is to use materials that are so open-ended that toddlers may use them in a variety of ways, depending on their interest and ability levels. (See Figure 12-1.)

Principle 3— Toddlers Initiate

For teachers who feel that teaching means telling things, working with toddlers requires a major adjustment in style. Rather than setting aside time during the day for "lesson times" when play is stopped and the teacher takes over, teachers observe toddlers and remain available to respond briefly during the times when toddlers indicate a readiness for conversation, assistance, or ideas from adults. By responding to toddlers' initiative, teachers reinforce toddlers in their "learning-to-learn" strategies, by far the most important lesson that could be taught.

When teachers observe toddlers engaging in aimless wandering behavior (different from the very purposeful wandering of toddlers intent on exploration), they may offer or suggest new interests to the children, then allow the toddlers to initiate their activity. For example, a toddler may be encouraged to notice the wood shavings and animals in the water table today.

Principle 4— Adults Observe

When some adults hear that they are meant to allow children to become the active initiators in learning through play, they interpret this to mean that their only role is to set up the environment and supervise for safety. This is to lose sight of the important role of observing: observing initially to learn the toddler's level of ability and interest, before making first decisions about materials; observing later to see how the child uses the materials and how best to respond to the toddler's initiative; using those observations to make next decisions about materials that may extend and reinforce the current learning; and continuing to observe at each step of the learning cycle.

Caregivers position themselves strategically to play areas for maximal observation. They observe while interacting, assisting, comforting, and tidying. (See Figure 12-2.)

Principle 5— Adults Scaffold

"Scaffolding" is a term used by Vygotsky, Bruner, and others to describe the specific process whereby adults support children to take a next step in their play (Vygotsky, 1962; Bruner, 1973). In effect, by their actions and/or suggestions, adults provide a skeletal structure of possibilities to which children can respond. In scaffolding, adults have to look to see what the child has achieved, and then consider several of the possibilities of learning that might build on this. An example of scaffolding might be when the toddler holds a plastic bottle filled with colored marbles out to the teacher. The teacher might say, "Shake the bottle," to help her discover the sound produced by this action; the teacher might take the bottle and pretend to drink, to encourage pretend play; or the teacher might roll the bottle on the floor toward the toddler, to help her notice how a bottle moves when rolled. "The result is more sophisticated behavior than the child could have performed all on her own" (McCune-Nicolich, 1984, p. 13).

Principle 6—Adults Play As Partners

In the small scenarios when toddlers approach adults, adults interact with them as partners, not as dominant leaders. Partners use the skills of observation and scaffolding, and wholeheartedly convey the impression of support and respect for the serious learning embedded in the play. They do this by positive attention and approval of active discovery. They convey partnership by pausing, turn-taking, and seeing things from the toddler's perspective. Partners pause long enough to follow the other's lead; think of it as a dance, where the best partner doesn't try to throw in several complicated new steps that might trip the other up! (See Figure 12-3.)

Planning

Figure 12–3 Adults play as partners. *Courtesy Methodist Home Child Development Center.*

Does all this emphasis on toddler initiative in exploratory learning and downplaying of teacher lessons mean that toddler teachers do not write lesson plans? Not at all. Effective toddler teachers definitely plan so as not to leave to chance the supply of varied, interesting, and appropriate materials. They recognize, however, that they are simply planning a variety of choices and experiences from which toddlers may choose an assortment of learning possibilities. Thus, they are not planning absolute blueprints for their own teaching actions, but instead are creating a bare framework of learning choices. Toddlers will choose which activities and materials attract them at a particular time, and will initiate their activities from the materials planned for by the caregiver. No child's play is interrupted to urge them to participate in activities planned by the teacher; toddler play is valued in its own right.

Planning is based on observed developmental levels. As teachers are familiar with physical, cognitive, and language landmarks, they are aware of where individuals in the group are in the developmental sequence, and are able to plan experiences that support the level achieved, and help children move on to the next level.

Planning takes into account the particular learning style of toddlers, with the pattern of brief interaction with materials, moving on to other activities, then returning to repeat the experience. While teachers plan appropriate materials and activities for the brief times when a small group of toddlers may come together to enjoy stories or songs, they recognize that the majority of learning time will be spent by toddlers in solitary exploration and self-determined tasks.

Planning is also based on observed interest. As teachers discover topics that are important to toddlers, they sustain that interest by extending their explorations with additional related learning experiences. If this sounds very much like the kinds of emergent curriculum that will be discussed in more detail in Chapter 13, that is because this is appropriate when modified for toddlers also. Many of the problems that occur in toddler classrooms are probably the result of teachers' thinking that toddlers are too young for any real learning and thus there is no need for real planning. Often in such a classroom, toddlers are simply left free to play with the collections of toys that adorn the shelves of most classrooms, unchanged for months on end. While there is nothing wrong with the typical collection of puzzles, shapesorters, balls, trucks, and hollow blocks—indeed, these are among most lists of appropriate materials—reliance on these items alone without planning to provide for variety, increasing levels of challenge, and

Talking about:	Things we do and use at home
Sensory table:	Cedar shavings, plastic scoops and hand rakes
Paint:	Using objects: pot scrubber, sponges
Water table:	Soapsuds and plastic dishes to wash
Manipulatives:	Tongs to put cotton balls in plastic jars
Puzzles:	Fisher-Price house with knobs (shows interior)
Blocks:	Foam blocks and small family figures
Dramatic play:	Babies and baby bottles, box of scarves
Special:	Butter crackers to sprinkle with sesame seeds
Consider:	Put train out for Ian?
	See if Jessica is still interested in climbing?
Stories:	*My Daddy and Me; Our Garden*
Songs:	"This Is the Way We Sweep the Floor"

Figure 12-4 Sample of planning ideas for toddlers.

toddlers' desire to create new effects leads to increased wandering behavior, shortened attention spans, increased friction among toddlers, and increased toddlers' reliance on adults to entertain them.

LeeKeenan and Edwards describe a project approach in planning curriculum for toddlers to allow for toddlers making connections between different experiences. For example, one of their projects worked with "water," with toddlers using water in many activities over a period of time, from washing babies to painting with water in spray bottles. They found that the connecting experiences allowed toddlers to comprehend the basic and related concepts, and use the vocabulary more extensively in their everyday play (LeeKeenan and Edwards, 1992).

A sample planning sheet for a toddler classroom might look like the one shown in Figure 12-4. Note that the teacher has planned for specific children's interest as well as for experiences that anyone in the group might enjoy. Note also that the plan is in the form of notations for teachers to follow as they prepare for the day. They will be prepared to initiate these adult-planned activities at opportune times, rather than having set times in which the activities must be done.

It should also be clearly stated that caregivers need to be ready to forego the planned activities for the day, depending on children's interest and receptivity. Teachers follow toddlers' leads in determining when and how to implement their planned activities.

Materials and Activities for Sensorimotor Learning

As noted in the section on planning, the emphasis for materials is on those that lend themselves to the kinds of sensorimotor exploration toddlers do, including

BUT WHAT ABOUT?

But what about some of my toddlers' parents who insist that we should really be learning something? How do I convince them that this is inappropriate?

Actually you agree; both parents and caregivers believe that toddlers should be learning something. The difference is in your understandings of how this learning actually happens. When an adult believes that toddlers learn only through direct instruction from adults, it is often very difficult to see the learning that is actually occurring. Your best strategy may be in making that learning become more obvious to parents.

Try using a camera to capture the active involvement of toddlers with their materials. Display these with appropriate notations on your parent bulletin board, or mount them in a photograph album, with explanatory notes, and send it home on a rotating basis. Use a tape recorder to capture some language interchanges or singing times. Make a display of favorite books shared recently.

Offer articles and books that explain toddler learning style and responsive teaching; parents who are readers often take information better from reading than from a personal source. Make available the NAEYC statements on developmentally appropriate and inappropriate practices in centers serving toddlers. Emphasize development of the whole child. Record development and share changes with parents in informal conversations.

Perhaps most importantly, invite parents to come and observe for periods during the day. Share your plans for the week based on your own observation and objectives. Call their attention to the real involvement of toddlers busy at self-chosen exploration. Play your usual role as consultant; then make an opportunity later to discuss this role of the teacher. Have them watch the self-help skills developing during the period before, during, and after lunch.

Have a morning in the toddler room videotaped, and plan a parent get-together to discuss what they see. Sometimes the support of other parents helps others look at new ideas.

Remember that imposing your views on parents will not change their opinions, but allowing them to have real opportunities to experience the learning that is happening may help them see the developmentally appropriate orientation you come from. Allow time for dialogue, and don't force agreement. Gonzalez-Mena (1993) refers to this issue in her fine book on multicultural issues in child care.

testing out all the characteristics of objects and finding new ways to use familiar items. This means the majority of materials need to be *open-ended*, that is, being open to use in a variety of ways, and able to be used in increasingly complex play.

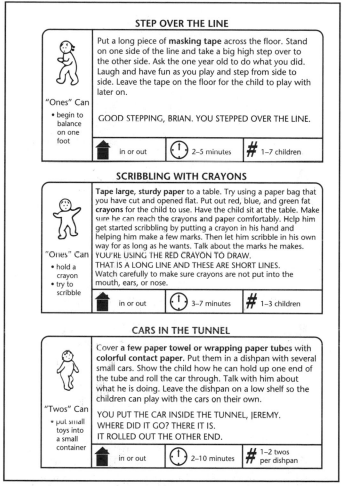

Figure 12-5 Sample of activities for toddlers. *Used with permission; from* Active Learning for Infants *by Cryer, D., Harms, T. and Bourland, B., Menlo Park, CA: Addison-Wesley Publishing Co., 1986.*

The following suggestions are by no means exhaustive. As you read, note other similar items you have seen used. Any good book on toddler education activities will add suggestions. (See Figure 12-5.) At chapter end, see Miller, 1984 and 1990, White, 1985 and 1988, Cataldo, Harms et al., 1987, Leavitt and Eheart, 1985.

Creative Corner

Toddlers will enjoy using:

- fat crayons, including the chunky ones homemade in muffin tins. Tape the paper to the table, or tie the crayons with yarn to the easel. Toddlers are less interested in having their own product than in making a scribble.

- finger paint, which may be homemade from a variety of recipes (see Miller, 1984), and used on trays, table tops, mirrors, windows, meat trays, or anything else that will help contain the mess.

- chalk and chalk boards.
- Play-Doh® (yes, it will be tasted).
- paint and varieties of brushes and other applicators.
- tissue paper and magazines for tearing.
- occasional opportunities for gluing, as long as teachers are willing to allow children to experiment with the stickiness. Small brushes and containers help.
- any kind of paper at all for use with these materials. Get castoffs from parents.

Manipulative Area

Many commercial items are appropriate for toddler fingers. A selection should include:

large Legos®

puzzles with single piece pictures, some with knobs

bristle blocks

plastic snap beads

large beads for stringing

shape sorting boxes

stacking or nesting toys

busy boxes (See Burton White's (1985) recommendations)

small table toys (See Figure 12-6.)

Household castoffs provide necessary variety. Manipulative toys can be made from:

an assortment of plastic containers and jars, lids, and tops, as from aerosol cans, and especially screw tops

canisters

clothespins

boxes and lids

egg cartons, L'Eggs® containers, and things to put in them

milk jugs

popsicle sticks

large nuts and bolts

belts and buckles

hinges, castors

sponges

wheels or other safe, large parts from broken toys

Used in any kind of combination, there are a lot of possibilities for manipulation here.

Figure 12–6 Small table toys for toddler manipulation are appropriate materials. *Courtesy CPCC Child Care Training Center.*

Sensory Exploration

Toddlers need regular access to materials for sensory exploration, and accessories to use with sensory materials. When teachers do not have access to commercially available water/sand tables, they can improvise with dishpans or baby bathtubs. Mess is minimized when children are given interesting accessories to suggest play more constructive than throwing. Having a broom, mop, and dustpan nearby will also help. Materials for the tubs include:

- sand, both indoors and outdoors, with accessories such as spoons, shovels, containers both big and small, funnels, strainers, shape molds, small dump trucks. Occasionally water can be added to the sand. (See Figure 12-7.)

- water, both indoors and outdoors, sometimes varied indoors with addition of color or bubbles, ice chips, and accessories such as boats, containers, egg-beaters, sponges, colanders, hoses or tubing, watering cans, basters, squeeze bottles, straws, things to wash.

- dry rice, cornmeal, oats, dried beans and macaroni mixtures, styrofoam bits, woodshavings, sawdust, cedar shavings, large stones, Easter grass, leaves and nuts, potato flakes, birdseed, coffee sand (coffee grounds mixed with sand). Yes, all of these things do need supervision so stones or beans don't get into noses or ears, but the variety is worth it.

- boxes or trays of other sensory manipulatives, such as sandpaper, fabrics of all kinds, ribbons, elastic, sticky papers, balls of yarn or masking tape; natural materials, like seeds, nuts, seed pods, bark, sea shells, sometimes arranged as games to match or compare.

- clear plastic containers with varieties of items inside such as sound-makers and other homemade shakers.

- collections of bells, whistles, and horns.

Figure 12–7 Sand with rakes, shovels and containers has endless fascination for toddlers. *Courtesy CPCC Child Care Training Center.*

Large Motor Play

Teachers will probably want to include some purchased equipment for large muscle play in their classroom requests. Items such as:

climber/slide combination

step arrangement

low, sturdy riding toys for foot propulsion

toys for pushing and pulling

tunnel

wheelbarrows and wagons

Other additions can probably be found, including:

large cardboard cartons to climb into or fill and push (see Figure 12-8)

inner tubes

balls

tree trunk sections to climb and pound on

old mattresses

piles of cushions to climb or jump on

things for throwing indoors—nerf balls, crumpled newspaper balls

things for throwing outdoors—whiffle balls, bean bags, with containers to throw in, such as old laundry baskets

Figure 12–8 Large boxes for climbing into, or filling and pushing, offer large motor challenges for toddlers. *Courtesy NationsBank Child Care Center.*

Construction Area

It is likely that toddlers are not yet ready for many experiences with the traditional wooden unit blocks of the preschool classroom. Instead they enjoy constructing with:

> sturdy cardboard blocks
>
> foam and fabric blocks
>
> teacher made blocks from boxes or milk cartons covered with contact paper
>
> giant Legos® (See Figure 12-9.)
>
> boxes of various sizes
>
> large cardboard or plastic tubes
>
> additions of props such as animals, people figures, or cars

Twos may begin using unit blocks to line up and carry around.

Housekeeping Area

Figure 12–9 Giant Legos® are easy for toddlers to use for construction. *Courtesy CPCC Child Care Training Center.*

For nurturing the first pretend kinds of play, toddlers need a clearly recognized house area that includes:

> a table and two small chairs, stove, stroller, and bed. Toddlers will be playing simple repetitions of home-based scenes, so they need a simply furnished area, easily recognizable.
>
> simple dress-ups, such as scarves, hats, grown-up shoes, purses and zipped travel bags, and a mirror to look in.
>
> toy or real telephones.
>
> a few pots, pans, dishes and big spoons: The real thing, rather than toys, appeals to toddlers.
>
> a small mop and broom
>
> dolls and baby blankets (leave out the doll clothes for a while; toddlers will remove them and then want you to put them back on—repeatedly). Make sure you have both boy and girl dolls, and dolls that represent ethnic diversity.
>
> realistic looking materials from home life. (See Figure 12-10.)
>
> empty food containers.

Book Area

In trying to encourage toddler interest in books, teachers will want to provide books they can handle themselves, as well as books for reading to toddlers. The area should include:

> board books (rather than cloth or plastic books, which are less easily cleaned and more difficult for toddlers to handle).
>
> homemade picture books, with stiff pages, useful to place in looseleaf notebook.
>
> photo album books, using either familiar photos or large magazine pictures for naming objects.
>
> flannel board with large figures for toddler use.

Again, watching the toddlers use all these materials will probably give teachers more ideas. A developmentally appropriate cognitive environment for toddlers provides for needs and interests of individual children as well as broad abilities of the group. Examples:

> Rosa added a firefighter's hat to the dress-up clothes, a new picture book featuring firefighters, and two new small firetrucks to the block

Figure 12–10 Realistic household items encourage beginning dramatic play. *Courtesy CPCC Child Care Training Center.*

area after Michelle repeatedly used her new word "fire" when the sirens raced by.

Realizing that DeJuan preferred not to put his hands in the shaving cream available to smear on the art table, she added some fresh paper to the easel, where two fat crayons were tied.

Noticing that Sarah had mastered the puzzles with one-piece shapes, she found some three-piece puzzles in the storage closet.

Cognitive development, then, is encouraged by the thoughtful preparation of an environment that encourages exploration and movement, using carefully selected open-ended materials and sturdy toys. Adults remain available, observing toddlers' levels of understanding, and responding promptly to toddler approaches to share discoveries or ask for help. They use these brief encounters to support curiosity and learning, to add related ideas, and to add language. Let's consider the adult's role in providing an optimum language environment for toddlers.

Principles of Teaching Language to Toddlers

Someone once said that adults teach two important things to toddlers: how to talk and how to eliminate. The difference between the two is that adults are frequently frustrated in teaching the latter, and have more success with the first because of the differences in methods of instruction! With toilet training, adults usually decide on a time for instruction, teach quite directly what to do and how to do it, and clearly let toddlers know when they have succeeded or failed according to adult standards. With language, however, most adults allow children to choose their time to begin speaking, teach quite indirectly and mostly by modeling, and are nearly always extremely positive with toddlers about any effort to speak at all. While this does bear thinking about (primarily for considering new tactics with toilet instruction!), adults who want to provide the optimum language environment for toddlers will become more conscious of behaviors that research has found particularly helpful.

Principle 1— Language Teachers Respond

If toddlers are to continue with language development, they need to perceive that their efforts at speech are important. If speech is not attended to by adults, toddlers quickly learn that language is not valued or necessary. Even when adults are unable to understand toddlers' first words, they use context and nonverbal cues to attempt to understand and respond appropriately. Even when adults are tiring of the persistent "Whatzat?" they respond patiently, knowing their key role in helping toddlers sort out labels for objects. Examples:

"Wuh," says Rodney, holding out his cup. "More juice, Rodney? You want more juice?"

"Muk wal." "Hmm," says a toddler teacher. "I don't understand. Show me."

"Whatzat?" "That's a mirror. *Mirror.*"

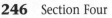

**Principle 2—
Language
Teachers Model**

Knowing that toddlers depend on adult speech for their example of vocabulary, as well as for extracting their own understanding of grammar usage, adults speak frequently, clearly, and distinctly to toddlers, enunciating more clearly than in ordinary speech, and emphasizing key words. Sometimes they repeat the child's word, with correct, emphasized pronunciation. This is done as a form of positive reinforcement, instead of a negative correction. They model not only the mechanics of speech, but also the logistics of conversation, making it clear when they are speaking to a particular child, and waiting for response before speaking further:

"Mok," says Jeffrey. "Yes, here's your *milk*," says his mother.

"Randy, here's your *jacket*."

"*Snack time*, Michelle."

**Principle 3—
Language
Teachers Simplify**

Adults simplify much of their speech so it is only slightly more complex than the child's current level. For example, if a child is speaking in two-word sentences, adults use about three words. Long, complex sentences are avoided:

"Time for jackets."

"More juice, Jennifer?"

**Principle 4—
Language
Teachers Expand**

One strategy known to be effective with toddler language is to expand on their original utterances, adding vocabulary and ideas. Expansions fill in children's missing words or offer more specific words, and extend ideas that children begin. Such expansions are important for both cognitive and language development:

"Ju," says Michelle, holding out her cup. "More juice. Michelle wants more juice," expands her caregiver.

"Want dat," says Sarah. "You want your bunny?" says Mom.

"Daddy car," says Peter. "Yes, Daddy went in the car. He went to work."

**Principle 5—
Language
Teachers Link
Words with Action
and Experience**

Toddlers learn vocabulary in a particular context. When gestures, pointing, and other nonverbal clues help children understand the meaning of words, their learning is assisted. When caregivers describe their actions and the activities of toddlers, the concrete context helps toddlers recognize meaning. Caregivers provide an abundance of objects, pictures, and experience in toddler environments to offer interesting things to stimulate communication:

"Shoes, Jennifer, please get your shoes," as the caregiver points to the shoes.

"You're playing in the soap bubbles, aren't you," as the caregiver puts her own hand into the soapy water.

"Where's the duck, Julio? Show me the picture of the duck," as they look at some bright pictures taped to the wall.

**Principle 6—
Language
Teachers Correct
Indirectly**

There is much for toddlers to absorb about grammar and word usage. In the process, they typically make mistakes by overgeneralization; for example, having deduced that plurals are formed by adding an "s," and past tenses by adding "ed," toddlers apply those rules in all cases, including irregular English words, producing such phrases as "my feets" (or foots), or "Daddy goed" or "wented."

Actually such constructions show clearly the toddler's amazing understanding of a number of grammar rules! It is most helpful when adults repeat the idea back, correctly phrased, rather then directly pointing out the mistake. Toddlers quickly self-correct, without feeling failure. Brazelton lists too much direct emphasis on correct speech as one possible reason for language delay (Brazelton, 1974). Examples:

> "Yes, Daddy went to the office."

> "You *do* have new shoes on your feet, don't you?"

Principle 7— Language Teachers Encourage Speech

Once toddlers have the ability to link sound and word, adults encourage toddlers to attempt speech. They do this by not immediately responding to a perceived need before the toddler has had a chance to verbalize it. They also encourage speech by asking questions the toddler can answer with a word or two. They do not frustrate toddlers, however, by demanding a word before they give an object to a child if the child is unable to speak.

Sometimes they encourage speech with the materials in the environment. There are toy and/or real telephones; there are puppets, and there are pictures and objects that intrigue:

> "Tell me what you want, Michelle."

> "Do you want one cracker or two?"

> "Hello? There's somebody who wants to talk to you, Danielle," holding out the telephone.

Principle 8— Language Teachers Talk Face to Face

Figure 12–11 Language teachers sing to encourage interest. *Courtesy NationsBank Child Care Center.*

Cawlfield has noted a time in toddlerhood she labels "Velcro" Time (Cawlfield, 1992). This is a short period, varying from toddler to toddler regarding age of onset and duration, when children's interest in independent exploratory play with toys is replaced by an interest in spending time with primary caregivers. During this time toddlers are obviously interested in language, watching caregivers' mouths, attempting to say words, bringing objects for labeling or comment, and enjoying having adults label pictures in books. As more vocabulary appears, toddlers seem to move back to a primary interest in toys. She hypothesizes that this short period has a linguistic purpose as well as an emotional one, and that caregivers would do well to feed this toddler desire to hear language directly and face to face with a familiar caregiver who can tune in to the individual language development:

> "Turtle," says Jennifer, when Bobby points to the picture in the book. "Turtle." He turns to watch her face.

> "Show me your nose," says Joe. Lee is sitting facing him on the carpet, and watching intently, as she touches her nose.

Principle 9— Language Teachers Sing, Recite, and Play Games

The reason traditional nursery songs, rhymes, and games have lasted is their appropriateness for language experiences of toddlers. The rhythm, rhyme, repetition, and linking of action and meaning help toddlers acquire understanding and vocabulary. (See Figure 12-11.) Examples:

> "Head and shoulders, knees and toes," sings LaToya, moving her hands so the toddlers can imitate her.

> As Anthony recites "Humpty Dumpty sat on the wall," Sarah and DeJuan wait with anticipation to "fall off the wall" along with the words.

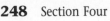

Favorite Books for Toddlers

Ahlberg, Janet and Allan. *Peek-a-Boo!*

Alexander, Martin. *Maggie's Moon*

Aliki. *Hush Little Baby*

Bang, Molly. *Ten, Nine, Eight*

Barton, Byron. *Airplanes*

Brown, Margaret Wise. *Goodnight Moon*

Bruna, Dick. *Miffy at the Zoo*

Burningham, John. *The Baby*

Campbell, Rod. *Dear Zoo*

Carle, Eric. *1, 2, 3 to the Zoo*

Carlstrom, Nancy. *Jesse Bear, What Will You Wear?*

Crews, Donald. *Ten Black Dots*

De Paola, Tomie. *Tomie De Paola's Mother Goose*

Fisher, Aileen. *Do Bears Have Mothers Too?*

Fujikawa, Gyo. *Mother Goose*

Galdone, Paul. *Little Bo-Peep*

Gibbons Gail. *Trucks*

Hill, Eric. *Spot's First Walk*

Hoban, Tana. *A Children's Zoo*

Holzenthaler, Jean. *My Feet Do*

Howard, Jane. *When I'm Sleepy*

Hutchins, Pat. *Titch*

Isadora, Rachel. *I Hear*

Komori, Atsushi. *Animal Mothers*

Krauss, Ruth. *Carrot Seed*

McMillan, Bruce. *Kitten Can*

Mack, Stanley. *Ten Bears in My Bed*

Maris, Ron. *Is Anyone Home?*

Martin, Bill. *Brown Bear, Brown Bear, What Do You See?*

Miller, Jane. *Farm Counting Book*

Oxenbury, Helen. *Friends*

Peek, Merle. *Mary Wore a Red Dress and Henry Wore His Green Sneakers*

Peppe, Rodney. *Circus Numbers*

Reiss, John. *Colors*

Rockwell, Anne. *Big Wheels*

Rojankovsky, Feodor. *Animals on the Farm*

Roy, Ron. *Three Ducks Went Wandering*

Speier, Peter. *Gobble, Growl, Grunt*

Tafuri, Nancy. *Who's Counting?*

Titherington, Jeanne. *Pumpkin, Pumpkin*

Watanabe, Shigeo. *How Do I Put It On?*

Wells, Rosemary. *Max's Bath*

Wheeler, Cindy. *A Good Day, A Good Night*

Wildsmith, Brian. *Animal Homes*

Williams, Garth. *The Chicken Book*

Winter, Jeanette. *Hush Little Baby*

Look for other books by these authors.

Figure 12-12 Favorite books for toddlers.

Principle 10— Language Teachers Read Books

The important association of word and picture helps toddlers increase their vocabulary. While most toddlers are not ready to sustain interest in actual stories until well into the second year (White, 1988), picture book sessions are important labeling sessions. In addition to vocabulary, the positive connection between books and pleasurable experiences is reinforced by book time with adults. A selection of toddler favorites is listed in Figure 12-12.

Group Time for Toddlers?

As caregivers hear the importance of books and songs for toddlers, it might be tempting to consider planning group times to introduce these activities to toddlers. For most of toddlerhood, children are unlikely to be able to sustain interest long enough for an organized group time to be very meaningful. The sheer logistics of trying to encourage a number of independent toddlers to occupy the same space and to sustain the quiet listening skills demanded by an organized group time are daunting. Generally, formal group times for toddlers are extremely frustrating for everyone involved.

Far better to form small, less formal groups by sitting on the floor with interested toddlers and beginning a singing session or looking at a picture book with those who are nearby. As the activity appears interesting, toddlers will wander over to join in. Just as they casually come, caregivers should be willing for them to casually leave when something else attracts them. For book sharing time, the adults in a room may find it advantageous to form small groups distant from one another. Often adults read to toddlers sharing space on their laps, rather than grouped in a distant semicircle as in a preschool group time. Sometimes it is helpful to read to a few toddlers seated in chairs at a table; this arrangement encourages staying a bit longer. The brief pleasure of sharing a song or singing game, like "Ring around a Roses" is a pleasant introduction to extended group participation appropriate for later on.

With toddlers, it is more important that they have pleasurable experiences with books and language games and songs than that they stay, sit still, and learn group time skills.

After many such experiences, the very oldest toddlers—those well into their third year—may be ready for short, more structured group experiences. Teachers may create half-circles, with a space clearly marked for each child, by a carpet square, for example. They will plan very short reading and music experiences, coaching children daily with group skills, such as sitting quietly, listening when others talk, and so on.

Things Not Seen in a Developmentally Appropriate Environment

When toddler caregivers find the best developmental match for toddler learning style, they avoid two extremes.

1. **Creating an environment without challenges or responses:** When caregivers decide that toddlers are "too young for any real learning," there is a danger of offering an environment that bores and stifles curiosity. Adults merely supervise toddlers in a sterile room, stepping in to referee the squabbles that are frequently the result of too little interest or novelty to otherwise occupy interest.

2. **Creating an environment that imposes structured adult-decided learning experiences:** When caregivers decide that toddlers are "not babies any more," this frequently translates into imposing rote learning experiences and dribbling down ideas from the preschool. The plans usually include producing some product to take home "so we can show our parents we're really teaching them something," which usually means adults have to do most of the "work" themselves—producing a ditto sheet of farm animals for toddlers to color, or gluing together the precut parts of an Easter bunny.

   Rote learning experiences do not match the active, self-initiated learning style of the toddler. While toddlers can sometimes parrot back the words taught by the flashcards (red, yellow, up, out, or whatever concept is pictured on the card and repeated by the adult), their true understanding is certainly questionable. Moreover, to coerce toddlers into such experiences usually requires trying to get them to sit and attend by persistent adult direction, often resulting in powerful toddler resistance. The question remains whether anything is gained by such cognitive practices.

Television and Video Viewing

Both White and Brazelton question the value of television viewing experiences for toddlers (Brazelton, 1974; White, 1985). While it is obvious that toddlers can and do learn from television—notice the words and tunes picked up from commercials, or the ability to "sing out the letters with tunes culled from Sesame Street" (Brazelton, 1974, p. 160)—learning is richer and much more individualized and meaningful in an interpersonal setting. While White acknowledges that toddlers may pick up some vocabulary from children's shows like Sesame Street, words that are not tied in to concrete action or meaning are just words. "If he never sees a single television program he still can learn language through you in an absolutely magnificent manner" (White, 1985, p. 172). The reliance in many centers on television as a curriculum event decreases the amount of active exploration time available for toddlers. Surely the most discouraging sight is to see toddlers being scolded for not sitting quietly through a television presentation; this seems the height of developmental inappropriateness.

Emphasis on Sitting to Learn

Toddlers are creatures on the move. Their drive to explore and to use their whole bodies, linked with an average attention span of about two minutes, means that toddlers learn to go and learn as they go. When toddlers are asked to sit and do, it is contrary to their nature. They much prefer to stand and move, even for stories and songs. Since they will be asked to sit to eat, that should be the one time of the day this is required.

SUMMARY

The natural sensorimotor learning style of toddlers demands responsive adult behaviors. These include: preparing interesting environments; observing as a basis for planning and interaction; playing as partners; using brief, child-initiated encounters for adding language and ideas. Individual, rather than group, learning experiences are emphasized. Toddler language is reinforced by adults who are careful to model, expand, correct indirectly, and simplify their speech patterns. Books and songs are important language experiences.

THINK ABOUT IT

1. Visit a toddler classroom. Notice the kinds of planning done by the teachers. What about planned group times? Does this suggest developmental appropriateness to you?

2. Observe the teachers. What behaviors do you see that suggest the characteristics of White's description of a consultant?

3. List the materials that are available for toddlers to use in their play. Note those that were suggested by the materials list in the chapter and those that are additional ideas.

4. Select one toddler and watch him or her at play. Record activity for a ten-minute period. What behaviors do you notice? What strategies does the toddler use to explore materials?

5. Note several examples of language interchanges between adults and toddlers. Which of the principles of language teaching discussed in this chapter do these illustrate?

6. What materials do you see in the room that would encourage language exchanges?

QUESTIONS TO REVIEW OBJECTIVES

1. Describe the characteristics of the last substages of sensorimotor development.

2. Discuss typical language development patterns of toddlerhood.

3. Describe the behaviors of a consultant, as defined by Burton White.

4. Identify several principles of teaching toddlers for cognitive development.

5. Think of as many materials as you can that are appropriate for toddler learning.

6. Discuss several techniques for nurturing toddler language development.

7. Identify several inappropriate practices relating to toddler cognitive/language development.

REFERENCES AND SUGGESTIONS FOR READING

Brazelton, T. B. (1974). *Toddlers and parents.* New York, NY: Dell Publishing Co.

Bruner, J. (1973). *Beyond the information given: Studies in the psychology of knowing.* NY: Norton.

Cataldo, C. (1983). *Infant toddler caregiving.* Reading, MA: Addison-Wesley.

Cawlfield, M. (1992, May). Velcro time: The language connection. *Young Children, 47(4),* 26–30.

Gonzalez-Mena, J. (1993). *Multicultural issues in child care.* Mountain View, CA: Mayfield Publishing Co.

Harms, T., Cryer, D., & Bourland, B. (1987). *Active learning for ones.* Reading, MA: Addison-Wesley.

Harms, T., Cryer, D., & Bourland, B. (1987). *Active learning for twos.* Reading, MA: Addison-Wesley.

Leavitt, R., & Eheart, B. (1985). *Toddler day care: A guide to responsive caregiving.* Lexington, MA: Lexington Books.

LeeKeenan, D., & Edwards, C. (1992, May). Using the project approach with toddlers. *Young Children, 47(4),* 31–35.

McCune-Nicolich, L. (1984, Spring). Infants don't pretend, do they? *Beginnings,* 10–13.

Miller, K. (1984). *Things to do with toddlers and twos.* Telshare Publishing Co.

Miller, K. (1990). *More things to do with toddlers and twos.* Telshare Publishing Co.

Piaget, J. (1951). *Play, dreams and imitation in childhood.* NY: Norton.

Vygotsky, L.S. (1962). *Thought and language.* NY: Wiley.

White, B. (1985). *The first three years of life.* New York: Prentice-Hall.

White, B. (1988). *Educating the infant and toddler.* Lexington, MA: Lexington Books.

Developmentally Appropriate Cognitive/Language Environments: For Preschoolers

*I*n her article "Why Not Academic Preschool?" Polly Greenberg responds to the following inquiry from a preschool director:

> I have looked into NAEYC's accreditation system to see whether I want to discuss getting into it with our board and staff. I see the obvious advantages.... Of course we seek educational excellence. We want to be the best.
>
> This is where I balk at accreditation. *We* believe that three- and four-year-olds can *learn,* and *expect* them too. Our parents are educated and would never put up with an inferior program where children just play (Greenberg, 1990, p. 70).

This statement summarizes the widest division between programs advocating developmentally appropriate practices for children, and those that stress more formal academic learning. The first implication of the director's statement is that learning is quite narrowly cognitive, overlooking the complex learnings for preschoolers already discussed in the physical, social, and emotional domains, as well as the importance of achieving positive self-esteem and attitudes toward life experiences. The second implication is that play is something rather trivial and time-wasting, indeed "inferior." The crux of the matter is differences in opinion about what young children should be learning and how they should be taught. In this consideration of developmentally appropriate cognitive/language environments for preschoolers, play takes a central position as offering the most appropriate curriculum and medium for learning. This chapter will examine central issues regarding play and the teacher's role in providing for optimum play experiences.

OBJECTIVES

After completing this chapter, students should be able to:

- discuss characteristics of preoperational thinking.
- describe characteristics of play that make it developmentally appropriate curriculum for preschoolers.
- identify three kinds of play and three kinds of knowledge identified by Piaget.

- identify and describe teacher behaviors in providing for play.
- discuss what is meant by *whole language,* and reasons for its appropriateness in the preschool language environment.
- describe eight components of the appropriate language environment.
- identify several developmentally inappropriate teacher practices.

Preoperational Thinking

As Piaget described the thinking and cognitive functioning of children ages two to seven or so, he called this stage the *preoperational stage,* meaning it is a time before children begin to be able to make truly logical connections in their thinking. During this time, "children are incapable of formulating or understanding true concepts, concepts that are reliable and stable, not in constant risk of contradiction" (Van Hoorn et al., 1993, p. 222). This is because, according to Piaget, young children reason from particular to particular rather than understanding how particular cases relate to the whole set of possible cases (Piaget, 1966).

In actuality, Piaget defined two distinct substages within the preoperational period: one from about two to four, where children are able to apply familiar action patterns to something outside themselves, and the next from four to seven, where there is more sophisticated cognition, enabling children to understand contingencies and relationships somewhat. Nevertheless, in both phases, the preoperational thought of preschoolers is limited in particular ways that have implications for those wanting to understand how these children best learn.

Centration　*Centration* is the tendency of preoperational thinkers to focus attention on one aspect of any situation, while ignoring all others. Thus their concepts are limited by one outstanding appearance or perception, to the exclusion of true understanding based on being able to consider the total picture. In Piaget's classic experiments, preschoolers were unable to understand that the amount of water did not change when poured from a short, broad beaker into a taller, thinner one where the water line appeared higher, even when they had watched the pouring from the first container to the second.

The ability to de-center is needed to be able to focus on details, while still keeping the whole in mind. This, after all, is the skill required in learning to read, to be able to perceive the individual letters as part of a word. Math operations require an understanding of transformations, impossible for preoperational minds.

Egocentrism　*Egocentrism* is part of this inability to center on more than one aspect of a situation at a time, according to Piaget. Thus egocentrism causes preschoolers to interpret every event in reference to themselves and makes it impossible for preschoolers to understand others' points of view or feelings. It is egocentrism that causes preschoolers to engage in conversations where they leave out vital bits of information, becoming impatient with those who do not visualize what they have in mind. It is also egocentrism that leads preschoolers to believe in animism, assuming all objects have the same lifelike characteristics they have experienced. This egocentrism is very developmentally appropriate for preschoolers.

It is only through multitudes of experiences and encounters with persons and objects that preschoolers slowly come to an ability to de-center, to gain wider understanding of their world.

Irreversibility

Irreversibility is another limitation of preoperational thinking. Preschoolers are unable to reverse their thinking to reconstruct mentally the actions that got them to the final point. This inability again contributes to centration; they are able to focus only on the end or beginning state, without understanding what happened in between.

Concreteness

Concreteness is another characteristic of preoperational thought. Young children are able to understand real objects, situations, and happenings they have actually experienced firsthand, but have difficulty with abstract ideas, things beyond their personal knowledge. This characteristic also ties them to literal interpretation of words and phrases. Much of the world of academic learning deals with abstractions; the numeral 5 is an abstraction until the child has had enough firsthand experiences with 5 to turn the concept into reality.

Understanding the abilities and limitations of preoperational thought has serious implications for matching learning style and ability for those planning curricula for preschoolers. Because of their facility with language (and their desire to please adults), preschoolers can be taught to repeat many of the conceptual words that some adults feel they should be taught. Many four-year-olds can count rapidly to 10 or 20, but get bogged down when asked to count pointing to objects, or to go get 10 napkins. And why is this? In Piaget's view children are active in constructing their own understanding of the world about them. They can't just gain knowledge by being given information or imitating others, but they bring what they already know to each new learning situation to try to make sense of new information. They take in information (assimilation) and they organize the information so it makes sense in relation to what they already understood(accommodation). As they manipulate, experience, do, interact, observe, play, and problem-solve, they move to true understanding of basic concepts. "Knowing requires spontaneous action, which takes the form of play: the self-initiated recreation of one's experiences in order to understand (assimilate) them" (Jones and Reynolds, 1992, p. 4). After enough meaningful, active experiences, young children achieve for themselves a sense of "ten-ness," or whatever concept it is that adults are hurrying to teach them. And they really understand it, because they have "constructed" their own real knowledge of it, rather than learning by rote someone else's abstraction.

This constructivist theory lies close to the heart of developmentally appropriate practice. (Constructivist theory refers to those ideas of Piaget and the cognitive researchers who followed: that intelligence and understanding are actively created, or "constructed" by the individual through interaction with elements of the environment.) If one accepts the notion that children's minds operate quite differently from those of adults, and that no amount of teaching will cause them to work the same way, then one is forced to call into question the traditional teaching-by-telling methods. Adults can tell, preschoolers can repeat back, but the learning remains superficial, not a part of the child's constructed cognitive reality. If construction of intelligence is viewed metaphorically as building a tower of blocks, the solid base is the sensorimotor information taken in during infancy and toddlerhood, and continuing during the preschool years. The next

Figure 13–1 Experiences, materials, and support enhance cognitive learning through active play. *Courtesy CPCC Child Care Training Center.*

part of the structure is the blocks added during the preoperational years, as children work/play through to understandings of how that information relates together. Once these basic concepts are formed, the building can proceed to the learning of academic skills that needs the foundation of conceptual understanding. The tower stands solidly. But if, in the rush to move children on to the intellectual tasks that are meaningful and measurable for adults, the preoperational blocks are added quickly and casually, or left out altogether, there is likelihood that the tower will topple, without the necessary sturdy underpinnings.

The implication of understanding the characteristics of preoperational minds in defining developmentally appropriate practice seems to be to find a medium for children to be able to actively construct their intelligence. That medium is play.

Through play, children actively re-create their experiences and understandings of the world, forming and linking their own concepts.

 It is in this stage (the preschool years) that the child first becomes a competent representer of experience rather than simply a doer of it. Human society and thought are built on the achievement of *representation*, which makes possible both looking back and looking ahead, rather than simply living in the moment, and communication removed in both place and time, rather than simply face to face. The exploration of the toddler is direct encounter, not representation. But the dramatic play of four- and five-year-olds is increasingly sophisticated representation of both real and imagined experiences (Jones and Reynolds, 1992, p. 4). *"*

The goal of developmentally appropriate preschool classrooms is to allow children to learn to *represent* their growing understandings orally and through action, by having experiences, materials, and support for their active cognitive learning through play. (See Figure 13-1.)

Play As Developmentally Appropriate Curriculum

The universality of children's play has attracted the attention of countless researchers and theorists over the years. There have been differences in basic assumptions about play, but there is agreement that play is significant in the development of children physically, socially, emotionally, and cognitively.

 Freud (1958) and Erikson (1963) emphasized the emotional significance of play, the expression and release of children's strong feelings; Piaget (1962) emphasized play's cognitive significance, the practice of known information; and Vygotsky (1967, 1978) emphasized its social significance, the rehearsal for adult roles (Isenberg and Jalongo, 1993, p. 32). *"*

Early childhood educators a half century ago affirmed the importance of play in classrooms for young children. John Dewey, Patty Smith Hill, and Susan Isaacs all supported play as opportunity for children to explore materials and develop concepts and problem-solving abilities, as well as enhancing social growth (Isenberg and Jalongo, 1993). Statements from the major organizations for early childhood professionals (Association for Childhood Education Interna-

Figure 13–2 These woodworkers are practicing skills of coordination, planning and project completion, cooperation and communication, among others. *Courtesy Avondale Children's Center.*

tional and National Association for the Education of Young Children) affirm that play is the medium through which children most appropriately develop in all aspects (Bredekamp, 1987; Isenberg and Quisenberry, 1988). Except for those parents and educators who feel that play is suspect because it doesn't seem to be "real work," play has wide recognition as the most appropriate medium for young children to develop knowledge and abilities.

What does play offer that makes it the most appropriate curriculum for young children? *Play provides for all areas of a child's development,* in a simultaneous and integrated way:

When Thomas and Will work together on a large structure in the block area, that they later call a space station, they are:

- cooperating and sharing ideas and conversation
- problem solving
- developing eye-hand coordination and fine motor skills
- working on an understanding of balance
- representing a concept symbolically
- extending attention span, task perseverance, concentration
- enjoying companionship and feelings of success; and more

Just consider other possible learnings, and which of the domains is being developed in such a play scenario. (See Figure 13-2.)

Play emphasizes learning as an active/interactive process: The interchange between Thomas and Will began with:

> Will: "But we can't live there, because people don't live in space."
>
> Thomas: "Well, but they live on space ships because I saw pictures. They were bouncing around."
>
> Will: (for whom this was obviously a new idea) "OK, but there's no bouncing on the space station, because then it would fall to the water. Here, this can be the water," as he runs over to get a piece of paper from the art shelf across the room.

Children who interact with other children are exposed to ideas they have to fit in with their own previous understandings. (See Figure 13-3.) Children who are free to move see the whole classroom as a learning environment.

Play presents highly motivated opportunities for learning, because children *choose* to participate in activities that are meaningful to them. "They choose whether or not to play, with whom, with what, where, how, and how long" (McKee, 1986, p. 186). They become open to the learning challenges because they have selected tasks they are interested in and are ready for.

> Thomas: "Oh no, that part fell off." The two boys stare at each other and at the structure.
>
> Will: "Here, I know. Put that big block on the corner. You hold it while I put the little one back on. See, that will do it."

A hundred lessons offered by a teacher on the concepts of size and balance could not have taught these two more than they taught themselves in their play.

Adults must be careful to distinguish between those kinds of adult-manipulated play that thinly disguise the adult's teaching/learning agenda and do not really allow children free choice of what and how they will play. For example,

Figure 13–3 Play allows for interactive learning. *Courtesy Avondale Children's Center.*

Figure 13–4 Practicing with pincers to sort colored pegs is an example of functional play. *Courtesy NationsBank Child Care Center.*

Montessori's fine materials may be used only in a particular way, in a particular progression of skills, as presented by the teacher. This does not provide for children's choice, creativity, or true play.

Play allows for differences in developmental ability, interest, and learning style. Within the choices prepared by the teacher, there are opportunities for children to play alone or together, to play with simple or more complex materials; to construct, create, match, manipulate, explore, and pretend; to succeed at whatever level they are. "It is reasonable to assume that where a single teaching method is used for a diverse group of children, a significant proportion of these children are likely to fail" (Katz, 1987, p. 3). No such failure occurs in play where children are able to find the activities best suited to them, their needs and interests.

In the center next to Thomas and Will, Julio is filling containers with red play dough. He pushes hard to see how much he can get in each container. Beside him Hilary and Anna chat about making pizza as they roll out and shape the play dough. Sam, at the end of the table, is making an "s" with his play dough, and excitedly points it out to Julio: "See Julio, that says 's' for me!"

Children who play can set their own tasks, and are likely to succeed at such self-assigned challenges.

Play is pleasurable. Children who are actively involved in activities they have chosen with materials they can use successfully show us the correctness of considering play as the appropriate curriculum for them. They are filled with energy, enthusiasm, and curiosity. They are excited by their discoveries and confident in their abilities. They do not have to be harangued or manipulated into staying with the task a little longer. Their self-esteem as learners and as people is nurtured.

Will and Thomas built for over 50 minutes. When the teacher announced it would soon be time to pick up toys, they asked if they could leave their building up to continue after outdoor time. The teacher agreed, noting it would have to be picked up before nap time, but she could take a Polaroid picture to show their parents at the end of the day.

Kinds of Play

As children move through the different stages or styles of social play described in Chapter 9, so too do they move through cognitive stages of play, according to theorists such as Piaget (1962) and Smilansky (1968). These stages begin at certain developmental stages, although they continue in some form throughout development. The stages follow.

Functional Play

Functional play is also called sensorimotor or practice play, and is most common in children in the first two years of life, though obvious in all later stages. Children repeat movements with objects, people, and language. (See Figure 13-4.)

Functional play is seen when:

- babies explore soft blocks by handling and mouthing them
- toddlers climb on every object they can possibly climb on
- four-year-olds finish a puzzle, and immediately dump out the pieces to begin again
- six-year-olds roller skate in every waking minute

Through such practice play, children achieve a sense of confidence in their physical skills. To repeat, this is the predominant form of play of infants and young toddlers.

Symbolic Play

Symbolic or representational play appears around age two, and continues in various forms into adulthood. Symbolic play includes dramatic play, in which we see children's mental ability to allow objects or words to stand for something else. Sociodramatic play is pretend play that involves other persons, allowing for interaction, planning, and verbal communication. Constructive play is evident when children plan and create objects. It is in this stage that children begin to represent their known experiences. Learning to master symbolic play is the major task of preschoolers; this is what clearly differentiates their play from toddler play.

> " To become a master player is the height of developmental achievement for children ages 3 to 5. Master players are skilled at representing their experiences symbolically in self-initiated improvisational drama. Sometimes alone, sometimes in collaboration with others, they play out their fantasies and the events of their daily lives. Through pretend play young children consolidate their understanding of the world, their language, and their social skills (Jones and Reynolds, 1992, p. 1). "

Symbolic play is seen when:

- a toddler holds a block to her ear and says "Hello"
- a three-year-old manipulates small figures in and out of a house, talking for each character
- several five-year-olds play shoe shop, with one child playing the role of store clerk, and two others coming to try on shoes
- a six-year-old works with clay to produce a model of his house

Games With Rules

Games with rules become part of the play of children school-aged and older. This play is dependent on children's understanding and agreement to use sets of pre-arranged rules. Logical thinking and social controls and skills are necessary for this stage of becoming "serious players." (Wasserman, 1990).

Ability to play games with rules is seen when:

- a group of seven-year-olds chooses teams for a game of kick-ball
- two six-year-olds play a game of checkers
- most of the ten-year-olds in the neighborhood participate on Little League teams

The preschoolers' inability to reason logically or move beyond egocentric thinking means that games with rules is a stage of play they are not yet ready for.

Piaget pointed out that there are basically three kinds of knowledge needed by young children. These are *physical, logical-mathematical,* and *social* knowledge. Physical knowledge is obtained from activities with objects that allow children to draw conclusions about the physical properties of objects. For example, through play children discover that cars roll quickly down an incline and that heavy objects sink in water. Logical-mathematical knowledge develops as children discover relationships among objects, people, and ideas. A child playing with blocks discovers that placing a longer one on the bottom provides a sturdier base than a shorter one. Play offers children the experiences necessary to construct these kinds of knowledge. Much of social knowledge is taught by other people directly, as children learn cultural and societal custom and expected behavior. Nevertheless, experiences with others in play allow children to apply the ideas they have learned from others in social situations. Play is the medium for developing these three kinds of knowledge, through the use of spontaneous oral language, and tools and materials for creative expression and investigation. Thus children can learn in the ways in which the competent preschool mind can succeed, rather than in the deficiency model of the academic preschool, that "demand premature practice of what one *doesn't* know how to do" (Jones and Reynolds, 1992, p. 5).

Teachers' Roles in Providing for Play

While a criterion for play is that it is spontaneous and freely chosen, this does not imply that there are not specific roles for teachers in supporting play. The underlying structure provides the optimum play learning environment for particular children at a particular time. Many of the teacher roles are played behind the scenes, setting a stage for the beginning point of play, and resetting it as the play unfolds and develops. Some of the roles involve more direct interaction, though even then the traditional image of the teacher as *teller* and *giver of information* (Bredekamp, 1987, p. 53) is replaced by the teacher as facilitator and guide. The roles we will consider include: creator of the environment; observer-and-recorder; planner; model; and responder.

Creator of the Environment

In Chapter 5 we considered the decisions teachers make in physical arrangements of the classroom space. Here we will consider briefly the rationale for using learning centers as the primary focus of play, and the creation of a positive atmosphere for play.

A developmentally appropriate classroom for preschoolers recognizes that much of their day needs to be spent in uninterrupted periods of play. Thus the environment is arranged into separate areas where children can choose their materials, activities, and playmates. The learning center approach supports active play because it provides for:

- **Choices:** There are enough separate play spaces in the room that each child has a choice of several play options.

- **Free movement:** The need to be active is provided for by the variety of options and styles of play provided. Children decide when they will move on to another activity.

- **Range of developmental differences:** With the variety of materials provided in each center, children with different interest and attention spans can be accommodated within a learning center arrangement.

- **Facilitating of play:** Because children take the dominant role in play in learning centers, teachers are free from primary instructional duties with a large group. They are then able to move about among children at play,

Figure 13–5 This dramatic play center has enough space to promote cooperative interaction. *Courtesy NationsBank Child Care Center.*

taking opportunities for effectively reinforcing the learning they observe, or extending and stimulating discoveries on an individual basis.

These points so far show little difference from the reasons for creating active areas for exploration in toddler classrooms. But as preschoolers are now ready for true symbolic and sociodramatic play, their interest centers make possible additional and more complex learnings:

- **Cooperative learning:** Most of the learning centers provide space for several preschoolers to play together at the same time, fostering language, interaction, and social skills. (See Figure 13-5.)

- **Initiative:** Children are the active agents in a learning center arrangement. They are encouraged to plan and initiate their own activities, not merely be passive followers of adult instructions.

The core centers (those always available for play) in a classroom for preschoolers most likely include: creative arts/construction; blocks; dramatic play; gross motor; math/manipulatives; science; language arts (reading and writing); and music. Depending on space and available adults, other centers may be occasionally available: woodworking; cooking; and sand, water, or other sensory exploration.

> Basic learning materials and activities for an appropriate curriculum include sand, water, clay, and accessories to use with them; hollow, table, and unit blocks; puzzles with varying numbers of pieces; many types of games; a variety of small manipulative toys; dramatic play props such as those for housekeeping and transportation; a variety of scientific investigation equipment and items to explore; a changing selection of appropriate and aesthetically pleasing books and recordings; water-based paint and markers, and other materials for creative expression; large muscle equipment.... (Bredekamp, 1987, p. 4).

With all of these materials, the goal is to have children represent and elaborate on their understandings of their experiences of the world.

The decisions teachers make about physical placement of centers, about the kinds, amounts, and developmental span of materials provided, and about a schedule that offers blocks of time for play are all important factors in creating a rich environment that helps children get started and keep focused on play.

An important role of the teacher in regard to the environment is to bring order to the surroundings, to make the play possibilities clear to children. As children play they mess up the teacher's order, transforming it to their own conceptions. The teacher accepts this "messing up" as a right and inevitable part of play, then re-creates the predictable order so children can again see play choices (Jones and Reynolds, 1992).

Perhaps the key ingredient of an environment that supports play is adult attitude. When adults convey their respect for the importance for play, they encour-

Figure 13–6 Play is supported by the presence of an interested, supportive adult. *Courtesy NationsBank Child Care Center.*

age children's meaningful involvement; children are extremely susceptible to adult opinion and attitude.

 [An] answer ... about what produced prolonged concentration and rich elaboration in play rather took us aback. It was the presence of an adult. I do not mean an adult "over the shoulder" of the child, trying to direct his activity, but one in the neighborhood who gave some assurance that the environment would be stable and continuous, but would also give the child reassurance and information as, if, and when the child needed it (Bruner, 1991, p. 80). **"**

Adult respect for play is shown by:

- showing obvious pleasure and interest in observing children at play (See Figure 13-6.)

- displaying relaxed playfulness in their interaction with children

- accepting children's invitations to play occasionally, and following their lead

- protecting play from interruption, including interruption by the teacher and schedule

- enriching their play with provision of appropriate materials

- encouraging children to talk about their play

- showcasing and interpreting their play to parents and others

Things Caregivers Should Not Do

It is quite obvious to children that adults do not value their play when they:

- supervise play indifferently, only coming close when intervention is necessary

- provide only limited time for play, and interrupt casually when there's something adults want to do or teach ("Put those blocks away now, it's time for our lesson")

- offer a cluttered, unattractive environment, with toys and materials that are in disrepair or unchanged over time

- speak of play in ways that belittle its importance and try to impress parents with the "real" learning offered instead ("We don't spend much time 'just' playing; we have set lesson plans and follow XYZ curriculum.")

Observer-and-Recorder

For teachers to understand how best to support children's play, they must become astute observers of children. Teachers have likely learned the general developmental characteristics of the age group with which they work. But the individual development of each child within the group, the particular needs, interests, learning style and preferences, can only be learned by teachers' careful observation.

" When a child is in your care, you must function as if you know who she or he is at any given moment. The danger is that you can delude yourself into thinking that in fact you do have that knowledge. You can reduce this danger by regularly observing and recording behavior, whether or not it fits your preconceptions (Clemens, 1983, p. 100).

Figure 13–7 Teachers develop strategies to permit ongoing observation and recording. *Courtesy NationsBank Child Care Center.*

Observing children at play allows teachers to practice taking the child's perspective, to ask themselves key questions. What is happening for the child in the play, what is the child's agenda? Does the child have the skills and materials needed to accomplish the intent? (Jones and Reynolds, 1992).

Observing is the only way to make appropriate decisions for curriculum and materials, based on what is noted about each child's special interests and developmental progress. Therefore, observing is a cyclical activity; teachers observe children's play initially to make assessments of individual needs, strengths, and interests. They then provide materials and activities they feel will challenge and support children's play. The observations on subsequent play help teachers continue to plan next steps for curriculum, and so on.

Observing is possible because of the learning center approach to classroom learning. Teachers are free to be able to take specific times to observe and record information because children are initiating their own learning. Teachers who realize the crucial importance of observing for planning individually appropriate experiences make observation a priority, not just something they "never have time for."

Teachers need to develop skills for observing and recording information in usable forms. They work on:

- strategies to support observing, such as designating times, keeping pencil and paper handy, using checklists to be sure no child or aspect of development is being overlooked. (See Figure 13-7.)

- setting particular goals and defining tasks for observation, such as making notes on three children each playtime, or observing for different ways the children explore the water and bubbles activity. They know that this will help keep them focused on observing.

- recording objective, nonjudgmental facts, concentrating on describing what happened and what was said and communicated nonverbally, without using words that express subjective opinion.

- including relevant information, such as date, time, and place of observation, and other children involved. This allows teachers to organize the records in notebooks or file boxes, to provide information over the year as children change and develop. (See Chapter 14 for discussion of developing portfolios.) Observing without meaningful recording loses value.

- using their observations to make tentative assessments and formulate goals for individual children. Teachers will read back through previous observations to search for growth and patterns, and to ensure that the whole child is being paid attention to.

Carefully recorded observations are valuable for reasons beyond planning appropriate curriculum, and assessing children's play. As teachers focus on observing the whole child, not just those aspects that are most disturbing, they see strengths and learn to appreciate children more. The question moves beyond the management question of "What can I do about him?" to more child-centered questions of "What interests him? What issues is he dealing with? What does he know? What might he learn next?" (Jones and Reynolds, 1992, p. 74). Observed patterns of behavior may help identify children with special needs who need more specialized assessments and assistance. Observations are also valuable in sharing information with parents and other staff members during conference conversations. Observations should form the basis of decisions that parents and

> ### From-To Progressions in Seventeen Related Areas of Early Learning
> - From sensing to sorting to symbolizing
> - From spontaneous to controlled, coordinated, self-directed and imitative movement
> - From babbling to language
> - From decoding graphic symbols to reading
> - From scribbling to writing
> - From experiencing to processing information
> - From magic to natural phenomena
> - From birds and berries to organisms and ecosystems
> - From lines, daubs, and smears to pictures
> - From making things to using simple tools and developing handicraft skills
> - From bouncing to dancing
> - From lalling to singing
> - From hearing music to listening to it
> - From awareness of others to getting along with them
> - From being taken care of to taking care of himself
> - From home and center to community
> - From "me" to "who am I?"

Figure 13-8 Seventeen sequences of preschool learning. *Adapted from* Preschool Teaching and Learning, *Catherine Landreth, 1972.*

teachers share about appropriate next steps for the children. Ongoing observation is a much more accurate method of assessing children's developmental levels than any test. (See the discussions on assessment and testing in Chapter 14.) Observation of children's progress and achievement helps to evaluate the program's effectiveness.

Planner   Spontaneous play and teacher planning do go together, although the concepts may sound contradictory. Developmentally appropriate curriculum is matched to what teachers know through observation about the particular children in a classroom. It is planned to start with where children are and take them in the direction of particular goals. It is not, however, based on narrowly defined objectives of "what children will learn," but rather on broad goals for preschool children. These include providing opportunities: to develop and practice various physical skills, both gross and fine motor; to hear and use oral and written language; to explore various media for creativity and discovery; and to practice the kind of interpersonal and social skills discussed in Chapter 9. All of these goals are met through play.

How do we make the curriculum of play more specific in its answers to the question, What can and should young children learn? Catherine Landreth, in her classic book about preschool learning and teaching, outlines seventeen different sequences of learning in from-to progressions, along with materials and activities of interest for each area of learning, and learning checklists for each area (Landreth, 1972). (See Figure 13-8.)

The list makes it obvious that teachers are helping children move from simple to more complex levels of understanding and acting, from general ways of acting on the world to more specific ones. Such broad objectives help teachers plan appropriate classroom experiences for preschoolers.

But it is the specific decisions teachers make about individual goals for individual children that helps them decide what materials and activities they will make available for children to use at any time. As we have said, teacher observation and parent input work together to help formulate individual goals. Example:

> The teacher of the four-year-olds has planned a variety of experiences involving water this week. She knows that Constance is particularly interested in exploring filling and measuring, so she has added a variety of measuring cups to the water table. Holly finds it difficult to work close to others, so the teacher encourages her to work cooperatively with just one other child on washing the tables. Terry is intrigued with bubbles, so the teacher makes soap available for a number of the activities. Individualized curricula comes from such teacher observations.

The ideas for particular curriculum interests comes from the children and the adults who know them and their interests, and have interests of their own they want to share with the children (Cassady, 1993). The adults who know them include the family, school, and community and its particular culture.

> Jerry's Dad had just come back from a fishing trip, and brought pictures of fish and some of his equipment to show to and talk with the children. The teacher expanded their unit on water to include learning about fish and other animals living in water.

Such a curriculum is called *emergent,* because it diverges along new paths as choices and connections are made, and is always open to new possibilities that were not thought of during the initial planning process (Jones and Reynolds, 1992).

One way to conceptualize this planning model is by using a *web*. With the creation of a planning web, teachers may add on the ideas that develop, and help visualize the connections that children may make between related concepts. Sometimes the webbing process represents the initial brainstorming on a theme that teachers may do in exploring possible choices for materials to introduce to children; sometimes it represents the activities and learning that arises spontaneously from the introduction of an interesting item. See Figure 13-9a and b to look at the evolution of a web. In either case, the web allows for the inclusion of later ideas and related interests to be added on. Such an open-ended approach to a theme functions as possible directions to follow, not a one-directional, linear approach. The traditional lesson-plan form, with slots for plans for each interest center (art, blocks, manipulatives, etc.) to be filled in from Monday to Friday, does not allow for spontaneous following of children's interests and ideas.

Theme planning at its best offers an array of activities built around a central idea. When children find a common thread around much of their play, they are able to make linkages between the individual bits of information to build concepts. An advantage of theme planning is that there is a variety of means of exploring a concept via different methods and media; if a particular activity does not interest or fit the specific learning style of a child, there are other methods of exploring the same idea. Themes also allow children to immerse themselves in a

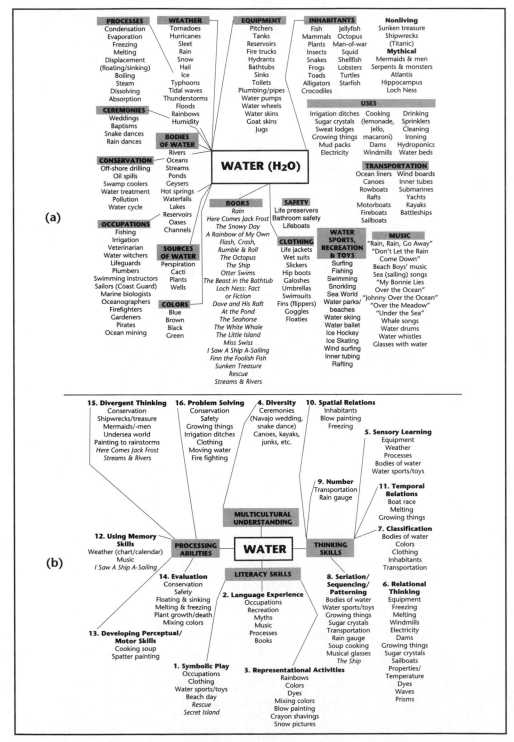

Figures 13-9a and b Evolutions of planning webs. *From "Curriculum Webs: Weaving Connections from Children to Teachers," by Susan Workman and Michael C. Anziano, January 1993,* Young Children, *48 (2), pp. 5 and 7. Copyright National Association for the Education of Young Children. Reprinted with permission.*

topic that is of deep interest to them. Play centered around a particular theme may last weeks, or even months, depending on sustained attention. (See examples of such sustained theme work in Chapter 17.)

Teachers also benefit from theme planning. Planning is easier when there is at least some initial focus for thinking. Teachers find that the brainstorming process, alone or jointly with co-workers, is invigorating, allowing them to continue personal and professional growth, and maintain their enthusiasm in the classroom. No teacher who plans with a theme/webbing emergent approach will be able to tell you before meeting a new class in September what he will be teaching the second week in November! Unfortunately, there are too many teachers using preplanned or prepared curricula who would be able to. This is *not* developmentally appropriate practice.

Themes come from teachers' ideas and from children's initiative and interest, from events and experiences, from cultural and community happenings. They are directly tied to children's real-life experiences, and are ideas that can be translated into hands-on action. (Themes evolving into the complex and sustained project approach will be discussed in Chapter 14.)

Many curriculum planning books are organized into study units built around theme topics. While some interesting ideas may be generated through these suggestions, it is more likely that merely copying the ideas from the books will force learning experiences into linear experiences without much passion. Using some suggestions for materials and activities as a starting place, and then carefully observing children's responses, questions, and play, results in subsequent planning that matches these particular children's interests and needs. Curriculum books may be most useful for ideas about interesting materials, after teachers have recognized the direction in which the children's interest is leading.

The most important caution for teachers involved in planning for preschoolers is not to become so caught up in their own plans and ideas; they must be able to let go of their ideas in favor of the children's responses. Good planning should allow for well-prepared starting points for children's play. Good teaching means modifying or even discarding plans as teachers continue to observe children's play. Good planning requires teachers to stand back and ask what they have found out as they have watched children's playful interactions with materials and activities. This thoughtful consideration inevitably leads to the next plans. "Through this process the curriculum keeps emerging and the teacher, together with the children, keeps learning" (Jones and Reynolds, 1992, p. 105).

Model   The teacher as model takes the role of a player. While children's play is self-initiated, there are times when teachers enter into the play. Their purpose in moving into the play is to support the play with the subtle introduction of ideas and information. This information is not given by telling, but by showing, modeling, and conversing. Teachers are most likely to play the role of model with younger preschoolers, or those less experienced in play. When children are short on ideas for play, teachers may enrich their thinking. Example:

Teacher: (entering the housekeeping area) Good morning, I was passing by and wondered if you were home so I could visit?

(Katie and Rachel have been silently manipulating dishes up to this point.)

Katie: Yes, you can. Sit there.

BUT WHAT ABOUT?

My director insists that the children in my classroom have some artwork to take home each day, and that it be related to the theme that we've been studying. A lot of the children frequently aren't interested in doing the art, and I usually end up having to virtually force them, doing most of it myself.

This may be one of the commonest issues facing teachers in preschool classrooms. The director and parents are most likely feeling that they want measurable proof that something has been accomplished each day, implying that "just play" isn't productive enough. Frequently, art that is specifically related to a theme is more of a crafted product made to match teacher specifications or models than it is a creative experience in which children select materials and create whatever they want. This lack of opportunity to initiate is one of just several reasons that this practice needs to be considered as developmentally inappropriate for preschoolers. The frustration involved in working to someone else's standards, the infringement on spontaneous choice, and the intrusion of teacher plans taking precedent over children's tasks are also negatives. The school's message to parents, who can usually figure out that these products are made with teacher instruction, is that teacher-dominated learning is the most valuable experience they can offer children.

This is such a large issue it deserves some thorough discussion among staff. The real crux of the matter seems to be how to make apparent to parents that children are truly learning through play that is respected. As staff direct their creative energies to helping parents be able to understand and appreciate the value of play, they can leave children free to create their own work. Newsletters, accounts of daily activities, pictures, anecdotes, parent visits and observation, workshops and reading for parents— there are many ways to get across to parents that real learning is happening, without mass producing unwillingly made art products.

There are some good ideas on this subject in an article by David Kuschner: "Put your Name on Your Painting, But ... The Blocks go Back on the Shelves." In *Young Children*, Vol. 45, No. 1, (November, 1989), pp. 49–56.

Teacher:	Thank you. Is it almost lunch time?
Rachel:	(bringing over a dish and handing it to teacher): Yes here's your lunch.
Teacher:	Oh, it looks great, what have you cooked for me? (pretending to eat)
Katie:	It's pizza.
Rachel:	With mushrooms.
Teacher:	Mmm. Are you going to eat too?

(Both girls sit down.)

(after a minute or two)

Teacher: Would your little girl like some pizza too? (pointing to the baby doll)

As the lunch scene unfolds, the teacher takes his leave, promising to come again. When he leaves, the children are busy feeding a couple of babies and chatting together. Teachers may not only model role behavior *for* children, they may model *with* young players.

The same teacher later notices Pia observing the play in the housekeeping area. He approaches and asks if she'll accompany him as he delivers a package to the household.

Teacher: Let's knock on the door and tell them the delivery man has a package for them.

Pia: OK. (He hands her the package.)

Teacher: Here we are. Knock loud and tell them their package is here.

Pia: (knocks and says) Your package is here.

(The children take the package from her.)

Pia: I've got another one. I'll go get it.

By involving themselves, teachers can help children understand the roles and possible strategies for play. They can also help sustain play by responding to the children's ideas. Example:

Katie: Hey, Tom, come and see us all dressed up.

Teacher: Wow, you look as if you're going someplace special.

Rachel: We are, we're going to New York.

Teacher: Hm, that's a long way. Who's going to look after your house while you're gone?

Katie: (looking around) Hey Pia, want to look after our house? We're going to New York.

Rachel: Yeah, and when we come back we'll bring you presents.

Pia: (happily) OK, I'll clean it up while you're gone.

The adult as model also enters the play to model problem solving as a way to sustain play: Rachel and Katie begin to argue over who will drive the train to New York.

Teacher: (pulling a chair over to their area) I hope this train for New York is going to leave soon. Nobody's even taken my ticket yet. And I've got a round-trip ticket, because I'm coming back later. What this train needs is a ticket-taker.

(Rachel and Katie look at each other.)

Katie: You can be the ticket-taker.

Rachel: OK, and then you can be when we come back.

This role of teacher as model is quite different from an intrusive adult who tells children what to do. This is not an adult who takes over and directs the play, or becomes so involved that children become an audience to the adult's sophisticated performance. This adult only introduces ideas or questions that children can develop from their own experience.

The teacher as model also enters play as an interested and supportive adult, not one following his own agenda. The model role is played briefly, as teachers move in and out of the play.

Responder

As teachers move about and observe children at their play, they see opportunities to reinforce and enrich children's learning experiences. In the role of responder, they individualize their response to their perception of what would help children build on their learning. Sometimes a response is an appreciative comment that puts in words what children have been doing and discovering.

> "The colors you used in your painting are very bright. It makes me feel like I'm wide-awake!"

> "Hmm. I see some very smooth clay. Looks like you pressed very firmly when you rolled it out."

Sometimes a response is a question that helps a child focus on his actions, or challenges to further exploration. Learning to ask good questions that really cause children to focus and reconsider is an important skill. Good questions are generally open-ended and divergent, questions that adults are genuinely interested in, and do not already know the answers to. Good questions cause children to question too, not just focus on giving the teacher the correct answer. (See Figure 13-10.)

> "Well, how *did* you make those pieces stick on top of each other?"

> "Hm. I wonder what would happen if you added more water to that mixture?"

Figure 13–10 Teachers who ask genuinely curious questions may challenge children to further exploration. *Courtesy CPCC Child Care Training Center.*

Sometimes a response is support as a child struggles with a difficult challenge:

> "That is a hard puzzle. I think you can do it. Take another look at the picture you're making. He's got one foot—where's the other?"

Sometimes a response is a suggestion or addition of more materials that could extend the play:

> "I wonder if you might like to find a friend who could help you work on balancing the scales."

> "Would this be helpful for your grocery store?" said while offering a new prop.

Figure 13–11 Adult presence supports explorations and stimulates deeper learning. *Courtesy CPCC Child Care Training Center.*

Sometimes a response is simply being available with focused interest to help children sustain their own activity and interest because of their perception that the adult values their involvement. (See Figure 13-11.) Example:

> The teacher sits near a group of children constructing in the block area. From time to time she comments on the activity. Mostly she watches and listens attentively. Her body language indicates attentive appreciation.

All such strategies may come under the heading of *scaffolding*, a term used to mean supporting children to move to more sophisticated behavior than they would be capable of without adult additions. Notice that all the possibilities of responding are focused on what children are presently doing. This is true responsiveness, not adults assuming the dominant role. Responses are open-ended and

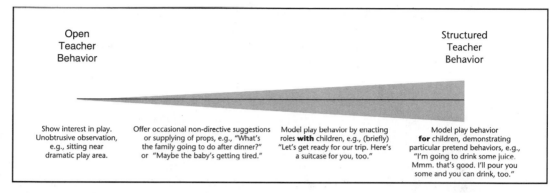

Figure 13-12 Continuum of adult environment in play. *Adapted from Wolfgang, 1977.*

tentative in nature, so that children may quite easily decide to disregard them in favor of their own initiative.

Wolfgang (1977) formulated a Teacher Behavior Continuum, that moves from the most teacher interaction behaviors to the least, depending on children's abilities to sustain their productive play. (See Figure 13-12.) As teachers perceive that children need their assistance and responses less and less, they are less actively involved in the play.

Things Caregivers Should Not Do

Developmentally inappropriate teaching roles include:

- heavy reliance on teaching as telling, on questioning children to see if they remember what they have been taught

- direct correction of children's errors or misunderstandings

- control of decisions about planning and learning

- static lesson plans or prepackaged curricula

- substituting secondhand learning experiences, such as pictures, videos, lectures, for firsthand experiences

Summary of Developmentally Appropriate Preschool Cognitive Environments

Play is the absolute stuff from which cognitive development in preschool children occurs, allowing them to actively create and represent their developing understandings of the world. This is a much more complex form of play than was possible for toddlers. Preschoolers who play in carefully planned learning centers using a variety of open-ended materials that have been selected to match their learning abilities and interests are able to construct their understanding of the world around them. In such an environment, adults: carefully observe; plan possibilities for active involvement of children with materials, playmates, and adults; prepare the environment; model play; and respond in ways designed to deepen and extend the learning experience. The appropriate emphasis is on children as active learners, with adults available as supportive resources. Skillful teachers make complex and rich play possible, and help children keep getting better at becoming adept players.

Language Environments

Figure 13–13 Whole language experiences include developmentally appropriate active, self-initiated writing activities. *Courtesy CPCC Child Care Training Center.*

Learning to understand the world and other people, and to represent that learning, involves language. Language is an inseparable part of the play and learning of the preschool classroom. By the age of three, children have accomplished amazing feats in language. They probably have a spoken (expressive) vocabulary of 900 to 1,000 words, and an understood (receptive) vocabulary of several hundred more. They are speaking in sentences that follow the grammar rules of their language, and they have mastered complexities, such as plurals and past tenses, with occasional tendencies to overgeneralize their understandings of grammar rules into such typical constructions as "feets" and "wented." They have generally learned to control the rhythm and fluency of their speech, with occasional nonfluency. They can generally pronounce enough words clearly enough that a stranger can understand about 75 percent of their utterances, and are good at understanding much of what is said to them. Considering it was only roughly two years earlier that they first produced sounds that had meaning to them, this is a remarkable accomplishment. And how did they achieve so much in such a short time? Without specific lessons or drills in language tutoring, but with opportunities to speak and hear others speak; with no pressure, but lots of time to experiment and experience.

" There's an old joke among teachers that holds that it's a blessing that educators and politicians haven't yet added speaking to reading, writing, and arithmetic as the "basics" of a standard education. If that should happen, the joke maintains, some social scientist somewhere would develop a curriculum, a lesson plan, and a basic text. Then the spoken word would be reduced to its component parts and given to babies and toddlers a step at a time. They would be expected to master the consonants first, then regular vowels. A long list of one-syllable words would be taught before two-syllable words could be attempted. Songs like "Sing a Song of Sixpence" and "This train is Bound for Glory" would be discouraged as potentially confusing and certainly inappropriate. And, of course, the result of all this expense and effort would be a generation that couldn't talk (Ayers, 1989, p. 108). "

Today, speaking and listening are seen as two of the skills related to language and literacy development, along with reading and writing. In past decades these skills were thought of as developing in sequence. Now, thanks to theorists, researchers, and practitioners who speak in terms of *whole language,* the belief is that there is a continual process of learning the various aspects of oral and written language, at the same time, and from birth.

While it is still jarring for some early childhood educators to consider reading and writing centers and activities as part of the appropriate preschool environment, the philosophy of whole language does not employ the skill worksheet and direct instruction approach; it removed from the developmentally appropriate active-learning style. (See Figure 13-13.)

In this section we will consider what whole language is, and practices in the preschool environment that facilitate development of all language and literacy skills.

Whole Language

Whole language is a philosophy rather than a prescribed set of activities. The set of beliefs is based on theory, research, and practice (Bird, 1987; Goodman, 1986, 1989; Pearson, 1990; Wells, 1986). The basic idea is that children are motivated to find ways of representing their experience; they try to represent it through play and action, and through communication. Children discover that communication meets their needs, brings pleasure and friendship, and helps them learn to understand their culture. As they are exposed to the literacy of adults at home and in the classroom, they discover that oral and written language are related, that print is another form of communication. Reading and writing are then viewed as part of a larger system for accomplishing their goals. In the same ways that children play to construct their own concepts about the world, so their active engagement with print helps them construct an understanding of how written language works. This awareness and motivation, along with adults providing meaningful literacy materials, activities, and support combine to develop what is called *emerging literacy* (Sawyer and Sawyer, 1993; Strickland and Morrow, 1989). There is no beginning point where children are asked to study language arts; instead they use language continually, experience how print language functions, and gradually move themselves into print media experiences. There is a continuity between all language experiences, from birth through the primary years, not a discontinuity of "now it's time to learn to read."

The whole language approach emphasizes the whole, not the individual parts. Some of the traditional ways that preschool and elementary children have been introduced to reading and writing are conspicuously absent. There is no clear-cut division between reading and writing lessons, between learning the isolated skills, such as letter-sound drills, or printing a row of "h," that might later lead to understanding the "whole" of how to read or write. There are no worksheets, no alphabet letter of the week, no practice of name writing, no rote counting to 100. Teachers use whole texts of children's literature as a method of introducing children to meaningful print, and then continue to use print as it functions in many ways in daily life. Reading and writing are important parts of daily activity, but no more important than the other play materials and experiences that bring children into dialogue and interaction with others. Oral language proficiency is seen as related to growth in interest in reading and writing, but is not a prerequisite; written and oral communication continue to develop in an interrelated manner. (See Figure 13-14.) Parents and teachers have a key role in encouraging spoken communication and in fostering pleasurable adult-child interaction related to print; they model literacy and its functions. It has long been recognized that children who come from homes where communication and literacy is valued and demonstrated move more easily into schooled reading and writing. The whole language philosophy brings some of these practices of literate families into the school, recognizing the developmental appropriateness of encouraging children's active participation in literacy activities. Schickedanz et al. (1990) make the distinction between academic content and academic methods, and suggest that the classroom bring the methods found to be effective in

Figure 13–14 Oral and print communication proceed together; these preschoolers are enjoying "reading" out loud to each other. *Courtesy CPCC Child Care Training Center.*

promoting literacy in the home into the preschool classroom. This is generally what the whole language approach does.

Components of an Appropriate Preschool Language Environment

The following components are part of any developmentally appropriate whole language environment for preschool children.

Conversations

Figure 13–15 Teachers use opportunities for conversation. *Courtesy NationsBank Child Care Center.*

Adults recognize the importance of direct conversation for giving children experience with oral communication and thought. The learning center approach to instruction encourages conversations among children at play. Teachers are also free to have individual conversations with children. In their conversations they ask questions that encourage children to think and to use additional language, and pick up on topics of interest to children. Adults foster communication by their attentive listening. They use every opportunity—meal times, transitions, play times—for personal conversation. They have materials in the classroom that encourage conversation; there is always something new and of interest to discuss, as well as telephones and tape recorders. They are particularly aware of giving opportunities to talk to quiet children who may need more encouragement to communicate. They recognize that children who speak and understand oral language well have some basic knowledge that will lead naturally to print media. (See Figure 13-15.) Silence is not valued in appropriate preschool settings; "when teachers instruct, children cannot speak" (Dumtschin, 1988, p. 20).

Acceptance

Teachers recognize that overt correction or judgment of attempts at oral or written communication may discourage children from making further attempts. "Controlling, directive language usually hinders…. A critical difference in mothers' speech to language-delayed children appears to be their approval or disapproval of their children's language" (Dumtschin, 1988, p. 19). They will not allow children's efforts to be mocked or belittled. They accept the added challenge that children have who come to school with a primary language or dialect that is not standard English usage. Recognizing that the child's language is part of who he or she is, they try to have them hear words they are familiar with. They use questions and interest to try to understand and clarify what children are attempting to communicate. They accept young children's "invented spelling" and explain to troubled parents its place in emergent language. They have faith in children's desire to acquire the skills and abilities used by important adults, so assume children will eventually correct themselves when exposed to good models.

Experiences

Teachers recognize that firsthand experiences provide the fuel for children's continued representation through play and communication. They arrange visits in the classroom and beyond in the community that will extend children's horizons and vocabulary, and then offer materials and time for children to re-create their experience.

Children who have had an opportunity to visit a skyscraper under construction come back to the classroom with words like architect, blueprints, beams, derrick, foreman. With paper and art materials, with clay, with blocks, with dramatic play props, with books, with tape recorder, and with writing materials, they will be able to communicate orally or with constructive, dramatic, or creative play about their experience. They may record the news of the event, with their own pictures or print, or watch as the teacher writes about it for the parent bulletin board.

Children's Literature

Figure 13–16 Watching the teacher at group time has helped this child learn how to read to her friend. *Courtesy CPCC Child Care Training Center.*

Reading good children's books, to individuals and to groups in the preschool classroom, plays a major part in the instructional part of the day. Teachers recognize that children must learn *why* people read; pleasurable experiences with books offer real evidence. They share books of all kinds: story books, including traditional stories; concept books; wordless books; books that invite participation; books carefully selected to mirror children's experiences; and books that convey acceptance of diversity in race, culture, socioeconomic circumstances, age, sex, and ability. Sometimes they read from big books that allow the children to see the print as the teacher reads and occasionally points out words. Children also have to learn *how* to read, and by watching the teacher they discover: that it is the print and not the pictures that is read; how to follow the print placed on the page; and how pages turn. (See Figure 13-16.) They read favorites again and again, and make the books that have been read to the group available for personal reading in the library area. (See Figure 13-17 for a list of preschool favorites.)

Favorite Books for Preschoolers

Look for these and others by the same author. The reference book *A to Zoo: Subject Access to Children's Picture Books* by Carolyn Lima will be helpful in finding more ideas, as will a listing for Caldecott award books.

Aardema, Verna. *Why Mosquitoes Buzz in People's Ears: A West African Folktale*
Allen, Pamela. *Who Sank the Boat?*
Arnosky, Jim. *Watching Foxes*
Asch, Frank. *Bear Shadow*
Brown, Marcia. *The Bun*
Brown, Margaret Wise. *Little Fur Family*
Burningham, John. *Mr. Gumpy's Motor Car*
Carle, Eric. *The Very Hungry Caterpillar*
Crews, Donald. *Shortcut*
Cummings, Pat. *Clean Your Room, Harvey Moon!*
Dabcovich, Lydia. *Sleepy Bear*
Ets, Marie Hall. *Gilberto and the Wind*
Flack, Marjorie. *Angus and the Ducks*
Freeman, Don. *Beady Bear*
Galdone, Paul. *Three Blind Mice*
Hadithi, Mwenye. *Hot Hippo*
Hoban, Tana. *A Children's Zoo*

Hoban, Russell. *Bread and Jam for Frances*
Howard, Elizabeth. *Aunt Flossie's Hats (and Crab Cakes Later)*
Hutchins, Pat. *Good-Night Owl!*
Keats, Ezra Jack. *The Snowy Day*
Keller, Holly. *Ten Sleepy Sheep*
Locker, Thomas. *Where the River Begins*
Long, Earlene. *Gone Fishing*
McCloskey, Robert. *Make Way for Ducklings*
McPhail, David. *Farm Morning*
Mack, Stanley. *Ten Bears in My Bed*
Martin, Bill. *Brown Bear, Brown Bear*
Mayer, Mercer. *Just Me and My Dad*
Polushkin, Maria. *Mother, Mother, I Want Another*
Rice, Eve. *Sam Who Never Forgets*
Rockwell, Ann. *First Comes Spring*
Sendak, Maurice. *Where the Wild Things Are*
Shaw, Charles Green. *It Looked Like Spilt Milk*
Steptoe, John. *Baby Says*
Tafuri, Nancy. *Have You Seen My Duckling?*
Westcott, Nadine. *Peanut Butter and Jelly*
Yolen, Jane. *Owl Moon*
Zion, Gene. *No Roses for Harry*

Figure 13-17 Favorite books for preschoolers.

Book Extenders

Teachers know that as preschoolers are engaged in literature experiences, they continue to see the relevance of print to their lives. Teachers provide materials and activities that allow children to continue processing the books they have heard read. The book area may include: flannelboard characters to act out stories; puppets; and taped stories to listen to while looking at the book. They may add props in dramatic play to play out stories that were read. They may add specific materials to the art area that might suggest making a visual representation of the story. Food experiences or cooking might follow particular books. See Raines and Canady (1989) for ideas about extending book experiences.

Print-Rich Environment

Figure 13–18 Teachers print lists, experiences, and conversations on wall charts. *Courtesy NationsBank Child Care Center.*

Figure 13–19 A print-rich environment may use labels on familiar objects. *Courtesy Avondale Children's Center.*

To learn the meaning and structures of written language, young children need to see print around them, used daily in meaningful ways. This is different from the decorative frieze of alphabet letters high on the walls of many classrooms that is usually just visual clutter. Teachers print, and let children know what they're printing. (See Figure 13-18.) They post print around the room in various ways. Children's names are printed on their cubbies, on their places at table, nap, and group, on the helpers' and attendance charts, on their art and stories, where children are also encouraged to write their own names. There are labels on the learning centers, and on the boxes of materials and the shelves. (See Figure 13-19.) There are printed charts that give children recipes, directions, rules, schedules, and keep track of progress in projects. Teachers and children discuss topics of interest and write their conversations down: lists of favorite songs and books; records of experiences, news, and events. There are sign-up sheets where children can sign up for turns at activities. There are signs that say: "This area is closed today" or "Trike area." There are shopping lists, lesson plans, and reminders. Children see parents and teachers communicate by notes, notices, notebooks, newsletters, and bulletin boards. Teachers help make the print explicit to children: "This says it will be Antonio's turn next." "This says we need to put in one cup of water." "This note from your mom says your Grandma will pick you up today. That word there—it says Grandma."

Part of the print-rich environment will be the inclusion of books as part of every learning center, not placed only in the library area. There may be books of famous artworks in the creative art center; counting books in the math center; informational picture and reference books in science; cookbooks, magazines, and telephone books in the home-living area (and relevant books for other dramatic play options); alphabet books in the writing center; books about builders and buildings in blocks (Beaty, 1992).

The print-rich environment reinforces for children the concept that functional, meaningful activities involve reading and writing.

Writing Center

A writing center should be one of the learning center choices in a preschool classroom. Teachers recognize that children learn to write by writing, just as they learn to talk by talking. This center would include materials that lend themselves to exploration of writing. Materials may include chalk and chalkboards, lined and unlined paper, stationery and envelopes, markers, crayons, pencils, pens, scissors, pads and notebooks of various kinds, index cards, typewriters, hole punchers, and staplers. An alphabet chart and other posters may give children something to model from; magnetic letters may be used for tracing.

As with books, writing materials may be added to centers other than the writing center. Materials to create signs and labels are appropriate in blocks; appointment pads for the doctor's office or hair salon; and lists and notebooks for the grocery store or office. Teachers discover that children find their own creative use for writing materials when they are available.

Many teachers who entered early childhood education in past decades, when having children form or use letters was disapproved of, definitely have to stop and consider the appropriateness of this addition when they see a writing center recommended for preschoolers. But when examined in the context of play to construct hypotheses and concepts as discussed earlier in this chapter, learning to write by writing makes sense. As children identify the areas where they want help and instruction, teachers can help them move on.

Group Time
The natural vehicle for communication in the preschool classroom is group time. Not only is group time an essential opportunity to learn skills and joys of group membership, it is also the occasion for teachers to introduce concepts and information. Bruner found that one such large group experience each day greatly enriched the individual play of children later that day (Bruner, 1991). Communication, both oral and written, lies at the heart of group time.

Oral participation and understanding is fostered by songs and chants; children's attention is gained more pleasantly through singing: "Where is Julio?" than by an impatient demand for his presence. Finger plays, action songs, and poetry are part of the rhythmic mix. Language games also foster both new words and ideas and confidence in speaking in a group, and in the risk-taking that is needed in an emergent language environment. Listening skills are fostered as the teacher presents books and other enjoyable experiences. Teachers concentrate on developing verbal and nonverbal methods of delivery that engage children's interest and participation. Group times may range in time from 7 to 20 minutes, depending on the experience of the preschoolers, and may go even longer as children participate more. They are planned carefully to provide for a balance of quiet listening and active participation. A sample group time plan for a group of threes and fours appears in Figure 13-20.

Activity	Purpose	Principle
Action song: Head and Shoulders, Knees and Toes	Familiar starting activity energizes and captures attention	Familiar cues help focus attention and remind of behavior pattern.
Rhyme: Sing, Talk, Whisper, Shout	Quietening activity encourages auditory discrimination	Change the pace from active to quiet before listening activity.
Book: *Ten, Nine, Eight,* by Molly Basog	Related to theme of families Encourage discussion of who puts children to bed at night and bedtime rituals	Book ties in with focus for learning this week. Portrays nurturing African American father; and inclusion of nonsexist materials, diversity of culture.
Record: Lullabies from around the world	Creative movement to soft, quiet music	Value of sharing ideas and experiences with group. Discrimination of quiet music for relaxing and movement.

Figure 13-20 Sample plan of a preschool group time.

Things Caregivers Should Not Do

A developmentally appropriate language environment does not include the following:

- Teachers who do most of the talking, demanding children's quiet attention
- Group times that consist mostly of repeating teachers' words, rote lessons on letter naming, and sound matching
- Worksheets and other teacher-led activities that suggest pushed-down curriculum of learning isolated skills for reading and writing
- Reading and writing skills taught as isolated from the active play context

SUMMARY

The developmentally appropriate language environment for preschoolers works from a whole language philosophy, emphasizing all forms of communication for children to represent their experiences and concepts to others. The use of language and language materials is completely integrated with active play. Teachers provide materials and experiences to encourage emergent literacy in oral and written communication. Children are encouraged to develop oral language and listening skills through conversations with playmates and adults. Teachers present attitudes of acceptance and confidence in children's desire to figure out communication skills. They use experiences, children's literature, book extensions, and a print rich environment to help children discover a need for reading and writing. They offer materials that help children practice writing skills and understanding. They plan group times that involve children in all aspects of communication.

THINK ABOUT IT

1. Visit a preschool classroom. What learning centers do you see? How are they set up and used? How do the teachers function during center time? How do your observations match the content of this chapter?

2. Write down examples you see of teachers having created a print-rich environment. What additions, if any, could be made?

3. Talk with two preschool teachers about how they plan for their classroom. What provision is there in their methods for including children's interests and specific goals for children?

4. Talk with two parents of preschool children about what they feel their children should be learning during the preschool years, and the style of classroom they would look for. How do their thoughts agree and/or conflict with the ideas about developmentally appropriate practice in this chapter?

QUESTIONS TO REVIEW OBJECTIVES

1. What is meant by preoperational thinking? Describe several characteristics of preoperational thought, and how they relate to preschoolers' learning style.

2. Identify several characteristics of play that make it the most appropriate curriculum for preschoolers.

3. Discuss three kinds of play and three kinds of knowledge described by Piaget.

4. Identify several teacher roles in providing for play, and describe ways teachers fill each role.

5. Discuss what is meant by the term *whole language,* and why it is appropriate for preschool language environments.

6. What are several necessary components of a preschool language environment. Describe as many specifics as you can.

7. Identify teacher practices that are not part of appropriate cognitive/language environments.

REFERENCES AND SUGGESTIONS FOR READING

Ayers, W. (1989). *The good preschool teacher: Six teachers reflect on their lives.* New York: Teachers College Press.

Beaty, J. (1992). *Preschool appropriate practices.* New York: Harcourt, Brace Jovanovitch.

Bird, L. (1987). What is whole language. *Teachers Networking: The Whole Language Newsletter, 1(1).* (reprinted from Jacobs, D. (ed.). In *Dialogue.* New York: Richard C. Owen).

Bredekamp, S. (ed.). (1987). *Developmentally appropriate practice in early childhood programs serving children from birth through age 8.* Washington, DC: NAEYC.

Bruner, J. (1991). Play, thought, and language. In Lauter-Klatell, N. (ed.), *Readings in child development.* Mountain View, CA: Mayfield Publishing Co.

Cassidy, D. J., & Lancaster, C. (1993, September). The grassroots curriculum: A dialogue between children and teachers. *Young Children, 48(5),* 47–51.

Clemens, S. C. (1983). *The sun's not broken, a cloud's just in the way: On child-centered teaching.* Mt. Rainier, MD: Gryphon House.

Dumtschin, J. (1988, March). Recognizing language development and delay in early childhood. *Young Children, 43(3),* 16–24.

Fields, M., Spangler, K., & Lee, D. (1991). *Let's begin reading right: Developmentally appropriate beginning literacy* (2nd ed.). New York: MacMillan Publishing Co.

Goodman, K. (1986). *What's whole in whole language.* Portsmouth, NH: Heinemann.

Goodman, K. (1989). Whole language research: Foundations and development. *Elementary School Journal, 90,* 207–221.

Greenberg, P. (1990, January). Why not academic preschool? (part 1). *Young Children, 45(2),* 70–79.

Isenberg, J. P., & Jalongo, M. R. (1993). *Creative expression and play in the early childhood curriculum.* New York: Merrill.

Isenberg, J., & Quisenberry, N. (1988). Play: A necessity for all children. *Childhood Education, 64 (3),* 138–145.

Jones, E., & Reynolds, G. (1992). *The play's the thing: Teacher's roles in children's play.* New York: Teacher's College Press.

Katz, L. (1987). *What should young children be learning?* Urbana, IL: ERIC Clearing House of Elementary and Early Childhood Education.

Kontos, S. (1986, November). What preschool children know about reading and how they learn it. *Young Children, 42(1),* 58–65.

Landreth, C. (1972). *Preschool learning and teaching.* New York: Harper and Row Publishing.

McKee, J. S. (1986). Thinking, playing and language learning: An all-in-fun approach with young children. In *Play: Working partners of growth.* Wheaton, MD: Association for Childhood Education International.

Pearson, P. D. (1990). Reading the whole language movement. *Elementary School Journal, 90,* 231–241.

Piaget, J. (1962). *Play, dreams, and imitation in childhood.* New York: Norton.

Piaget, J. (1969). *The language and thought of the child.* New York: World Publishing.

Raines, S. C., & Canady, R. (1989). *Story s-t-r-e-t-c-h-e-r-s-: Activities to expand children's favorite books.* Mt. Rainier, MD: Gryphon House.

Sawyer, W. E., & Sawyer, J. C. (1993). *Integrated language arts for emerging literacy.* Albany, NY: Delmar Publishers Inc.

Schickedanz, J. A., et al. (1990, November). Preschoolers and academics: Some thoughts. *Young Children, 45(1),* 4–13.

Smilansky, S. (1968). *The effects of sociodramatic play on disadvantaged preschool children.* New York: Wiley.

Strickland, D., & Morrow, L. (eds.). (1989). *Emerging literacy: Young children learn to read and write.* Newark, DE: International Reading Assoc.

Van Hoorn, J., et al. (1993). *Play at the center of the curriculum.* New York: Merrill.

Wasserman, S. (1990). *Serious players in the primary classroom.* New York: Teacher's College Press.

Wells, G. (1986). *The meaning makers.* Portsmouth, NH: Heinemann.

Wolfgang, C. (1977). *Helping aggressive and passive preschoolers through play.* Columbus, OH: Merrill.

Zeece, P. D., & Graul, S. K. (1990, Fall). Learning to play: Playing to learn. *Day Care and Early Education,* 11–15.

Developmentally Appropriate Cognitive/Language Environments:
For Primary-Aged

*F*ive-year-old Samantha says proudly, "I can write my name."

Six-year-old Aaron says, "See my story? That says, 'We went to the farm.' (We wnt to th frm.)"

Seven-year-old B.J. says, "I hate school. All we do is boring stuff." The math papers he brings home show signs of lots of corrections.

Seven-year-old LaKeisha says, "I can read almost this whole book. Except some of the hard words. It's my favorite; it's about dogs."

Children in the early school years seem so very different from the preschoolers they recently were. Their leaner, stronger bodies and increased muscular strength allow them to participate energetically in physical activity and games. Their confidence away from adults allows them to enter the world of friends and children's fun. They pour into and out of their school buildings with varying degrees of enthusiasm and excitement, eager to succeed in the world of the grown-ups, or fearful of the new and unfamiliar expectations. There are serious cognitive norms and patterns to live up to. Most of us are familiar with the story of the first grader who came home in tears at the end of the first day because she hadn't learned to read yet. But in their inner cognitive world, these primary-aged children are still closely linked to the preschool years in ability and style of thinking and learning. Preoperational thinking and learning dictates clear implications for decisions in primary cognitive/language environments. Learning and language are always closely linked, and in the early primary years, the emphasis in both children's and adults' minds is on learning to use the skills of written language.

During the primary years, the society places inordinate emphasis on acquiring these cognitive skills. Stressing the cognitive and minimizing attention to other aspects of children's development may be a root cause of some of children's failures in school experiences. While this chapter will focus on cognitive/language aspects, the discussion connects with earlier discussions of all areas of development.

OBJECTIVES

After completing this chapter, students should be able to:

- identify the implications of preoperational and concrete operational thought for primary cognitive/language environments.

- discuss readiness testing as related to developmentally appropriate practice.
- describe components of implementing integrated curricula in primary classrooms.
- discuss reading in developmentally appropriate practice.
- describe aspects of a developmentally appropriate writing program.
- identify developmentally appropriate aspects of a primary math curriculum.
- compare effects of achievement testing and assessment, and describe the role of assessment in a developmentally appropriate primary classroom.

Preoperational and Concrete Operational Thinking and Developmentally Appropriate Practice

In Chapter 13 we considered the various characteristics of the stage of preoperational thinking as defined by Piaget, seen in children from about ages two through seven or so. To review, these characteristics include: centration, or focusing on one perception at a time; egocentrism in thought; irreversibility; and concrete thinking. All of these characteristics limit children's abilities to learn about abstractions and through methods related to abstractions, such as learning through someone else's words, or through being asked to find mental solutions to problems. It is this fact of still being mostly capable of preoperational thought during the early school years that keeps school-aged children linked with the preschool period, and so unsuited for the learning tasks and methods of the typical elementary school classroom.

Slowly during the primary years, children move into the stage of *concrete operational thought.* At this time they acquire the mental ability to think about and solve problems in their heads, no longer needing physical contact and manipulation of objects to be able to learn. They are still limited in their ability to think about purely symbolic or abstract ideas, and need real things to think about. "Accordingly, while children can use symbols such as words and numbers to represent objects and relations, they still need concrete reference points" (Bredekamp, 1987, p. 64). This means that a key feature of developmentally appropriate cognitive practice is curriculum for primary-aged children that is based on the provision of many developmentally appropriate materials for children to explore and think about; things that are relevant, interesting, and meaningful to the children themselves. It is also developmentally appropriate for teachers to recognize that some thinking skills, notably mathematical skills, are beyond children who are only developing concrete operational thinking. Some kinds of learning and lessons are delayed until after the primary years, for easier learning and less risk of failure. Yet, according to a study completed by the Educational Research Service, the majority of kindergarten programs today attempt to teach children formal academics using formal methods (Coletta, 1991).

Moving out of the egocentric thought of the preoperational period is dependent on interaction, conversation, and communication with other children and adults. Developmentally appropriate practice demands, therefore, that children be given opportunities to work in small groups on common activities that provide the basis for communication and interaction. Children's abilities to reason are strengthened by such opportunities for group work and conversation.

Teachers realize that one of their key roles is to "facilitate discussion among children by making comments and soliciting children's opinions and ideas" (Katz in Bredekamp, 1987, p. 64). Learning how to stimulate children's language is a vital component in the cognitive/language environment.

Every child is on an individual timetable of moving between the preoperational and concrete operational stages. Only teachers who are familiar with characteristics of thinking in the two stages and aware of likely responses of children within each stage will be able to match most appropriate learning experiences and materials for each child. (See Chapter 17 on Scarborough schools, for an account of teachers who use Piagetian tasks routinely to help assess children's developmental levels for planning curricula and instruction.)

Other Aspects of Readiness for School Learning Tasks

Young children's eyes often have difficulty with tasks essential to reading, such as focusing quickly, tracking, moving beyond the midline, etc. It is not until age eight that most children have enough control of eye muscles to do what is demanded of the eyes in reading; much nearsightedness is blamed on doing too much close up work too soon. More than 3,000 studies made by the American Optometric Association present consistent findings that young children's eyes should not be strained with much reading at least for the first six to eight years, and even afterward should be restricted to 15 or 20 minutes at a time, to allow rest through refocusing their eyes on distant objects (Seefeldt, 1990). It is considered quite usual for children to reverse written letters and numerals through age seven (Uphoff, 1989).

The lack of fine muscle control makes pencil and paper work difficult for young children. Watch the awkward methods of holding a pencil used by many children in first and second grade classrooms to corroborate the truth of this statement; unfortunately for many, this early pencil grip becomes a handicap that slows their writing for the rest of their lives. Uphoff states that "tasks for four- to six-year-olds which call for extensive writing of small *(less than 4 to 6 inches in height)* letters or numbers are likely to create such lifelong handicaps for up to 40-60% of children" (Uphoff, 1989, p. 5).

Social skills vary in any group of young children. The average primary classroom has one adult for every 25 to 30 children; many children may have come from preschool arrangements where the ratios were about half of that, or from home or care arrangements where it was even less. This makes a lot more children with whom to learn to cooperate and share, to take turns and wait to listen; for many children, becoming comfortable in a social setting offers the first challenge to be resolved before being able to concentrate on tasks of formal cognitive learning.

Emotional comfort and security affect children's readiness to learn. Many of the factors mentioned above create physical and emotional stress that may manifest itself in a variety of ways, including toilet accidents, the physical symptoms such as stomach aches and nausea, collectively known medically as "school phobia," inability to pay attention, and general distress and unhappiness. The cogni-

---

Ready for Kindergarten

I don't understand the focus,
Somehow it seems misplaced and wrong,
As when the melody being played
Does not match the song.
I thought schools were for children,
Not children for schools,
Perhaps we have dropped the pieces
Confused the rules.
Wasn't kindergarten envisioned
As a supportive place to learn,
Not a sweathouse for young children
With intricate competencies to learn?
Look at the advice given to parents,
At what young children need to know,
So that children will be ready for kindergarten,
Ready before they go.
Assessment-taking tips
The eventual entrance test.
Of physical adeptness, social skills
And academic readiness.
I don't understand the focus,
Somehow it seems misplaced and wrong,
As when the melody being played
Does not match the song.
A sweathouse for young children
The notion seems absurdly wild
But I don't hear many voices asking,
Is kindergarten ready for your child?

Figure 14–1 What does it mean to be "ready for kindergarten?" *Used with permission of author, Sigmund A. Boloz. Copyrighted.*

tive environment must take recognition of all of these aspects of the whole child when considering "readiness to learn."

Readiness

Unfortunately "readiness" has often come to mean many things other than recognition of the unique development of the whole child. Around the country, readiness has been equated with children's scores on an variety of entrance tests. America's children are tested; over 55 million standardized tests of achievement, competency, and basic skills are administered each year by state and local mandate. This figure does not include the additional 30 to 40 million given in compensatory and special education. In addition, two million or more screening tests are given each year to obtain an "objective" measure of children's readiness for kindergarten and prekindergarten (Neill and Medina, 1989). The subject of readiness testing needs to be explored here in the context of developmentally appropriate practice. (See Figure 14-1.)

As noted above, educators and administrators use the term *readiness* to mean very different things. The discussion on readiness has been closely tied to schools' attempts to improve their accountability. Often, this has meant a way of excluding children who fail to demonstrate certain skills, and therefore might be expected to be less successful in first learning experiences. If there are particular expectations of what skills and abilities children should possess prior to school entry, readiness is really a method of *gatekeeping* (Willer and Bredekamp, 1990). Readiness defined in this way expects children to meet the demands of the schools, not the other way around. This seems grossly unfair to children who have unequal access to early experiences that can or cannot enhance their individual development, and who certainly need the opportunities to be in supportive classroom environments that will accept them as they arrive.

The urgency to have children "ready" for school is a result of the changed academic demands of the primary classrooms. "Children entering kindergarten are now expected to have already acquired the skills that used to comprise the entire year's curriculum!" (Willer and Bredekamp, 1990, p. 23). Rather than itself serving a readiness function of socialization in the environment for future schooling, kindergarten has become an experience for which children need to be ready before they come (Charlesworth, 1989). When they are unable to meet these higher standards, more of them fail (Balaban, 1990; Walsh, 1989). Readiness tests then become one of the school system's methods for trying to make beginning primary students older; when children are evaluated as "unready," schools hold children out of school for a year, thus raising the age for school entry. Another option is to enter transitional classes—prekindergarten, junior first grade, etc.—with children's futures based on the scores of readiness tests (Walsh, 1989).

Tests for readiness are often based on single dimensions, such as "knowledge of letters and numbers" (NAEYC, 1990, p. 23) that ignore strengths in other areas. The interrelationships of social skills, physical development, and emotional adjustment are ignored by such tests. Readiness tests that examine the existence of certain basic skills as prerequisite for later learning are based on the misconception that "children's learning occurs in a sequential, hierarchical process."

❝ In fact, children's acquisition of higher order thinking processes and problem-solving abilities occurs in tandem with and may outpace acquisition of basic skills. For example, children are able to comprehend and compose far more complex stories than they can read or write.... This does not mean that the acquisition of basic skills is unimportant; rather, focusing solely on isolated skills deprives children of the meaningful context that promotes effective learning (NAEYC, 1990, p. 22). *❞*

When administrators and communities rely on test scores as indicators of determining school readiness, they ignore the fact that the tests are neither valid for all children, nor reliable in their results (Bredekamp and Shepard, 1989; Charlesworth, 1989; Meisels, 1987). One of the most widely used and respected tests is the Gesell School Readiness Screening Test. Criticized on the basis of poor reliability and validity, the test is also criticized as being based on an outdated theory of child development (Meisels, 1987; Walsh, 1989), though these charges are refuted by the Gesell Institute (*Young Children,* 1987).

> Tests without reliability and validity are inherently untrustworthy and should not be used to identify and place children. We do not know if such tests provide different results when administered by different testers, whether children from certain socioeconomic or ethnic backgrounds are disadvantaged by them, or whether they are strongly related to some stable, external criterion or outcome measure ... that permits the test results to be interpreted and the findings to be generalized (Meisels, 1987, p. 5).

Despite the lack of data indicating reliability and validity on all major available tests, many of them are used arbitrarily for placement decisions. "For instance, in 1988 the Norwood-Norfolk school district in New York assigned 61 percent of incoming kindergartners to the 2-year track called developmental kindergarten on the basis of a single administration of the Gesell test" (Bredekamp and Shepard, 1989, p. 17).

Side effects of relying on readiness test information that is invalid are: that children who need special services are often overlooked; that some children are erroneously labeled "at risk;" that parents are alarmed, teachers and administrators upset, and resources wasted (Meisels, 1987). In many communities readiness tests are confused with tools for accurate developmental screening; at best, readiness tests "should be used to facilitate curriculum planning, not to identify children who may need special services or intervention" (Meisels, 1987, p. 5).

When readiness is also equated with being able to sit quietly at desks to listen to the teacher's lesson, inappropriate curricula and teaching practices that do not recognize current knowledge about children's style of learning go unchallenged. Walsh points out the narrowness of the kindergarten curriculum. When leaving, children are expected to be able to do four things: sit still, pay attention, recognize and write numbers, and recognize and write letters (Walsh, 1989).

In the NAEYC position statement on school readiness, adopted in July 1990, three critical factors that must be included in any discussion of school readiness are identified: the diversity and inequity of children's early life experiences; the wide range of variation in young children's development and learning; and the degree to which school expectations of children entering kindergarten are reasonable, appropriate, and supportive of individual differences (NAEYC, 1990). The statement emphasizes making schools responsive to individual needs, rather than demanding that children be ready to fit into "rigid, lock-step distinctions between grades," (NAEYC, 1990, p. 23). Developmentally appropriate practices offer children continuous progress through the primary grades, with teachers responding to individual variations among children with individualized curriculum and teaching practices. In such a system, there is then no need for transitional classes; every child progresses individually (Brewer, 1990; Uphoff, 1990). Readiness then becomes a concept applied to schools, administrators, and teachers: Are the schools ready to ensure the success of every child who enters, meeting each where he or she is? Readiness includes teachers trained in child development and early education who are able to plan and implement child-initiated learning experiences, small group activities, integrated lessons, and active hands-on learning with a variety of materials and activities. Readiness also

Figure 14–2 Class size that permits observation and instruction of individual children is a crucial element for DAP. *Courtesy Scarborough School Department.*

includes class size reduced to the point where individualized instruction and observation are feasible. (See Figure 14-2.) Readiness also includes investment in classroom equipment and materials. But in the words of the position statement, readiness does not include using "labeling and sorting mechanisms as a sieve," (NAEYC, 1990, p. 23) allowing too many children to fail.

> We must be particularly concerned about policy that is less about improving early schooling and more about sorting children at a very early age, on reducing variation, on narrowing what gets taught and to whom (Walsh, 1989, p. 389).

Cognitive/Language Goals of Primary Education

> The primary grades hold the potential for starting children on a course of lifelong learning. Whether schools achieve this potential for children is largely dependent on the degree to which teachers adopt principles of developmentally appropriate practice (Bredekamp, 1987, p. 66).

All children, free of physical disability, illness, or abuse, arrive at school eager to learn and confident they will succeed (Bredekamp, 1987, p. 66). The number who fail, are held back, need special assistance, lose confidence in their abilities to learn, and eventually drop out, is far too high in a country that prides itself on and needs an educated citizenry. This fact alone suggests that our goals are not being met. What are the basic goals for primary-aged children?

1. Ensure that children have successful early experiences in learning. Lifelong patterns are being set, and children's self-esteem and feelings of confidence as learners are critical. This relates to the previous discussion: Are children being put through the stress of tests to be told they are not ready for the skills of school, or are the schools preparing to meet them as they arrive and take them on to their next successful step? When schools rely on competition and comparison among children, children's confidence as learners is put at risk.

2. Ensure that children play active roles in their learning. To feel themselves to be competent learners, children must perceive their importance as decision-makers, initiators, and active participants in primary classrooms.

3. Ensure that children develop dispositions toward learning (Katz, 1988). Dispositions are different learning from skills and knowledge. They are "habits of mind, tendencies to respond to situations in certain ways" (Katz, 1988, p. 29). An example of a disposition is curiosity; it is not a skill or a piece of knowledge. Children must acquire the disposition or inclination to use the skills they acquire. There is a big difference between having the skills and having the disposition to be a reader. Much evidence suggests that too much emphasis on developing narrow skills in children through drill and rote learning may threaten children's dispositions to use those skills: "I *hate* reading," when what is hated is the school's method of teaching reading.

4. Ensure that children have appropriate learning opportunities to develop basic competencies of literacy and numeracy. Continuing to develop competence in communication as well as the basic skills required for further

Figure 14–3 Developing basic skills in numeracy is an important part of primary learning. *Courtesy Scarborough School Department.*

instruction in the knowledge deemed essential by culture and communities are part of primary learning. (See Figure 14-3.)

5. Ensure that children have opportunities to continue developing their individual and personal interests. Educators recognize that children's motivation for learning is an intense desire to make sense out of their own unique world. These interests extend beyond the purely cognitive, and broaden the narrowly defined subjects of curriculum. Howard Gardner has proposed a theory of multiple intelligences, each following its particular developmental path (Gardner, 1983 and 1991). Schools need to consider their roles in optimizing the development of various kinds of intelligence, which may include linguistic, musical, logico-mathematical, spatial, bodily-kinesthetic, personal, and social intelligence.

How best to meet these goals will be explored as we discuss basic components of what is considered developmentally appropriate practice for the cognitive/language tasks in primary-aged classrooms.

Components of Developmentally Appropriate Cognitive/Language Environments

Integrated Curriculum

The traditional separation of subject areas in the curriculum, with segments of time allotted for each, implies that children construct their understandings of the world in a separated, linear fashion. In fact this is not so; children learn by making connections between ideas and experiences, between learning skills needed to be used in a meaningful context that is of interest to them. Isolated facts about related subjects seem irrelevant, important only to the teacher, not likely to catch children's interest and extend their confidence or dispositions toward learning.

How do primary teachers integrate curriculum? There are several practices relevant here.

Themes. The learning is organized around large themes, rather than on particular subjects. This is quite different from say, what a teacher in a traditional primary classroom might do on the subject of Valentine's Day (Gamberg et al., 1988). Here the children might read a story about it, discuss the story, learn a Valentine's song, write and illustrate stories or poems about what Valentine's Day means to them, and paste their math work on red valentines. The next week they do something quite different. Although the focus is on a topic of interest and combines several school subjects, this approach falls short of what is meant by theme study that truly integrates curriculum in primary classrooms.

Theme study forms the core of developmentally appropriate learning activities in primary classrooms. The theme defines what is the center of attention, incorporates many subject areas within it, and develops over a long period of time. Some subjects, math for example, cannot be fully included in theme work, because the theme studies do not always offer enough exposure to the concepts. Whatever fits naturally into the theme is included; what does not is dealt with separately. But a large amount of time each day and week is devoted to activities related to the theme. Theme activities may take up a large part of the curriculum, and be pursued several times a week. The theme may be integrated into learning centers, or form the basis for most classroom curriculum activities.

Real theme study involves in-depth work over time. Many classrooms spend months or even the full academic year pursuing their interests. Other criteria for theme study include:

- Topics are of great interest to the children
- Topics are related to the surrounding community
- The topic is broad enough that it can be divided into smaller subtopics that also interest the children
- The relationships of subtopics to the wider context can be made clear
- The topic lends itself to extensive investigation of real situations, materials, and resources, to comparing and contrasting ideas
- The topic encourages rich cross-disciplinary work (Gamberg et al., 1989)

For example, an appropriate theme for primary-aged children living in rural Maine or Oregon might be "The Forest." A selection of subtopics might be: the growth cycles of trees; kinds of trees and their uses; harvesting lumber; history of lumbering; forest animal families; habitats; ecological issues. It is obvious that each of these subtopics offers a wide scope for study. Children studying kinds of trees and their uses might draw different kinds of trees, make charts that indicate the wood products of each, use carpentry and measuring skills to make some things from wood, and write letters to wood product companies as part of their research. Children's interests and questions will be a force in determining the direction the theme study takes.

Eleanor Duckworth refers to the learning process for children as the "having of wonderful ideas." She says:

> There are two aspects to providing occasions for wonderful ideas. One is being willing to accept children's ideas. The other is providing a setting that suggests wonderful ideas to children—different ideas to different children—as they are caught up in intellectual problems that are real to them (Duckworth, 1987, p. 7).

While the topic and not the academic subject is emphasized, there are still ample opportunities for incorporating the traditional subjects in the children's learning. Children involved in theme study use reading, writing, spelling, math, and creative arts to explore and record their thinking and observations about content usually involving science, social studies, and health. As particular skills are needed for the projects of the study, they are taught. In this way children understand the purposes of reading, writing, and math skills. Yet the theme study is undertaken because the content is important to know; it is not just a

> ...thin excuse for teaching children to perfect their recognition of words, spelling, punctuation, and so forth. These skills are indeed learned but not through drill. They are learned because they are identified as necessary tools for achieving another purpose (Gamberg et al., 1988).

In-depth study organized around themes has also been called the project approach (Katz and Chard, 1989). As children participate in projects to gain a "deeper and fuller sense of events and phemenona in their own environment and experience" (Katz, 1989), they get extensive and varied practice in analyzing and questioning. By so doing they develop confidence in their own intellectual powers and strengthen their disposition to go on learning. This is the result of a challenge to the idea that there are just two alternatives of curriculum for the early childhood years: an academically oriented curriculum or the traditional approach of kindergartens that emphasizes socialization and play. "Teachers throughout the early years tend to overestimate children academically but underestimate them intellectually." (Katz and Chard, 1989, p. 5). The project work complements and enhances what children learn from spontaneous play as well as from systematic instruction. Wonderful ideas are built on other wonderful ideas that improve learners' understanding of the world around them and strengthen their dispositions to go on learning.

Joint Planning. Integrated curriculum involves joint planning by teachers and children. Children are involved in identifying topics that are of great interest to them, but this does not mean that the classroom curriculum is solely dictated by children's whims. Theme study is a focused study, guided intentionally by teachers. Children and teachers collaboratively select projects, plan activities, and decide what materials are needed.

Teachers are very likely to make initial decisions about the overall themes, since they know the characteristics of themes that will prove successful for in-depth study. Teachers also do preliminary research on resources of print, materials, people, and places within the community that would support project research. They also plan ideas and classroom activities to introduce the topics.

Figure 14–4
Brainstorming sessions will help teachers select appropriate topics for extended theme study.
Courtesy Scarborough School Department.

The children may be involved in a process of brainstorming—free-flowing discussions to identify what children already know or have experienced about a topic. Brainstorming questions that they do not know may also guide teachers and children in selecting the topics they want to study with more depth. (See Figure 14-4.) With such curriculum development, subjects are not being covered, but are being uncovered, as Duckworth (1987) says.

Children are encouraged to make their own decisions and choices about the work to be undertaken: What it will be, how it will be undertaken and with whom, and how will their learning be represented and shared with others? Thus, through the theme study/project approach, primary-aged children learn not only about the theme itself, but also how to be active participants in their learning, how to plan and organize their study. The disposition to engage in thought about active learning is being established.

❝ They are not passively following someone else's instructions. Instead, they are required to consider alternatives and make their own decisions based on reasons they can explain and justify. They are learning to become independent and critical thinkers (Gamberg et al., 1988, p. 30). *❞*

Collaborating in small groups. In an integrated curriculum, teachers create situations where children collaborate in small groups to work on individual projects. Group work is valuable both socially (see Chapter 10) and cognitively. Research indicates that peer interaction can foster cognitive development by allowing children to attain new skills and reconfigure ideas through discussion. Collaborative efforts increase the amount of time children work on a task,

Figure 14–5 Children learn to fulfill responsibilities to the group for project completion. *Courtesy Scarborough School Department.*

since peer presence prevents children from giving up on difficult tasks and makes work more enjoyable (Azmitia, 1988). Working together facilitates acquiring knowledge and skills, since different members bring different skills and interests to the activity. Verbal interaction among the children makes a rich basis for extending ideas and supporting efforts. As they learn to express their learning to others, children truly process their understandings. Children benefit from the feedback they give and receive with group members.

Sometimes children select their work partners; sometimes teachers suggest groups to children for social reasons or to complement learning styles. By working together on projects, children exert powerful influences on one another's work habits; when certain behaviors of an individual are a problem for the group, it is the group's responsibility to find appropriate ways of changing those behaviors. Children learn that they can be useful and contributing members of a work group, and that they have a responsibility to that group in pulling their own weight. (See Figure 14-5.)

Obviously not all experiences in the primary classroom are group activities, though most of the project work in studying themes is productive in groups. An example of a solitary activity may be writing in a journal, although children are free to consult with one another about spelling and ideas.

Teachers as facilitators. When using an integrated curriculum, teachers function as facilitators in addition to being instructors. In effect, the teacher is removed from center stage, and many of the functions of the teacher are taken up by the group members. However, teachers are not less involved in or less accountable for children's learning. What does the teacher do in an integrated curriculum?

The teacher does the advance preparation, choosing theme topics and gathering resource materials for classroom activities. "Projects are often initiated and developed in response to teachers' suggestions, questions, or materials."(Trepanier-Street, 1993, p. 26). It is important that the teacher be curious and enthusiastic, and open to learning new ideas and following children's lines of questioning. Because the individual interests of children help guide the direction of projects, teachers will probably find that the same theme undertaken in different years with different groups will take quite different directions. Teachers will not necessarily know initially all of the information that the children will gain from the projects undertaken, but model the role of interested and active learner themselves. When the teacher is learning along with the children, the importance and seriousness of their work is emphasized.

Teachers prepare the environment for project work, adding interesting and relevant materials to interest centers for choice times, displaying other resource materials, and displaying records of finished project work. Preparation continues as the project progresses, as various possibilities, needs, and interests emerge. Preparation may include planning for relevant field trips, classroom visitors, and follow-up activities. Teachers ensure that there is a rich variety of materials and activities that will stimulate and extend children's interests. They schedule time so children have extended, concentrated periods to become involved in their project work.

Teachers prepare children to work in groups. They may help them select working partners, and remind children of their responsibilities to others in group functioning. Students do not automatically know how to work with others in a constructive fashion, and need to direct conversation about this subject. Teachers may help children define their roles within the group, so everyone has a part to play for which he or she is suitably skilled (Cohen and Benton, 1988).

Teachers act as resource persons. Being a resource person means being available to teach skills as the need arises in the activity. Literacy or math skills needed for the project to progress are embedded in a meaningful context. The teachers' job is not to tell children everything, but to help them locate information and figure out how they can find their answers. As they oversee the children's busy activity, they see where support is needed at any time.

Teachers help themselves and the children keep track of the children's works in progress. They may make charts of the brainstorming and plans, listing the steps of the group project so that children can keep progressing in an organized way. They make observations and notes on children's interests, abilities, and difficulties, to guide them in meeting individual needs for assistance and to discover what the children are ready to learn. They keep samples of children's work for assessment of progress and planning of next steps in curricula and instruction.

They question, to help children clarify their thinking and be able to express their learning verbally and in writing. A question may be the impetus for children to take another step in their work. They give feedback, guidance, and encouragement, and they provide opportunities for children to summarize and display their learning to peers and parents.

They hold individual conferences with children to assess their progress in learning and thinking, and to help children learn to evaluate the quality of their own work. Teachers schedule reading, writing, or math conferences with individuals during the times when children are busy at their own work. Usually such conferences are held on a weekly basis, to help both teacher and child plan the next learning events.

As facilitators, teachers also provide direct instruction as they see that children need skills and are ready to acquire them. Such instruction is usually offered individually or in small groups, and uses the child's chosen reading, writing, or math interest as a basis for the instruction, instead of lessons from standard texts. Teachers who use integrated curricula find themselves in the midst of busy, active groups of children, rather than standing at the front of a classroom teaching lessons determined by a textbook. (See Figure 14-6.)

Figure 14–6 Teachers using DAP will not always find themselves teaching the whole group from the front of the classroom. *Courtesy Scarborough School Department.*

Things Caregivers Should Not Do

In classrooms that stress imparting measurable content and skill acquisition rather than meaningful content gained through an active process of learning, these less appropriate practices will be found:

- Primary emphasis is on reading and math, with specific lessons taught each day, and children progressing through workbooks and basal readers.

- Curriculum is divided into separate subjects, such as social studies, science, health, and are taught only as time is available after the reading and math skill lessons.

- Little time is left for "enrichment" activities such as projects and learning centers.

- Emphasis is on teacher instruction, and pencil-and-paper practice of skills at desks.

- Student conversation is discouraged as disruptive to teacher lessons and quiet seat-work.

Language and Literacy

Brian Cutting, a noted New Zealand educator, points out that children learn to talk successfully, naturally, and with apparent ease well before they go to school. There are several contributing factors to this:

- No one expects children to fail at the task.

- Children are responsible for much of their learning, instead of being given daily lessons from a manual of learning to talk broken down into successive steps.

- Children practice for a long time, amidst an environment that is patient, tolerant of "mistakes," and delighting in their early attempts.

- There are no tests of talking.

" If we really wanted to make learning to talk a non-success story, the easiest way would be to design tests that would set a standard which all children would be expected to reach. We all know that such procedures would be futile for children learning to talk. So why do we use similar procedures for children learning to read and write? (Cutting, 1991, p. 65). *"*

The development of language and literacy in the primary classroom is seen as a continuum of earlier experiences. The goal of the language and literacy program in the primary years is for children to continue to develop their ability to communicate orally and through reading and writing. Basic tenets of the whole language approach are that spoken and written language interact and influence each other, and that all phases of language development are experience-based. Children learn about reading and writing through observing these skills being used and through using them themselves. Writing and reading are taught simultaneously and are experienced as an integrated part of the total curriculum, not just at assigned times. Oral language skills of listening and speaking are integrated into every aspect of the classroom day. The physical environment is arranged to enhance interpersonal communication. For purposes of clarity only, reading and writing will be discussed separately below.

Reading. Children are given an understanding that the purposes of reading instruction are to enjoy reading as an activity and to develop strategies to construct meaning in a text.

To foster enjoyment of reading, teachers:

- Provide time each day for children to look through books, read and be read to, using a carefully selected variety of high-quality children's literature, poetry, and nonfiction books (See Figures 14-7 and 14-8.) Example:

  Today in Mr. Bryant's first grade, he reads a book about trains as part of their theme study. Before lunch, he reads a chapter of *Charlotte's Web*, their ongoing book. There is a half hour library period in the classroom each morning, when children read their own selections.

- Provide adults, older children, or "reading buddies" to read to children:

  The fourth graders come in to the first grade three times a week to read with individual first graders.

Figures 14–7, 14–8
Teachers regularly read to children ... and provide opportunities for individual reading of good children's literature.
Courtesy Scarborough School Department.

- Help children write and/or illustrate their own books of stories, riddles, classroom experiences:

  Each child writes his or her own page for a class book about trains. Each page is illustrated. When the book is finished, it will be available in the library area for personal reading.

- Provide activities related to stories, such as dramatic play props, flannel boards, puppets, and creative art materials.

The dramatic play center might have engineer hats, train tickets, maps, and railway signs. The art center may have a selection of sticks, straws, etc., that have been used to make three-dimensional representations of trains on tracks.

- Use the school library and attractively set up library area of the classroom for children to choose their own books regularly.

- Provide books that have meaning related to classroom themes and projects, so children can experience the function of reading to gain information.

- Provide materials at a variety of ability levels—wordless picture books, familiar books, books with illustrations that closely match the text, songs and poems that rhyme and have a definite rhythm, books that have portions of the text repeated frequently—in the classroom, so each child can experience success at his or her own level.

To help children develop strategies to construct meaning in reading, teachers:

- Read predictable stories to children regularly, encouraging children to join in with the reading whenever they can (shared reading).

- Use "Big Books" with text large enough to be seen and followed.

- Help children use their own knowledge of language to predict the language of the author, to use their knowledge of the context to get clues about meaning. Example:

  The teacher in a K-1 class reads again the classroom big book *Brown Bear, Brown Bear* to her group. Then children happily join in as she hesitates and points to the next illustration: "... an ORANGE FISH looking at me."

- Have children draw, write, and dictate their own stories, for their own reading:

  For their writing/drawing experience after the book, the teacher suggests they create their own book about some of the animals in *Brown Bear, Brown Bear*. Anthony is writing a story called *Purple Horse*.

- Write and post charts, lists, and experience stories so children are familiar with the text:

  After their trip to the zoo, the teacher writes down the words of each child to describe their favorite animal. After each child's words are printed on the chart paper, she reads it aloud to them, and they join in: "And Anthony said...."

- Encourage children to focus attention on what the text means:

    When Julio is puzzled by a word, the teacher asks him to look at the picture and see if that gives him an idea. To Erica she says: "What do you suppose that little girl feels like when her mother goes to work?"

- Encourage children reading together to help one another with meaning:

    She suggests that Ricky might like to read the story with Julio, to help him figure out some of the hard words.

- Help children who have already been introduced to reading in a natural literature context to develop the skills and subskills needed to accomplish the larger goals of reading:

    "Look at that word carefully, Julio. It starts with an …? That's right, an "h." That sounds like…?"

- Develop an awareness of phonics through interaction with meaningful text, such as pointing out sounds in a song or poem:

    "Hop, Hop, Hop" recites the teacher, emphasizing the beginning sounds as she points to the printed words of the poem.

- Hold reading conferences to discuss reading and have children read to one another. By analyzing children's miscues, teachers can help each individually:

- Use reading purposefully to help children acquire the information or the pleasure they want.

The developmentally inappropriate practices in primary classes related to reading include:

- teaching reading as a distinct subject, with time in reading groups and workbook practice taking up much of the instructional day

- emphasis on skills and subskills being directly taught as ends in themselves, with no context of meaning other than being necessary to pass standardized tests

- reading instruction beginning with a focus on letters and sounds of words, rather than looking at language as a whole

- focus of the reading program is the basal reader, used in the reading groups, (and everyone knows which children are reading the lowest level book)

- absence of reading or listening to children's literature regularly

- much time spent listening to other children read or be corrected in their reading, asking artificial workbook questions, or doing boring workbook pages

Writing. As with reading, children in primary classrooms that use the whole language approach need purposes for writing, and plenty of time to practice it and learn the skills. Again the assumption is that this aspect of language is learned developmentally by making approximations of what children see others doing in writing, and that continual practice will gradually help them reach the correct form and usage over time. (Remember, the analogy of how infants learn to produce oral speech, at first sounding quite unlike adult speech, and gradually coming to resemble the speech they hear around them.)

Children in primary classrooms need to see adults writing regularly, to realize this as an important means of communication. And children in primary classrooms need to write a great deal every day to get better at doing it. In primary classrooms the process of writing is more important than the finished products, which may indicate varying degrees of understanding of the way grammar, spelling, and punctuation work. What is important is the child's decision about what to write and how to express it. The traditional methods of drill and repetition to teach skills of handwriting and spelling are not the goal of writing in the primary classroom. Instead, the goal is to create a disposition to enjoy expressing thoughts in writing.

This is often one area that adults who do not understand the concept of beginning with the whole and working down to the individual skills often have trouble with, seeing the incorrect spelling and grammar as something that should be corrected at the beginning, so that children do not develop bad habits. "How will he learn to spell correctly if she lets him spell like that?" "I can't believe she lets him bring home a paper with so many mistakes." (Dailey, 1991, p. 21). Parents need to be introduced to concepts of developing reading and writing through whole language practice, so that they can be supportive and appropriate in their responses to children's work.

Beginning writing skills are nurtured by:

- Opportunities to observe adults and older children writing frequently, so that they can see that writing has purpose, and that there are conventional forms to learn in writing letters and words. Example:

  Miss Edwards uses chart paper on a large easel at morning meeting time to print the daily news. She talks about what she is doing. "I'll put a capital letter here because I'm starting a new sentence."

- Opportunities to learn firsthand that writing is one of the vital ways people communicate with one another:

  "I'm writing a note to your mother, Quiana, to thank her for the cookies she sent us for snack."

- Functional print in the classroom that encourages both reading and writing:

  A sign on the Art center says: "Needed: 4 people to wash brushes and tidy the shelves today. Sign up here."

  A sign in the meeting area says: "Write your name here if you have news to tell today."

- Individual mailboxes in the room encourage children to communicate with one another in writing:

  Miss Edwards adds stationery and envelopes to the materials in the writing center.

- Adults taking children's dictation to describe their creations or experiences:

  "That's an interesting picture you made, Seth. Would you like to tell me the story about it, and I can write the words down."

Figures 14–9 There is time to write every day. *Courtesy Scarborough School Department.*

Stages of Invented Spelling

1. String of letters:
   ("This says Dear Mommy")

   HTP†

2. Beginning sounds only:
   ("My Cat")

   MC

3. Beginning and ending sounds:
   ("My Cat")

   Mi CT

4. Beginning, middle
   and ending sounds:
   ("Dear Mommy")

   der mome

Figure 14-10 Stages of invented spelling.

- Time to draw and/or write every day, including time to discuss ideas with peers and teacher, time to plan how to proceed in the writing, time to work with writing implements and to figure out how words are spelled, and time to share their writing by reading it out loud to a partner or group. (See Figure 14-9.) Example:

  > Every morning after the meeting and story, Miss Edwards's class has writing time. The children each have a writing folder and a notebook where they keep their on-going writing projects. They sit together at tables, and frequently discuss their writing with one another. "How do you spell dinosaur? I'm writing a story about a dinosaur that gets lost." "I'm going to put a friendly dinosaur in my story; I don't like scary dinosaurs." "I'll read you my story when I'm done. You won't be scared."

- Experiences and events that encourage and necessitate writing: notes about project plans and progress; project reports; questions for field trips and classroom visitors; thank-you letters and letters to gain information; games, riddles, and jokes; signs, posters, and fliers; messages for friends' mailboxes; lists of favorite things; stories and journal entries:

  > Jennifer used her writing time to write a letter to the zoo with a question about what they feed the zebra. DeMario adds a joke to the book of jokes he's writing. LaQuisha and Annie work together on a list of the books they like the best.

- An atmosphere of acceptance of all attempts to express themselves, without undue correction of scribbling, letter formations, "invented" spelling, grammar, word spacing, or punctuation. (See Figure 14-10 for stages of invented spelling.) When any corrections are made, they are made orally, and only incidentally as opportunities present themselves:

> When Briana shows her dinosaur story to the teacher, "dinosaur" is spelled "DNSR." Her teacher comments on the dinosaur's adventure only, while enunciating the word dinosaur very precisely, and tells Briana she enjoyed her story. Later she notices that Briana has added an "E"—"DNSER."

- Resources children can use independently to assist their writing, such as picture dictionaries and word lists, and materials to help create finished books to establish authorship.

- Encouragement to keep their own personal style of expressing themselves, rather than fitting into some prescribed mold of approved writing (Hubbard, 1988). Children are expected to choose their own topics, and make decisions about length, organization, and style:

> Kim's writing demonstrates her concern for small creatures; her story today is about a lost puppy. Wally has a scientific curiosity, and writes extensively about his observations. Jill's sense of humor comes through in her writing, which she almost always finishes with the words "HA HA."

- Portfolios of children's written work maintained over time, for teachers to use as assessment of children's understanding and abilities, and to share with parents during progress conferences. (See further discussion on portfolios later in this chapter.)

- Regular writing conferences between teacher and child, to discuss finished work and work in progress. Such individual attention helps teachers work with developing the skills individual children need, as well as supporting and learning unique styles and interests.

Children's developmental progress as writers is hindered when teachers:

- emphasize quality of penmanship as "writing" lessons

- teach writing as grammar rather than a form of expressing ideas

- emphasize correction of errors in children's work so that the work "looks like a battlefield full of casualties" (Gamberg, et al., 1988, p. 201)

- use writing as a punishment or drill practice (a page of M's; a page of "I will not talk out loud")

- use workbook pages extensively

Math Skills. As primary-aged children slowly leave the stage of preoperational thought and move to understanding concrete operations, they are assisted in this development by opportunities to explore and discover logico-mathematical relationships by acting on concrete objects. Young children need opportunities to use number concepts and skills to explore, discover and solve meaningful problems. The emphasis in developmentally appropriate primary classrooms is on "developing the thinking that underlies children's ability to read and write mathematical symbols" (Kamii and Kamii, 1990, p. 138). In addition to needing concrete materials to handle, children need time

BUT WHAT ABOUT?

I've been trying to move away from basal readers and workbooks in my first-grade classroom, but the problem is that the parents get all upset when the work they see is mostly drawings with a few letters and difficult-to-decipher words on it. How am I going to be able to change if their reaction is so negative?

The parents of children in your classroom undoubtedly attended schools where the emphasis was on skill acquisition, using methods of formal teacher instruction of various subjects, with textbooks and workbooks for each. Understandably they are confused when the system seems so very different for them; this does not look like the education they experienced. Remember that parents can be either your most outspoken opponents or your staunchest supporters: The difference is in how well they understand the benefits of offering their children developmentally appropriate curricula and methods. Teachers and administrators who want to get parent support must commit themselves to educating and offering information that helps parents understand that the activities are purposeful, designed to meet overall learning goals in the primary years that go beyond mere skill acquisition. As parents come to understand the goals of learning to become independent thinkers, writers, and readers, of learning abilities to work cooperatively and autonomously, and, most importantly, of developing self-confidence and pleasure in their abilities to learn, they will see direct benefits to their children.

How to educate parents? In as many different ways as you can, since parents also have their own individual styles of learning. Give parents articles and excerpts from books that explain the concepts of whole language. See if you can find a teacher who has successfully used these techniques for a time, who can talk about the results that have occurred. Welcome parents into your classroom as observers and/or volunteers, so they can see excited children busily at work. Videotape, photograph, make audiotapes, and use these materials at parent discussions. Give children rotating turns to take home a "Writer's Briefcase" filled with paper and notebooks, crayons, markers, stencils, envelopes, clipboard, scissors, pencil sharpeners, stickers, and gummed labels. Include an article for parents that explains the reading/writing process and a letter describing the process used in your classroom so parents can get a better understanding of what is happening in the classroom. Let parents who are becoming believers share examples and incidents involving their children's responses to learning in developmentally appropriate ways. Make collections (portfolios) of children's work that indicate progress and learning of different skills over time, and share these with parents during progress conferences. Keep doing what you're doing, and keep aware of informing and exciting parents as well as their children. Children need to feel that their parents have confidence in their teachers and classrooms.

to make the mental connections that help them discover relationships. "Young children think better when they physically act upon objects" (Williams and Kamii, 1986, p. 25).

Figures 14–11 Teachers are constantly observing and asking questions, as part of ongoing assessment. *Courtesy Scarborough School Department.*

An important goal of primary mathematics curricula is to help children develop confidence in their ability to think things through.

> To assess children's confidence in math, a visitor can walk around the classroom while children are completing a worksheet and stop to ask individual children, "How did you get this answer?" (pointing to a correct answer). Many children immediately reach for their erasers, indicating their lack of confidence in their own ideas (Kamii and Rosenblum, 1990, p. 149).

Developmentally appropriate practice for primary-aged children related to math includes:

- Opportunities to develop number concepts by action in contexts that are personally meaningful to children, such as planning materials needed for a group activity, playing games with peers, and cooking. (See Figure 14-11.) Examples:

  Rosa's group is making cookies to share with the whole class today. "Three cups of flour," she says. "That's only two. You need to add one more."

  "You rolled five," says the teacher. "Count out five spaces."

  "This is Juanita's sixth birthday. We'll need six stars to paste on her crown, six candles for the cake, and six balloons for decoration."

- Daily life experiences in the classroom for children to use mathematical concepts, such as taking attendance, preparing for snack, table-setting, distributing materials, and enforcing the number of children allowed in each center.

  "See if there's a chair for everyone at the table, please Yolanda."

  "How many children are absent today, Jodi?"

- Opportunities to solve practical problems, investigate, and make decisions by themselves.

  "We have six cupcakes left, and there are ten children. How can you divide them so that everyone gets a fair share?"

  "He thinks you have more of the blocks than he does. How can you see if that's true or not?"

  "Heather said 3 + 5 = 9. Do you think that's right? How can you check?"

- Many objects to classify, seriate, create patterns, count, add and subtract, weigh, and measure. Some objects include traditional math manipulatives such as Cuisenaire rods, dominoes, cards, lotto and bingo games, board games, table cubes, geoboards, and parquetry blocks. Teachers use their own creativity, community resources, and theme ideas to collect objects for classroom manipulation. Examples include: nuts, seeds, pebbles, sea shells, keys, bolts and screws, poker chips, miniature toys, bottle caps, buttons, play money, golf tees, and stamps. Math-related tools are included in interest centers: various kinds of balances and scales, rulers and measuring tapes, scales, stopwatches, kitchen timers, and egg timers.

- Mini-theme projects that use math skills, such as building, cooking, measuring, that provide a context for math. Such a mini-theme could be setting up a restaurant business, with math activities ranging from planning, buying and cooking the food, and selling the food, calculating the price and the profit or loss.

There is a detailed and fascinating account of such a venture and its integration of math into the theme studies in a primary classroom (Chili Enterprise Ltd.) in Gamberg et al., 1988.

- Opportunities to work together on solving math problems, in noncompetitive activities that encourage discussions of the thinking that led to the answers.

    Tasha and Bradley are figuring out how many cookies they will have to make for each child to get two. Tasha's method is to draw two cookies beside everyone's name and add up all the cookies. Bradley lines up thirty poker chips on the table and takes two away every time he mentions a child's name. At the end, Tasha has a number and Bradley has two piles of poker chips. Tasha explains why her idea worked.

- Mini-lessons for individuals and/or small groups, as teachers discover areas children are ready to proceed in math learning:

    The teacher sits down with Tasha and Bradley to show them how to form a column of 2's for addition.

- Classroom investigation activities, such as taking surveys (What pet do you have at home? What is your favorite topping for pizza?), measurement assignments (See how many cups of sand fill the bucket), calendar graphs (How many sunny days, cloudy days, or rainy days did we have this month?) help children become deeply involved in meaningful math (Perlmutter, et al., 1993).

- Much time devoted to playing math games as a vehicle for the repetition needed for children to learn number recognition and value:

    Cynthia and Robin are playing War, each turning over a card and the one with the higher card claiming it, until all the cards are gone, and the winner is the one with the most cards. Stephen and B.J. are ready for Double War, where each turns over two cards, and the winner is the one with the highest two-card total (Kamii and Kamii, 1990).

The developmentally inappropriate practices listed below help neither children's acquisition of math skills, nor their confidence in their problem-solving abilities. Such practices include:

- a math program that focuses on the math textbook, accompanying workbooks, practice sheets and board work

- a separate time for math instruction each day, unrelated to any other curriculum subject or classroom activity

- teacher correction as children's only method of learning whether their answers are correct or not

- correct answers as the focus and goal, rather than attempting to understand children's methods or thinking

- little time for hands-on activities or materials
- competition as a primary method of motivating children to learn math facts (e.g. Row 4 against Row 2)

Assessment vs. Achievement Testing

When tax dollars in large quantities are spent on education, the issue of accountability naturally arises. Unfortunately, one of the most expedient methods of proving to the community that schools are doing their jobs is by publishing children's scores on achievement tests. "Attempts to make schools accountable through achievement testing have resulted in 'doing more of what has not been working, and doing it earlier in children's lives'" (Katz in Kamii, 1990, p. 163). When widespread testing comes into prominence, the result is a "narrowing of the curriculum, a concentration on those skills most amenable to testing, a constraint on the creativity and flexibility of teachers, and a demeaning of teachers' professional judgment" (Meisels, 1989, p. 17). The common phrase is that teachers find themselves "teaching to the test" (or indeed teaching *the* test), with the specter of tests looming over the lives of children throughout the year. The inappropriate expectations and stress of artificial test situations take a toll in the healthy development of young children, and result in too many children thinking of themselves as failures (Cutting, 1991). Achievement tests are designed to make half of the children tested come out below the average (Kamii, 1990); children developing more slowly than others, for whatever reason, are labeled and designated in a lower percentile, and everyone knows what they got on the test! Achievement tests work by comparing a group of children of the same grade level at one point in time, whereas to evaluate a child's progress in learning, the comparison needs to be made between his knowledge at one point in time to his knowledge at a later point in time. While quality early childhood programs readily accept the principle of accountability in establishing the value of the program in maximizing children's potentials, they reject the narrow focus of achievement tests (and readiness tests, as discussed earlier in this chapter). Teachers who are advocates of developmentally appropriate practice need to continue to press and educate about the dangers and ineffectiveness of achievement tests.

Observation-based assessment is, however, essential to providing curriculum and instruction that is both age appropriate and individually appropriate; assessment is, in fact, completely integrated with curriculum and instruction. While achievement tests usually work to the detriment of the child, often resulting in tracking, exclusion, or labeling on the basis of limited factors, assessment results in benefits to the child such as necessary adjustments to curriculum or more individualized instruction. Assessment demonstrates children's overall strengths and progress, instead of focusing on their wrong answers, what they do not know. Assessment supports, rather than threatens, children's feelings of self-esteem. Children are encouraged and taught skills to participate in self-assessment, rather than being the passive recipients of an outsider's narrow method of evaluating them.

The purpose of assessment is to provide teachers with information needed to plan appropriate experiences for individuals and groups to support development in all domains, to know how children are responding to curriculum and teaching techniques, and to have a body of information to communicate to parents, as they confer to make plans for children's progress.

> We need to evaluate in order to know what level of development a child has reached in various aspects of learning, what attempts the child has made to learn, and what areas the child has mastered. Evaluation helps us see what experiences the child needs in order to make progress and in what areas the most effort should be put. Basically, evaluation helps provide us with a plan for teaching (Gamberg et al., 1988, p. 216).

Assessment is an essential component of a teacher's role, since it is teachers who will make use of the information. But this does not mean that teachers function alone in the assessment process. Assessment involves joint effort and communication between teachers and children, between parents and teachers, between the larger school and community. Each member has information and insights to offer the others.

Assessment involves devising methods of regular observation of children, and recording that information systematically for future use.

Methods of Regular Observation

Systematic observation for assessment occurs in the classroom, during the variety of typical learning activities, in the usual circumstances, rather than in any specially set up situation that detracts from the natural learning environment. Teachers observe children's performance and activity during real interest center times, group work, and literacy experiences. They have conversations and individual conferences with children to gain additional insights into their style, rate, and interest in learning. Thus, there is minimal intrusion into children's normal routines and developmentally appropriate activities. Teachers do all of this over periods of time, so that they put together a consistent picture or pattern about a particular child, rather than a single observation that may or may not be representative of the child's actual accomplishment or ability. They are careful to observe for information in all the interrelated domains of development, knowing that a single observation may yield insights in several separate areas. They are aware that assessing is not comparative; that is, the assessment of an individual child takes into account diversity of learning in style and rate of learning, recognizing that family and cultural influences need to be considered. Assessment gives a picture of where each child is now, in relation to where he or she used to be.

For example, as the first-grade teacher focuses this morning on Maria, she is busy at the writing center. There are several children working near her, but she does not converse. She appears very intent on her work. She switches the pencil from her right to her left hand, and pauses frequently to rest her hand. She leaves the area to find a book in the library. The teacher observes her finding a word, then continuing to write her story. She displays quiet pleasure when the teacher comes over to ask her to read her what she is writing. Maria reads: A MTHER luks FTIR hir BBE (A mother looks after her baby). As the teacher makes notes in Maria's file later, she notes: Comfortable near other children and with adults, though does not initiate conversation. Perhaps the language? (Maria's parents speak Spanish with her at home.) Concentration good, and finds resources independently. Still having difficulty with pencil grip, and possibly handedness. Has progressed with her invented spelling to using some internal vowels. Confident and interested in her reading/writing. Interest in babies. (Maria's mother has several younger children at home.) The implications for the teacher for planning future work with Maria include pencil skills, working with her bilingually, and planning a pairing with an outgoing child. A plan is evolving, as her progress and interests are noted.

Teachers have time for regular observation because of playing a facilitator role rather than directing all of the learning experiences in the classroom. As children are actively involved with reading, writing, math, theme work or interest center times, teachers circulate among them, asking questions, encouraging efforts, and always observing. Assessment is so essential to developmentally appropriate practice that it must be built into the routine each day. Teachers find their own methods for ensuring a focus that involves each child in the classroom. They may select several children to observe during the day, or during a particular activity. They devise quick methods of note taking, such as keeping a roll of gummed labels in a pocket for making brief notes through the day, then dating them and sticking them in children's folders at the end of the day. If there is more than one adult teaching in the classroom, teachers may divide observation tasks, or confer with colleagues about their separate observations.

Recording Information Systematically

Teachers use a variety of tools for compiling assessment data on children. These may include: videotapes and audiotapes; checklists for literacy and numeration skills, social skills, work habits, or other developmental aspects; anecdotal notes; student portfolios. Meisels refers to a Work Sampling System™ (Meisels, 1993). The three complementary components are developmental checklists, portfolios, and summary reports, offering a record of both learning and instruction.

Portfolios. Portfolios may contain collections of representative work of children that illustrates their progress and achievements, such as: periodic, dated samples of drawing and artwork; samples of writing, including ideas and plans; tape recordings of their reading that can be analyzed for mistakes and self-corrections; lists of books and stories read. Certain core items, or examples of repeated work, may be collected from each child several times a year (Meisels, 1993). Children are encouraged to add their own selections of work that they feel show their progress to the portfolios. Teachers may keep working portfolios, later condensing them to show representative progress, perhaps creating exit portfolios to move on with students.

Portfolios present *primary resources* for consideration by parents, teachers, and children. In portfolios the work itself is presented as tangible evidence of progress for parents and children, rather than having to rely on teachers' reactions to the work, as might be presented in anecdotal reports or checklists. Teachers, parents, and children learn how to look at work as part of a developmental continuum, evidence of children's use of skills in a meaningful context. (See SACUS, 1991, for further discussion on the uses of portfolios in developmentally appropriate assessment of young children.)

Another method of recording may be to keep tapes of children talking with the teacher about specific questions that will help evaluate their progress in thinking logically, or their understanding of, and attitude toward, their reading.

Teachers often devise their own questionnaires or descriptive checklists related to the continuum of specific competencies they are working on with children. For example, a teacher questionnaire to document literacy competencies might include these components: knows directional conventions—left-right, top-bottom; understands consistency principle, same word is spelled the same way; knows twelve or more letter sounds (Engel, 1990). Teachers may decide on a series of books of different levels to use for observing specific reading competencies. A social skills descriptive checklist might ask questions in areas like: evidence of the child's ability to work cooperatively with others, and evidence of tolerance toward others' mistakes, and constructive help of others.

Periodically, teachers review their folders and documentation of children's progress to summarize progress and interests to date. This forms the basis for understanding where the child is before making plans for future instruction. It is also useful to do this before parent conferences or year-end reviews, or when making anecdotal written reports to parents. Regular opportunities for sharing information between teachers and parents about children's overall progress are a part of the assessment process. This communication, sometimes oral and sometimes written, focuses on descriptive, narrative accounts, using specifics from teacher observation. Because this kind of reporting focuses on children's overall strengths and progress from the last reporting period, it is supportive of parents' relationships with, and confidence in, their children. There is no absolute standard of grades or percentiles that indicates readiness to move on, so children's progress is continuous through sequential curricula.

Things Caregivers Should Not Do

Confidence and success as a learner and feelings of security within the school setting are threatened by developmentally inappropriate practices such as:

- evaluating young children only by testing and ranking them against a standardized group norm that assumes all children will achieve the same academic skills at the same chronological age and grade level

- testing all subjects regularly in the classroom, and emphasizing test scores as indications of success or failure

- reporting progress to parents using letter or numerical grades, comparing primary-aged children to others in the same class or to national averages

- promoting (passing) or retaining (failing) children who have not reached the minimum numbers on tests measuring reading and math skills, with the attendant effects on self-esteem

SUMMARY

Primary-aged children are supported in developmentally appropriate classrooms that recognize their active and experiential methods of learning. Appropriate practices that facilitate their development of reading, writing, and mathematical skills include: integrating the curriculum so that skills can be learned in a meaningful context; using a theme/project approach so that children can become autonomous learners; using whole language methods to help children progress in literacy skills; and individualization of teacher instruction to promote early success. The use of readiness tests to determine beginning eligibility and/or tracking, and achievement tests to decide later placement leads to narrow academic approaches in primary classrooms. Ongoing teacher assessment, however, is an essential component of determining the direction of curricula and instruction.

THINK ABOUT IT

1. With a group of classmates, brainstorm a list of potential theme topics for primary-aged children in your community. Refer to the criteria on page 289 to select your most appropriate choice. Create a list of suitable subtopics that might interest children.

2. Do some preliminary research on the resources you would make available for theme study—children's literature and nonfiction books, pictures and posters, field trips, visitors, other classroom materials, and possible activities. Share this with your classmates.

3. Make a collection of creative math manipulatives that could be used in primary classrooms.

(Include at least ten to twenty in each of several categories.)

4. Read more about whole language activities that develop language and literacy skills in primary classrooms. (See list of references at chapter end.)

5. Where possible, identify primary classrooms in your community that are using developmentally appropriate practices such as theme study for integrated curricula, literature-based reading instruction, and daily writing for expression. Talk with the teachers and/or visit their classrooms to see them at work. Identify practices that are different from traditional primary classrooms.

QUESTIONS TO REVIEW OBJECTIVES

1. Discuss the implications for developmentally appropriate classrooms of understanding characteristics of preoperational and concrete thought.

2. Identify goals of the cognitive/language primary environment.

3. Identify the components of an integrated curriculum.

4. Discuss whole language practices for development of language and literacy skills in: **a.** reading; and **b.** writing.

5. Describe practices of a developmentally appropriate math curriculum.

6. Contrast the effects of achievement testing and assessment, and describe the importance of assessment in planning developmentally appropriate cognitive/language primary environments.

REFERENCES AND SUGGESTIONS FOR READING

Azmitia, M. (1988). Peer interaction and problem solving: When are two heads better than one? *Child Development, 59,* 87–96.

Balaban, N. (1990, March). Statement to the Montgomery County Council. *Young Children, 4(3),* 12–16.

Bredekamp, S. (1987). *Developmentally appropriate practice in early childhood programs serving children from birth through age 8.* Washington, DC: NAEYC.

Bredekamp, S., & Rosegrant, T. (eds.). (1992). *Reaching potentials: Appropriate curriculum and assessment for young children* (vol. 1). Washington, DC: NAEYC.

Bredekamp, S., & Shepard, L. (1989, March). How best to protect children from inappropriate school expectations, practices, and policies. *Young Children, 4(3),* 14–24.

Brewer, J. A. (1990, September). Transitional programs: Boon or bane? *Young Children, 4(6),* 15–18.

Charlesworth, R. (1989, March). "Behind" before they start? Deciding how to deal with the risk of kindergarten "failure." *Young Children, 4(3),* 5–12.

Cohen, E. G., & Benton, J. (1988, Fall). Making groupwork work. *American Educator, 12,* 10–17.

Coletta, A. (1991). *What's best for kids: A guide to developmentally appropriate practices for teachers and parents of children age 4-8.* Rosemont, NJ: Modern Learning Press.

Curry, N. E. (1990, March). Presentation to the Pennsylvania State Board of Education. *Young Children, 4(3),* 17–23.

Cutting, B. (1991, May). Tests, independence and whole language. *Teaching K-8,* 64–66.

Dailey, K. A. (1991, Spring). Writing in kindergarten—helping parents understand the process. *Childhood Education,* 170–175.

Duckworth, E. (1987). *"The having of wonderful ideas" and other essays on teaching and learning*. New York: Teachers College Press.

Engel, B. S. (1990). An approach to assessment in early literacy. In Kamii, C. (ed.), *Achievement testing in the early grades: The games grown-ups play*. Washington, DC: NAEYC.

Fisher, B. (1991). *Joyful learning: A whole language kindergarten*. Portsmouth, NH: Heinemann.

Gamberg, R., et al. (1988). *Learning and loving it: Theme studies in the classroom*. Portsmouth, NH: Heinemann.

Gardner, H. (1983). *Frames of mind: The theory of multiple intelligences*. New York: Basic Books.

Gardner, H. (1991). *The unschooled mind: How children think and how schools should teach*. New York: Basic Books.

Genishi, C. (ed.). (1992). *Ways of assessing children and curriculum: Stories of early childhood practice*. New York: Teachers College Press.

Hayes, L. F. (1990, March). From scribbling to writing: Smoothing the way. *Young Children, 4(3)*, 62–69.

Hills, T. W. (1993, July). Assessment in context—teachers and children at work. *Young Children, 48(5)*, 20–28.

Hubbard, R. (1988, March). Allow children's individuality to emerge in their writing: Let their voices through. *Young Children, 4(3)*, 33–38.

Kamii, C. (ed.). (1990). *Achievement testing in the early grades: The games grownups play*. Washington, DC: NAEYC.

Kamii, C., & Kamii, M. (1990). *Negative effects of achievement testing in mathematics*. Washington, DC: NAEYC.

Kamii, C., & Rosenblum, V. (1990). *An approach to assessment in mathematics*. Washington, DC: NAEYC.

Katz, L. (1988, Summer). What should young children be doing? *American Educator*, 28–33, 44–45.

Katz, L., & Chard, S. (1989). *Engaging children's minds: The project approach*. Norwood, NJ: Ablex Publishing.

Meisels, S. (1987, January). Uses and abuses of developmental screening and school readiness testing. *Young Children, 4(2)*, 4–6, 68–73.

Meisels, S. (1989). *Developmental screening in early childhood: A guide* (3rd ed.). Washington, DC: NAEYC.

Meisels, S. (1993, July). Remaking classroom assessment with the work sampling system. *Young Children, 48(5)*, 32–40.

NAEYC. (1990, November). Position statement on school readiness. *Young Children, 4(1)*, 21–23.

National Association of Elementary School Principals. (1990). *Early childhood education and the elementary school principal: Standards for quality programs for young children*. Alexandria, VA: Author.

Neill, D. M., & Medina, N. J. (1989). Standardized testing: Harmful to educational health. *Phi Delta Kappan, 46(8)*, 688–697.

Perlmutter, J. C., Bloom, L., & Burrell, L. (1993, Fall). Whole math through investigations. *Childhood Education, 70(1)*, 20–24.

Raines, S. C., & Isbell, R. (1994). *Stories: Children's literature in early education*. Albany, NY: Delmar.

Schweinhart, L. J. (1993, July). Observing young children in action: The key to early childhood assessment. *Young Children, 48(5)*, 29–33.

Seefeldt, C. (1990). *Continuing issues in early childhood education*. Columbus OH: Merrill Publishing Co.

Southern Association on Children Under Six (SACUS). (1991). *The portfolio and its use: Developmentally appropriate assessment of young children*. Little Rock, AR: Author.

The Gesell Institute Responds. (1987, January). *Young Children, 4(2)*, 7–8.

Trepanier-Street, M. (1993, Fall). What's so new about the project approach? *Childhood Education, 70(1)*, 25–28.

Uphoff, J. K. (1990, September). Extra-year programs: An argument for transitional programs during transitional times. *Young Children, 4(6)*, 19–21.

Uphoff, J. K. (ed.). (1989). *Changing to developmentally appropriate curriculum successfully: 4 case studies*. Rosemont, NJ: Programs Educational.

Walsh, D. J. (1989). Changes in kindergarten: Why here? Why now? *Early Childhood Research Quarterly, 4*, 377–391.

Willer, B., & Bredekamp, S. (1990, July). Redefining readiness: An essential requisite for educational reform. *Young Children, 4(5)*, 22–25.

Williams, C. K., & Kamii, C. (1986, November). How do children learn by handling objects? *Young Children, 4(1)*, 23–26.

SECTION FIVE

Guest Editorial by Linda Espinosa

In my work with preschool and primary teachers, I am often painfully reminded of the need to respect teachers' need for understanding and support as they struggle with the demands of changing what they do before they have had the time to internalize the beliefs underlying the approach. My failure to give teachers adequate time to come to their own understanding of what is developmentally appropriate, combined with my haste for all teachers to enthusiastically embrace my ideas, resulted in several emotionally charged sessions. I learned that I cannot impose my beliefs and desires on other teachers, but I can provide the conditions and access to knowledge that allow teachers to come to their own conclusions about the need for change and the strength to struggle with personal change (Espinosa, 1992, p. 166).

Guest Editorial by Burchfield and Burchfield

Each person, and each school staff, must go through their own process of change, learning, and discovery to determine what developmentally appropriate practice means to them and how it can be implemented in their classroom and community. Parents are an important part of the process and must be involved if they are to buy into this new vision of the way schooling should look. Mistakes are learning opportunities for adults, just as they can be for children. Risk taking must be encouraged, and results should not be judged too quickly. The results of change take time to be effective, profound, and long lasting (Burchfield and Burchfield, 1992, p. 158).

Steps Toward More Developmentally Appropriate Practice

Introduction

In this section we will consider the process of moving through change to more developmentally appropriate practice. Teachers are not involved by themselves. Change involves parents, administrators, and others in the community. Principles and strategies for involving others in dialogue about developmentally appropriate practice will be considered, as well as patterns for implementing change in individual classrooms.

Helping Teachers Change to More Appropriate Practice

"My principal says I'm going to have to change my curriculum to fit in with more hands-on learning."

"I've been teaching ten years, and I've got things pretty well figured out, and then here they go with this DAP."

"Something's just not working well. I spend most of my time trying to figure out ways to get them to pay attention."

"There's got to be something the matter with a system where so many children have to repeat kindergarten."

Whether teachers have chosen change, or had change thrust upon them, the process of moving toward more developmentally appropriate practice in their classrooms is neither simple nor swift. There is much for teachers to learn, and much to decide. It can all seem overwhelming at first consideration, and tempting to postpone action until some more opportune time—say, well into the twenty-first century. But when change is either desirable or inevitable, teachers may find it useful to consider some helpful attitudes and actions. This chapter will present ideas to help teachers deal with changing to more developmentally appropriate practices in their classrooms.

OBJECTIVES

After completing this chapter, students should be able to:

- identify reasons why change is difficult.
- describe actions that are part of a fifteen-point plan for teacher change.

Change Is Difficult

Human beings are creatures of habit. Behaving in accustomed ways brings the security of familiar actions, with no great need to make potentially risky decisions, or even think too hard about what to do and how to do it. Moving beyond the usual way of acting necessitates learning new patterns of behavior, new skills, and facing new situations. Since most teachers are currently teaching as they have been taught to, and believe they were doing the best they can and should do, becoming mentally ready to change requires some shifts of thinking, which may be quite shaking to personal self-confidence. If I need to

311

change, what does that imply about what I have been doing? Rather than face such a question, many teachers avoid change.

When working in an educational setting, teachers are connected closely with others. Change is made even more complicated, because decisions made by just one teacher may need support and approval from administrators, other teachers, parents, and others in the community. This sometimes makes the prospect of change seem too complex to be undertaken. Realistically, the implementation of change takes a good deal of time, and involves considerable stress. Since teachers have personal lives as well as their professional lives, finding additional time often seems an impossibility and adding stress is often unwelcome.

It is not surprising, then, that teachers sometimes hesitate before embarking on actions to change the practices in their classrooms. But the alternative is even more frightening. Beyond the classrooms educators and communities identify and discuss failures in the school systems, and professional organizations outline current understandings of developmentally appropriate practice. Teachers are then faced with the realization that to make no changes puts the children they care for at risk for educational and personal failure. The need for change seems inevitable.

A Fifteen-Point Plan for Change

There are at least three dimensions of change that exist for teachers. Teachers will be learning to use new or revised materials, to use new teaching strategies and activities, and to alter their beliefs and values (Espinosa, 1992). All three types of change must be addressed.

There is no magic formula to make change painless. In fact some of the turmoil associated with transitions is a desirable part of the growing process. In addition, change can be less traumatic when teachers and their supervisors are aware of a number of helpful steps. There is not a precise order to these stages; it is not a prescription to follow, leading neatly from one accomplishment to the next. The work of one area continues simultaneously with the work of another. But awareness of some of the necessary aspects of a plan for change will benefit all.

Recognize Feelings   It is inevitable that adults facing the prospect of changing their teaching practices and environments will experience a number of emotional responses. As they identify and accept their feelings, they will be more easily able to deal with them.

One feeling teachers will feel is *anxiety.* Teachers will be nervous with the prospect of starting over to learn and try new things. Some teachers have likened it to the first days of student teaching, when they were unsure whether they could perform as expected. Trying new practices raises the possibility of failure. Teachers feel that their performance will be very much open to others' scrutiny, either through administrative or parental monitoring. Naturally, much of the initial concern is about how change will affect the individual. Self-doubt and worry is a common response when faced with a need for change; anxiety accompanies self-doubt.

If the idea for change has come from powers beyond individual teachers, there is a likelihood of feeling some *resentment.* Asking teachers to change raises inevitable personal questions about their past practices, to which they have been personally committed and have devoted their time and energies. It may be a more difficult process for this group of teachers, who will initially be more reluctant to change, or even to move through the steps of this plan. Recognizing their resentful feelings, and the reasons for them, is important.

Another emotion experienced by some teachers is *guilt*. Some teachers may have recognized that certain classroom practices were not in children's best interests, or that programs needed improvements. But in the face of institutional indifference and the very human inertia that accompanies role overload, they have maintained the status quo. Other teachers feel guilt because they are not really "teaching" the children any more, and are still adjusting to this new concept of teaching as facilitator of learning. Rather than becoming bogged down by guilt over past inadequacies or present roles, teachers need to focus that emotional energy on present and future possibilities.

Mixed in with these more difficult emotions may be the feeling of *excitement*. Facing new challenges and learning experiences offers teachers a chance to grow both personally and professionally. Excitement continues as they begin to see new responses in the children they care for.

When emotions, especially negative emotions, are not recognized, accepted, and expressed, they have a debilitating effect. Even when recognized this variety of feelings makes the time of change stressful and uncomfortable. Listen to a teacher express how she felt during the first year of instituting changes:

> Never having coped well with sudden decisions and change, I was an emotional wreck. I felt physically ill, out of control, and I pictured myself jumping off a high diving board, not knowing where or how I'd land.
>
> The first year was such a growing yet painful year....
>
> In spite of seeing so many good things happening, I did not have the confidence at the time to really enjoy the changes. I worried about everything.... I was also thinking, "I'm not sure that I can truly change, that I will ever feel happy and comfortable in this new role.... (Humphrey, 1989, pp. 18–19).

The teacher's story ended happily, however, not just in the expanded learning experiences for children in her classroom, but for the teacher herself, who finishes by thanking the children who have helped her become "a little more flexible, a little more spontaneous, and a little more willing to risk becoming 'me,' whoever that is" (p. 21). In recognizing and dealing with the emotional responses that accompany change, teachers learn to become more fully human and authentic persons. (See Figure 15-1.)

Figure 15–1 Change can bring expanded learning experiences for teachers as well as children.

Affirm Self

It is too easy, when faced with the need for change, for teachers to evaluate themselves and their past practices with an overly negative eye. In the rush to learn and implement new actions, they too frequently discard too much—throwing out the baby with the bath water, as it were. Instead, it is important to value and affirm much of their professional judgments and experiences.

For confidence in the new situations ahead, teachers need to trust and value themselves, and their abilities to offer good things to children. Moving to more developmentally appropriate practice is not a negation of what has gone before.

Instead, teachers need to view it as another step in expanding their professional expertise and learning, building on what has preceded it in time. There has been good in what has gone before; it is important that this be affirmed.

When administrators ask teachers to institute changes, it is especially important that teachers receive the implicit messages that they are trusted and valued by their supervisors. Trust and value is conveyed when teachers are given ultimate control of the change process and decisions that affect their lives, and are supported as they make decisions thoughtfully. The opposite message is given when administrators make arbitrary declarations that past practices have been deficient, and unilaterally order changes to be implemented immediately. Giving prescriptions does not affirm persons; giving options does. When teachers are given prescriptions, they feel out of professional control, and self-esteem is damaged. It has been stated that "as you do unto teachers, so will they do unto children" (Espinosa, 1992, p. 164). Developmentally appropriate practice is also applicable to adults.

A useful technique for teacher self-affirmation is to write some autobiographical material, such as answers to questions like, What are my particular strengths in working with young children? What is unique about my personal teaching/ interaction style? It is helpful for teachers to recall past experiences that have succeeded, where their professional abilities have helped children. Keeping a journal has been helpful for a number of teachers, to have a vehicle for sorting out their feelings and values.

One of the functions of a teacher support group during the time of change may be as a forum for such affirming of individuals, by the group as well as personally. When teachers are affirmed by others who are familiar with their work and style, they gain important insights and confirmation from their peers. Here the questions are, What do you most appreciate about _____'s work with children and families? What are the parts of _____'s performance that should not change?

Define Values

As a starting point in the learning/changing process, teachers need to define the present concepts and beliefs that are the foundation for their teaching practice. Developmentally appropriate practice is a unique product of developmental knowledge and individual needs, and this holds true for everyone involved, adults and children alike. Thus, teachers need to work from a solid base of certainty about the basic principles that will undergird their teaching practice. Change is easiest when teachers perceive the changes as consistent with their values. They define for themselves answers to key questions such as the nature of learning, children's capabilities, and teachers' responsibilities: What do I value most highly, and how does/will this influence my actions with children and families? The answers will be unique for each teacher, and are necessary to making decisions about classroom practice.

Again, the process of defining values may be either an individual or a group activity.

Define Preliminary Tasks and Goals

The confusion of change is lessened when teachers focus on precise understandings of what it is they want to accomplish. It can be overwhelming to combine goals of particular practices in which change will be implemented with preliminary goals of considering philosophical issues. Change will take place best when time is taken for gradual, organized, and thoughtful change.

The preliminary goal is for teachers to reflect "on their current practices and [make] their own decisions about what would work for them given their own abilities and preferences, the needs of the children, and the expectations of the schools and communities in which they work" (Hatch, 1992, p. 54).

Teachers have choices to make, and the preliminary task is to define these choices. As teachers identify the areas of concern within their own classrooms, they begin to see the benefits of potential change. These benefits provide motivation toward change.

Find a Support Base

The stress and complexity of change may be overwhelming if teachers attempt to go through the process on their own. Teachers who are involved in change, and their administrators, need to recognize the crucial importance of providing teachers with a support group during the process. The support group may include other teachers who are undergoing the same process of change at the same time. It may include parents who are eager to learn more as they support teachers who are trying to improve their children's educational experiences. It may include experienced mentor teachers, sometimes in individual pairings, who can help teachers with their knowledge and expertise. It may include administrators as sources of additional support. It may include teachers of younger and older children, to encourage communication about continuity. Whatever the size or composition of the support base, teachers need the security of knowing there are others who want to help during the time of change. Teachers should make the defining of the support group as an early priority in the process of considering change.

The support group may function informally or meet regularly with specific agenda plans. The essence of the support experience is a medium for frank and comfortable expression of the feelings and experiences of the change process. Peers and parents alike may function as a vehicle for feedback on ideas and questions, for brainstorming strategies and concerns. The sense of commonality will reinforce teacher confidence.

Acquire an Information Base

The best source of confidence for teachers moving to implement more developmentally appropriate practice is as much knowledge about what they are doing as they can acquire. Teachers do what they know how to do. To move to more developmentally appropriate practice, teachers must understand why the change is necessary, what the change "looks like," and how to become proficient at the new practices (Espinosa, 1992). Understanding and believing in the underlying theoretical assumptions is essential to successfully moving to DAP.

Teachers must use every resource available to them. Membership in local and national professional early-childhood organizations brings opportunities for meetings, conferences, workshops, as well as current information in journals. Meetings and discussions with peers enhances their communication and mutual understandings, and helps teachers feel they are not the only ones trying to move toward more appropriate practice. Reading everything they can about developmentally appropriate practice and ways of implementing it stimulates personal thinking.

Sometimes administrators will arrange for staff development to assist their teachers. Successful staff development uses a variety of methods, including lectures, hands-on activities, expert visitors, and time for reflection about current practices. Demonstrations, visits to model programs, coaching of experts and/or peers will support opportunities for teachers to gain the knowledge necessary for making their choices among practices. Staff development needs to emerge through a consensus process, rather than being imposed.

The knowledge base gives teachers confidence, as well as specific possibilities of practices they may choose to institute in their classrooms.

One Thing at a Time

When teachers who have implemented changes to more developmentally appropriate practice are asked to give advice about how to get started, the consistent response is to begin by focusing on one area at a time (Hatch, 1992).

> The rationale for such an approach is that change involves risk and uneasiness for teachers and sometimes creates confusion and uncertainty for [primary-aged] children. By keeping changes within one area, anxiety-producing factors are reduced and made more manageable than when large-scale change is introduced all at once (Hatch, 1992, p. 55).

One change at a time is less personally threatening for teachers. They feel more in control when most of their classroom still functions in familiar ways. The one-change-at-a-time approach allows teachers to devote their complete attention to planning, implementing, and evaluating the new practice, still comfortable with the rest of the routine. For example, a teacher might decide to work on changing the schedule, freeing up larger blocks of time for child-initiated free choice activities. Or another teacher might concentrate on changing outdoor play time, planning so that it no longer is an unplanned-for time to just let off steam, but rather another learning environment with rich possibilities for children's play. While these teachers concentrate on thinking about the schedule and the outdoor learning environment, everything else in the classroom proceeds as it has.

It is important that teachers be encouraged to think of the one-thing-at-a-time approach. Otherwise, if they are thinking they must change all or nothing, the task appears too insurmountably large to act on.

Think Even Smaller

Thinking about only making one change at a time helps teachers narrow their focus, but breaking the task down into even smaller steps helps give teachers a specific plan for action. "Changing the outdoor environment" is broad and general. A teacher with such a goal may plan specifics to be done as part of this overall purpose. For example:

1. Observe children's play for a week or so, defining their preferred physical activities, their other interests outdoors, their social interaction patterns, their favorite equipment, the causes of disagreements.

2. Using both individual observations and developmental age norms, consider some of the possible goals for this group in the outdoor environment.

3. List all the present equipment and materials available for outdoor play. Define the gaps. Bring the children into the conversation.

4. Inform parents and the community of goals for enriching the outdoor play environment.

5. Identify resources in the community for obtaining supplemental materials and equipment.

6. Plan specific changes to be added, in the order they will be added.

7. Plan a work party to prepare materials.

8. Adjust schedule to provide for a larger block of outdoor time.

9. Institute plan and observe play for new ideas.

10. Let parents and the community know about how the new playground arrangement is working. Record examples of the outdoor learning environment at work. Enjoy these efforts before moving on to the next plan.

Planned changes may be even smaller steps than these. For instance, a teacher might decide to make some signs and add some props to the tricycle area only, and to observe the effect of that action. The small step approach "builds positive momentum by giving teachers and children successful experiences along the way to major change" (Hatch, 1992, p. 56). If small changes are not effective, they are easy to adapt or modify.

Some teachers prefer to make an overall plan for their classrooms, then break it into smaller incremental steps. For example, a teacher's overall plan might look like this:

1. Make plans for observation schedule.

2. Analyze each interest center for how it functions, necessary materials, space, and plan improvements accordingly.

3. Organize storage for children's accessibility.

4. Begin system to help children plan choices.

5. Involve parents in helping locate and prepare materials.

6. Add a writing center.

Each item in the overall plan would clearly have to be broken down into sequences of specific actions. Breaking big changes down into smaller steps is another strategy to make change less frightening.

An Individual Pace   Having a sequential plan like the one outlined above offers security to teachers who want to organize their thinking, and evidence to administrators and parents that the changes will be carefully thought out and organized. It is important, though, that teachers proceed through the steps of the plan at their own pace, taking as long as they need with each step, to be comfortable. Teachers need to be supported to take as much time as they need to feel satisfied with their efforts and learning. It takes time to lay the proper groundwork through observation and goal-setting, to identify appropriate materials and activities, to make children and their families comfortable with new routines and ideas, to observe and evaluate the results of the new practices, and to adapt as considered necessary. Rushing not only increases the likelihood of making mistakes because of poor preparation or lack of time to make the best decisions, but it also diminishes teachers' feelings of being in control.

Set Goals   As teachers set their individual pace, they need to devise strategies to keep their eyes firmly on the goal ahead. Setting and working toward specific goals is something teachers do in their work with children. They need to use that same technique in moving themselves toward specific actions to take in implementing more developmentally appropriate practice. Many teachers have found it helpful to set themselves a goal of trying one new thing a month (Hatch, 1992; Greenberg, 1991). The specific goal can be modified (one new thing every two months) if teachers find the original goal was not realistically matched to their individual pace. Whatever the comfort level, having such a goal helps keep teachers focused on the tasks at hand, and prevents timidity or complacency from stopping progress.

Bring Parents Into the Process

Developmentally appropriate practice defines parents as active participants in helping teachers make good educational choices for their children. Whether parents have been previously involved in developmental partnerships with teachers or not, their active involvement is what teachers who are moving to more developmentally appropriate practice will strive for.

Teachers involve parents at the outset of any process of change. They will be involved initially in discussions of proposed changes in the classroom, offering their insights and concerns as important guidance. They may be involved as part of an ongoing support effort for the teacher. They may be involved in helping teachers identify, obtain, organize, or prepare developmentally appropriate materials, or in helping create and put together interesting learning centers and classroom activities (Greenberg, 1991). The involvement of parents can support the efforts of teachers in improving learning experiences for their children. Teachers benefit, of course, but parents also benefit by learning more about appropriate learning experiences for their children, and feeling essential to the process.

Enjoy the Successes

As teachers give themselves permission to set their own pace for implementing change, they should also allow time for enjoying the results of their work, and sharing the results with others. Allowing time to observe, to sit back and watch the children's responses to changes in their learning environments gives teachers the opportunity to affirm that the changes are important, that the effort is worth it. Taking the time to realize what results from the changes allows teachers to learn from the children, and to be strengthened in their desires to continue to push for the best.

Successes can be enjoyed by sharing them with others who are touched by the process. The support groups of peers and parents need to hear specific examples of classroom changes. Other teachers, administrators, and parents need to visit the classroom to enjoy watching the new learning opportunities. Children need to have opportunities to express visually and/or graphically their pleasure with the classroom changes. Bulletin board notices and pictures will help spread the word to anyone who visits the center. As Polly Greenberg says, "Celebrate! See how far you've moved toward developmentally appropriate practice!" (Greenberg, 1991, p. 33). And teachers should not wait until all changes are completed before the celebration. Enjoying the successes as they appear will give teachers increased motivation to continue.

Adapting Is a Skill

Good teachers quickly learn to discard even the most carefully crafted plans in favor of learning/teaching opportunities that present themselves in the doing. So, too, will teachers, who are involved in moving toward more developmentally appropriate practice, use that same flexibility to depart from their planned sequence in favor of changes that seem more logical, easier, or relevant at any given time.

When Teacher A was working through his plan for enriching outdoor learning opportunities, he discovered through observation that much of the children's time outdoors was spent in digging for worms and insects in the sand box. It was such a compelling interest that he decided to enlarge the indoor science area (previously a rather dusty and unused area displaying a heap of pine-cones, sea-shells, and rocks) to include a terrarium in which he added a supply of insects from his back yard. Along with magnifying glasses and some books about insects, the science area quickly became an area filled with curious children. Most of the teacher's energy that week went toward enriching the science experiences indoors, rather than working through his planned sequence for changes out-doors. Teacher A used observations of the children's play to create an interesting learning environment, adapting from his previous focus on the outdoors alone.

In just the same way, teachers will realize that their path toward developmentally appropriate practice consists of choosing from a variety of options, and their paths may be quite distinctly different from other teachers who started on the journey at the same time. They continually adapt their knowledge and try out what makes sense to them from among the array of practices they learn about. As they learn from doing, they will make personal adaptations that seem to work for the right reasons, for their children and themselves.

Some adaptations result from the feedback teachers get about the changes. Mechanisms for obtaining prompt, constructive feedback from parents, colleagues, and administrators need to be instituted. Teachers need this feedback to help them in their evaluation process.

Think Continuum

As has been stated earlier in this book, there is no all or nothing about developmentally appropriate practice. Instead, it is more useful for teachers to consider that there is a continuum between the most developmentally appropriate and the most developmentally inappropriate practice, and their current practices are located somewhere on the continuum (Hatch, 1992; Kostelnik, 1993). As they move along the continuum from one side to another, they are more closely approaching methods more suited to the natural learning style and needs of the children they teach.

For example, Teacher A's transition in learning opportunities on his playground might be represented by the following table:

Materials and Equipment		
Only playground equipment	Some choices added	Many choices, for creative, constructive, dramatic, scientific, and gross motor play
Teacher Role		
Supervision	Occasional interaction	Close observation, facilitation of children's learning

Teachers who think about the continuum toward more developmentally appropriate practice won't be quite so harsh in evaluating themselves, and will find ways to make small changes to move themselves in the direction of matching their classroom practices to more of what is defined as excellent educational practice for young children.

Focus on Rewards

More than one teacher has been heard to threaten that it would be preferable to leave the teaching profession rather than to have to submit to more change. And if it were change for the sake of change itself, this sentiment is quite understandable. But this change is for the purpose of nurturing optimum development of the potential in all of the children cared for in schools and child care centers, and incidentally enriching and promoting the development of the adults in their lives. When teachers and parents recognize the important positive benefits for all children—their success in both learning and developing a sense of capability as learners—the rewards are obvious.

For adults, there are opportunities to develop their own potential to become real, to accept themselves as fully human, with opportunities to grow and opportunities to admit their mistakes and create fresh beginnings. A spokesperson for the Reggio Emilia model of education for young children said that when things are not good for children, they are also not good for adults.

 It is an attitude of circularity. Therefore, "to educate" means additionally and above all "to be educated" through relationships with children in the same way one is educated through relationships with adults…. If we abandon this pretense of education based solely upon the capabilities and skills that children ought to acquire, we would give ourselves the gift of opening up the great potential of the unexpected (or the not expected) and of the uncertain (or the not certain). This means to be open to change, to that which is new, to others and to the child (Rinaldi, 1992, p. 7). **"**

The rewards of changing to better learning environments for children include rewards for adults.

Change is hard. But it is necessary, and can be very worthwhile in challenging teachers to reach their own potentials. In the next chapter, we will consider ways teachers can enlist the support of others in the community as they embark on this process of change.

SUMMARY

As teachers move toward more developmentally appropriate practices in their classrooms, they are helped by recognizing fifteen ideas. Among these ideas are the importance of both the support of others and knowledge, and of specific goals and plans, implemented at a pace teachers choose for themselves. Parents are an integral part of the process of change. Teachers need to recognize and express some of the very mixed feelings provoked by the prospect of change, and to validate their own judgments and experiences.

THINK ABOUT IT

1. If you work or observe in a classroom for young children, identify one practice that would be at the top of your list to change to more developmentally appropriate practice. Discuss the idea with your classmates. Together, brainstorm a list of steps that could be implemented in moving toward more developmentally appropriate practice.

2. Talk with a parent who has a child enrolled in an early childhood program. Ask them to identify a change they think would improve the learning environment for that child.

3. If you are in a position to effect a change, keep a journal documenting: your planning and decisions about the change; your feelings throughout the experience; the responses of children and other adults to your change; the ideas this particular change gives you for future changes.

QUESTIONS TO REVIEW OBJECTIVES

1. Discuss reasons why change is difficult.

2. Recall as many of the fifteen points discussed in this chapter as you can. Then discuss them fully.

REFERENCES AND SUGGESTIONS FOR READING

Espinosa, L. (1992). The process of change: The Redwood City story. In Bredekamp, S., & Rosegrant, T. (eds.), *Reaching Potentials: Appropriate Curriculum and Assessment for Young Children* (Vol. 1). Washington, DC: NAEYC.

Greenberg, P. (1991, November). Make a difference! Make your program more developmentally appropriate. *Young Children, 47(1)*, 32–33.

Hatch, J. A. (1992, September). Improving language instruction in the primary grades: Strategies for teacher-controlled change. *Young Children, 47(6)*, 54–59.

Humphrey, S. (1989, November). The case of myself. *Young Children, 45(1)*, 17–22.

Kostelnik, M., Soderman, A., & Whiren, A. (1993). *Developmentally appropriate programs in early childhood education.* New York: Macmillan.

Rinaldi, C. (1992, July 24–26). *Social constructivism in Reggio Emilia, Italy. Presentation prepared for the Images of the Child Symposium.* Newton, MA: Mt. Ida College.

16

Helping Parents and Communities Understand Developmentally Appropriate Practice

I'd like to let the children in my class choose more of their activities, but the parents would have a fit."

"My director says our families just aren't ready for the changes that would be necessary with developmentally appropriate practice."

"Our community demands accountability."

"The school board just won't accept children playing."

Comments such as these abound when teachers explain why they continue to use classroom practices, curricula, and environments that the professional standards indicate are not developmentally appropriate for young children. The understanding is that parents and communities speak with powerful voices when it comes to setting the standards in schools and programs for young children. There is no question that the successful implementation of standards of developmentally appropriate practice depends on positive acceptance and support of others. But using hesitance as the rationale for maintaining programs that do not offer the best environments for children is unacceptable. Teachers of young children must be advocates for children and their parents: watching out for, defending, and nurturing their best interests. This advocacy role includes educating parents and communities about what is in children's best interests, and lobbying for their active partnership in working toward those goals. In many cases, when teachers define the composition of the community they must convince of the merits of DAP, that community includes fellow teachers, administrators, school boards, as well as the general citizens who may or may not show active interest in early childhood education. In this chapter we will explore both reasons and methods for helping parents and communities understand and accept the need for developmentally appropriate practices in their children's schools.

While the emphasis here will be on teachers' participation in processes of involving parents and the community, it is recognized that frequently today the impetus for change comes from administrators, school boards, and parents. In these cases the principles remain the same, with teachers becoming involved in supporting the initiatives of others.

OBJECTIVES

After completing this chapter, students should be able to:

- describe the reasons parents are welcomed as partners in developmentally appropriate programs.
- identify teacher attitudes and behaviors related to parental/community acceptance of DAP.
- describe issues involved in parental/community acceptance.
- discuss general strategies for teachers promoting DAP.
- identify specific strategies related to each of the issues.

Home-School Relations

The NAEYC guidelines on DAP suggest three major reasons why early childhood teachers must work in partnership with families and communities, communicating regularly with children's parents. The partnership is essential to achieve individually appropriate programs.

Guideline 1: "Parents have both the right and the responsibility to share in decisions about their children's care and education" (Bredekamp, 1987, p. 12).

The family is the crucial environment during early childhood. Children are dependent on their families for "identity, security, care, and a general sense of well-being" (Bredekamp, 1987, p. 12). No matter how many hours children are with teachers in early childhood programs for education and care, their parents are the most important people in their lives. No teacher should ever lose sight of that fact. The task of the schools is to provide the support and knowledge that enables parents to do their job in the best possible way.

As the schools support family efforts, maximum communication between parents and teachers is essential to facilitate understanding and respect for the contribution of each party. Children benefit from greater consistency in their guidance as teachers and parents work together to plan for major socialization tasks. They also benefit from the most advantageous educational placement, made with input from both their parents' and teachers' knowledge of their individual needs.

For too long families have been largely excluded from the educational institutions serving their children. The message that parents may have received was, "Bring them to us, say good-bye, and we'll educate them. After all, we're the professional educators. And if they don't do well, it's likely something you've done (or not done) at home, since we know what we're doing!" This practice was itself developmentally inappropriate, failing to recognize the primary position of the family as the main source of nurturance for children. The more developmentally appropriate interpretation of seeing the schools as one of a constellation of community supports for families to function optimally reverses the old error and brings the family directly back into the picture, with an active voice in what happens to their children.

Guideline 2: "Teachers share child development knowledge, insights, and resources as part of regular communication and conferences with family members" (Bredekamp, 1987, p. 12).

The mutual sharing of information and insights about the individual child's needs and developmental progress helps both parents and teachers. As parents understand more about general child development knowledge, and teachers learn more about specific conditions with an individual child, there is an increase in the mutual ability to formulate specific plans and problem solve concerns. Mutual respect grows with increased communication. There are benefits for everyone—children, parents, and teachers—when there is regular communication. Professionals and parents work from different points of view and different knowledge bases. Acceptance and acknowledgment of these differences is essential.

It is beyond the scope of this chapter to discuss the many methods teachers may initiate to establish communication systems with families. For an in-depth resource on this topic, read the author's book that focuses completely on this subject: *Home, School, Community Relations: A Guide to Working With Parents* (Delmar Publishers Inc., 1992).

Guideline 3: "Teachers, parents, agencies, programs, and consultants who may have educational responsibility for the child at different times should, with family participation, share developmental information about children as they pass from one level of program to another" (Bredekamp, 1987, p. 12).

For optimum development, continuity of educational experiences is essential. Such continuity occurs only when communication about children's needs, style, and accomplishments is part of the process when children move on. Professional communication both protects and supports parents and children at times of change.

The standards define the necessity for inclusion of parents as full partners in the education of their children. As outlined above, the reasons for this inclusion are to promote communication that will increase both parent and teacher knowledge of the developing child, to facilitate mutual support and planning, and to ensure continuity of educational experiences. Teachers take the initiative in establishing and maintaining frequent contact with families.

As is proper with developmental appropriateness, the standards do not define precisely the ways in which parents are to be included, as these vary from one program to another, depending on factors such as: family structure; program structure; parental language, culture, and education; parents' work schedules and geographical location from the school; program goals and needs; and children's ages. Parents may: be occasional or regular visitors and/or observers; assist in classrooms or with individual children; provide materials or other learning resources for schools; come for conferences or have visits made to them at home; be involved with tasks related to school/classroom maintenance; raise funds and/or make program decisions. Whatever their actual roles, participation of families is seen as an integral and essential element of any developmentally appropriate program for young children.

Facilitating Understanding of DAP

As you will recall from the discussion in Chapter 1, families and communities have had their own reasons for viewing with scepticism developmentally appropriate programs for young children. The concern about failures of the educational system at large has increased demands for emphasis on the purely cognitive aspects of education, for development of specific skills and subskills that can be readily identified on standardized tests. Teachers, administrators, and their boards feel increasingly pressured to demonstrate accountability for educational budgets or fees paid by parents; results from standardized tests and easily recognizable learning (recitation of colors, shapes, counting, etc.) are a demonstrable means of proving effectiveness of programs.

Child development knowledge is not something that is part of common understanding, either by persons within the educational community, or outside it. A majority of university schools of education focus more on methods of educating children than on understanding the children themselves. Teachers and administrators educated both in decades past and present may represent the varying strands of child development/early childhood approaches, so a common knowledge base cannot necessarily be assumed (Elkind, in Brown, 1982).

Any parent will freely admit that the knowledge necessary to rear children does not come with them in the form of a direction book, or in the form of innate wisdom conferred with parenthood. Thus the average citizen falls back on what he or she remembers of early education, which is probably the sit-and-learn school of instruction most of today's adults experienced as elementary school students. So it is entirely understandable, given the combination of concern about student achievement and lack of child development knowledge, that the community at large, the educational community, and parents in particular are bewildered by the appearance and style of developmentally appropriate early childhood programs.

In the role of child advocate, it is essential that early childhood educators accept the challenge of communicating with other adults to help them understand developmentally appropriate practice. Teachers must understand how to gain respect and acceptance in their communities for the kind of programs that they know will benefit children.

Teacher Attitudes

Particular teacher attitudes and behaviors are prerequisite to working with parents and the community to gain acceptance for developmentally appropriate practice.

Confidence Teachers who want to promote acceptance of DAP need to believe wholeheartedly in the philosophy themselves. The absolute belief that children must have optimum environments to reach their individual potentials will carry many teachers through the sometimes difficult and sensitive discussions required to enlist the support of others. Teachers must believe in the practices, and in their own abilities to create developmentally appropriate environments.

This confidence comes in a number of ways. Teachers must immerse themselves in the literature related to developmentally appropriate practice. By reading books, articles, brochures, and professional journals, they become even more convinced that this is the way to go. They also gain the information that will help them become more confident spokespersons for the philosophy of DAP. Membership and attendance in professional organizations also increases teachers' knowledge base, while providing feelings of support within a community of professionals with similar goals. Of course there are uncertainties, especially as teachers themselves move to change toward more developmentally appropriate practice. But through the uncertainty teachers must be unswerving in their faith that this is the philosophical base that early childhood education must have. The confidence they generate will be positive in its influence on others. "We must show confidence; otherwise, we cannot expect affirmation by parents" (Roosen, 1992, p. 81).

Acceptance   Confidence does not mean that teachers are so filled with an air of professional importance that they are overbearing and dogmatic. The best writings on developmentally appropriate practice convey the honest sense of humbly puzzling through some real thorny philosophical and practical issues; there is no impression of haughty, this-is-the-only-right-way professionals looking down their noses at folks who don't immediately embrace their viewpoints.

Teachers will be able to work through processes of understanding and discussion with others as they recognize and respect the real desires of other adults to give children the best learning opportunities, and the real reasons for their concerns and questions. Concerns and questions should not be interpreted as resistance, but as evidence of real desire to create the best situations for children. The right to disagree, argue, and work through differences is inherent in our society; in fact, the dialogue contributes to strengthening and clarifying of the final compromises. It is easier for teachers to accept opposite viewpoints if they recognize these two ideas: that most others genuinely want the best for children, and that the process of discussion and clarifying by itself will strengthen the final product. Teachers who accept these premises will not feel they must change the world and everyone's mind within a particular time frame. They realize that pushing to force issues or agreement only makes for bad feelings, and are able to allow time for changed thinking and perceptions. Accepting the legitimacy of others' concerns and questions allows teachers to be patient and understand this as a mutual learning process.

Acceptance allows teachers to also accept themselves as human beings, with all that this implies in emotional ups and downs, dissatisfactions, mistakes, and discouragements. Seeing the opportunity to move to developmentally appropriate practice as an opportunity for personal as well as professional growth helps teachers accept themselves and others as being part of a large and challenging process.

Risk Taking   For teachers who are trying to move toward more developmentally appropriate practice, there are few certainties. Moving into new territory always means leaving behind the security of being in a predictable and known place. Teachers must be willing to take risks, to face the possibility of criticism and the certainty of making mistakes. Just as developmental appropriateness defines the need to consider individual answers for particular needs and situations for children, so too will teachers have to find answers for their unique situations, learning by trial and error. Remembering that children depend on professionals as advocates for their interests helps even the most hesitant teacher develop personal strength to take risks on their behalf.

Susan Humphrey has written a sensitive article describing some of her fears and feelings as she tried to change to more developmentally appropriate practice in her kindergarten classroom:

> " What would the principal think if he walked in and saw these children playing and moving freely from one activity to another? What would parents think when their children proudly brought home these odd-looking creations they made on their own.... What would first grade teachers think when they found out I was no longer "getting children ready" for first grade? It was an exciting but worrisome year, and I felt as though I were involved in some sort of subversive activity (Humphrey, 1989, pp. 18–19). "

Trust-building

When teachers leave themselves open to new ideas, they display a willingness to be vulnerable. Revealing that vulnerability to parents and others in the community is a way of building trust. Parents and the community must know and trust teachers who are introducing them to new ideas. Teachers do what they can to help win parents' trust; helping them get to know the teacher as a person is one way of building trust.

Trust works two ways. Teachers reveal themselves as vulnerable, learning persons to help build parents' trust in them. Teachers must also trust parents to make decisions that are good, once they are given information and empowerment. When there is mutual trust, mutual support can develop.

Communication

Teachers who actively enlist the support of parents and the community must be able to articulate clearly the philosophy of developmentally appropriate practice. They learn and practice verbal and nonverbal skills of communication, learning how to listen to and interpret others' communication as well as speak clearly. They communicate in ways that include and invite, not in ways that exclude and divide. The point of the communication ultimately is to educate, to turn "caring people into wise people" (Smith, 1990, p. 9), who have the information they need to understand the benefits of DAP. But there are not only facts involved in this process; emotions color adults' interpretation of facts. When parents are made to feel powerless in educational systems, the information they are given is filtered through their feelings and biases. When administrators or other teachers feel that their professional wisdom and experience is questioned and threatened, they react with defensiveness. Teachers must become adept at responding to others' emotional reactions, and empathizing with them. Recall the discussion on active listening techniques in Chapter 9; these techniques apply with both children and adults, in situations where feelings need to be responded to and released before other communication can proceed.

In the atmosphere of creating a dialogue, teachers try to avoid sparking a philosophical argument. They do not try to tell others what they should or should not be doing, but attempt to create a shared interest in further conversations about the goal of working together toward educational excellence. Teachers must be honest, without operating behind peoples' backs, mindful of not provoking defensive, closed responses by errors in communication.

Greenberg points out that there are specific words and phrases that are best avoided as teachers try to open dialogue with others. She suggests avoiding the phrase "developmentally appropriate" with administrators and other teachers, since it may act as a red flag of something that has become a buzz phrase in the academic community. Since the phrase smacks of professional jargon for parents, it is best to avoid it with them as well. Instead she talks about "enriching and expanding" current subjects or curricula (Greenberg, 1992). With parents she mentions "further individualizing," "strengthening the present curriculum," "enriching learning materials;" all these phrases are positive and build on present goals of parents and others. Words to avoid are words like "change," "different," "experimental," and "a new approach." Such words unsettle and frighten people unnecessarily, and make less receptive to the communication that follows. It is human nature to want to know: "What's the matter with the old ways? Haven't they worked just fine? Are they saying what we did wasn't right?" The last thing teachers working for change want to do is present an "us against them" feeling. This is one place where the goal is not to "lick" them, but to have them join in. Teachers who take the time and trouble to learn effective communication skills will be more able proponents of developmentally appropriate practice.

Key Issues

As professional educators try to help parents and the community understand the need to move to more developmentally appropriate practice, there are several key issues that must be addressed. Identifying the issues is a first step in planning strategies.

Separate Viewpoints

Everyone who could be involved in a debate on education approaches the subject from a different angle. Parents approach the subject of education from an intensely personal vantage point. For them, the key question is, "How will this help my child?" Administrators have their own concerns: "How can I justify the community expense of my educational program?" Teachers focus on, "What should I be teaching this child? What do *I* think, and how does that fit with what others are asking me to do? What do I already know and do?" The community at large wonders, "How do we best prepare the work force and citizens we will depend on?" The key issue is how to combine these separate viewpoints into one that is comprehensive of all. The energy of all can then be directed to provide a unified answer.

Trust

The issue of separate viewpoints leads directly to the issue of trust. When interests are perceived as distinct and different, the groups involved tend to view others as opposed to their best interests. Their actions are then directed to safeguarding their interest, protecting their turf, as it were. The thinking seems to be that, "I'm the only one who cares about this issue, so I have to keep my focus on my question and interest alone." Such a perspective is divisive in its narrowed approach. Participants on all sides of a debate have to come together in an attitude of trusting that will open themselves to others, assuring them that their individual questions will become the questions of the group.

Change

Very few people actually welcome change, and most actively resist it. "Better the devil you know than the devil you don't" is an expression that applies here. Even if they can see that the present educational systems have minor flaws or major defects, it is at least the system they know and are comfortable with. Familiar patterns of behaving and thinking do not require new efforts and learning. In

---

Principles That Enhance Acceptance and Success of Change

1. Involve all who are impacted by change in the planning and decision making.

2. Reduce competition among the groups involved.

3. Demonstrate the practicality of the change.

4. Help participants see that change will improve their status.

5. Recognize the unique roles of individuals involved in change.

6. Center leadership for change on group members who already have recognition.

7. Acknowledge and build on the values of the group.

8. Make the intentions and direction of change appear as guided efforts, rather than chance.

9. Continue evaluation of the change long after initial implementation.

10. Include extensive communication, additional training as needed, support services, and regular reporting.

Figure 16–1 Principles for any change process. *Adapted from Uphoff, 1989.*

our modern world, most people are fairly busy, and the prospect of having to spend more time and energy in learning about new ideas and developing new plans for action is quite daunting. Without the familiar understandings and guidelines, people feel adrift and incompetent. Change represents a challenge to individual self-esteem, and people do what they can to protect their self-esteem. Change, then, will be avoided, unless people can be led to see that it is in their best interests. (See Figure 16-1 for a summary of key principles for any change process.)

Knowledge Base   It would be misleading to suggest that there is no disagreement within the early childhood educational community about learning and development theories. It would be simpler if there were one theory or one method that has the full support of all researchers. (See Chapter 1.) But this is not so. The proponents of other theories of learning have their voices. Those who argue about the vital importance of including computers in preschool classrooms, for example, are as definite about the need for technological education as some spokespersons for developmentally appropriate practice are in denouncing computers as plugged in, MTV-generation worksheets. It may be that those approaching the question from different theoretical bases will not be able to agree; or it may be that, as David Elkind suggests, it is time to unite the separate strands of child development research and educational practice. In either case the issue is that "when researchers and practitioners interact, they lack a common language and a common outlook on what is important and what is real" (Elkind in Brown, 1982, p. 4). Finding ways to explore commonality is the issue here.

And if the knowledge base of professionals is varied, the knowledge of parents is largely a matter of remembered experience, news headlines and magazine articles, and oral traditions. The issue of offering information to parents in ways that do not suggest professional superiority is important.

Principles for Enlisting Support

Being convinced that they want to provide developmentally appropriate learning environments for young children is not enough; teachers must develop plans of action to enlist the support and involvement of parents and others in the community. No matter what the circumstances and what the issue, teachers will find it helpful to keep some general principles in mind.

Prepare   No matter how strong the enthusiasm, enthusiasm alone will neither move administrative mountains nor change community minds. Teachers need to take time to prepare information, materials, and plans. They need to plan ahead, to see what the action plan in the classroom and out in the community will be. They need to do their reading and research, not only to learn more about principles of DAP, but about how changes have been implemented in other communities. (See Uphoff, 1989; Burchfield and Burchfield, 1992; Espinosa, 1992.) Imagining what the questions will be allows for advanced preparation of answers. Figuring out the potential sources of resistance helps teachers plan how to involve opponents in discussions at the outset. Teachers who have taken the time for thorough preparation will show a confidence that is contagious.

Find Support   Being the only voice crying in the community is an extremely lonely thing. Before opening the discussion to the community, teachers should try to enlist support of others interested in educational excellence via DAP. Teachers should begin with informal conversations with other teachers and with parents. As they share articles and information, they will find others who are immediately interested. It is important to have allies to plan and discuss with, and to share the task of communicating the information and vision of DAP. The joint dialogue as others are included enriches and strengthens teachers' plans of action.

Slower Is Better   Jumping in with both feet ready to run may actually mire the process down. When people are overwhelmed, many tend to get paralyzed with confusion or concern that prevents action. Teachers should remember that they have undergone a process of learning about DAP and becoming ready to act. They need to allow plenty of time for others to become first ready to learn, and then ready to absorb new information and draw conclusions about the implications of the information. Teachers of young children are accustomed to thinking about children's readiness to learn, and finding ways to facilitate their becoming interested and ready. This same principle holds true for adult learning.

As the process of dialogue moves toward plans for action, this same principle of going slowly holds. Programs fail when participants try to do too much, too quickly.

Include, Don't Exclude

Eventually, teachers will have to concede that they can't win everyone over to their viewpoints. But in the beginning, they truly don't know who will or who won't get on the DAP bandwagon. Teachers need to remember that it is much easier to work with people than against them. Others can be partners or adversaries. Teachers must not make assumptions that particular persons will not agree unconditionally. Everyone deserves to be given a chance to learn more. If teachers create an atmosphere of openness, not an impression of trying to slip their programs in behind someone's back or in the face of opposition, they are less likely to incur strong resistance. Alienating administrators or citizens at the outset makes for heavy going down the stretch. Some who will never be converted to the DAP viewpoint might still allow teachers to make changes in their classrooms, provided they haven't been alienated by being excluded from the discussions. Again, teachers should remember that dialogues are richer when the various viewpoints are included.

Persist As a Realist

Schools and programs won't be changed in a day, or even a year. Teachers committed to making their classrooms more developmentally appropriate need to realize that change creeps in little by little, not with a big, disruptive bang. The meetings that seem to bear no fruit one year need to be continued the next. Teachers need to adopt a philosophy of settling in for the long haul, not becoming discouraged because initial efforts are not as productive as anticipated.

But persistence should be tempered with optimistic realism. While teachers might like to see all children experience the benefits of learning in developmentally appropriate classrooms, that hope is beyond their immediate control. What is within their power to affect is the learning experiences of the children within their own classrooms. As discussed in Chapter 15, teachers need to realize they can make changes within their own areas of responsibility, even as they are working toward bigger changes.

Strategies to Resolve Issues with Parents and the Community

By keeping focused on the issues that provide the main sources of contention, teachers can formulate specific strategies that have been effective for others.

Strategies Focused on Separate Viewpoints and Trust

Since the issues of seperate viewpoints and trust are so closely linked, they will be discussed together here.

Bring the different groups together. Everyone deserves a chance to be heard, and to hear the viewpoints of others. The distinct components of those involved with children's education need to be assembled; teachers, parents, administrators, boards, civic and business leaders, and others in the community, need to be involved in initial discussions. Organizers find times that enable everyone involved to attend meetings, even if it means holding some meetings during the day and others in the evening. It is important that all groups be brought into the process at the same time, at the outset. Bringing groups in separately increases the lack of trust that is inherent when different initial interests become obvious. The groups who come together later may feel that others have collaborated and excluded them.

Many methods of advertising the meetings need to be used: TV and radio spot announcements, newspaper articles, school notice boards, personal invitations, announcements to church and other local groups. The community needs to know that there is interest in improving things for children in schools, and to become excited about their possible participation in such a project.

Create a positive atmosphere. As the initial group meets, it is important that a positive atmosphere be created. Participants should not feel they are meeting together in a problem-laden crisis atmosphere; this is likely to make people defensive. Instead, the approach that is helpful is to work from strengths. As parents, teachers, and others identify the current strengths of the educational programs, a positive framework is created. From this beginning it is appropriate to move to discussions of additions that could promote optimum conditions and excellence. Accentuating the positives at the beginning allows for development of a spirit of collegiality and mutuality, a prerequisite for trust.

Provide for group integration. The larger group may remain divided, at least mentally, into the separate strands of specific interest groups, unless effort is made to dissolve the arbitrary boundaries. Creating small groups composed of several members of each of the distinct subgroups—for example, teachers, administrators, parents, community members—to work on common discussion or investigation goals creates a feeling of unity in common tasks. It is also easier to express opinions in a smaller group than in a large one. Knowing one another is facilitated by the smaller group; personal comfort is necessary to express beliefs freely and honestly. The concept of brainstorming allows for an atmosphere where everyone is comfortable making contributions, of there being no wrong answers or preset agendas. Group integration avoids the "us against them" problem.

Provide for a common focus. When people with different perspectives and questions come together, their interaction is facilitated by giving them a common focus. In the case of developmentally appropriate practice, the common focus is the best interests of children. Asking the groups to articulate specific comments and questions about children's learning needs and styles helps participants move from their personal issues to a focus that may unite them for future goal setting and planning. Some groups have found it helpful to use the published guidelines as a focus for thinking through their own specific practices in their programs. Using an outside source such as the NAEYC guidelines removes the subject from the personal realm, and gives the group a specific starting point. Trust develops as the group members exposes themselves to new material, and through the learning experience of working to interpret it. Defining specific task goals for the small groups prevents straying into less productive conversations, although it should be emphasized that everyone's contribution is important.

Allow time to explore issues. It is tempting for teachers who are already committed to concepts of developmentally appropriate practice to feel the group should move quickly to an agenda of implementation. But time spent in exploring beliefs, experiences, questions, and issues is time well spent. The group will not be able to move on productively unless they themselves have become committed to the concepts of a need for a change. As members feel they are pressured to adopt someone else's ideas, their resistance will grow. It is better to allow enough time for the establishment of group comfort, for initial conversations, and for moving to work on the initial tasks. During the introductory processes of group meetings, teachers may discover some strong advocates and spokespersons for children's issues. As the voices strengthen, widespread support and mutual trust will be a positive by-product.

Strategies Focused on Change

Start with consensus. The concept of change is frightening and unsettling for most everyone. It is important to find ways of minimizing the stress involved. One important way is to gain maximum acceptance and approval of change. For those involved to support plans for change, they need to have plenty of time to discover that the proposed changes are consistent with their present position and values. Feeling that change offers personal or professional advantages over a former system allows adults to accept the inevitable difficulty that accompanies change. As changes are proposed within positive frameworks of present status, those involved will find it less threatening.

Make a plan. The group may identify a number of concrete changes that are necessary in order to institute developmentally appropriate practices in the educational program. Too much change at any one time is counterproductive, producing too many issues and concerns simultaneously. It is important for new strategies to be identified at the outset in an overall, long-term plan, which will then be initiated gradually. Knowing what the overall plan entails allows participants to realize that their viewpoints have been acknowledged, even though the plans may be for implementation later in the timeline. Concrete, realistic plans provide security during times of change. It is important to start from the philosophical base to make specific plans.

Move slowly. Initially, implementing only one or two changes will prevent stress. It is better to change only one practice, allowing enough time for preparation, organization, thorough exercise, and evaluation. Doing one change well gives the participants feelings of confidence for future changes. Going slowly also helps the community feel they are not having change thrust upon them faster than they are ready to proceed.

Keep everyone involved. The more the community is involved in change, the likelier the changes will proceed as planned. Teachers and administrators need to keep both the goals and the plans in the public eye, using newsletters, newspaper articles, and local television and radio programs. The group meetings that began the process should continue, as a vehicle for giving information and soliciting feedback. During the times when teachers are implementing change in the classroom, support is essential. The more people feel that this change is something they have actively participated in, both in the decision making and the doing, the more likely they will be to support it. The community should be brought into the schools regularly, to see what is actually occurring.

Strategies Related to Knowledge

Inform, inform, inform. Teachers who have become educated in the philosophy of developmentally appropriate practice have an obligation to share that knowledge with parents and the community they are trying to influence. If teachers do not adequately do this, their efforts will be weakened. It is important that those who are new to the ideas realize that they are not just the ideas of a few local teachers who want to change things. They need to understand "there is a universe of theoreticians, researchers, policymakers, teacher educators, administrators, teachers, and parents out there who think as you do" (Greenberg, 1991, p. 32). Teachers need to share articles, brochures, books. They may offer lending libraries to parents and colleagues; they may distribute ideas in newsletters and copy articles that are appropriate. They may summarize articles and have them translated when parents and the community have various language backgrounds. They may use videos available from professional organizations, or invite guests who have had experience with implementing DAP. Later they may arrange classroom visits for group members to observe developmentally appropriate classrooms in their community or elsewhere. They share studies and reports of communities that have tried to implement more developmentally appropriate practice (Uphoff, 1989). They do all of this, and continue to think of innovative ways to bring information to the attention of those they are trying to influence. They remind themselves of the variety of learning styles, and make assortments of informational options available. They are mindful of time constraints on busy people, and do not present burdensome overloads.

Inform as partners. There is a delicate strategy necessary in giving information to others, whether they are professionals or lay persons. If teachers offer the information as partners united by their common interest in children, they offer it in ways that allow the other adults to accept the information without being turned off by a superior manner, or a feeling they have been belittled. Comments such as: "Know you'll be interested in this"; "Here is some information that might help us in our discussion"; "Thought this book about establishing learning centers might help us" are inclusive approaches that allow teachers to spread information about developmentally appropriate practice in ways that are more likely to be accepted (Greenberg, 1991, p. 33).

Integrate information and practice. Recognizing that humans do not live in the abstract: teachers must allow opportunities for members of the community to discuss the practical implications of the information they are receiving. If others—most likely other teachers or administrators—have information that presents alternative theories or viewpoints, teachers accept that information, and work to see if there is a common ground for reconciling the viewpoints. All information is accepted, without feeling a need to screen out that which disagrees with the DAP approach.

Keep information flowing. As changes are instituted within educational programs, there is still a need for information. As observations, assessments, and evaluations are made, this information should be readily available to the involved community. Teachers must remember that valuable insights result from the analyses and questions of others.

When dealing with the idiosyncrasies of human nature and people with a variety of information and experiences influencing their perspectives, teachers should expect that there is no magic strategy that will miraculously win universal support for the philosophy of developmentally appropriate practice. Nevertheless, attention to meeting peoples' needs for trust, involvement, and knowledge permits them to contemplate and support change. It is not easy, but it is worthwhile.

SUMMARY

Parents must be included in developmentally appropriate programs for young children, as resources for understanding individuality, as partners in setting goals and assessing children's progress, and planning for continuity of educational experiences. Specific teacher attitudes and behaviors are important in promoting acceptance

of developmentally appropriate practice. In planning strategies to promote acceptance, teachers need to recognize specific issues that involve parents and the community, and plan strategies to help with each of these issues. Persistence and optimism is important.

THINK ABOUT IT

1. Find out if there have been teachers in your community involved in trying to implement more developmentally appropriate practices in their classrooms. If there are, try to talk with them, in class or out, about their experiences. What successes and failures did they have in trying to gain support from parents and the community? What progression of steps did they take?

2. With your classmates, plan a hypothetical initial meeting for introducing concepts of DAP to parents and the community. What methods would be used to encourage a positive group atmosphere, and build feelings of participation and trust? What information, if any, would be given?

3. Role-play the dialogues that could occur when the following situations take place in meetings with parents and the community:

   a. A school board member asks: "What I want to know is, how will these changes you're talking about help improve our overall test scores in the state?"

   b. A parent asks: "With so many kids failing kindergarten, maybe the real problem is with our teachers? Maybe we need to look at the training they're getting."

   c. An administrator asks: "Are you telling me we'll have to increase our budget for new materials?"

QUESTIONS TO REVIEW OBJECTIVES

1. What are the three major reasons in the standards for including families in developmentally appropriate programs?

2. Describe several teacher attitudes and behaviors necessary in promoting DAP.

3. Identify four issues that are involved in gaining parental and community acceptance of DAP.

4. Discuss the general strategies helpful for teachers trying to promote DAP.

5. Discuss specific strategies that can help with each of the issues discussed in question 3.

REFERENCES AND SUGGESTIONS FOR READING

Black, J. K., & Puckett, M. B. (1987). Informing others about developmentally appropriate practice. In Bredekamp, S. (Ed.), *Developmentally appropriate practice in early childhood programs serving children from birth through age 8.* Washington, DC: NAEYC.

Bredekamp, S. (1987). *Developmentally appropriate practice in early childhood programs serving children from birth through age 8.* Washington, DC: NAEYC.

Burchfield, D. W., & Burchfield, B. C. (1992). Two primary teachers learn and discover through a process of change. In Bredekamp, S., & Rosegrant, T. (Eds.), *Reaching potentials: Appropriate curriculum and assessment for young children* (vol. 1). Washington, DC: NAEYC.

Elkind, D. (1982). Child development and early childhood education: Where do we stand today? In Brown, J. F. (Ed.), *Curriculum planning for young children.* Washington, DC: NAEYC.

Espinosa, L. (1992). The process of change: The Redwood City story. In Bredekamp, S., & Rosegrant, T. (Eds.), *Reaching potentials: Appropriate curriculum and assessment for young children* (vol. 1). Washington, DC: NAEYC.

Gestwicki, C. (1992). *Home, school, community relations: A guide to working with parents.* Albany, NY: Delmar Publishers Inc.

Greenberg, P. (1991, November). Make a difference! Make your programs more developmentally appropriate. *Young Children, 47(1),* 32–33.

Humphrey, S. (1989, November). The case of myself: Teaching as a limiting activity. *Young Children, 45(1),* 17-22.

Roosen, J. (1992, July). Reflections of a teacher. *Young Children, 47(5),* 80–81.

Smith, M. (1990). Excellence and equity for America's children. In McKee, J. S., & Paciorek, K. M. (Eds.), *Early Childhood Education 90/91.* Guilford, CT: Dushkin Publishing Group, Inc.

Uphoff, J. (ed.). (1989). *Changing to a developmentally appropriate curriculum successfully: 4 case studies.* Rosemont, NJ: Programs Education.

A Look at Developmentally Appropriate Programs

O ne concept that has been stressed throughout this book is that the standards for developmental appropriateness are not intended as an exact prescription, but as philosophical guidelines and questions. As teachers, administrators, and parents make decisions for individual children and specific educational programs, they create their own developmentally appropriate environments and curricula. Each will have things in common with other developmentally appropriate programs, and each will be the distinctive product of the thoughts and efforts of the particular decision makers.

Because one method of learning to apply new information is to observe working models, it seems valuable to examine different programs that are working from principles of developmental appropriateness. Schools and centers for young children that offer fine examples of developmental appropriateness may be found everywhere in this country, as well as in other countries. Students may be fortunate enough to have opportunities to teach or observe in such classrooms. The author welcomes learning of names and addresses of such programs, for future visits and writing. Please write to her care of the publisher. Two programs have been chosen for description in this chapter. The preschools in the town of Reggio Emilia in northern Italy have received international attention increasingly in the last decade as child- and family-centered programs of excellence for children aged birth through six years. As more and more professionals have visited and studied the programs, they have become the source of ideas for stimulating the redefinition of developmental appropriateness (Bredekamp, 1993). The school system in Scarborough, Maine, has been cited for excellent work with nongraded multi-aged groupings, parental choice, theme/project in-depth study, and individualization.

It is intended that, as students read of these programs serving children from birth through age eight, they will find common questions, and interesting possible solutions as they find their own way toward more developmentally appropriate practice.

OBJECTIVES

After completing this chapter, students should be able to:

- describe the components of different developmentally appropriate programs for young children.

The Schools of Reggio Emilia

Figure 17–1 The physical beauty and attention to detail in the environment at Reggio Emilia is remarked on by visitors. *Courtesy Betty High Rounds.*

Immediately after the end of World War II, under the leadership of some committed parents, preschools opened in the northern Italian town of Reggio Emilia. Today there is government support (12 percent of the town's annual budget) for thirty-five schools serving children ages three to six years and infants up to age three, about 47 percent of the town's preschool population and 33 percent of its infants.

There are several features about these schools that have captured the attention of the education community. Leading the list is the philosophy of children's active collaboration with adults to construct their expanding understandings of their world. Also noteworthy is the children's use of many kinds of symbolic language to express this understanding and involvement with the world around them. An exhibit entitled "The Hundred Languages of Children" has toured through Europe since 1984, and in America, beginning in 1987. The images presented by the children's art are truly astounding, provoking questions about young children's creative capabilities. Visitors to the centers comment on the physical beauty and attention to detail in the classrooms and buildings. (See Figure 17-1.)

Beyond the beauty there are components of the programs that deserve closer scrutiny in a consideration of educational excellence. A recent article in *Newsweek* magazine named a representative school from Reggio Emilia as one of the Ten Best Schools in the World, with much for us to learn from it (*Newsweek*, 1991). While it is necessary to caution that the Reggio concepts could not be transported to America without modifications to account for cultural differences, such a model of excellence must be considered. Some of the components to be discussed here include: programs that are child-centered, that is, based on the child's relationship with his or her environment and others; the environment as teacher; children's interests and expression as curriculum projects; teaching roles and relationships; a sense of community, seen in teachers' collaboration with colleagues and the integral involvement of parents.

Child-Centered Programs

At the heart of the Reggio Emilia philosophy is a dedication to the principle of the rights, potential, and strengths of children. Children are seen as "rich, strong, and powerful ... with rights rather than simply needs ... a unique and unrepeatable subject ... seeking completion" (Rinaldi, 1992, p. 3). Children are full of power and value, and are able to educate not only themselves but also to educate adults through their relationships with them. Adults at Reggio value their interaction with children as opportunities for adults to also develop their personal potential. This contrasts with the philosophy implied in many programs that children are weak, with many needs that adults must supply. (See Figure 17-2.)

> *It is thus necessary to abandon the desire to shape the behavior of children to conform to our own image of childhood, because by doing so we tend to bend the identity of the child to mirror our own adult identity. What should never be forgotten is that each child bears a unique initial blueprint towards life. Therefore, the existence of a child cannot be reduced to some plan to carry out, nor can it be shaped according to preconceived objectives and rigidly established schedules (Rinaldi, 1992, pp. 6–7).*

Figure 17–2 A concrete evidence of the philosophy that children are powerful is shown in these baby beds. Note the low side, so crawlers can get out of bed and join the group when ready. *Courtesy Betty High Rounds.*

The concept of the reciprocality of adult-child relationships is emphasized as a third alternative to the two more usual attitudes of relationships between adults and children: either adults dominating children or children dominating adults. This is child-centeredness where both child and adult grow to fuller potential, as partners.

Children are not all expected to do the same thing, and their originality is valued. They are given the time they need. Activities may go on for hours, days, or months. They are given time to stop and figure out what they have done and what they will do next. It is the child's active learning task to construct their own understandings, and interaction with the adult guides this learning process. Teachers become immersed in children's ideas, not simply centered on their own.

The Reggio approach maintains that children seek communication and interaction with others from the start, as their way to experience authentic growth. This assumption demands that children feel supported in their right to this interaction, and also feel themselves to be an integral part of the relationships and communication within the school.

> *Children must feel that the whole school including the space, materials and projects, value and sustain their interactions and communications. Children need and love to see that adults—parents and teachers—interact and communicate with them but also among themselves* (Rinaldi, 1992, p. 4).

Adults convey the message to children that their work and learning are taken seriously. Objects of interest to children, from their homes or recent experience and creation, are beautifully displayed in classrooms and hallways. The centers reflect children's home and cultural lives, with items from real kitchens for decoration and play things. Teachers and children continually adjust the space to reflect their interests.

Environment as Teacher

Visitors to the Reggio schools come away talking first about the environments as places with personality, reflecting the personal and cultural history of the children and adults who share the space (Gandini, 1991). The educational significance of thoughtfully designed spaces is part of the Reggio philosophy as expressed by an early leader, Loris Malaguzzi:

> *We value space because of its power to organize, promote pleasant relationships between people of different ages, create a handsome environment, provide changes, promote choices and activity, and its potential for sparking all kinds of social, affective, and cognitive learning. All of this contributes to a sense of well-being and security in children. We also think that the space has to be a sort of aquarium which mirrors the ideas, values, attitudes, and cultures of the people who live within it* (Gandini, 1991, p. 6).

The rooms are beautiful, with an attention to aesthetic detail of color, light, plants, reflections, and arrangements of objects, in such often overlooked areas as bathrooms, kitchens, hallways and entrances. Natural objects and items from home experiences are displayed as a record of recent events in the children's lives. The cultural life of the community is reflected in the objects hanging on the walls. Children's expression, in many media and beautifully arranged, is displayed as an ongoing commentary on current and past projects undertaken by

Figure 17–3 The program at Reggio Emilia emphasizes the importance of the environment as the "third teacher." *Courtesy Betty High Rounds.*

children. Teachers' photographic records of children's learnings activities are also displayed along with the children's work, to inform parents and to stimulate more thinking by children. (See Figure 17-3.)

The emphasis on artistic creativity is seen in a central *atelier* with an abundance of all manner of art supplies where an *atelieriste* (a teacher trained in individual arts) works with the children, as well as a mini-atelier in each classroom, with supplies and space for children to work on long-term projects. There is space enough for children to create together; one of the goals for children at Reggio Emilia is for them to experience teamwork and collaboration in the creative process—to produce something beyond what any one child could produce.

The planning of space includes more than the physical setting, as teachers consider the social environment as well. There is a central gathering area, or *piazza*, in each school, where children of different ages can play together. The classrooms for the separate age groups and the atelier open off the piazza; so does the kitchen, with large windows to allow children to observe. (They often assist as well.) Each classroom has a large central area for children and teachers to meet together, emphasizing interaction and mutual learning. Bathrooms are decorated to recognize their function as social gathering places. There is evidence of encouraging personal communication; small boxes with each child's name serve as personal mailboxes children use for giving one another gifts and messages. Each school also has space in the entry way where parents and families can gather. Gardens and courtyards extend communication spaces. The environment is made homelike and comfortable for children and adults. "The layout of physical space in the schools encourages encounters, communication, and relationships" (Gandini, 1993, p. 6).

Children are assigned to classes of twenty-five that stay together, deepening relationships with their two teachers, for three years. The environment at Reggio is carefully constructed to meet social goals of promoting community, as well as providing for creative stimulation and cognitive reflection. Teachers realize:

> *...the fundamental role played by the school environment, i.e. the rooms, furnishings, materials, equipment, and toys. It is essential that the environment can provide conditions for being together and being separate, can handle large meetings and small intimate gatherings; is capable of providing a sense of security as well as a desire for adventure, and can answer the children's needs and rights but also those of adults. The environment thus becomes a third teacher, that is able to work with the teaching team, but also, as both container and content, has the potential to replace the teachers (Rinaldi, 1992, p. 10).*

Children's Interests As Curriculum

At the core of Reggio Emilia's curriculum are projects devised as outcomes of children's initial interests. An initial experience may be planned by the teachers in their efforts to help children explore their cultural heritage or their physical surroundings, or it might be the result of a spontaneous happening, responded to by the teachers. Almost any experience that intrigues children can become the basis of the project. The projects are undertaken in great depth and detail, using a variety of investigative methods and a variety of visual and graphic forms to express the learning experience. The interaction of teachers and children in planning the projects allows learning to become rich, complex, of many forms,

Figure 17–4 Children take the initiative in their projects, while adults support, observe, and document. *Courtesy Betty High Rounds.*

taking directions which no one has predetermined. Teachers support the children's active learning with encouragement, observing, finding ways of helping them organize their ideas, supplying materials. But the driving forces behind the projects are the children's curiosity and their pride of accomplishment.

Projects may last for days or months, in the belief that long periods of time allow both children and teachers to stay with an idea. Projects may involve the entire class or only small groups of children, and may be of three types: those resulting from children's natural encounters with their environment; those that develop from mutual interest of teachers and children; and those that are initiated by teachers based on observed cognitive/social needs of one or more of the children (New, 1990). (See Figure 17-4.)

It might be best to illustrate the Reggio Emilia project approach by the story of the investigation of the lion, made fairly well known now by the videotape made in Reggio in 1987: *To Make a Portrait of a Lion.*

The teachers planned a trip to the historic center of Reggio Emilia, to the busy market square, presided over by a stone lion. The video captures the children's instant fascination with the statue, as they touched it, climbed on it, and explored it from all angles. The teachers had brought along sketching pads for the purpose of recording the children's perceptions. Back at the school, the children had opportunities to talk about the lion, and to explore the photographic images made by the teachers. As the project continued, children worked with clay, with paints, with puppet props and costumes, to continue to re-create their experiences. The lion became the basis for a rich and extended project experience.

Integral to this process is the creative use of materials by children to represent and communicate their learning. The creative activity is not imposed on the child; the creative experience starts from a desire of the child. Lilian Katz comments that several of the things we can learn from Reggio Emilia are related to the creative project work. An intriguing thought is that the teachers "seem to have higher expectations than most of us in the United States of young children's abilities to represent their thoughts, feelings, and observations with the graphic skills they already have at hand, namely drawing, painting and other graphic arts" (Katz, 1992). Another interesting idea is that when children are using their drawing or other work as a basis of more discussion and learning, they "attend to it with great care," not needing to take it home every day, but allowing the thinking about the project to build. Finally, the direct experiences and support that children receive in artistic expression from their atelieriste "does not necessarily inhibit children's abilities or desires to use the media for abstract, creative and imaginative expression as well."

Providing experiences, creative media, and skills as possibilities to express thoughts and concepts is a goal at Reggio Emilia. (See Figure 17-5.) Loris Malaguzzi comments:

Figure 17–5 Creativity is valued as a means of expressing thoughts and concepts. (Note also the teacher documenting the activity.) *Courtesy Betty High Rounds.*

" What we like to do is to accompany a child as far as possible into the realm of the creative spirit. But we can do no more. At the end of the path is creativity. We don't know if the children will want to follow the path all the way to the end, but it is important that we have shown them not only the road, but also that we have offered them the instrument—the thoughts, the words, the rapport, the solidarity, the love—that sustain the hope of arriving at a moment of joy. (Goleman et al., 1992, p. 83). "

Teacher Roles and Relationships

Figure 17–6 Adults are available as resource people, and for warm interaction. *Courtesy Betty High Rounds.*

"The adult should not try to teach the child anything which the child could not learn on his/her own" (Rinaldi, 1992, p. 6). This idea moves beyond the traditional role of teacher as speaker, transmitting information, competencies, and skills, to the concept of the teacher as "listener" (Rinaldi, 1992). Teachers are listeners and observers in any good developmentally appropriate program, asking questions and reflecting on the responses to know what materials and ideas children can use to expand their understanding. But teachers at Reggio create incredible depth to their listening and observing. They routinely take notes and photographs and make tape recordings of children's play and discussion. These records are the basis for hours of discussion with other teachers each week. The documentation allows them to focus on children's flow of ideas and questions, as well as to help them illustrate to children and parents what is being learned and how.

Listening challenges adults—teachers and parents—to be available as "resource people to whom the child can (and wants!) to turn" (Rinaldi, 1992, p. 5). But as resource people, adults do not simply satisfy or answer questions, but help children find the answers, and "more importantly still, to help them ask themselves good questions" (Rinaldi, 1992, p. 6). The adults realize that they are incomplete without the child's interaction, that as the adult educates the child, so too the child educates the adult. The emphasis is on the child in relation to other children, to teachers, and to parents. (See Figure 17-6.) Interaction between teachers and children gives importance to the role of each in the learning process.

Collaboration With Other Adults

 The school is a system of communication, socialization, and personalization, a system of interactions in which the three inseparable and integrated subjects of education—children, educators, parents—are primarily involved. To carry out its primary task, the school cannot worry about and be involved only in the children's welfare; it must also pay attention to the teachers' and parents' welfare. The system of relationships is so highly integrated that the well-being or the lack of well-being by one of the three protagonists is not merely correlated with that of the others, but it actually depends on them. This well-being is closely linked with the quantity and quality of awareness they have of the reciprocal rights, needs and pleasures and the occasions for meetings and get-togethers that form a natural part of a system of permanent relations.

The participation of the families is an integral part of the educational experience (Rinaldi, 1992, pp. 8–9).

In the three years that children remain together in Reggio Emilia infant and preschool classrooms, parents and teachers have time to develop real partnerships. From the historic beginning, parents have been deeply involved with the schools of Reggio Emilia, and they see this participation as a right. They meet regularly with classroom teachers, in small groups with other parents, and for parties and entertainment. They make decisions on the managing council. They participate actively in the day-to-day life of the school, influencing it with the culture of their individual families, and being influenced by its visions and experiences with their children. Albums are created for each child, for family members and school personnel to fill with notes, photographs, anecdotal observations, for communication back and forth between home and school, to document the child's progress, and to give children evidence of the importance adults place on their lives (New, 1990).

There is the feeling of a large extended family. Parents share family recipes with the cook, and form stable relationships with other young families, effectively multiplying the community of adults available to children, and supporting the schools.

"This community of adults shares the understanding that no one has a monopoly on deciding what is best for the children" (New, 1990, p. 6). Both teachers and the community recognize that this kind of ongoing dialogue is complex and difficult, but that differences of opinion become a resource instead of a problem. Teachers and parents consider that separation from one another is a hindrance both to adult and child development.

This model of school life being based on family and community relationships is another point from the Reggio approach that Katz believes should impact our thinking in applying some of their learning here at home. When communities make real commitments to young children, much can be accomplished.

The sense of community is extended to collegial relationships as well. A fundamental Reggio principle is that a team of at least two teachers is essential for the development of complex dialogue about children. Each week several teachers review the documentation, communicate their own perspectives about the children, and arrive at a shared interpretation. The richness of community interaction affects every aspect of the schools at Reggio Emilia. There is a reciprocity of relationships that develops back and forth between teachers and children, parents and teachers, teachers and teachers, parents and children, and the community, when there is commitment and continuity of contact over time.

Sue Bredekamp, in considering the power of the schools at Reggio, reflects that their practices

> ...have gone beyond DAP, at least in its current incarnation, especially in their emphasis on the social construction of knowledge and their articulation of the teacher's role as co-constructor with children and documentor of the learning process. (Bredekamp, 1993, p. 13.)

She describes challenges for early childhood educators in America. These are: to reclaim the image of the competent child; to promote conceptual integrity in programs and experiences for children and adults; to refine our definition of developmental appropriateness; to balance standard setting with questioning; to reflect on professional development; and to expand our understanding of the roles of the teacher. Perhaps the greatest influence of the schools at Reggio Emilia on American early childhood education may be to stimulate thinking and discussion among early childhood professionals in considering the most appropriate practices.

The GOLD Program in Scarborough, Maine

A developmentally appropriate program in the school system in Scarborough, Maine, has turned national attention on education in this picturesque small city (NASBE, 1991 and 1993; Kostelnik, et al., 1993). Located just outside Portland, and home of generations of farming and fishing families, as well as a newer influx of city-dwellers, Scarborough had been considered one of the weaker school systems in the area, featuring highly structured traditional classrooms, using old textbooks and lots of workbooks. When a new superintendent came on the scene in the mid-1980s, the school board responded to requests from parents for some options within the schools. The result was the GOLD program, begun in 1986, and recognized by educators and the community as highly successful. GOLD is an acronym for Grouping for Optimal Learning Development, first used in explaining the program description when applying for a state early childhood grant. From primary through middle school (K–8), parents may choose to enroll their children in a multi-aged ungraded program that tries to match learning materials, activities, and expectations to each child's developmental level. They may also choose the more traditional grade-level system; classrooms for both options are located within the same schools. As the director of curriculum and instruction describes the GOLD program, "It is not an It or a Kit; the program is not one of education's fads." It has a solid foundation, based on Piagetian research; there is a research-based reason for everything they do. Changes in GOLD classrooms and communication among all teachers within the system have effected improvements for all children, no matter which program their parents have chosen.

In this section we will look at the developmentally appropriate practices instituted in the GOLD primary classrooms, and then consider the reasons for Scarborough's success in making large-scale additions and changes in the structure of their educational offerings. The developmentally appropriate practices to be discussed are: multi-aged groupings; theme teaching and integrated curriculum; teachers' roles; and parental choice.

Multi-Aged Grouping

Scarborough defines multi-aged groupings as "the placement of differing chronological ages with the same teacher(s) for more than one year" (Scarborough, 1991). The schools are divided into GOLD Primary (ages five to eight), GOLD Intermediate (ages eight to eleven), and GOLD Middle School (ages eleven to fourteen). Scarborough feels the three-year age span is important in removing any concept of gradedness, thinking that with just a two-year span, teachers would be tempted to think in terms of the older and the younger division. Parents are asked to commit to placing their children for the full sequence of three years in the program so that children get the full benefit of the way the curriculum is organized; both the ungraded and graded programs offer the same concepts and skills to the children, but not necessarily at the same time or in the same order. (See Figure 17-7.) The family groupings allow for continuity and comfort with teachers, parents, and children. In this time when social change affects many families, children have real stability within these classrooms. In addition, the three-year span of ability necessitates that teachers come to understand each child as an individual learner, to help each acquire the knowledge and skills needed. Children who spend such a long period of time together learn

PRIMARY PHASE CURRICULUM

Graded

	Social Studies	Science/Health
K	Me and my family	Five Senses
		Water
		Seasons
		Health
1	Homes and neighborhoods	Pond/Woods
		Seasons
		Magnets
		Sound
		Construction: Simple Machines
		Health
2	Neighborhoods and community	Ocean
	Introduction to mapping	Light/Shadows
		Weather
		Rocks/Minerals
		Health

Ungraded

Theme Cycle (1 theme/year)	Social Studies	Science/Health
Farm	Farm as a part of our community (products and occupations)	Construction (simple machines)
		Pond-farm ponds and animals
		Weather/seasons
		Health
Forest	Forest as a part of our community (products and occupations)	Light/shadow
		Sound
		Rocks/minerals
		Forest
		Health
Ocean Community	Me and my family	Water
	Homes and neighborhoods	Five senses
	Neighborhoods and community	Magnets
		Ocean
		Health

Figure 17–7 A comparison of the subject material of three primary years in graded and ungraded classrooms. *Used with permission of Beth Bellemere, Scarborough School Department.*

to care for and support one another, to cooperate and work together. Children learn from one another, both socially and cognitively; the age range of students means access to a wide range of interests, thinking, skills, and modeling. Student interaction is valued as a source of expanded learning opportunities.

The ungraded environment supports the development of high self-esteem and feelings of capability as a learner. Children are able to progress at their own rate along a three-year skills continuum of literacy and math skills carefully monitored by teachers. The individualized programs are extremely responsive to children's particular needs. Kindergartners (five's) in the state of Maine are only in half-day programs. The children in the ungraded primary program know that some of their friends are "half-day" and some "full-day"—this is the children's own distinction. At some point in the year, if teachers perceive that a five-year-old has met the criteria needed to stay all day (e.g., not becoming fatigued, able to sustain activity for longer periods, etc.) teachers may suggest to parents that the child become a "full-day" student. On the other hand, there may still be children who are best suited to half-day attendance even at the beginning of their second year in the program. If students have not yet achieved certain "benchmark" skills on the skills continuum at the end of three years, parents and teachers will consider a fourth year in the multi-aged grouping. Not "just another way to retain" a child, children given the additional time do not suffer the blow to self-esteem as well as the boredom that usually occurs when spending an additional year in traditional graded settings. These children know their teachers and most of their classmates, are looked up to as "the big ones," and, since curriculum experiences are ever-changing, they are exposed to new learning opportunities, not going back through the same old reader. The GOLD program finds that the multi-aged groupings help them "continually find ways to push the boundaries for children."

Functioning in the multi-aged classroom helps children become independent learners. As they study the differential effects of the GOLD and the graded programs, administrators have devised a number of questionnaires for children and their parents. Children were asked, "If you had a problem you couldn't solve, what would you do first? If that didn't work, what would you do next?" They were given a number of choices, such as using other resources, asking a teacher, etc. The children in the multi-aged programs looked for help from a variety of people as resources, and would ask the teacher as a last choice. The children in the traditional classrooms would seek help from the teacher first.

One outcome of the multi-aged grouping that had not been looked for was discovered the first day of the second year of the program. The "old" children from the year before showed their new friends around the room, pointing out interest centers and activities. After an hour or so of this, they came to the teacher, already a familiar friend, and asked for the work to begin. Over a three-year period, teachers are literally gaining months normally lost to teaching in getting to know children and familiarizing them with the classroom.

Theme Teaching and Integrated Curriculum

The developmental foundation for the nongraded curriculum is the understanding that children construct their own knowledge through learning experiences matched with their developmental level, and that they need to be able to make connections in learning and applying skills and concepts in new situations. The curriculum in the GOLD program is theme based, allowing interconnections among different subjects (reading, writing, math, science, social studies, health, and art). Children work on projects in groups, sharing their knowledge and skills. Teachers use whole language methods to encourage children in emerging literacy skills. During the first year of implementing the program, teachers utilized short themes, lasting two or three weeks, integrating math and science.

The Year of the Forest

Trees	Wood and Paper	Animals	Geography and Ecology
Light, shadow, color	Sound	Animals tracks and camouflage	Rainforest
Trees	Simple machines	Light, shadows and reflections	Rocks and minerals
Plants	Construction	Feelings and relationships	Forest pond and water
Safety (from strangers)	Safety (fire)		
Seasons	Seasons	Seasons	Seasons
Five senses	Five senses	Five senses	Five senses

Figure 17–8 An example of the year-long theme for the year of the forest, with smaller branches of learning. *Used with permission of Beth Bellemere, Scarborough School Department.*

During the following summer they had opportunities to observe in English primary schools using multi-aged groupings, and came away convinced that there was learning power in year-long, comprehensive themes.

The primary teachers considered the local environment of the school community and the children's interests, and decided on three themes for their three-year sequence: the Farm, the Forest, and the Ocean. (See Figure 17-8.) The existing curricula decided on by K–12 teachers was pulled apart to fit within the themes. Free-flowing planning of both children and teachers helps a web of related activities evolve. Skills are developed as outcomes of the activities and interests. For example, while studying the forest, children may write letters to a Maine wood products company, exchange Maine products with a school in Ari-

Figure 17–9 Children of various ages work together at tables, not at individual desks. *Courtesy Scarborough School Department.*

zona, work out the dimensions of a log cabin, and study the ages of trees by counting the rings (The Scarborough K–8 Non-Graded Model, 1991). Such learning experiences are not reliant on workbooks and worksheets; learning may be reported orally, illustrated, or described in writing in classroom books. Themes allow children to develop their own interests and capabilities, and to move deeply into a topic. As highly motivated, independent learners, children initiate questions, find their resources, make their plans, and communicate their knowledge.

The classroom environments are arranged to encourage children's active involvement and interaction with materials and with peers. They work together at tables rather than desks (see Figure 17-9), and choose from a variety of interest centers each day with materials carefully chosen to help children move into activities related to the theme interests. Children also take frequent field trips, using the community as a learning environment related to their themes, with activities to follow up the experience. A key word to summarize all of this is *integration*—children see and make their own connections, continuing to construct their knowledge of the world.

Teacher Roles

Figure 17–10 Teachers assess children on their understanding of a series of Piagetian tasks, in order to plan appropriate curriculum. *Courtesy Scarborough School Department.*

Teachers within the GOLD program, originally all volunteers from within the existing system, have undergone a metamorphosis in their thinking and functioning in the classroom. Supported by inservice training and administrative backing, they have become facilitators in addition to being instructors.

They begin by administering a series of Piagetian tasks to each child in the fall and again in the spring, to learn where children are in the stages of cognitive development. This enables teachers to provide learning experiences that are an appropriate match. (See Figure 17-10.) As children work, teachers observe and record data, using their own systems, such as notebooks, checklists, and index cards. They focus not only on the Piagetian information about cognitive growth, but also accumulate anecdotal data to help understand the child's level of development in physical and social/emotional aspects. The teachers themselves identified the need to be trained in observation skills and techniques as the program progressed. Another need they identified related to the teacher's role as facilitator was to be trained in asking questions. As they question children about their work, teachers gain valuable insights about present level of comprehension and future needs. Teachers prepare activities they think will interest children and move them along in their skills and knowledge. They help make displays of students' learning, to confirm their experiences.

They may teach lessons to individuals, to small groups, or to large groups. (See Figures 17-11 and 17-12.) Math skills are taught in three ways. There is a formal math lesson each day, with children grouped according to skill; teachers may cooperate to send some of their children to be with another teacher if a different skill level is needed. Math is incorporated into center times as well, and used as part of the theme study.

Teachers recognize that a classroom filled with active learners each functioning at his or her own level makes a major change in their role with the children, to become a supportive resource person. In one sense this makes teachers' tasks easier, for learning is coming from a variety of sources over a longer period of time, not just from the teacher. Teachers recognize the learning from child to child, for example, and are relieved of the time pressure that most teachers acknowledge in the spring of "getting the children ready" for the next grade. But

The Working Portfolio

The **working portfolio** is kept in the classroom and is meant to be a compilation of the child's growth over time. Some work may be sent home at the end of the quarter or at the end of the year. Some may accumulate for the length of time the child stays in the classroom. These decisions will be made as the faculty refines the portfolio process. While we experience this process firsthand, some changes will certainly be made as we gain knowledge and experience. The following lists are suggestions of what will be considered for inclusion in a child's working portfolio:

Writing: journals, writing folders, weekend news, published books, computer stories, handwriting samples, shared writing, directed writing, notes, letters, thank you notes, science reactions, theme or subject-related journals (farm, math, etc.), labeling examples, spelling work, center record sheets, center recording sheets, lists.

Science, Social studies, Health: observational drawings, sorting work and recordings, journals, center recording sheets, recipes, classification work, brainstorming lists, field experience records.

Art: drawings (observational, free, teacher directed, child choice), sewing, 3-D work, paintings, prints, self portraits, puppets, story boards and aprons, prints, weavings, cut and paste activities.

Math: center recording sheets, sorting, seriating, patterning tasks, graphs (individual, group, child generated, teacher directed), game boards, geoboard work, classifying, problem-solving strategies.

Reading: book lists, word lists, literary passages, Marie Clay checklist, cloze packets, book reaction sheets, attitude inventory, word and letter recognition sheets, book projects, reports, poems, word families, word search, published books, tape of the child reading or retelling a story, phonics work, a copy of a page of text the child reads comfortably.

Figure 17–13 A sample list of materials for a working portfolio. *Used with permission of Beth Belle-mere, Scarborough School Department.*

Figures 17–11, 17-12 Teachers may teach individuals, small groups or large groups. *Courtesy Scarborough School Department.*

on the other hand, teachers recognize their responsibility; they must ensure that children move through the three-year skills continuum, so their skill in assessing children's progress and planning appropriate experiences and learning opportunities is critical.

Assessment in the Scarborough system is coordinated and comprehensive, and is used to monitor children's progress, plan for them, and share information with parents. In addition to the information gained by systematic observation, teachers engage in individual reading, writing, and project conferences with children. They collect samples of children's work for assessment of contents and change over time. Individual children keep work in a working portfolio. See Figure 17-13 for a sample list of what is likely to be found in the working portfolio. These materials are shared with the child and his or her family at conference time. Some work may be sent home at the end of the quarter or the year; some may accumulate for the length of time the child stays in the classroom. Parents are told at the beginning that they will not get daily evidence of learning activities, but will get narrative reports and portfolio conferences.

There are four periods of formal reporting to parents each year. Conferences are held in the first and third report periods. At the second and fourth, GOLD teachers send home anecdotal written reports. In addition, parents know that the teachers keep records of the child's progress on the three-year skills continuum, and that parents have access to this at any time.

The director of curriculum and instruction reports that teachers have blossomed within their new classroom roles, many of them going on for advanced degrees, and all of them becoming confident spokespersons for their program, one she refers to as "teacher-owned."

Parental Choice

One of the primary motivations for developing the GOLD program was to respond to parents' requests for educational choices for their children. The school administrators recognized that choice comes with having at least two things that are different, though both offering the full range of academic learning. Parents not only have the option of two different structures and philosophies of learning situations, but they are also empowered to be able to make appropriate choices for their children. The school system assists them with ideas on how to make the decision, but does not make the choice for them.

The school district offers a program in March for the parents of incoming five-year-olds. The information centers on thinking about children and their unique learning styles and interests. Slides are shown to illustrate different classroom learning experiences, and parents are given a questionnaire to help them think through some crucial questions about their children's learning style and their own values for their children. Parents are reminded there is no "best answer," and the programs are not presented as a polarity, but the process is meant to help parents make thoughtful choices. Questions focused on children include: Does your child prefer to sit in chairs or sit in a variety of places? Does your child usually keep working on something of own interest, work for awhile then turn to something else, or work best when reminded by an adult? Does your child have many own interests, get interests from other children, or ask adults for ideas? Parents are asked to consider whether they prefer their children to have a different teacher each year, or the same teacher for more than a year; whether they prefer to have their children learn certain skills each year or are comfortable to have them gain the skills in a three-year block of time, and so on. They are given until June to decide. The program administrator commented that one sign of success in helping parents make developmentally appropriate decisions for individual children is that some parents choose different programs for different children in their families.

Because parents have made their own choices about placement in the GOLD program, parents in both systems are happy and supportive of the programs. In both programs parents are invited to visit and become as involved in their children's classrooms as they are able. Because of the emphasis on active learning experiences, outside visits, and classroom visitors in the GOLD program, more parents are likely to become involved on a regular basis.

These four aspects of the Scarborough GOLD program work together to create developmentally appropriate classrooms for young children. One of the goals of the program planners was to improve educational opportunities for all children in both options, and this in fact is what has happened. Teachers from both options work together to review curriculum and plan staff development. The inservice training for GOLD teachers was open to all teachers. The shared dialogue has brought more developmentally appropriate practices into the already existing program as well.

At a time when educators and communities alike are recognizing the need for widespread changes in current education practices, how did Scarborough succeed in instituting very widespread and innovative changes? Several factors deserve consideration.

Reasons for Implementing Change

Change in Scarborough was not entered into arbitrarily or simply for the sake of change, nor for the opportunity to attract national attention to the school system. (While they have held several large workshops and been invited to present their program several places around the country, Scarborough administrators and teachers are not in the business of proselytizing, but put their energy into building a superb program, and are happy to share what has happened.) The reason for change was to improve the quality of education for all children, based on what is known about children's development. The solid foundation on research principles keeps the program firmly centered on children and their needs. For the first four years, a Piagetian expert (Dr. Pat Arlin of British Columbia) came in to consult and have dialogue.

The second reason for change was to respond to parental request. This brought community support to the concepts being offered.

Community Support

In Scarborough, the members of the community were not unwilling, passive recipients of change decreed from authority on high. Instead, at least part of the community was initially ready to accept the changes, since they were initiated at their request. Those parents and teachers who were not interested or supportive of the change had the option of remaining with the system already in place. The teachers who were selected for the program initially were all volunteers, whose only requirement be that they commit two years to the program and be willing to go to England (more about this shortly). By not excluding the teachers in the existing program, Scarborough avoided a sense of polarization; teachers in the graded system sometimes suggest to parents that they might consider the GOLD program for their children.

The administration was careful to keep the community participating in evaluation of the program, and informed about the results. Parents were given opportunities to evaluate their children's progress and their satisfaction. Budget facts were available, indicating that the GOLD program was actually less costly to run, since fewer consumables like workbooks are needed. As the program administrator said, "The degree to which you are trying to make change is the degree to which you will cause a reaction." Change has not always been smooth, but the opportunity to have the option of participation or not has been helpful in avoiding major problems with acceptance.

Inservice Education and Support for Teachers

Rethinking classroom practices and learning new techniques is exhausting and stressful, hard work. The teachers in Scarborough were given intensive inservice training of one or two days a week for months during the school year, and several weeks in the summer before instituting the program. They were taken to observe in English primary schools and do college study in England the summer after their first year. The training for the GOLD program continued for the first five years of the program, open to all teachers. This allowed teachers to identify some of their own needs for training after their first experiences in the changed settings.

Multi-Aged Grouping

Student Outcomes

- High self-esteem and self-assurance
- Cooperative, work together
- Caring and supportive of others, high level of tolerance
- Self-initiation, self-motivated, independent learners, questioners
- Acquire skills, knowledge, concepts in useful contexts
- Know how to plan and "find out," how to use resources
- Persevere, risk-takers, flexible, use variety of decision-making strategies, creative
- Able to analyze, draw conclusions, make inferences
- Able to solve problems in real contexts, make connections among learnings
- Able to communicate learning in a variety of ways; highly verbal
- Develop individual interests, take responsibility
- Learn from others, learn in a variety of ways and places

Teacher Outcomes

- Understand children as a whole child, trust children more
- Reflect upon instructional practice and can articulate own practice
- Put research into context of children's learning
- Respect diversity in adults and children
- Build upon colleagues' strengths, respect styles
- Raised expectations of self
- Increased self-confidence
- More analytical about curriculum—what we teach and why
- See selves as learners
- More flexible
- "See possibilities that weren't there before"

Figure 17–14 There are benefits for both children and teachers in a nongraded, multi-age grouping. *Used with permission of Beth Bellemere, Scarborough School Department.*

The school administrators were completely supportive of the challenges teachers faced, and acted as buffers for them with the community, allowing them time to build both their skills and their confidence. The administrators were so closely involved with the teachers' experiences that they were able to make immediate responses to even the smallest issues. For example, as the first three-year sequence was drawing to an end, teachers began to comment on how difficult it would be to lose some of the children they had been with so closely over time. The administrators met with the teachers to discuss healthy transitions for children and adults, and there have been no difficulties since. The successful program is proof of the success of the teacher training and support, as is the fact that no teacher has been willing to leave a GOLD classroom, and others would like to enter into the program.

Responsive Adaptations

Another positive factor in the Scarborough system was the administrative responsiveness and flexibility in making changes for improvements after the program was instituted. An example of this is that the two programs were largely separated geographically at first. Classrooms for the GOLD program were in different schools from the already existing program. Now they are in the same schools. The administrators have been more careful in recent years to ensure that both programs receive equal attention.

Because of the attention to these four factors, along with a group of committed teachers and administrators, children in the school system in Scarborough, Maine, have access to admirably developmentally appropriate classrooms. The system seems to work well for the children and adults involved. (See Figure 17-14.)

Note: The GOLD program has developed a short informational video and booklet about their program. For more information, contact Beth Bellemere, Director of Curriculum and Instruction, Scarborough School Department, P.O. Box 370, Scarborough, Maine 04070-0370.

SUMMARY

Both of these programs have succeeded in providing developmentally appropriate and responsive programs for children and families over time. They have based their practices thoughtfully on developmental theory and observation of individuals, involving families, and facilitating the development of curricula related to children's interest and the particular community. Other programs will benefit by considering the sources of their success.

THINK ABOUT IT

1. After reading about the schools in Reggio Emilia, identify key elements that are part of the earlier discussions about developmentally appropriate practice.

2. As you evaluate a preschool setting in your community, ask yourself these questions raised by the consideration of practices at Reggio Emilia:

   • How do children influence the classroom environment?

   • What provisions are there in the setting that enable children to engage in activity deeply?

   • Where and how do opportunities for collaborative peer interaction take place?

   • Any other questions raised by your reading and discussion with your classmates (Adapted from questions offered by Lella Gandini in a handout, later published in an article by *Scholastic Pre-K Today*, Oct. 1992)

3. After reading about the GOLD program in Scarborough, Maine, identify key elements that are part of the earlier discussions about developmentally appropriate practice.

REFERENCES AND SUGGESTIONS FOR READING

a. Reggio Emilia

Benham, E. (1992, October). The power and value of the child and Reggio Emilia: A model in creativity. *Scholastic Pre-K Today, 7(2)*, 5, 81–5, 84.

Bredekamp, S. (1993, November). Reflections on Reggio Emilia. *Young Children, 49(1)*, 13–17.

Edwards, C., Forman G., & Gandini, L. (eds.) (1993). *Education for all children: The multisymbolic approach to early education in Reggio Emilia, Italy.* Norwood, NJ: Ablex.

Gandini, L. (1991, March/April). Not just anywhere: Making child care centers into 'particular' places. *Child Care Information Exchange, 85,* 5–9.

Gandini, L. (1993, November). Fundamentals of the Reggio Emilia approach to early childhood education. *Young Children, 49(1),* 4–8.

Goleman, D., Kaufman, P., & Ray, M. (1992). Playful schools that work: Creativity—Italian style. In *The creative spirit.* New York: Dutton.

Katz, L. (1992, Fall). What can we learn from Reggio Emilia? *Innovations in early education: The international Reggio exchange, 1(1).*

Malaguzzi, L. (1993, November). For an education based on relationships. *Young Children, 49(1),* 9–12.

New, R. (1990, September). Excellent early education: A city in Italy has it. *Young Children, 45(6),* 4–10.

Rinaldi, C. (1992, July 24-26). *Social constructivism in Reggio Emilia, Italy. Presentation prepared for the Images of the Child: An international exchange.* Newton, MA: Mt. Ida College.

The ten best schools in the world, and what we can learn from them. (1991, December 2). *Newsweek.*

To make a portrait of a lion. Comune di Reggio Emilia. [Video] (1987). North Andover, MA: Early Childhood Exchange.

b. GOLD program, Scarborough

Kostelnik, M., Soderman, A., & Whiren, A. (1993). *Developmentally appropriate programs in early childhood education.* New York: Macmillan Publishing Co.

NASBE. (1993). *Building good schools for young children right from the start.* Arlington, VA: Author.

National Association of State Boards of Education. (1991). *Caring communities: Supporting young children and families.* Arlington, VA: Author.

The Scarborough K-8 non-graded model. (ERIC document no. 333984). (1991). Scarborough, ME: Scarborough School Department.

Index